Colección Támesis

SERIE A: MONOGRAFÍAS, 189

A COMPANION TO MODERN SPANISH AMERICAN FICTION

DONALD L. SHAW

A COMPANION TO MODERN SPANISH AMERICAN FICTION

TAMESIS

First published 2002 by Tamesis, London

ISBN 1 85566 078 4

Tamesis is an imprint of Boydell & Brewer Ltd
PO Box 9, Woodbridge, Suffolk IP12 3DF, UK
and of Boydell & Brewer Inc.
PO Box 41026, Rochester, NY 14604–4126, USA
website: http://www.boydell.co.uk

A catalogue record for this book is available
from the British Library

Library of Congress Catalog Card Number: 99–045411

This publication is printed on acid-free paper

Printed in Great Britain by
St Edmundsbury Press Ltd, Bury St Edmunds, Suffolk

CONTENTS

To Mariella, Andrew and Silvia

Chapter 1

ORIGINS

George Santayana used to say that to understand means to perceive patterns. In the following chapters no serious attempt will be made to follow the example of Brushwood and others whose aim was to be inclusive and to mention as many writers of fiction as possible. What such an approach tends to produce is a kind of dictionary of names with a little connective tissue between the individual entries. Here instead, the aim will be to sketch out the broad outlines of the successive phases of fiction in Spanish America, using the work of representative writers to illustrate the developing patterns. It is assumed that at any given moment there tends to be among writers a certain consensus, or possibly just a majority view, with regard first of all to the human condition. This often translates itself into a view of reality, so that as the world-view changes, the attitude to reality tends to change with it. In turn, new narrative strategies and techniques tend to be invented or borrowed in order to figure forth the shift. This is one of the main dynamics driving on the processes of literary development. We do not know with any certainty why basic outlooks change, bringing change in literature, though we can speculate about new spiritual, intellectual, social and economic influences which may be operating. What we can see is that changes take place and, allowing for a great deal of simplification in the process, can be roughly charted. To understand a writer's work, then, it usually helps to be able to situate her or him in relation to what seems to be the prevailing world-view of the times and the evolving literary responses to it. This is, reduced to its essence, the approach to be followed here. If it is objected that this is a 'history of ideas' approach, with some formalistic trappings, the author can only reply that it seems to be a mainstream approach and that it is probably a good springboard to more sophisticated ones.

In 1965 the Paraguayan novelist Augusto Roa Bastos wrote: 'Si es cierto que la literatura hispanoamericana nace con el Descubrimiento, es decir, con las Crónicas, la verdadera literatura americana nace con el surgimiento de las literaturas nacionales.'[1] In other words, however much it may be true, as

[1] Augusto Roa Bastos, 'Imagen y perspectivas de la narrativa latinoamericana actual', *La novela hispanoamericana*, ed. Juan Loveluck, 3rd edn (Santiago de Chile, Universitaria, 1969), pp. 193–211, p. 202.

Carlos Fuentes affirmed in a speech in honour of Rómulo Gallegos in 1977 that Bernal Díaz's *Crónica verdadera de la conquista de la Nueva España* was the 'antecedente secreto de toda la narrativa hispanoamericana', it was just that: an antecedent. Similarly while it is possible to make a case for *El carnero*, written in the 1630s as a chronicle by the Colombian Juan Rodríguez Freyle (1566–1640) but not published until 1859, or for the *Lazarillo de ciegos caminantes* (1773) by a Spanish official, Alonso Carrió de la Vandera (1715?–78?), as to some degree fictional narratives, the argument that they can be regarded as novels is not persuasive. This leaves *El Periquillo Sarniento* (1816) by José Joaquín Fernández de Lizardi with pride of place as the first real novel to be published in Spanish America. Not surprisingly, it was an example of an old genre, the Picaresque, moved to a new setting.

Even so, the work is full of observation of contemporary Mexican reality and realist detail. Like all picaresque novels, it is told retrospectively by a narrator who has the benefit of hindsight (and in this case conversion), so that there are necessarily two levels in the narrative. On one level we are offered a brilliantly satirical account of aspects of Mexican society based on the numerous expedients Periquillo has recourse to in order to survive without having learned a trade or acquired the will to work. On the other, from the standpoint of the experience he has gained, he comments, usually moralistically, on the incidents. These are selected and manipulated by Lizardi (who got into plenty of trouble for his pains) to mount a comic attack on political, social and religious abuses, chiefly those associated with the Church and the professions. Periquillo is at different times a novice in a monastery, a card sharper, a doctor's assistant, a chemist's assistant, a sexton's helper and so on, which brings him into contact with a range of more than eighty characters drawn from all ranks of society. The emphasis is on hypocrisy, deception and charlatanism.

Noël Salomon, commenting on the novel from a left-wing social perspective, makes some interesting points. One is that, by contrast with the lack of confidence in humanity characteristic of the traditional Spanish picaresque, Lizardi, a son of the Enlightenment, sees man as rational and educable (though this is rather less true of Lizardi's other picaresque novel, *Don Catrín de la Fachenda*, 1832, which Salomon does not consider). Another is that Lizardi is not only interested in moral satire, but also in direct social criticism. There are sharp attacks on the idle nobility and on social privilege, on entails, which tied up land unproductively, on an economy which is based on mining rather than agriculture, on racial discrimination and exploitation of the poorer classes. A third is that not all the educated characters whom Periquillo meets are there to be satirized. Some provide a contrast with the bulk of their fellow citizens because of their awareness of the need for social change. On these grounds Salomon concludes that Lizardi's criticism 'contribuyó objetivamente a la toma de conciencia nacional del pueblo mexicano en un momento decisivo de su historia'.[2] Lizardi was not concerned to produce a well-shaped literary artefact. The novel is perforce episodic, with the constant on-stage presence of Periquillo as its unifying factor. He hardly evolves until his change of heart at the end. Before that he alternates between cunning and folly, pretentiousness and self-ridicule, enterprise and cowardice as the incidents require, though he is not without occasional flashes of decency and generosity, which portend his final conversion. His shifting fortunes allow him to observe and participate in the life-styles not only of the middle class, to which his mother thinks she belongs – and this is the origin of his problems – but also, inevitably, of the underworld of Mexico City into which we are given fascinating insights. The satire reaches its peak when Periquillo is shipwrecked on a Pacific island and, in semi-Swiftian fashion, is called upon to describe and justify the ways of his society to a Chinese chieftain. The latter's comments reflect Lizardi's hostility to so much that he saw around him and are more effective than the moralizing commentaries which Lizardi regularly inserts into the narrative at other times. We notice that Periquillo's final salvation is based, not so much on growing moral awareness as on fear of the consequences if he does not change his life-style. Two of his companions, Aguilucho and Januario, come to sticky ends. He, on the other hand, has the good fortune to find in Manila a kindly employer who offers him the opportunity to reform. The work is essentially didactic, but not for that reason dull. Its style, though usually loose and unpolished, can at times be refreshingly direct and vernacular. But it has been rightly said that *Ei Periquillo Sarniento* comes at the end of a genre which goes back to the Spanish *Lazarillo de Tormes* (1554) rather than beginning something new. What was needed was a change of sensibility, and that only came with Romanticism.

The interpretation of the Romantic movement is still a matter of ongoing discussion and frequent controversy. Generalizations are therefore risky. But for the present purpose it may be said, with much simplification, that the movement in Europe had two broad and ill-defined wings. Both grew out of a sense that a variety of factors, out of which we commonly select for special emphasis the Rationalism of the Enlightenment, which underlay the Encyclopedia Movement in France, and the ideological and social impact of the French Revolution and the Napoleonic Wars, had led to a pattern of disintegration of values. There seemed be be, especially among the intellectual minority, a loss of confidence in the older world-view, based on the idea of a fatherly world according to design, inherited from Christian teaching, and in the assumptions which went with it. Both groups of Romantics, those whom we may call more traditionalist and those who were in some ways more 'pro-

[2] Noël Salomon, 'La crítica del sistema colonial de la Nueva España en *El Periquillo Sarniento*', *Cuadernos Americanos* 138 (1965), 166–79, p. 169.

gressive', and even subversive, wished to see the process of disintegration reversed; the traditionalists like Scott, or in Spain, Zorrilla, by a return to the values of an idealized past; the progressives, like Byron, or in Spain, Espronceda, by a new synthesis. In the new world-view, a high value was placed on the emotions generally, and on human love above all. There was considerable overlap between writers belonging to the two broad wings of the movement, especially in Spain, where the struggle against the Napoleonic invasion had reinforced Nationalistic values even among the progressives and libertarian ideals even among some traditionalists. Both groups tended to accept the need to find new forms of literary expression. In Spanish America, Romanticism coincided with the Wars of Independence and their aftermath. This skewed the movement towards the exaltation of Liberty and patriotic endeavour and, in the newly liberated countries, towards the need for a 'civic' literature, designed to help meet the need to 'hacer patria', to disseminate and tread in the ideals for which the wars against Spain had been fought. The failure of love sometimes symbolized or was closely associated with the failure of those and similar ideals. Thus in *Sab* the failure of Carlota's marriage coincides with her realization that, as a woman, she is as enslaved by marriage as Sab was on her father's plantation, despite the nobility of soul which both incarnate. Masiello writes à propos of *Amalia*: 'Doomed marriage as a metaphor for failed political unity is a major preoccupation in the book',[3] and in *Clemencia* the betrayal of love goes hand in hand with the betrayal of Mexico. The darker side of Romanticism, its *mal du siècle*, despair, and existential questioning, which some critics regard as its fundamental legacy to modern times, though sporadically present, did not really develop significantly in Spanish America until near the end of the century. This was to affect Romantic fiction profoundly.

In another sense Romanticism was to be the great inaugural movement in modern Spanish American literature. For this reason: in the period before Romanticism, the idea was to address a notionally universal audience using universal themes. Local settings and references were inevitable but were not usually considered significant in themselves. With Romanticism, all that changed. For the first time it became recommendable to exploit 'local colour'. From Scott's kilted highlanders to Hugo's black slave Bug Jargal and Mérimée's Spanish gypsy, Carmen, exotic figures from the margins of society emerged triumphantly into literature. This meant that there was now a place for the gaucho, for the Indian, and in the Caribbean, for the black slave. 'Americanist' literature was now possible and desirable. With it came a flood of Spanish American *pintoresquismo*, which survived through Regionalism practically as far as the early Boom. So much so that Carlos Fuentes, early in

[3] Francine Masiello, *Between Civilization and Barbarism* (Lincoln and London, Nebraska U.P., 1992), p. 30.

his career, declared that: 'El problema básico para nosotros los escritores latinoamericanos es superar el pintoresquismo.'[4] Carpentier, in his first novel *Ecue-Yamba-O* (1933), was still affected by it and had to learn to eliminate it. Still, even now, some nationalist critics tend to stress the need for what is often called 'especificidad', in contrast to 'cosmopolitanismo', and the need to keep Spanish American literature attuned to conditions in Spanish America. Their views go back to the Romantics.

The first monument to 'civic' Romantic fiction is the famous short story 'El matadero' (1838?) by Esteban Echeverría (Argentina, 1805–51). Set in the slaughterhouse area of Buenos Aires during the dictatorship of Rosas (1835–52), it begins with what appears to be a *costumbrista* description of the butchery of a bull. But this opening is not-so-subtly manipulated to include symbolic details which express the author's criticism of the regime and turn it into a preparation for and prefiguration of what is to come. A young middle-class figure comes into view and is at once recognized as a 'Unitarian' opponent of Rosas's government, which the red-handed rabble support. He is reviled and attacked, and ultimately dies a victim to the dictator's repulsive and barbarous partisans. The first two-thirds of the tale, though characterized by biting sarcasm and irony, are more loosely written than the climactic section. Once this begins, however, the language becomes more precise and economic, and the technique almost cinematographic. Foster, in an original approach, points out that the story contains a series of Christ-related motifs, begining with the fact that it all happens on a Good Friday. Associating the stockyard with Calvary, he sees the events of the tale as figuring forth a mockery of Christian love. However, he emphasizes that the context is one of purely human values and argues convincingly that it is the 'use of inverted religious motifs' to attack the unholy alliance of Church and authoritarian State under Rosas and the bestiality of the society it produces, which is significant.[5] We shall see in a future chapter how Asturias developed this technique in *El Señor Presidente* and later how it surfaces again in Donoso and others. Pupo-Walker points out that '*El matadero* no puede encasillarse en los moldes de géneros establecidos'.[6] It contains elements of *costumbrismo*, Realism and even Naturalism, as well as being essentially allegorical. It stands in proud isolation, far in advance of the literature around it.

Facundo (1845) by Domingo Faustino Sarmiento (Argentina, 1811–88) has to be regarded as the foundational novel in modern Spanish America, not

4 Cit. Mario Benedetti, 'Carlos Fuentes', *Homenaje a Carlos Fuentes*, ed. Helmy F. Giacoman (New York, Las Américas, 1971), p. 95.

5 Foster, David W., 'Paschal Symbology in Echeverría's "El matadero" ', *Studies in Short Fiction*, 7.2 (1970), 257–63.

6 Enrique Pupo-Walker, 'Originalidad y composición de un texto romántico: "El matadero" de Esteban Echeverría', in his *El cuento hispanoamericano ante la crítica* (Madrid, Castalia, 1973), p. 38.

least because it launched explicitly the grand old theme of Civilization versus Barbarism (already implicit in 'El matadero') which dominated whole areas of fiction in the continent at least until the middle of the twentieth century. We shall see it turn up again in Azuela, Gallegos and Asturias and it is present behind much of the work even of García Márquez. Sarmiento had to face the fact that the Wars of Independence had been followed not, as in North America, by the establishment of democracy and progress, but by anarchy and dictatorship. In *Facundo* he attempts to discuss the problem in terms of a new, Argentine, and by extension Spanish American, *modo de ser* which has produced struggle and violence, political and industrial incapacity and authoritarian governments, instead of fulfilling the ideas of the Independence movements. His approach is essentially deterministic: a combination of geographical, historical and racial factors are responsible for spawning savagery instead of civilization. Having established this postulate, he selects the figure of Facundo Quiroga, a barbarous local land-baron and leader of an army of irregular gaucho cavalry, with which he terrorized and dominated a large area in the interior of the country. He was the principal rival of the dictator Rosas while the latter was on his way to power, and eventually had to be treacherously eliminated by him.

Thus *Facundo* is a kind of fictionalized biography of a representative figure of barbarism, by means of which Sarmiento hopes to illustrate and explain the problems of his country and of his continent. It is, to borrow Fredric Jameson's phrase, the first great 'national allegory' in Spanish American fiction, to be followed by many others. In the course of it, Facundo emerges as a figure of mythic stature (indeed quite different from the historical figure, but nobody cares – the myth has conquered the man). Myth is often more important than reality, never more so than when it shapes a nation's self-perception, and this is the case in the present instance. But there is a price to be paid. *Facundo* belongs to a pattern of Cultural Reformism based on the notion of changing people by enhancing their awareness, rather than changing concrete conditions. Not that Sarmiento was blind to the latter need. He and his group of reformers believed in setting the barbarous gauchos to eliminate the barbarous Indians in the hope that both would largely disappear in the process. Then Argentina could be repopulated, preferably by white Anglo-Saxon immigrants, thus disposing of the racial problem. The geographical problem could be overcome by improving transportation, and the political instability by preparing a suitable Constitution. Finally education, to which Sarmiento dedicated his chief energies, would do the rest. But the *modo de ser* on which Sarmiento bases his approach is perilously close to being an *alma de la raza*, something not entirely explicable in simple deterministic terms, but instead an epiphenomenon interacting mysteriously with other forces. If that is what it is, something inherently negative in the racial makeup, as subsequent writers have sometimes assumed, it is stubbornly resistent to change and a source of discouragement to observers. What

Sarmiento put into circulation is responsible for a great deal of pessimism and ambiguity of outlook in later writers whose novels bear on the various national situations.

Facundo has often been regarded as a structurally inadequate work which suffers from what Fishburn calls 'a failure to synthesize the ideological message with the aesthetic content'.[7] But not all critics agree. Ernesto Sábato, himself a novelist and an explorer of Argentine problems, has described it as an 'obra sociológica e históricamente equivocada, pero novelísticamente genial'.[8] Indeed if its defects were as glaring as has sometimes been argued, it would hardly have achieved the immense success it has enjoyed. In fact, it has a formal arrangement dictated by Sarmiento's aim and a regular development dictated by the subject. The first phase of the novel contains two mutually modifying and complementary sections. One is in part *costumbrista*, dealing nostalgically with the picturesque life of the gauchos out on the pampa and corresponding to Facundo's formative years. The other is a historical excursus explaining his entry on to the national scene. The pattern is milieu > moment > man. This pattern is further developed in Part II until the novel's centre of balance is reached, after which we pass from causes to effects (Facundo's short-lived triumph as the incarnation of barbarism) and to the emergence of the counterforce, Rosas, who engineers Facundo's fall and murder in a superbly dramatic sequence of events. Part III is an epilogue; but it is not a mere appendage. It shows us the final consequences of all that has gone before. While Rosas is systematically working out and putting into devilish practice Facundo's methods, the progressive *Asociación de Mayo*, to which Sarmiento belonged, has come into being and represents Argentina's best hope for the future. The organization of the book is coherent not only in its broad outlines but also in most of its subordinate aspects.

Two points still need to be emphasized and another re-emphasized, because of their importance for the future of fiction in Spanish America. First, *Facundo* is a novel which in reality sets the values of the city against those of the great rural interior. This dichotomy will remain significant and re-emerge in the twentieth century as the predominance of the rural environment in the Regionalist novel is challenged, in the end successfully, by writers after Arlt. Onetti, his great successor and the author of the first recognizable Boom novel, is often regarded as the writer who brings fiction back to an urban environment in the mid-twentieth century, though not now to the city as the home of civilized values. Second, *Facundo* is an essentially hybrid work mixing novelistic episodes with historical and other forms of interpretation which could be thought of as more like essay-material. This characteris-

[7] Evelyn Fishburn, 'The Concept of "Civilization and Barbarism" in Sarmiento's *Facundo*. A Reappraisal', *Iberoamericanisches Archiv* 5. 4 (1979), 301–308, p. 304.

[8] Ernesto Sábato, *El escritor y sus fantasmas*, 3rd edn (Buenos Aires, Aguilar, 1963), p. 42.

tic, shared for similar reasons by Mármol's *Amalia*, was one of the two novels' important legacies to many future novels in Spanish America. As recently as 1994, Colás was obliged to make the point that the characteristic hybridity of much Spanish American fiction makes it difficult to apply to it an unmodified concept of Postmodernism.[9] Third, 'El matadero' and *Facundo* together illustrate a tendency which will become rooted in Spanish American fiction to present the national situation (and even life itself) in dualistic terms of a struggle of good versus evil, right versus wrong, in which evil and wrong triumph. It is true that happiness has no history and that almost all great art arises out of the contemplation of suffering. It is true that, as Vargas Llosa once memorably asserted, optimistic writers are liars. Even so we cannot overlook the intense pessimism which surrounds the beginning of fiction in modern Spanish America, and which goes on resounding through so much later narrative. *Americanismo* is in a sense contaminated at its source.

The central Romantic formula for fiction (and drama) was love, crossed by fate, ending in death. This is what we see in the major romantic novels we are now about to discuss. The trick was to find a convincing way to convert mere bad luck into adverse destiny and so raise the level of the narrative, thematically at least, to that of high literature, by making it appear to contain a comment on the human condition. There are several ways to do this, from making the various mishaps so consistent that fate could be seen operating through them, or by using a symbol of fate, such as Isaacs's *ave negra* in *María*, or by making a direct reference to fate itself. But it has to be clearly understood that adverse fate is the opposite of Divine Providence. It is extremely difficult to believe in both. The novelists with whom we are about to deal failed to recognize this contradiction, or if they did, to handle it adequately. This is one of the reasons why Romantic fiction in Spanish America is not nowadays a popular subject of study.

The first still highly regarded novel by a Spanish American author after Lizardi's *El Periquillo Sarniento* was *Sab* (1841) by Gertrudis Gómez de Avellaneda (Cuba, 1814–73). Her poetry is now largely forgotten and her plays are museum pieces, but *Sab*, which deals with slavery, the subjugation of women and the superiority of natural virtue over socially accepted canons of behaviour, came back into the mainstream of critical attention in the later twentieth century, as interest in slavery narratives and above all in feminism became widespread. Set on a slave plantation in Cuba, *Sab* is the story of a heavily idealized, intelligent and noble-minded, light-coloured mulatto slave, who, brought up alongside his owner's angelicized daughter Carlota (as well as being probably her cousin), is hopelessly in love with her. She, however, blinded by an innocently exalted dream of love, consents to marry a

[9] Santiago Colás, *Postmodernity in Latin America. The Argentine Paradigm* (Durham and London, Duke U.P., 1994), p. 17.

commercial-minded, not to say avaricious, young Englishman, Enrique Otway, to whom her father's ward Teresa is also strongly attached. Thus the three themes of the novel are romantic illusion, the injustice of slavery (including domestic conjugal subjection of women) and the greedy attachment of patriarchal male society to wealth and purely commercial values. Although Jackson is correct in accusing Avellaneda of depicting a black protagonist with white features and of playing down (like Isaacs) the sufferings of the slaves,[10] this is a profoundly courageous and radically transgressive novel for its period. It contains an open attack on both slavery and patriarchy (critics are surprisingly divided on the first issue, but there can no real question about where Avellaneda stood on the issue of the injustice of the system), and the only example of its time in fiction in Spanish of an (almost) black hero who aspires to the love of a white, upper-class woman. Not only that, but, as Sommer cogently indicates, gender coding is reversed, with Sab passionate and sentimental, i.e. 'heroic to the extent that he is feminized', while Teresa 'gives up romantic infatuation for principled passions' (like a man, presumably) and is even willing to throw in her lot with the slave.[11] This implicit acceptance of miscegenation is the novel's boldest defiance of social prejudices. All three figures, Carlota, the compulsorily submissive wife, Teresa, the illegitimate poor female relation, condemned to humilliation and frustration, and Sab, the slave, are victims of a cruel, oppressive and materialistic society. At the national level the novel can be seen as an allegory of Cuba, exploited by rapacious foreigners and betrayed by the indolence of its oligarchic class, symbolized by Carlota's weak and incompetent father. At a more universal level, Sab can be seen as yet another example of mankind seeking fulfilment through the ideal of love, but being prevented by a fatal obstacle, in this case symbolized by Sab's mixed race status and his position as a slave.

The difficulty facing Avellaneda in *Sab*, bearing in mind that the novel is set in its own times and not in some safe legendary or medieval past, is to make Sab's passion for Carlota credible, yet at the same time non-threatening and acceptable to contemporary readers. It is precisely in order to do so that Avellaneda lays herself open to Jackson's present-day criticism of the way she underplays Sab's racial characteristics. Sab, as virtually every critic has pointed out, is a variant of the Romantic 'noble savage'. His character is built around utter devotion and self-sacrifice. He not only saves the life of his rival Otway but also, when he wins the National Lottery, he gives the proceeds to Carlota to make up the dowry that Otway demands. His stirring letter, written as he is dying, carries most of the direct commentary on the plot and the bulk

10 Richard L. Jackson, 'Black Phobia and White Aesthetic in Spanish American Literature', *Hispania* 58 (1975), 467–80.

11 Doris Sommer, *Foundational Fictions. The National Romances of Latin America* (Berkeley, California U.P., 1991), p. 121.

of Avellaneda's impassioned rebellious and anti-conformist ideology. Although he makes some ritual references to his 'destiny', Avellaneda avoids presenting Sab directly as a victim of fate (but Alberto Gutiérrez correctly recognizes that 'la esclavitud desempeña el papel del destino implacable que ha de convertir al protagonista en un héroe trágico'[12]) since her quarrel is with society and human prejudice, both in his case and that of Carlota. The novel's often quoted key phrase is: '¡Oh!, ¡las mujeres! ¡Pobres y ciegas víctimas! Como los esclavos ellas arrastran pacientemente su cadena y bajan la cabeza bajo el yugo de las leyes humanas',[13] eventually to be echoed by Bombal, Mistral and Storni. However, it is hard for the reader to overlook the conflict between the novel's consistently religious tone and the events which take place. Like Isaacs, Avellaneda clings to the notion of a Providential world, while filling her novel with evidence to the contrary.

José Mármol (Argentina 1817–71) wrote the typically bombastic, patriotic and libertarian poetry of his time, but is remembered above all for *Amalia* (1855). What 'El matadero' does on a tiny scale, *Amalia* attempts to do on a vast scale. Told from the point of view of the threatened minority of Unitarian opponents of Rosas, it deals in often minute detail with life in Buenos Aires under the dictatorship and the attempts at conspiracy of a group of upper-class young people at the time of Lavalle's abortive invasion attempt in 1840. It has two dimensions and three strands of plot. The first of the two dimensions is the purely novelesque one, the love-and-terror story of the central fictional characters, Eduardo Belgrano and Amalia, the lovers, with their friend and protector Daniel Bello, whose beloved Florencia is safe in exile, allowing him freedom of action. The second dimension is the historical one, the evocation of the dictatorship with a huge amount of description, historical exposition, analysis, satire, propaganda and, naturally the entry into the novel of actual historical characters, in particular Rosas, his diabolical sister-in-law, María Josefa, his charming daughter Manuelita, and a gallery of courtiers, hangers on, and bit-part players both Unitarian and Federal. It may be said at once that one of the criticisms of the novel is that the historical characters, especially some of the secondary ones, are far more convincing and successfully depicted than the highly idealized central figures.

The three strands of plot are: first, the one centred on Eduardo and Amalia, the tragic love plot; second, the love story of Daniel and Florencia, which is of less importance and really a re-make of the first; and third, the activities of Daniel, as a kind of lone Romantic superman, directed against Rosas and his minions.

In the novel Mármol runs up against serious problems, not least because

[12] Alberto Gutiérrez de la Solana, '*Sab* y *Francisco*: paralelo y contraste', *Homenaje a Gertrudis Gómez de Avellaneda*, eds. Rosa M. Cabrera and Gladys B. Zaldívar (Miami, Universal, 1981), pp. 301–17, p. 311.

[13] Gertrudis Gómez de Avellaneda, *Sab* (Madrid, Cátedra, 1997), pp. 270–71.

anyone reading it would be likely to know that Rosas's regime survived triumphantly for more than a decade after the events of 1840 described here. Even then it collapsed because one of his henchmen turned against him and not because the ideals of the conspirators who take part in the action of the novel prevailed. The projected invasion by Lavalle to topple Rosas never got under way, and the conspiracy to support it fizzled out. Moreover Eduardo is not the central male figure. He is elbowed aside by Daniel, whose actions constitute an intrigue and not a real struggle. Sommer, among others, points out that Daniel has by no means broken his bridges with *federalismo*. His quarrel is with the brutality of the regime rather than with its ideology. Hence perhaps Mármol's positive presentation of Manuelita Rosas and the important fact that the union of Amalia, who is from Tucumán in the interior, and Eduardo, who is from Buenos Aires, implies a possible reconciliation of city and hinterland. Sommer also makes a good point when she writes that '*Amalia* assumes a social chaos in the absence of legitimate power, and therefore sets about to construct a legitimate nation/family from the elements in flux' (p. 92). The counterforce operating against the lovers, led by María Josefa and Mariño, emerges only sporadically and does not grow into a cumulative development. In any case the plot elements are often almost submerged by the welter of historical exposition and interpretation both by the third-person narrator and by a number of the characters. *Amalia* rambles; it lacks unity and coherence. But some dramatic incidents are splendidly carried off and there is a sense of reality about the writing which lifts it at times to the level of Scott, Hugo and Manzoni. *Amalia* is, in other words, one of Henry James's 'loose baggy monsters', a typical nineteenth-century three-decker with seventy-nine chapters. It has a strong beginning, but comes to a premature climax at the end of Book II and the opening of Book III, after which it loses momentum until the final climax, when the lovers, newly married, perish.

The juxtaposition of love and death is characteristically Romantic. The third element, destiny, is not emphasized, though Amalia believes herself fated to destroy all who love her. Political fanaticism takes the place of fate, which, in a sense limits the range of the commentary. *Amalia* is the first great novel of dictatorship to be published in Spanish America and was to be followed by many more. Among them would be Asturias's *El Señor Presidente*. Asturias himself acknowledged a distant debt to Mármol's example, but, unlike the latter, introduces a deeper dimension into his depiction of despotism which lifts it above the merely political. This existential element which derives from subversive Romanticism is in the end what *Amalia* lacks.

Unlike *Amalia* which is essentially plot-centred and full of incident, in *María* (1867) by Jorge Isaacs (Colombia, 1837–95) not much happens. The hero, Efraín, falls in love with his father's ward, María, while they are still children. His love is intensified when he returns from boarding school, but is threatened by María's bouts of epilepsy. In deference to his parents, Efraín goes to London to complete his education and is unable to return before María dies. The story is told chiefly by Efraín in the first person after her death. *María* is held to be the most popular nineteenth-century Spanish American novel and continues to be republished. It is an idyll, set on a slave plantation in the lush valley of the river Cauca. This allows Isaacs to introduce lyrical descriptions in which the moods of Nature, in characteristically Romantic fashion, are used functionally to reflect the emotions of the characters and to identify María with Efraín's deep love of his home-region. All the major characters, including even a potential rival to Efraín, are highly idealized, and this is above all the case with regard to the lovers and Efraín's close family. The question, then, inevitably arises: if these people as so nobly high-minded, so virtuous, chaste, devoted and religious, why is the love of Efraín and María condemned to waste and destruction, with suffering for all involved? There is no moral flaw or failing in the lovers to justify what happens to them. The mishap that overtakes them is completely arbitrary and, in fact, is specifically associated with adverse fate by Isaacs himself through the use of the *ave negra* symbol. While this is the most explicit, it is not the only one. Critics have overlooked the implicit symbolism of the frustrated journey up river towards the plantation made by Efraín near the end of the novel. Since Heraclitus, rivers have been used to symbolize life. Efraín is struggling desperately against the stream to reach his love. He finds death awaiting him instead. This is a very powerful symbol reinforcing that of the sinister bird. In all three of the novels under discussion, the love affairs which are central to the stories end unhappily. All three seem to contain some symbolic message about life which is in the end sad. But we look in vain for what it is. We see the workings of an unjust destiny, which implacably condemns the most pure and worthy human feelings, but we are offered no satisfactory commentary on it. There is no anguish, no outcry, only melancholy and resignation. Isaacs, above all, surrounds the events of the novel with a profoundly Christian atmosphere. But can we avoid noticing the unresolved contradiction between a loving God and an evil fate?

The outwardly Romantic features of *María* include, most of all, the outpouring of rapturous emotion on the theme of youth and love, which is never allowed to be dislodged from first place in the author's priorities; the references to the *ave negra*; the emphasis on the natural background and on local colour (the rustic wedding and in general the descriptions of the picturesque life of the plantation workers and Efraín's more humbly situated friends); and the mood of melancholy. Unlike *Amalia*, *María* is well-constructed and unified. Several critics, including Brushwood, have emphasized how even the parts of the novel which might seem to break its unity are actually extensions of the love theme. We have mentioned Nature's functional role; but in addition Brushwood, in *Genteel Barbarism*, points out that 'The Nay story and the Braulio-Tránsito idyll are metaphors of the María-Efraín love that enhance the meaning of the novel' (p. 106).

Sommer's attempt to explain the novel in socio-political terms as the swan-song of a semi-feudal planter class is a possible, but somewhat strained, interpretation based more on biographical data about Isaacs than on the novel itself. It illustrates her failure to understand the inherent contradiction of the novel, to which she refers at the outset of her chapter, in terms of the contradiction inherent in Romanticism itself, especially in Spain. *María* belongs to that wing of traditionalist Romanticism which Fernán Caballero inherited from her father Böhl de Faber and which, while using the trappings of Romanticism, was primarily concerned to shield readers from any of the subversive 'disolvente' ideas imported by the opposite wing of the movement. The idea of cosmic injustice was one of them.

Clemencia (1869) by Ignacio Manuel Altamirano (Mexico, 1834–93) has the same allegiance. Extravagantly praised – almost every historian of Spanish American literature who mentions it ritually echoes Carlos González Peña's remark that Altamirano was the greatest (Mexican) writer of his time – it is virtually unstudied even by modern Mexican critics. Altamirano was practically the founder and first theorist of modern Mexican fiction. Praising the examples of Echeverría and Mármol among others, he called for consciously *americanista* literature. It would be one which would teach, especially patriotism and morality, as well as history and right-thinking social doctrines. Ironically, as a theorist and critic, he felt obliged to seem slightly contemptuous of the 'simple cuento de amores', in which, he declared, 'no deben buscarse más que elevación, verdad, sentimiento y elegancia de estilo', but above all morality.[14] *Clemencia* is set in and around Guadalajara during the French occupation of Mexico (1864–67). The main figures are two young officers in the Mexican army in conflict with the French: the handsome, dashing and popular Enrique and the disagreeable and mean Fernando. In Guadalajara they each fall in love, with Isabel and Clemencia respectively, but both women are in fact attracted to Enrique. The novel turns a first corner in chapter eleven when the latter drops the mask and emerges as a cynical womanizer and, worse still, a man consumed with ambition and greed. Fernando is revealed at the same time to be the Romantic idealist:

> Yo creía que el amor era uno de los grandes objetos de la existencia; yo creía que la mujer amada era el apoyo poderoso para el viaje de la vida; yo creía que sus ojos comunicaban luz al alma, que su sonrisa endulzaba el trabajo, que el fuego de su corazón era una savia vivificante que impedía desfallecer.[15]

Clemencia turns a second corner in chapter eighteen when Clemencia also

[14] See Ralph E. Warner, *Historia de la novela mexicana en el siglo XIX* (Mexico City, Robredo, 1953), p. 50.

[15] Ignacio M. Altamirano, *Clemencia* (Mexico City, Porrua, 1944), p. 65.

reveals her true feelings, after using Fernando as a stalking horse in her pursuit of Enrique.

Thereafter it becomes apparent that the latter is about to betray not only Isabel's love for him, but also his country, since he is in league with the French. Fernando, however, discovers his treachery and his rival is condemned to death. But, in a final romantically melodramatic reversal of fortunes, Fernando sacrifices both life and honour to liberate Enrique, who is promptly promoted to colonel in the French-led forces. Clemencia remorsefully takes refuge in a convent. Characteristically, chapter thirty-six is entitled 'La fatalidad' and in it Fernando mouths the commonplaces of *mal du siècle*:

> Creo una fortuna que me fusilen. Estoy fastidiado de sufrir, la vida me causa tedio, la fatalidad me persigue y me ha vencido, como era de esperarse . . . yo no sé si en buena filosofía estará admitida la influencia de la Fatalidad . . . pero el hecho es que sin haber hecho nada que me hubiese acarreado el castigo del cielo, que sintiéndome con el alma inclinada a todo lo noble y bueno, he sido muy infeliz y he visto cernerse siempre la tempestad de la desgracia sobre mi humilde cabaña, al tiempo que he visto brillar el cielo con todas sus pompas sobre el palacio del malvado.
> (pp. 220–21)

It is not at all clear what we are supposed to make of these words, which portend the novel's unexpectedly bitter and ironic finale. Clearly, Altamirano here is engaged in a last minute attempt to convert Fernando's repeated misfortunes into indications of the hand of destiny. But if destiny can operate like this, what conclusion is the reader to draw? Apparently that the way to thwart adverse fate is by heroic self-sacrifice, irrespective of the fact that in this case, the sacrifice merely contributes to the triumph of evil. It is difficult not to conclude that *Clemencia* shows evidence of a certain degree of ideological confusion.

It has to be kept constantly in mind that in Latin America (and most of Europe) before the 1860s to write about real life as it was actually lived was not an option. The directly observed reality of everyday life and behaviour was thought of as commonplace, depressing and demoralizing. The tiny literate audience contained a large sector of women readers, and it was thought that they and others needed to be shielded from the spectacle of things as they really were. The camera had to angled: reality had to be prettified, idealized or exoticized; suffering and hardship had to be presented, not as part of the nature of things, but as the result of sin or evil. Thus writers turned to history for novelesque and romanticized plots, as in the case of *La novia del hereje* (1846) by Vicente Fidel López (Argentina, 1815–1903), the forerunner of many others throughout the century and beyond. Or, as we have just seen, they turned to national allegories and sentimental romances. Here and there, as in Sarmiento's gallery of denizens of the pampa ('el baquiano, el rastreador, el payador'), or in Isaacs's presentation of the life of the humble folk living near Efraín's father's plantation, we see examples of *costumbrismo*, the depiction of picturesque types and their life-styles. This was another camera angle which permitted the writer to seem to be dealing with the real, while in fact presenting only the more acceptable, more droll, less sordid, aspects of it. *Costumbrismo* (which survived into the Regionalist novel of the twentieth century and was, for example alive and well in Ciro Alegría's prettified depiction of the Peruvian Indians in *El mundo es ancho y ajeno* [1941]) is a very complex phenomenon. It had its 'civic' side, in aiding the literate public to achieve national consciousness. It helped that public to understand part of what their nationality involved, through coming to terms with the 'otherness' of other areas, other classes, other life-styles, in the same country. It might at times contain the presupposition that the way in which people visualized their national reality could affect the way they behaved as citizens. It could satirize, usually affectionately, some older aspects of societal behaviour. It could moralize. It involved a certain degree of achievement of national self-awareness through the discovery that these new nations had marked individual characteristics, even if these were not always positive. What it did not normally do was to contain references to the harshness and complexity of real social conditions. As a rule it was intrinsically non-threatening to the status quo.

Costumbrismo flourished everywhere in Spanish America throughout the nineteenth century, peaking in the work of writers like Tomás Carasquilla (Colombia 1858–1940), with *Frutos de mi tierra* (1896), but above all in the *Tradiciones peruanas* (1872–1910) of Ricardo Palma (Peru, 1833–1919). All *costumbrismo* tends to look backward, usually to the recent past, with a certain amused, sometimes wry, nostalgia. The originality of Palma, which was imitated all over the continent, lay in his exploitation of historical *costumbrismo*. This was not only for entertainment. Every self-respecting country needs a national tradition. Post-colonial countries have to create one. This is where writers, already engaged, as we have seen, in the civic task of promulgating national ideals, were able to make a further contribution to building a sense of nationality. Palma and his many followers and imitators embraced this function, ransacking the past for relevant material. He adapted the *tradición*, which flourished in Spain and had its roots in folklore, to make it into a historical anecdote which had nothing to do with the Romantic tendency to create a heroic, idealized past into which to escape from the present. His *tradiciones* are closely connected with the establishment of *peruanidad*. Higgins reminds us that at the beginning of 'Un virrey y un arzobispo' he pens a brief lament on Spanish America's 'ignorance and disregard of its own past'.[16] In the end he published more than five hundred of them, the bulk

16 James Higgins, *A History of Peruvian Literature* (Liverpool, Cairns, 1987), p. 68.

being set in eighteenth-century Lima, when it was the splendid viceregal capital. Typically, he would select some piquant, 'human interest'-type event and develop it into a well-crafted short narrative, often in three parts. The first part would whet the readers' curiosity, but the climax would be postponed until after a short, didactic, historical digression, to be followed by the often dramatic outcome. Thus 'Las orejas del alcalde' begins by introducing the licentious mayor of Potosí and his abuse of power to punish a poor, but noble, rival, who threatens vengeance. But then follows: 'Hagamos una pausa, lector amigo, y entremos en el laberinto de la historia', which introduces some details about the Viceroy at the time. And then we read: 'Al siguiente día . . .' and find out what the vengeance consisted in. Similarly in 'Pan, queso y raspadura', the battle of Ayacucho is announced, but not allowed to commence, until Palma has paused to introduce the members of the Council of War who decided to begin the action.

This is not to suggest that the *Tradiciones* are all cut to a similar formula. Palma was out to entertain and he does so by ringing the changes on a wide variety of different ways of bringing history alive. In addition, at a time when fictional style was often fustian and overburdened with long solemn periods, a glance at almost any page of the *Tradiciones* shows crisp, agile sentences and short, rapid-fire paragraphs, 'light and gay like castanets' was how Palma described it. But most of all the style is enlivened by sly, playful, sometimes slightly sardonic humour, underlining the piquancy of the anecdotes and not infrequently the relevance of what is being recounted to Palma's own times. We recognize a tone of disenchantment with contemporary Peru, especially with its politicians and high Church functionaries, which finds expression in what has been called Palma's aggressive irony. Nonetheless, Palma was bitterly attacked in the next generation as a reactionary whose obsession with the past distracted attention from the need to modernize the country. Certainly *costumbrismo*, while it contributed to a greater sense of nationality, tended to avoid seeing reality in all its complexity and problematicness. For the beginning of this we have to turn to the dawn of Realism.

Further Reading

For this and subsequent chapters the best general source books are:

Dictionary of Literary Biography, vols. 113 (1992) and 145 (1994) (Detroit, Bruccoli, Clark, Layman). Detailed and illustrated entries on individual writers by leading critics.

Foster, David William and Altamiranda, Daniel, *Spanish American Literature* (New York, Garland, 1998), vols. 3–5. Essays in English and Spanish on major writers from Romanticism on.

Hart, Stephen, *A Companion to Spanish-American Literature* (London, Tamesis, 1999). A first-class general introduction.

Moss, Joyce and Valestuk, Lorraine, eds., *World Literature and its Times*, vol. 1, *Latin American Literature and its Times*. On individual works, stressing the historical background.

Smith, Verity, ed., *Encyclopedia of Latin American Literature* (London, Fitzroy Dearborn, 1997). A massive work of reference both on authors, themes and individual texts. The best in the field.

Brushwood, John S., *Mexico in its Novel. A Nation's Search for Identity* (Austin, Texas U.P., 1966). Dated but useful.

Lichtblau, Myron I., *The Argentine novel in the Nineteenth Century* (New York, Hispanic Institute, 1959). Also dated but a handy overview.

Suárez-Murias, Marguerite C., *La novela romántica en Hispanoamérica* (New York, Hispanic Institute, 1963). The only work of its kind on this neglected period. We need a new one.

Spell, Jefferson R., *The Life and Works of José Joaquín Fernández de Lizardi* (Philadelphia, Pennsylvania U.P., 1931).

Alba-Koch, Beatriz de, *Ilustrando la Nueva España: texto e imagen en 'El Periquillo Sarniento' de Fernández de Lizardi* (Cáceres, Extremadura U.P., 1999).

There is almost no good modern criticism of Lizardi in English.

Foster, David W., 'Paschal Symbology in Echeverría's "El matadero" ', *Studies in Short Fiction*, 7.2 (1970), 257–63.

Mercado, Juan C., *Building a Nation: The Case of Esteban Echeverría* (Lanham, University Press of America, 1995).

Katra, William H., *Domingo F. Sarmiento: Public Writer (Between 1839 and 1852)* (Tempe, Arizona State U.P., 1985).

Shaw, Donald L., 'Concerning the Structure of *Facundo*', *Iberoamerikanisches Archiv*, 6.3 (1980), 239–50.

Harter, Hugh A., *Gertrudis Gómez de Avellaneda* (Boston, Twayne, 1981). The Twayne series books are intended to be systematic introductions for English speakers. They vary greatly in quality, but have improved since the mid-1980s. This is adequate.

Kirkpatrick, Susan, *Las Románticas: Women Writers and Subjectivity in Spain, 1835–1850* (Berkeley, California U.P., 1989). Includes Avellaneda because of her residence in Spain.

Brushwood, John S., *Genteel Barbarism. Experiments in the Analysis of Nineteenth-Century Spanish American Novels* (Lincoln, Nebraska U.P., 1981).

McGrady, Donald, *Jorge Isaacs* (New York, Twayne, 1972).

Magnarelli, Sharon, *The Lost Rib: Female Characters in the Spanish American Novel* (Lewisburg, Bucknell U.P., and London, Associated University Presses, 1985). A pioneering book on what is now a hot topic.

Brushwood, John. S., *The Romantic Novel in Mexico* (Columbia, Missouri U.P., 1954). Dated but still useful in default of anything better.

Compton, Merlin D., *Ricardo Palma* (Boston, Twayne, 1982).

Tauzín Castellanos, Isabelle, *Las tradiciones peruanas de Ricardo Palma: claves de una coherencia* (Lima, Universidad Ricardo Palma, 1999).

Chapter 2

REALISM, NATURALISM AND *MODERNISMO*

The ideal of the Realists was to depict reality as it would be if they were not there. But this, of course, is simply an ideal. In the first place, all narrative is necessarily selective. In order to make them interesting, events have to be organized into a pattern, which means making reality seem much tidier and directly comprehensible than it ever is. In the second place, the organizing agent, the writer, is conditioned by his or her own sex, temperament, experience, belief system, class situation and period, so that the pattern can never be 'objective'. Realism, in other words, is a matter of intention, on the writer's part, to be 'true to life'. Thirdly, we have to recall that, until quite recently, whole areas of experience were more or less taboo, the area of sexuality being chief among them. When we stop to think of the immense influence of sex on behaviour, it is hard to accept that nineteenth- and early twentieth-century Realism was in fact realistic in any full sense of the word. When we also stop to think that the earlier Realists, before human psychology began to be systematically investigated, often tended to underplay the subconscious, subrational drives and motivations of human conduct, we realize that we have to be careful how we understand the term. Finally, as Borges pointed out, language is by its very nature successive. It can only describe events one after another, whereas reality is simultaneous. All the same, Realism marked an important shift of literary sensibility. There was no longer any need to angle the camera quite so obviously towards a prettified reality, even if some areas had to be largely avoided.

The Realists took it mainly for granted that the task of the novelist was to present the fictional world in a way which (the reader was called upon to realize) reflected more or less faithfully a pre-existing reality against which the behaviour of the characters and the verisimilitude of the episodes could somehow be checked and which was somehow more authoritative than the copy. They adjusted their techniques accordingly. Form in fiction is often a metaphor. The characteristic Realist novel form, in which an omniscient narrator recounts events and human reactions to them as if both were by and large rationally explicable, makes up a reassuring metaphor of an intelligible world, even if the events in question do not have a happy outcome. One of the great differences between nineteenth-century fiction and twentieth-century fiction, as we shall see, is that, in the twentieth century, that reassuring metaphor is frequently replaced by a disturbing one which questions the very basis on which Realism rests. The writer who spelled out the basis of this shift most explicitly in Spanish American literature was Borges, as we shall see.

Meanwhile the transition from Romantic romances to the early Realist novel is clearly visible in *Martín Rivas* (1862) by Alberto Blest Gana (Chile, 1829–1904). To see how this is the case we need only compare it with *La gran aldea* (1884) by Lucio V. López (Argentina, 1848–94), while recalling at the same time that Altamirano's *Clemencia* was not to be published for another seven years. In other words, before Romantic fiction had fully run its course, and while *costumbrismo* was still evolving, Blest Gana's ground-breaking novel had already appeared. López's *La gran aldea* begins as an autobiographical account of the childhood and youth of its narrator in the Buenos Aires of the later nineteenth century. Looking back to the early 1860s, the narrator writes categorically: 'No había entonces realismo.'[1] Even Dickens was still unknown. European literature was represented by Henri Murger, Théophile Gautier and Alfred de Vigny, that is, by the Romantics. Twenty years later however, that is, shortly before López's novel was published, Maupassant was already on the scene. But not for López: what we find in *La gran aldea* is urban *costumbrismo*. The picture of 'las tiendas de antaño' in chapter five, while not written with as sharp a pen as Larra's, is quite worthy of Mesonero Romanos. But Mesonero had written his *Escenas matritenses* half a century before! López knew that Romanticism was finished, and says so categorically in chapter nine; but he does not quite make it into Realism. Blest Gana does much better. He too makes no bones about presenting Romanticism as an obsolete movement. Chapter thirty-two is the key chapter. In it Don Fidel Elías, a 'sectario de la religión del comercio', discusses the marriage of his daughter, Matilde, with his wife, who happens to be reading *Valentine* (1832) by the French Romantic George Sand. He regards the marriage as 'un buen negocio', while her head is full of 'romántico arrobamiento'.[2] Needless to say, in the end, Don Fidel prevails.

In Romantic fiction, marriage may take place, as in *Amalia*, but is rarely if ever consummated, for that would destroy the effect of the underlying metaphor. Love has to be tragic. But in Realism, so often associated with the rise of the middle class, the emphasis shifts from love to marriage. Fate is no longer the issue; society and social mores are what matter. There is tragic love in *Martín Rivas*. Martín's friend, Rafael, is deeply in love with Matilde, but is too poor to aspire to her hand. Worse still, he has fathered a child with a lower-class girl. When she hears about it, Matilde rejects him outright and he goes out to die heroically in the cause of freedom. She eventually marries the rich but witless suitor whom her father has lined up for her and (alas) seems

[1] Lucio V. López, *La gran aldea* (Buenos Aires, Plus Ultra, 1965), p. 84.
[2] Alberto Blest Gana, *Martín Rivas* (Paris, Bouret, 1924), I, pp. 345–46.

quite likely to be as happy as the somewhat cynical Blest Gana thinks married couples ever can be. The outline of a romantic situation is still there, but it is undercut by middle-class morality. This is merely a sub-plot; the main plot is also a love story, that of Martín and the haughty Leonor. Jaime Concha, in his excellent introduction to the English translation, rightly speaks of Blest Gana's 'system of exclusions and preferences'.[3] The novel is so strongly influenced by Balzac and Dickens as to be almost derivative. Martín is intended to be one of Balzac's *hommes d'élite*, characterized essentially by intelligence and willpower, who take on society, as Rastignac does Paris at the end of *Le Père Goriot*, and overcome the obstacles to their social mobility. He comes from the impoverished lower middle class and is initially a dependent in the mansion of the *nouveau riche* Don Dámaso, a usurious financier who would like to be a senator. The real difference between Martín and Rastignac is that, whereas Balzac lays the emphasis on willpower (that obsession of nineteenth-century France and early twentieth-century Spain), Blest Gana lays it on nobility of character. 'What in fact Blest Gana lays out before us,' Concha writes, 'is Martín Rivas's class apprenticeship and an itinerary for social ascendency' (p. xxx). But this is only partially correct (to say nothing of the fact that Concha presumably means 'ascent'). When we read that Martín 'como los antiguos caballeros, se lanzaba a lo más crudo de la pelea' [i.e. the revolt of 1851 in which Rafael is killed] 'llevando en su pecho la imagen y en sus labios el nombre de Leonor', we see that Fernando Alegría was right to call this a work of 'romantic realism'.[4] The novel is not a social novel but a novel of love in a social setting. Martín carries off the heiress at the end and is set to scale the heights of bourgeois Chilean society, but he gets there by unselfishly lending a hand to everyone in his circle who needs it even when it momentarily compromises his reputation. As a result, when he is condemned to death as a revolutionary, everyone rallies round to save him, with the formerly disdainful Leonor in the lead. The legacy of the Romantic romances is seen in his idealized personality traits: he is in fact quite close to Fernando in *Clemencia*. Both are condemned to death, after showing themselves as exceptionally self-sacrificing and noble. But the metaphor has changed because the world-view has changed: one cannot struggle successfully against fate but one can struggle successfully against social obstacles by self-help (albeit in this case of a rather special kind).

Again in contrast to López's *La gran aldea*, *Martín Rivas* is an early example of the well-made novel. The main plot consists of a series of interlocking love affairs, but ones in which money and social class play the role of (a now not so adverse) fate. The function of each of these is to bring out

3 Jaime Concha, 'Introduction' to *Martín Rivas* (Oxford U.P., 2000), p. xxiii.

4 Fernando Alegría, *Nueva historia de la novela hispanoamericana* (Hanover [New Hampshire], Ediciones del Norte, 1986), p. 54.

aspects of Martín's fundamental friendliness and moral integrity. Blest Gana carefully constructs the plot like a mechanism around this young pseudo-Balzacian provincial so that time after time he can step in and save the day. Meanwhile we follow with real interest the gradual, well-orchestrated shift in Leonor's attitude to him until his life is on the line at the end. To provide comic relief we have a series of Dickensian older characters, headed by the ineffable Doña Bernarda Molina and her scoundrelly son, Amador, *gente de medio pelo*, who represent Blest Gana's 'excluded' group, lower-class people who are up to no good. They contrast with his 'preferred' group, Martín and Rafael. The latter, despite Rafael's indiscretion, stand for a professionally educated, younger generation ready to take over from the coarser-grained, ignorant businessmen who are their elders. As in *La gran aldea*, a class who are little better than jumped-up shopkeepers face a new class of 'hombres nuevos pobres'. In Blest Gana's novel, as Brushwood points out, the 'happy ending' symbolizes the two classes reaching an accommodation.[5] López, on the other hand, though his novel deals with the same class of *nouveaux riches*, and drops strong hints of intra-class, inter-generational rivalry, does not develop the theme. Instead he stitches together his picturesque vignettes of life in old Buenos Aires with a creaky, melodramatic story of a greedy young woman marrying a foolish old man for his money and coming to grief. What matters to him in the later part of the novel is to excoriate the self-important vulgarity of a new-monied upper bourgeoisie, not to analyse social change and renewal. We notice a very clear shift of tone and intention from the earlier *costumbrismo* to the later social criticism, which marks the turn towards Realism. As was to be the case in the next century, the bourgeoisie enjoyed being pilloried and rewarded the writers who undertook the task. López became a Deputy and later a Minister, just as Eduardo Mallea and Agustín Yáñez, for example, who in Argentina and Mexico both had hard things to say about the middle and upper classes, were both given plum jobs with Unesco. We should not overestimate the importance of social criticism in literature. The directing class can usually absorb it with ease.

It is perhaps worth noting at this point that the criticism of the novels under discussion here is generally of very indifferent quality. This is partly because this is not a fashionable area to write about and therefore does not attract much thoughtful and competent criticism, but chiefly because confusion reigns in the matter of nomenclature. We read of 'costumbrismo realista', 'realismo naturalista' and the like on all sides, with the result that a novel like *La Bolsa* (1891) by Julián Martel ([pseudonym of José Miró] Argentina, 1867–96) is commonly written about as if it were a Naturalist work, simply because it was published after *Sin rumbo* (1885) by Eugenio

[5] John S. Brushwood, *Genteel Barbarism* (Lincoln and London, Nebraska U.P., 1981), p. 81.

Cambaceres (Argentina, 1843–89), who is much closer to the Naturalist movement properly so called. There is in *La Bolsa* none of the nostalgic *costumbrista* evocation of a bygone, still predominantly *criolla,* Buenos Aires, as there had been in López's *La gran aldea* only seven years previously. But, despite the arguments of Morales,[6] equally there is little that is genuinely Naturalistic, even by the standards of Argentine Naturalism, the peculiarity of which will be mentioned presently. *La Bolsa* is basically a Realist novel of observation and commentary in terms of social criticism, without any of the caricaturesque fun-elements present in *Martin Rivas* and *La gran aldea*. These are now replaced by bitingly hostile sketches of the dangerously insidious fauna inhabiting the financial district of Buenos Aires. There are no significantly deterministic elements, nor anything to bring to mind Zola's *Le Roman expérimental* (1870).

La Bolsa is one of a group of novels inspired by the Buenos Aires Stock Market crash in 1890. Its theme is the destruction of a well-intentioned, decent, family man who allows himself to be corrupted by the frenzy of speculation that overtook Buenos Aires in the late 1880s. Although its subtitle is 'Estudio social', it is in fact a moral fable. Luis Glow, the central figure, is an honourable man, but through weakness of character he is tempted into dishonest stock manipulation. Jitrik is right to point out that Martel believed he saw in the boom and bust of the Stock Market a way to explain what was happening in the country as a whole. He is no less correct when he suggests that Martel and his fellow novelists neither recognized nor understood properly the economic processes, typical of old-style bucaneering capitalism, by which they were surrounded.[7] Martel saw the problem in simplistic moral terms of 'los que carecen de moral social' and 'los que, por el contrario, respetan todo lo respetable',[8] which produces a rather schematic approach to characterization. Glow and his less scrupulous associates are presented as the outward manifestation of the contamination of Argentina by grossly materialistic values which Jewish and immigrant influence and the good times had caused to triumph over traditional attachment to honourable dealing.[9] The danger is not just to business, but to the nation itself: 'Allí donde el dinero abunda', Glow insists, 'rara vez el patriotismo existe' (p. 111). The description of the reception at the Glows' mansion in Part I, chapter 8, is designed to depict the luxury and folly of the middle and upper classes, which were about

6 Carlos Javier Morales, *Julián Martel y la novela naturalista argentina* (Logroño, La Rioja U.P., 1997), e.g. p. 95.

7 Noé Jitrik, 'El ciclo de la Bolsa', in Various Authors, *Historia de la literatura argentina* (Buenos Aires, Centro Editor de América Latina, 1980), II, pp. 159–66.

8 Julián Martel, *La Bolsa* (Buenos Aires, Emecé, 1942), p. 163.

9 Though slanted towards the presentation of the immigrant 'parasites', as Martel chose to see them, Evelyn Fishburn's chapter on *La Bolsa* in *The Portrayal of Immigration in Nineteenth Century Argentine Fiction (1845–1902)* (Berlin, Colloquium Verlag, 1981) is probably the best recent piece of criticism of the novel.

to plunge the country into a fearsome crisis. *La Bolsa* is structured symmetrically around the crash, which occurs in the middle of the novel between Books I and II. As Book I reveals the causes, Book II hurries on to the effects. Glow, betrayed and abandoned by his business associates, is utterly ruined and goes mad. *La Bolsa* is not a great novel. But it illustrates the fact that Spanish American Realist and Naturalist writers were characterized by a continuing explicit attachment to the moral idealism we already met with in Blest Gana's *Martín Rivas* but which is largely absent from the French movements.

Martel in real life, like Martín Rivas in fiction, belonged to that class of impoverished but professionally educated young men whom López tells us in *La gran aldea* were struggling up into the bourgeoisie. Like so many of the poor relations of the upper classes, he internalized their outlook and above all their prejudices to the point at which, as Fishburn implacably points out, it falsified his vision of reality. Cambaceres, by contrast, came from the ranks of the oligarchy itself, but defied its traditional values, attacking the Church (which he wished to see separated from the State), joining the Freemasons, living openly with a demi-mondaine, whom he only married after they had had a child, and writing a series of scandalous novels, best sellers in their time in Argentina, which provoked a storm of indignation and protest. He was instantly numbered among the Naturalists, not least by his friend and fellow-writer Miguel Cané, who savagely criticized Cambaceres's *Música sentimental* (1884) and *Sin rumbo* (1885), from a more or less Realist standpoint.

With the benefit of hindsight, we can see that Naturalism had two salient characteristics. On the one hand, the Naturalists felt that the process which had begun with the Romantics' use of local colour and *pintoresquismo*, and which had developed through *costumbrismo* to Realism, had not yet completed its evolution. If the Romantics and the *costumbristas* had screened out the more sordid, crude, violent and degraded aspects of human behaviour, and especially sexual behaviour, and if the Realists had accepted them only within certain narrow limits, the Naturalists felt that the time had come to angle the camera more specifically towards them, regarding them as a new area of observation for fiction to colonize. This is the aspect of Naturalism which survives in some areas of modern fiction, drama and cinema. When, for example, the characters in Pavlovski's *El Señor Galindez* (1973) are seen on the stage preparing to torture a naked girl in full view of the audience, we see in one sense a form of Neo-Naturalism. On the other hand the Naturalists tended to believe strongly in hereditary determinism, reinforced by ambiental determinism, as the principal factor influencing behaviour. Although the former is back in fashion, as a result of studies of twins, and although sociologists have always been attracted by the notion of environmental determinism, this pseudo-scientific aspect of Naturalism is now regarded as reductive and simplistic and has disappeared from modern literature.

Cané seized on the first characteristic, ritually vilifying 'el naturalismo de Zola' as deliberately emphasizing what is coarse and disgusting, and criticized Cambaceres for aligning himself with it. He himself advocated what he called 'naturalness' (*naturalidad*), not Naturalism, defining the former rather feebly as 'el esfuerzo por interpretar, no reflejar la naturaleza, en toda su verdad, dentro de las exigencias del arte mismo'.[10] Cymerman rightly castigates Cané for his confused thinking. By contrast, Cambaceres defined Naturalism as follows:

> Entiendo por naturalismo, estudio de la naturaleza humana, observación hasta los tuétanos. Agarrar un carácter, un alma, registrarla hasta los últimos repliegues, meterle el calador, sacarla todo, lo bueno como lo malo, lo puro si es que se encuentra y la podredumbre que encierra, haciéndola mover en el medio donde se agita . . . sustituir a la fantasía del poeta o a la habilidad del *faiseur*, la ciencia del observador, hacer en una palabra verdad, verdad hasta la cuja. (Cymerman, p. 42)

As we see, this does not go beyond advocating carrying Realism to its logical extreme, which is the positive side of Naturalism, in the sense of reflecting in fiction as wide a panorama of reality as possible and not leaving anything out. In fact, in *En la sangre* (1887) he goes rather further than this, and assumes that 'la ciencia del observador' will rest on a basis of determinism.

Characteristic of the kind of confused writing about this period in Argentine fiction is Bazán-Figueras' comment that 'Cambaceres se resiste a recurrir a una narrativa tradicional y, por lo tanto, a la tendencia naturalista-ochentista',[11] She goes on to base this judgement on the fact that he advocated 'el recuento de la verdad "hasta los huesos" ', which is precisely one of the two things which all the Naturalists advocated. What underlies her judgement, however, is the realization that *Sin rumbo* is in a way quite different from earlier fiction (but not in a sense that removes it from the category of Naturalism). Throughout the nineteenth century the intense negativism of one area of Romanticism (represented in Spain by the cosmic protest of Rivas's *Don Alvaro* and Espronceda's significantly titled *El diablo mundo*) gradually percolated through different strata of educated thinking, sending out cultural shockwaves. These produced chronologically a fierce reaction against 'el romanticismo malo' on the part of traditionally minded people in the period following the movement, then attempts to combat pessimism and despair through philosophical renovation (*Krausismo* in Spain, and, to some

[10] Cit. Claude Cymerman, *Diez estudios cambacerianos* (Rouen, Rouen U.P., 1993), p. 77.

[11] Patricia Bazán-Figueras, *Eugenio Cambaceres, precursor de la novela argentina contemporánea* (New York, Lang, 1994), p. 73.

extent thereafter, Positivism, which proposed a progressive, no nonsense, scientific attitude excluding cosmic speculation) and finally, in literature, movements orientated towards Art for Art's Sake, with heavy emphasis on 'the Ideal', designed to combat the heritage of negative Romanticism. But in the meantime that heritage (initially a largely unconceptualized, emotional outcry on the part of a minority of Romantics, said to suffer from *Weltschmertz* or *mal du siècle*, terms which still cause much misunderstanding) had been reinforced from several directions but chiefly by the input of Schopenhauer. The latter's influence, which was dominant in wide areas of Hispanic culture from Cambaceres, through Barrios and Neruda right up to Borges, has not been adequately recognized, still less systematically studied. It was extremely strong in French Decadentism, which in turn influenced *Modernismo*, and, of course, in Naturalism. The first great monument to it is *Sin rumbo*. There is no doubt that *Sin rumbo* is a Naturalist work and was recognized as such from the time of its publication, on the grounds that it emphasized the more sordid and ugly side of human behaviour, hitherto under-represented in Spanish American fiction. It is the story of a young, idle, wealthy member of the landowning class, afflicted with a sense of the futility, not just of his existence, but of existence generally. To those who are familiar with the Spanish Generation of 1898 and its horror of 'la nada' and 'la enfermedad de lo incognoscible', and with its postulate of *abulia* (borrowed from France where a similar outlook was prominent), this theme will be perfectly familiar. But *Sin rumbo* was published in 1885, two years before Unamuno's greatest existential crisis, sixteen years before Azorín's *Diario de un enfermo*, which is in many ways its Spanish equivalent, and seventeen years before the key year of 1902 which saw the publication of Azorín's *La voluntad* and Baroja's *Camino de perfección*, both of which are extremely relevant in this connection. Bazán-Figueras is quite correct to see in Cambaceres a precursor of later Argentine fiction, but mainly in the sense that he was the first major writer to express the kind of existential malaise that we find again in Mallea, Borges, Sábato and others. It led Mallea, as we shall see below, to postulate a generalized existential crisis afflicting his generation, and led Sábato to call for and practise a 'metaphysical' type of fiction as a response to it. When in my *Nueva narrativa hispanoamericana*, I included existential pessimism as an integral part of much Boom writing and a certain degree of renewed optimism among some Post-Boom writers,[12] I was provisionally suggesting that what began with *Sin rumbo* took at least until the mid 1970s to run its course.

The key chapters of the novel are not therefore the one in which Andrés, the world-weary central character, rapes the daughter of his faithful and

[12] See my *Nueva narrativa hispanoamericana* (Madrid, Cátedra, 6a edición ampliada, 1999), e.g. pp. 242 and 262.

devoted *capataz*, or even the one at the end in which he rips his belly open. Both of these are Naturalist incidents in the sense that they are distasteful, disgusting and in the second case horrible. The really important chapters are five and seven in which Andrés's world-view is made manifest, first by the omniscient author and second by his own words. In chapter five Andrés is described as 'abandonado a su negro pesimismo, minada el alma por la zapa de los grandes demoledores humanos, abismado el espíritu en el glacial y terrible 'nada' de las doctrinas nuevas, prestigiadas a sus ojos por el triste caudal de su experiencia', and in seven he voices publicly his Schopenhauerian creed: 'Dios no es nadie; la ciencia es un cáncer para el alma. Saber es sufrir; ignorar, comer, dormir y no pensar, la solución exacta del problema, la única dicha de vivir.'[13] Religion, plainly, is not an option for Andrés. Which others remain? Baroja in Spain, faced with the same problem in *Camino de perfección* (1902) and *El árbol de la ciencia* (1911) postulates three: love, the ethical ideal, and action limited to the small area of society in which an average individual can make some difference through his or her own efforts. None of these worked, and Baroja finally opted for withdrawal from society and seeking a fragile serenity in relative seclusion. Cambaceres is much more extreme. The ethical ideal, which he uses as a stick in his next novel to beat the non-*criollo* Genaro with, is (as the more traditional Cané immediately pointed out) never even considered. Action, too, which Andrés is well situated by his wealth, position and education to undertake, is not presented as a possibility, and Cambaceres is too impatient to explain why. Love, but not sexual love, is for him the only option facing Andrés. The latter, having raped Donata, has an adulterous affair (on her part) with an opera singer. But this only exacerbates his spiritual problem, leaving him 'sin rumbo en la noche negra y helada de su vida' (p. 321) and already contemplating suicide. Here, and elsewhere in the novel where suicide is mentioned as a possibility, we are in the presence of a 'prepared effect', in this case a prefiguration of the ending which helps the reader to accept it in all its eventual horror. But the 'dynamism' of the narrative technique, which Schade rightly praises, also plays Cambaceres false. The great shortcoming of the novel is his impatience at the beginning to get the plot moving. This leads him to deny Andrés the stages of psychological development which would explain and justify his existential despair. He is already enmeshed in it from the start and we are simply required to accept it. We are not 'shown' what the 'triste caudal de experiencia' was, which caused him to internalize so completely the teachings of the 'grandes demoledores humanos'; we are are merely 'told' that it was there operating. We are not shown why other possibilities of self-regeneration fail. As a result, *Sin rumbo* can be described as a psychological novel gone awry, because its author took his fences too

13 Eugenio Cambaceres, *Sin rumbo, Obras completas* (Santa Fe [Argentina], Castelvi, 1968), pp. 288 and 294.

fast. It portends the absence of the *roman d'analyse* from future Spanish American fiction.

At the technical level, it is interesting to contrast *Sin rumbo* with Isaacs' *María*, published only eighteen years previously. There we saw that all the characters (even Efraín's rival for the hand of María) are idealized, along with Nature itself, whose lush, tropical richness symbolizes life warmed and vitalized by the sunshine of love. Here instead everyone, with the exception of the *capataz*, Ño Regino, his daughter and Andrés's daughter by her, all of whom are presented as too primitive either because of babyhood or background to be included, are systematically denigrated. In fact, as Fishburn has demonstrated, they are animalized. By the same token, Nature, in this case the Pampa, is seen symbolically in chapter thirty as a life-threatening adversary. Characteristically Cané, in his review of the novel, complains that Cambaceres passes over the 'colorido', that is, the possibility of exploiting the *costumbrista* picturesqueness, of the rural scenes that he incorporates. The complaint precisely illustrates the step forward which Cambaceres was making. Schade has affirmed that the lean and concentrated narrative method of *Sin rumbo* makes it a classic, unrivalled before Azuela's *Los de abajo* in 1915. He points to a number of factors which contribute to its impact. These include the careful structuring of the narrative, divided into sections of 13, 13, 6 and 13 chapters, alternating between Buenos Aires and the Pampa; the brutal, bloody sheep shearing at the beginning and the brutal, bloody suicide of Andrés at the end, which frame an implacably cruel story; the speedy pace and dramatic rhythm of the action and the important role played by active verbs, especially those of rapid movement. Schade also mentions the symbolism of the seasons, especially Spring, but he seems to have overlooked the fundamental symbol of *Sin rumbo*, which is the agonizing death of Andrés's daughter, Andrea. As with the death of Luisito, in Baroja's *El árbol de la ciencia*, the arbitrary destruction of an innocent existence calls into question all comfortably positive interpretations of human destiny. In this case, Andrea's death is not only abstractly symbolic, but it is also profoundly ironic, since only she had reconciled Andrés to existence. In *Sin rumbo*, the malevolent fate which we have seen threatening the lovers in the Romantic romances, now emerges as an intrinsic part of life. For the first time we see reassuring metaphors of the human condition (the survival of love after death in Isaacs and Altamirano, the happy ending of Blest Gana's *Martín Rivas*) explicitly replaced by a disturbing one. In that sense *Sin rumbo* prefigures, not just later Argentine fiction, but much of later Spanish American fiction generally.

Because we know next to nothing of Andrés's early life and family there is no room in *Sin rumbo* for the other aspect of Naturalism, hereditary determinism, to be seen operating. But as if to prove that Cambaceres was a fully fledged Naturalist, this force becomes dominant in *En la sangre* (1887).

This is the story of Genaro, the son of poor, degraded, Italian immigrants who manage by cruel self-denial to send him to the University, where he gains a law degree by cheating. After his father's death, he packs his mother off to Italy and with cold cynicism forces his way into a landowning family by getting the only daughter pregnant. But he quickly loses in speculations the wealth he thus acquires and at the end of the novel reveals his brutal and violent nature by striking his wife. The difference from *Sin rumbo* is that in this case we are told from the first page why Genaro is like he is: he comes from racially inferior human stock: 'esa ingénita tendencia que lo impulsara al mal . . . Obraba en él con la inmutable fijeza de las eternas leyes, era fatal . . . estaba en la sangre eso, constitucional, inveterado, le venía de casta como el color de la piel, le había sido transmitido por herencia, de padre a hijo, como de padres a hijos se transmite el virus venenoso de la sífilis.'[14] As he gradually inserts himself into respectable society, his environment changes, but it cannot alter his inherited characteristics.

The 'deep theme' of *En la sangre*, however, is not this. It is that Genaro inherits his evil nature from his immigrant family. By 1895 immigrants were pouring into Argentina at the rate of more than 100,000 a year and already constituted a third of the population. Inevitably they began to be seen as a threat to traditional Argentine values and to the hegemony of the old landowning oligarchy. The consequence for *Sin rumbo*, which is written from the standpoint of a member of the oligarchy, is that the physiological is converted into the moral. Genaro clearly inherits positive as well as negative qualities from his parents: dogged effort, self-denial and business sense, the latter seen when he visits his in-laws' hacienda and is put out by the casual and wasteful way in which it is run. But these are either shown as overwhelmed by his greed, ambition and brutality or denigrated as un-*criollo*. Cymerman (p. 159) quotes David Viñas's comment that Cambaceres turns Naturalism, which was originally a movement aimed against the bourgeoisie, into a critique of the working class. This is clearly correct: Cambaceres instrumentalizes both aspects of the movement, the ugly and the determinist, to defend the class he belonged to, the decay of which, paradoxically, had been suggested in Andrés in *Sin rumbo*. One of the key epidodes in *En la sangre*, the rape of Máxima, Genaro's future wife, can be seen symbolically. Whereas in *Martín Rivas*, *La gran aldea* and even *La Bolsa* (though Glow has immigrant antecedents), the upper classes are infiltrated by 'nuevos hombres' from below, this merely represents a natural form of gradual renewal by assimilation, an injection of new blood. In *En la sangre*, by contrast, Genaro forces his entry into the upper class in a way that could be seen as representing the rape of Argentina by greedy and unprincipled immigrants. Similarly in the next generation Fuentes's Artemio Cruz forces his entry into the

[14] Eugenio Cambaceres, *En la sangre*, *Obras completas* (Santa Fe [Argentina], Castelvi, 1968), pp. 419–20.

Mexican landowner class by obliging Don Gameliel to allow him to marry his daughter Catalina, symbolizing the take-over of the country by the lower-class victors of the Mexican revolution. *En la sangre* is clearly intended to be a wake-up call by Cambaceres to his class. In retrospect we can now see that it was unnecessary. The Latin American oligarchies have proved surprisingly resilient, except in Cuba, where the new one is based on power and not on wealth. It was not to be the last important novel written in defence of old *criollista* values, as we shall see in the next chapter when we briefly discuss Güiraldes's *Don Segundo Sombra.*

If Cambaceres represents the dawn of Naturalism in Spanish American fiction, the later work of Federico Gamboa (Mexico, 1864–1939) represents its sunset. This is because, while a key theme in Naturalism is degeneration, Gamboa's last novels, *Reconquista* (1908) and *La llaga* (1910) are concerned with individual regeneration. Gamboa's *Santa* (1903), on the other hand, the most successful novel in terms of sales beween Isaacs's *María* and Gallegos's *Doña Bárbara* in 1929, was Naturalism's high noon. It was clearly inspired by Zola's *Nana* (1880), also the story of a high-class prostitute. When a consignment of the French edition of *Nana* arrived in Buenos Aires, it sold 1500 copies in a matter of days. We can be sure that it had the same runaway success in Mexico, whose literary culture was just as much French-orientated. The two questions which dominate criticism of *Santa* are: to what extent can we regard it as a full-blown Naturalist work? And is it in some sense a 'national allegory?' To understand the novel, we have to begin from Gamboa's view of the human condition, which was always profoundly ambiguous. Intellectually, he was clearly influenced by the Schopenhauerian pessimism of the times. In *Suprema ley* (1890) it is voiced by the elderly don Eustaquio when he remarks: 'La vida, para mí, es un enorme ferrocarril lanzado a todo vapor, pero sin maquinista ni guardafrenos. Dentro de él caminamos todos, grandes y chicos, sin que sepa nadie adónde parará ni cuál es el objeto del misterioso viaje.'[15] In *Metamorfosis* (1899), Chinto compares our existence to that of a tiny, frail boat amid hurricane-lashed seas (p. 615). In *Santa* itself, Santa's blind devotee, Hipólito, reflects: 'se nace, se vive y se muere sin que comprendamos palotada' (p. 871). But Gamboa's few serious critics recognize that, despite this, he retained his religious beliefs which, indeed, became stronger towards the end of his life. In other words, although he allowed himself to dive into the murky waters of *fin-de-siglo* existential negativism, he always kept firm hold of a life-line.

Prostitution is a subject, not a theme. A real Naturalist would have turned it into a theme by trying to show, with as much clinical detachment as might be, how Santa was driven to embrace and persevere in such an existence by a

[15] Federico Gamboa, *Suprema ley*, *Novelas* (Mexico City, Fondo de Cultura Económica, 1965), p. 457.

combination of hereditary and environmental factors. Gamboa makes only a half-hearted attempt to establish this pattern. There is a passing reference to the presumption that 'en la sangre llevara gérmenes de muy vieja lascivia de algún tatarabuelo que en ella resucitaba con vicios y todo' (p. 758), that is, to a negative hereditary influence and, of course, the environment (her family who reject her after her seduction; the Church which refuses to help her, and so on) presses upon her. But, as Fernández-Levin emphasizes: 'Gamboa se contradice contínuamente culpando y disculpando las acciones de Santa.'[16] Once dishonoured, she makes no attempt to find work, but makes her way directly to a brothel in Mexico City. From the scene of her seduction on, Gamboa, like Cambaceres, fulfils the other requisite of Naturalism, in that we are spared few disgusting details, though Santa dies of cancer, unlike Zola's Nana, who dies more significantly of syphilis. It is this combined emphasis on sexuality and on squalor of all kinds that links *Santa* to Naturalism. But it should not wholly distract our attention from the fact that other aspects of the novel weaken the link.

Santa does not really struggle against her lot. When she finds a certain stability, as the mistress of the toreador El Jarameño, she throws it away. Gamboa swings between blaming 'la maldad infinita de la vida y de los hombres' (p. 854), the irresistible strength of the sexual impulse, and the implacable pressure of society, all of which seem to lie behind Santa's reflection: 'Si me parece que me empujan y me obligan a hacer todo lo que hago' (p. 794). What reveals Gamboa's ambivalence is that he does not present these factors as inescapable, impersonal forces. From beginning to end of the novel, he does not hesitate to pass harsh moral judgements on characters and on their behaviour. But, more especially, he introduces a Hugoesque sub-plot with the horribly deformed and blind Hipólito playing Quasimodo to Santa's Esmeralda. He is hideous but morally salvageable; she is physically adorable but morally irretrievable. Although he briefly succumbs to lust, his dreams of Santa reveal a still Romantic idealization of love which jars with the rest of the novel and gives it that 'hybrid' appearance which, in sundry guises, often characterizes Spanish American fiction.

Fernández-Levin asserts categorically that Santa 'representa la gradual decadencia moral y política de México' (p. 30). She notes the presence of two of the pillars of the *porfiriato*: Santa is seduced by a soldier and the Church offers her neither refuge nor support after her fall. Suprisingly, Fernández-Levin overlooks the role of Gamboa's criticism of the legal system in this context. The same critic interprets the characters Ripoll and El Jarameño as representatives of *cientificismo* and *caudillismo* respectively and sees Santa's situation as symbolizing the exploitation and abuse of the country under the

[16] Rosa Fernández-Levin, *El autor y el personaje femenino en dos novelas del siglo XX* (Madrid, Pliegos, 1997), p. 33.

regime of Díaz. This is a possible reading of the novel and has the advantage of turning its subject into a theme at one level of reader reception. But, of course, this is not the only level at which we perceive meaning in the narrative. Brushwood, rather incautiously, alludes to *Santa*'s 'carefully developed story line and rich symbolic code'.[17] Of the latter there is no doubt; even Nature functions symbolically in the novel. But there is room for difference of opinion about the organization of the plot. *Santa* uses a straightforward biographical approach divided symmetrically into two parts of not very different length. The chapters are unusually similar to one another in length and are conceived as individual, self-contained, narrative units each responsible for a share of the narrative. There is no overlapping and each chapter has its own climax. In other words this, Gamboa's fourth novel, is a highly professionalized job. After the exposition in chapters one and two, we have a rising sequence of three chapters. These are followed by the central interlude in chapter one of Part II, the longest chapter, which is virtually a story within a story. Then follow two chapters of a falling sequence, accelerating very rapidly in the novel's penultimate chapter, after which we have the ending on a note of contrasting sentimentality. We are conscious of a string of episodes rather than of a meaningful evolution. There is no counterforce in the novel and hence, though there are moments of drama, there is no sustained conflict and hence no suspense. The murder and trial scene in Part II have no organic connection with the plot as a whole and are introduced for the purpose of social criticism. In other words, the absence of a well-defined theme, or the fact that the national allegory supplies the only thematic element, means that the plot has an arrangement, but lacks a satisfying pattern.

In his attack on Cambaceres's novel, *Música sentimental*, published in 1884, Miguel Cané insisted that society had to be offered 'el espectáculo constante de las cosas bellas' and 'la prédica incansable del ideal', if it were not to collapse into utter degradation (Cymerman, pp. 85–6). Although Cané was not strictly speaking a *Modernista*, he was voicing a central aspect of their creed. In Spain, a couple of years later, Valera struck at the very root of Realism. '¿Qué provecho nos trae el retratar la verdad si la verdad es siempre inmunda?' he asked revealingly. And specifically in terms of fiction: 'Si la novela se limitase a narrar lo que comúnmente sucede, no sería poesía, no nos ofrecería un ideal, ni sería siquiera una historia digna, sino una historia sobre falsa, baja y rastrera.'[18] We should notice the curious fact that in Spanish America Naturalism and *Modernismo* were contemporaneous movements. By the middle 1880s, Zola had been publishing for more than twenty years and his work had sparked off violent controversies both in Spain and Spanish

[17] *Genteel Barbarism*, p. 158.

[18] Juan Valera, 'Apuntes sobre el nuevo arte de escribir novelas', *Obras de Don Juan Valera* (Madrid, Aguilar, 1949), p. 657.

America. Those hostile to Naturalism were the heirs of the *bien pensantes* who had earlier berated the more subversive Romantics. When it became clear that Catholicism was only sporadically able to inspire works which might offset the pessimism and interest in the all-too-real towards which fiction was moving, the possibility of wheeling out the ideal of Beauty to act as a barrier in the path of such development became attractive. We can even see it operating on the Realists and Naturalists themselves. All we need to do is to turn back to the descriptions of tasteful, aristocratic luxury connected with Glow's mansion and the reception he gives there, in *La Bolsa*, or with Andrés's *garçonnière* in *Sin rumbo* and compare them to the emphasis on 'objetos de arte y de lujo' and the descriptions of sumptuous meals and parties in Silva's *De sobremesa*. The function of the descriptions may be different, but the attraction towards a world of lovely things and distinguished people, where the all-too-real has no place, is the same.

This is not the place to discuss in any detail the meaning of *Modernismo*, beyond remarking that critical attitudes towards the movement underwent a considerable change in the last thirty years of the twentieth century. Previously regarded as a movement (always to be carefully distinguished from European and Anglo-Saxon Modernism) characterized by devotion to the ideal of beauty and the search for formal perfection in poetry and prose, *Modernismo* has now come to be seen as a movement which took that direction in order to seek refuge from what Silva in *De sobremesa* calls 'este fin de siglo angustioso' and Díaz Rodríguez in *Ídolos rotos* calls 'este malhadado fin de siglo'. It is now normal to see in *Modernismo* the link between Romantic despair and the existential anguish of much of twentieth-century literature in Spanish America, especially in poetry.[19] If the Platonic triad Beauty= Goodness=Truth is correct, then to contemplate Beauty is to have Goodness and Truth added unto you. This is the conviction which underlay *Modernismo* at the deepest level, and which made it seem possible to reach a reconciliation with life through the cultivation of what Cané, Valera, Darío, Rodó and others referred to as 'el Ideal'. What this meant was that Beauty was so indissolubly connected with other life-enhancing ideals that it was capable of leading its devotees out of *fin-de siglo* negativism.

Criticism of José Martí (Cuba, 1853–95) is so bedevilled by Cuban Nationalism and by old-fashioned ideas about the meaning of *Modernismo* that it is difficult to situate him correctly within the movement. What is indis-

19 The literature on the topic is vast. Recommendable are the compilations of Luis Iñigo Madrigal, *Historia de la literatura hispanoamericana, II. Del neoclasicismo al modernismo* (Madrid, Cátedra, 1987) and Richard Cardwell and Bernard McGuirk, *¿Qué es el modernismo?* (Boulder, Colorado, Society of Spanish and Spanish American Studies, 1993), with contributions by major critics, José Olivio Jiménez, *Estudios críticos sobre la prosa modernista hispanoamericana* (New York, Eliseo Torres, 1975) and Stephen Hart, 'Current Trends in Scholarship on *Modernismo*', *Neophilologus* 71 (1987), 227–34.

putable is his innovatory impact on prose style in Spanish both in his declared ideas and in his practice.[20] Unfortunately his output of fiction is limited to a hastily written novella, *Amistad funesta* (sometimes also known as *Lucía Jerez*) (1885) which is usually seen as the inaugural *Modernista* novel. And with good reason; for, despite the haste with which it was produced, and the limitations imposed by the editor of the womens' magazine for which it was intended, it incorpated the *Modernista* adoration of Art and Beauty. 'Mejora y alivia el contacto constante de lo bello', Martí insists, at a time when 'Todo en la tierra, en estos tiempos negros, tiende a rebajar el alma'. 'Conviene tener siempre delante de los ojos . . . objetos bellos.'[21] These assertions are followed by a purple passage describing the *antesala* of Ana's house, full of objects with artistic, literary and exotic associations. The characters are divided into those with 'almas superiores' and those with 'alma escasa', the former led by the noble, generous, loving and self-sacrificing Juan Jerez. Is he, then, the first *Modernista* fictional hero? Not quite, and for the same reason that it is difficult to place Martí fully within *Modernismo*. Martí detested his times, because they were dominated by materialist values, by corruption, by abjection; but not because he was seriously afflicted by *fin-de-siglo* pessimism: the despair inherited from certain areas of Romanticism and intensified by Schopenhauer, Hartman and others. Unlike Darío or Silva, Martí had an answer: the 'moral passion' and the high-souled patriotism and faith in his fellow men that led him to his death in the cause of Cuban Independence. He was a tortured individual, but what tortured him was not 'el mal metafísico'. He loved beauty and associated it with 'the Ideal', in his case the ethical ideal, and this shielded him.

Amistad funesta, is therefore outwardly *Modernista* but inwardly Romantic. Not for nothing are *Amalia* and *María* mentioned as favourite reading matter of Sol del Valle. The plot is one of growing jealousy on the part of Juan Jerez's cousin, Lucía, which leads her to murder Sol, her rival for his love. Phillips correctly reminds us that 'El gran problema que tiene que resolver el novelista del modernismo es cómo lograr ese delicado equilibrio entre las necesidades interiores de un género que obliga al autor a mover acciones, contar vidas y crear mundos y el afán de escribir una prosa artística elaborada las más veces con ideales de poesía'.[22] Martí does not quite solve the problem. The narrative rhythm of *Amistad funesta* is slow and impeded by beautiful but static descriptivism. The novel unfolds like a beautiful tapestry until the sudden melodramatic ending in which human passion breaks

20 Indispensible in this connection is Ivan Schulman, *Símbolo y color en las obras de José Martí* (Madrid, Gredos, 1960).

21 José Martí, *Lucía Jerez*, ed. Manuel Pedro González (Madrid, Gredos, 1969), pp. 82–83.

22 Allen W. Phillips, 'El arte y el artista en algunas novelas modernistas', *Revista Hispánica Moderna* 34 (1968), 757–75, p. 757.

into the idyllic world of goodness and beauty surrounding the angelic, dying Ana, as if to tell us reluctantly that the truth (of human behaviour) is something else again.

Form in *Amistad funesta* is still conventional. An omniscient narrator tells us what has happened, intervening at intervals with obtrusive (usually moral) commentary. What has changed is the style, characterized by greatly enhanced use of figurative language and symbolism, in each case operating functionally to increase the impact of the events on the reader. The novel begins with colour symbolism, white for joy, love and innocence, crimson for passion and eventual crime. This is not just ornamental; over and over again symbols, especially of roses and broken flowers, are used to comment on the action and to prefigure its violent end. Symbolism is also used to contribute to characterization: Juan, for example, is associated repeatedly with the symbol of the eagle, and Ana with stars, flowers and opals. The same is true of the rich, visual imagery, which seems at first designed to delight the senses through the evocation of beautiful and opulent sights. But as we examine the wealth of figures of speech we see that they too are highly functional. Psychological, moral and social commentary is conveyed predominantly by means of metaphor and simile. This is 'poetic prose' in the best sense of the words; poetic devices made to earn their living, not just by adding their own beauty to what is already beautiful to contemplate (the loves and tendernesses of adorable young women), but by harnessing the expressive power of poetry to the task of enhancing meaning. Finally, it is worth underlining the forgotten fact that this is one of the first Spanish American novels, if not the first, to introduce the note of Feminism, declaring woman to be at that time 'una esclava disfrazada', obliged by 'un recato gazmoño' to suppress her thoughts, impressions and emotions (p. 90). This is not the only time the *Modernista* novel seeks to comment on its social context.

Mayer-Minnemann summarizes the characteristics of the *Modernista* novel as follows: the protagonist is normally an aesthete in conflict with his surroundings; there is usually a significant relationship between the latter and Spanish American reality as perceived by the author; the novel concentrates on the central character and his feelings and sensations and finds techniques to express them; the style represents a reaction against the generally less ornate style of Realism/Naturalism. Clearly *Amistad funesta* does not fully qualify because neither Juan Jerez nor Lucía is developed enough to fit the pattern of the later *Modernista* hero/heroine. Even so, we notice that Juan is a poet and lover of beauty who rejects the materialism and moral abjection of the society in which he lives, who suffers from a pre-anguished 'melancolía dolorosa' and elevates femininity into an Ideal. Most of all we see in Martí's only work of fiction the new *Modernista* style. So it is that only with *De sobremesa* (1895?, not published until 1925) by the famous poet José Asunción Silva (Colombia, 1865–96) that we see an example of fully developed *Modernista* fiction. For forty years it was practically ignored; but its complete re-evaluation since the1970s is evidence of the great change that came over criticism of *Modernismo*. Nowadays it is recognized as a key text both for the movement itself and for the *fin-de-siglo* in Spanish America.

Palmer has pointed out the importance of its form.[23] The frame is a reading of extracts from the diary of the protagonist, José Fernández, to a group of friends. The diary describes part of his past adult life and his quest for a meaningful ideal on which to base his existence. But on two occasions Fernández either stops reading or is interrupted by his friends. In each case the reappearance of the frame-situation at a crucial point in the narrative is designed to underline Fernández's failure to fulfil his hopes. The novel's theme is not only his growing self-awareness and changing perception of life, but also his inability to achieve a satisfying life-orientation. Probably influenced by Huysmans's *A Rebours* and French Decadentist fiction generally (but also by Naturalism since he emphasizes heredity), Silva presents Fernández as a manic-depressive, alternating between 'ímpetus idealistas', thirst for knowledge, grandiose dreams of action and orgiastic pleasure on the one hand, and aboulic inactivity on the other. He himself is well aware that what is lacking in his life is a spiritual principle. He finds it incarnated in a mysterious, idealized woman, Helena, whose disappearance converts the action of the novel into a quest to find her afresh. By the middle of the novel he is self-aware enough to record: 'Estoy harto de lujuria y quiero el amor; estoy cansado de la carne y quiero el espíritu.'[24] By centreing his novel on this quest for the Ideal, Silva believed that he was in line with what he called 'el renacimiento idealista del arte, causado por la inevitable reacción contra el naturalismo estrecho y brutal que privó hace unos años' (p. 210). Now, he asserted: 'el lector no pide al libro que le divierta sino que lo haga pensar y ver el misterio oculto en cada partícula del Gran Todo' (p. 211). The Uruguayan Carlos Reyles makes the same point in his essay 'La novela del porvenir' (1897). *De sobremesa* is not a successful novel of this sort. After realizing that the root of his problem is the collapse of religion, Fernández has run out of options. The latter part of the novel is largely composed of erotic episodes through which he tries to escape from his insight, though earlier ones have revealed that this is not the way out. Finally he discovers Helena's symbolic grave. We should not overlook the fact that the novel ends in the same existential impasse as Cambaceres's *Sin rumbo*.

Most of the criticism of *De sobremesa* has been concerned with its content. Palmer, however, has emphasized at the structural level, not only the importance of the double return to the frame-situation, but also of the arrangement of Fernández's love experiences around the central pivot, the

[23] Julia Palmer, 'Some Aspects of Narrative Structure in José Asunción Silva's *De sobremesa*', *Revista Interamericana de Bibliografía* 41 (1991), 470–77.

[24] José Asunción Silva, *De sobremesa*, *Obra completa*, 2nd edn (Barcelona, Biblioteca Ayacucho, 1985), p. 180.

meeting with Helena. Similarly Montserrat Alas has shown that the novel contains a coherent system of symbols which contributes to its unity as a literary artefact.[25] Without accepting the hyperbolical claims on its behalf made by Villanuevo-Collado in the late 1980s, we can agree with Phillips that '*De sobremesa* es, pues, clave y testimonio de toda una época' (p. 760).

For Juan Jerez in *Amistad funesta* woman is symbolic: 'él, en la mujer, veía más el símbolo de las hermosuras ideadas que un ser real' (p. 72). Clearly the same is true of Helena in *De sobremesa* and we find a similar situation in *Idolos rotos* (1901) and *Sangre patricia* (1902) by Manuel Díaz Rodríguez (Venezuela, 1868–1927). But the spiritual ideal symbolized by woman was not the only ideal pursued by the male protagonists of these novels. Juan Jerez as a lawyer defends the cause of the downtrodden Central American Indians. Fernández at one point dreams of becoming an enlightened dictator and regenerating Colombia both economically and politically. Tulio Arcos in *Sangre patricia* goes a step further and actually joins a band of revolutionary guerrillas (inevitably called 'la falange del ideal') and only when direct action on behalf of the community fails, seeks (but like Fernández is prevented by her death from finding) fulfilment through an idealized woman. This shift reflects Díaz Rodríguez's own awareness that progressive political activism in the Venezuela of Cipriano Castro, dictator from 1900 to 1908, and of Juan Vicente Gómez, whose regime lasted from 1908 until 1936, was quite futile. Díaz Rodríguez's forgotten essay, 'Paréntesis Modernista, o ligero ensayo sobre el modernismo' (1910), was one of the first to protest against the tendency to view the movement in terms of mere stylistic renovation. In it he declares *Modernismo* to be 'un movimiento espiritual muy hondo' and like Silva alludes to the neo-mysticism of the *fin-de-siglo*, the vain search for new spiritual values to replace those of Christianity, as the key to understanding the movement. But part of the originality of his two major novels is that in them, the *Modernista* quest for life-enhancing values is intimately bound up with the collectivity.

The theme of *Idolos rotos* is in fact that of the failure of Cultural Reformism either to benefit the Motherland or to fulfil the aspirations of the artist. In that sense this novel is the natural introduction to *Sangre patricia* a year later in which that failure, in the absence of any alternative ideal, leads directly to Tulio's suicide. '*Idolos rotos* es pues la historia de una desilusión', Olivares affirms, before demonstrating that the novel is in many respects a national allegory.[26] Alberto Soria, a young sculptor, is called back from Europe on account of the mortal illness of his father. He finds not only his father, but also his Fatherland dying, rotted internally by political parasitism and threat-

25 Montserrat Alas, 'José Asunción Silva, *De sobremesa*. Etapas de una búsqueda simbólica', *Rilce* (University of Navarre), 4.1 (1988), 9–15.

26 Jorge Olivares, *La novela decadente en Venezuela* (Caracas, Armitano, 1984), p. 57.

ened externally by the growing power of the United States. He and his artistic friends, who form an embattled 'ghetto de intelectuales', surrounded by incomprehension and hostility, attempt to begin a process of national regeneration through art and literature. But the outbreak of a Revolution, expressive of the continuing barbarism of the country, pre-empts their actions and in the course of it, the sculptures in the *Escuela de Bellas Artes*, including those of Soria, are symbolically destroyed. Soria draws the conclusion that activity on the national scale is hopeless and that he had sacrificed his pure devotion to art in vain. At the end of the novel he voices the great *Modernista* commandment: 'El supremo deber de un artista es poner en salvo su ideal de belleza.'[27]

Associated perplexingly with the problem of Venezuela are the series of incidents which place Soria, like Silva's Fernández, between surrender to eroticism and attachment to an idealized figure of womanly chastity. One of the manifestations of the deep pessimism shared by both the Naturalists and the *Modernistas* (and, of course, equally visible in the contemporary Spanish Generation of 1898) is the tendency towards aboulia, lack of willpower and energy, revealed by many of the movements' fictional heroes. Afflicted with a sense of national and personal crisis (the former being in large measure a projection of the latter) and hungering for sensations rather than ideas or emotions (a major component of the *Modernista* mindset), Soria is unable to find refuge in his creative talents and allows himself to be lured into a destructive relationship with Teresa Farías, a *femme fatale* figure borrowed from French Decadentist fiction, but here incorporated into the allegorical pattern of the narrative as a symbol of the devastating effect on the artist of living in contemporary Venezuela. Only by tearing himself away from his homeland at the end of the novel, can Soria hope to regain the allegiance to the artistic ideal which may give meaning to his life.

The work of all the writers of *Modernista* fiction, of which we are glancing at only a representative sample, was affected by two factors operating together. One was the process of socio-economic change we have already seen referred to in *Martín Rivas* and *La gran aldea*. This was the ongoing challenge to the old landowning upper-directive class by a new commercial and professional class. The *Modernista* novelists saw this in terms of the triumph of sordid materialist values over those which they attributed to a (mythicized) 'procer' aristocracy born of the *criollo* liberators of their countries. The other was the collapse of traditional religious and rational absolutes, which left (for them) Art and Beauty as the only barriers against pessimism. At one level, *Sangre patricia* can be seen, like *Idolos rotos*, allegorically, as representing the suicide of a patrician class which has lost its *raison d'être*. Tulio Arcos has shot his bolt before the novel even begins. He

[27] Manuel Díaz Rodríguez, *Idolos rotos* (Paris, Garnier Hermanos, 1901), p. 348.

has participated in a failed rebellion and been exiled. Action, in other words, is already no longer an option. Art and love remain. The former here is represented by the plump, happily married, deeply Christian Alejandro Martí. Because he has the gift of faith, it is implied, he is able to be 'un creador de belleza y un maestro de la voluntad',[28] that is, the polar opposite of Silva's Fernández or Díaz Rodríguez's heroes who are haunted by their sensuality, aboulia and failure to devote themselves consistently to artistic creation. Love, like libertarian action, on the other hand, has been excluded as a source of salvation already; in this case by the death of Belén, Tulio's bride, at sea, while she was crossing to Europe to consummate their marriage by proxy. This, it is hinted (p. 60), could be seen as an example of cosmic irony: God's mockery of man's aspiration to happiness. Be that as it may, the novel is the record of Tulio's inability to get over his loss and of his subsequent suicide, when he throws himself overboard to join Belén, while he is returning to Venezuela to take up afresh the military struggle against oppression. Belén, more than being a flesh and blood woman, symbolizes, perhaps more than any other *Modernista* feminine figure, an unattainable ideal of beauty. Gullón, whose article is one of the few which attempts to deal with technique in *Modernista* fiction, recognizes that here we are in the presence of a *Modernista* archetype: 'El narrador está convocando una mujer bella, de tal género de belleza que tiene algo de sobrenatural, no es un ser de carne y hueso . . . La *diosa* se convertirá en *visión de sediento*, espejismo, por tanto, sin realidad verdadera.'[29]

Olivares points out that technically the narrative evolves on two planes. One is dominated by the characteristic dynamic of most nineteenth-century fiction, logical causality (which, in the twentieth century, was to be significantly questioned). The other plane is that of Tulio possessed by, and eventually destroyed by, his dream of finding peace and reconciliation by joining Belén beneath the sea. Here the causation is psychological, symbolic and perhaps 'magical'. Even more than in the case of *De sobremesa*, an obtrusive code of colour symbolism links aspects of the novel together: gold, white and blue being positive, scarlet, purple and black negative, and sea-green ambivalent. Once more there are purple passages of what Oscar Wilde called 'jewelled style', characteristic of the *Modernista* desire to embellish a reality which otherwise seemed, as Fernández complained in *De sobremesa*, 'mediocre', 'trivial', 'insignificante' and 'despreciable' (p. 181). But these emebellishments do not hide the 'abyss', that buzz-word of the *fin-de-siglo*, which yawns when 'El Ideal' seems to have been irretrievably lost.

The last famous *Modernista* novel, at one time thought of as the best, was

[28] Manuel Díaz Rodríguez, *Sangre patricia* (Madrid, Sociedad Española de Librería, [no date]), p. 89.

[29] Germán Gullón, 'Técnicas narrativas en la novela realista y en la modernista', *Cuadernos Hispanoamericanos* (1974), 83, 173–87, p. 286.

La gloria de Don Ramiro (1908) by Enrique Larreta (Argentina, 1873–1961). It was translated into French in 1910 by none other than Remy de Gourmont himself. Until the 1940s it retained considerable fame. But the contemptuous reference to the 'españoladas' of 'el doctor Rodríguez Larreta' by Borges in 'Pierre Menard, autor del Quijote' gave the final blow to a prestige which was already collapsing. Already in 1904 with *Dionysos* by the Venezuelan Pedro César Dominici, for example, *Modernista* fiction had sought in the past a setting which lent itself to verbal embellishment and in which the search for the Ideal could be presented with more conviction and hope of success than in the present. Larreta chose, in the years after the catastrophe of 1898, which brought about a certain sense of solidarity with the humiliated mother country, to research and write a novel whose background was Spain of the Golden Age. Its hero, Don Ramiro bears a certain family resemblance to the modern heroes we have mentioned. Jansen correctly writes that 'toda su existencia se caracteriza por un fracaso motivado por la desproporción entre su ideal y su personalidad'.[30] But his ideal of glory, inherited from the Renaissance, and the ambivalence of his character, to which his inheritance of Moorish blood at a time of fanatical attachment to *limpieza de sangre* strongly contributes, cannot be convincingly related to the spiritual emptiness and the yearning for an Ideal with which to fill it, characteristic of literary sensibility at the end of the nineteenth century. The novel is superbly evocative of the Golden Age, but the values it harks back to are as obsolete and irrelevant to the 'ache of modernity' which had arrived on the scene with *Modernismo* as those of *Don Segundo Sombra* were to be (in a different context) twenty years later. Unlike the other *Modernista* novels we have glanced at, *La gloria de Don Ramiro* is highly novelesque and plot-centred. Ramiro becomes a spy on the local *moriscos*, takes a *morisco* girl as a lover, betrays her and them, observes a plot against Phillip II, kills his rival for the hand of a local beauty, kills her in turn, and becomes successively a religious anchorite and then a bandit in Peru. There he is redeemed by Santa Rosa of Lima and dies a Christian death. Even if we are willing to see in Larreta's presentation of the crisis in Spain under Phillip II an allusion to the crisis of the end of the nineteenth century in the West, and in Ramiro's vacillation among personal glory, sensuality and religion a reflection of the dreams of power, erotic adventurism and spiritual problems of the earlier *Modernista* central characters, none of which is very persuasive, Ramiro himself is not aesthetically orientated and his salvation at the end by a Saint is hardly relevant to modern spiritual disquiet. The *Modernismo* of *La gloria de Don Ramiro* in other words is chiefly restricted to the character of Don Alonso Blázquez Serrano, a Golden Age lover of beautiful art-objects, and to the

[30] André Jansen, *Enrique Larreta* (Madrid, Cultura Hispánica, 1967), p. 107.

sumptuous colourist descriptions which the novel shares with its counterparts already mentioned.

Brief mention remains to be made of two other significant examples of *Modernista* prose. The first is *La guerra gaucha* (1905) by Leopoldo Lugones (Argentina, 1874–1938). The second is 'El hombre que parecía un caballo' (1915) by Rafael Arévalo Martínez (Guatemala, 1884–1975). In *La guerra gaucha*, Lugones harks back to the 'tradición' perfected, as we saw, by Ricardo Palma. Once more the aim is to 'hacer patria' by means of twenty-two anecdotic *tradición*-type stories of the War against the Spanish in the North East of Argentina during the struggle for Independence. The Argentine patriots are represented by gaucho irregular cavalry, operating with the support of the local people against the 'godos'. Ghiano points out Lugones's epic intention, his romantic vision of history in which the 'people' play the primary, heroic, role, the mythification of the patriots and the negative presentation of the Spanish.[31] But even he has to concede that the content of the work has not been what chiefly attracted critical attention. The significance of *La guerra gaucha* within *Modernista* narrative lies in the way Lugones carries the poetic prose associated with the movement to an extreme. All critics, with the exception of Phillips,[32] tend to support the view expressed by Roberto Giusti in 1911 that *La guerra gaucha* is 'admirable e ilegible'. Even Eduardo Mallea, who did not fully share that view, referred in *Notas de un novelista* to 'esta devoración del sujeto por el agente'. A short example will suffice to illustrate what he meant: 'La evanescencia verdosa del naciente desleíase en un matiz escarlatino, especie de aguita etérea cuyo rosicler aun se sutilizaba como una idea que adviniese a color' ('Güemes'). The *Modernista* stress on beautiful sensations, especially visual ones, is intensified by the recherché vocabulary (which Lugones had to explain in notes to each section) and by the final simile. Ornamentation is combined with unusual verb-forms and strained, effectist figurative language, until the reader, at first impressed, presently becomes irritated and finally rebellious. What is functional in Martí here comes to seem merely decorative. This principal historical importance of *La guerra gaucha*, therefore, is to show how the 'artistic' prose of *Modernismo* could run to seed.

One of its last hurrahs was Arévalo Martínez's highly acclaimed 'El hombre que parecía un caballo'. The story is a fantastic allegory. The narrator, perhaps thinking of Darío's:

31 Juan Carlos Ghiano, *Análisis de 'La guerra gaucha'* (Buenos Aires, Centro Editor de América Latina, 1967).

32 Allen W. Phillips, 'La prosa artística de Leopoldo Lugones en *La guerra gaucha*', *Estudios y notas sobre literatura hispanoamericana* (Mexico City, Cultura, 1965), pp. 73–104.

> El Arte puro como Cristo exclama:
> *Ego sum lux et veritas et vita*
> ('Yo soy aquel', *Cantos de vida y esperanza*, 1905)

yearns to find in his new-found friend, the poet Aretal, 'un mensajero divino'. There is an unbroken continuity here with *De sobremesa* and *Ídolos rotos*. The *Modernista* quest for a spiritualized Art, so heavily emphasized by Silva and Díaz Rodríguez, re-emerges here with increased intensity. The narrator, longing to draw on Art for spiritual enrichment, sees the poetic soul of Aretal as a source of the water of life. At the beginning of the tale Aretal is seen consciously as the long-awaited bringer of the good news of the gospel of Art but, at the narrator's subconscious level, as having some of the characteristics of a horse, that is, of a beast. The rest of the tale, using the now familiar *Modernista* high style, full of imagery and symbolism no less functional than in Martí, charts the gradual discovery by the narrator that his intuition is correct. The underlying symbol is that of the centaur, popularized by Darío in 'Coloquio de los centauros' in *Prosas profanas* (1896). This presents mankind as part human, part animal, and the two elements as harmonious and inseparable parts of a whole being which can only find fulfilment when the impulses of both are recognized as potentially positive sources of spiritual insight, in line with Darío's doctrine of *panerotismo*.

The narrator, though a great admirer and disciple of Darío, who is mentioned in the story as 'el Oficiante de las Rosas', cannot accept this view. It has been suggested that, since Aretal's character was based on that of the overtly homosexual Colombian poet Miguel Angel Ossorio, whose pen-name was Porfirio Barba-Jacob, the real theme of the tale is concerned with Arévalo Martínez's feelings of attraction-repulsion to his gay friend or even to gayness itself. Such a reading is perfectly plausible; but it is probably not the reading that does the fullest justice to the tale's great originality. Another less reductive reading perceives the theme as having to do with the mystery of the personality and the latter's ability to reveal different facets of itself to different people. This is Reedy's view.[33] It is extremely persuasive and converts the story into a striking psychological study using a symbolic technique. But 'El hombre que parecía un caballo' has to be seen primarily in its *Modernista* context. Here it is dominated by the narrator's longing to 'asomarse a Dios' through Aretal's devotion to Beauty and through finding spiritual nourishment, renewed ardour and sense of human harmony in 'el divino templo de aquella alma hermosa'. The tale pivots near the middle, however, and the second part shows Aretal changing from an angelic messenger to a bestial individual on to whom the narrator had merely projected his own allegiance to Beauty and the Ideal. There is an insistent technique of

[33] Daniel R. Reedy, 'La dualidad del "yo" en "El hombre que parecía un caballo" ', *El ensayo y la crítica literaria en Iberoamérica* (Toronto, Toronto U.P., 1970), pp. 167–74.

re-emphasis and symbolic use of the colour red to bring out Aretal's 'vacío moral', the fact that 'no tenía espíritu', that he possessed an 'alma animal' in contrast to the narrator's 'dios interno' still thirsting for what he now knows Aretal cannot provide. Still, although Aretal rushes away into the 'Desierto' (capitalized) of a life of abjection, the narrator, confident that the poet's residual 'elevada mentalidad' will eventually get the better of his animality, forcasts his 'redención'.

The *Modernista* quest has failed once more. But we must notice, first, how 'El hombre que parecía un caballo' confirms its existence as the deep theme of *Modernista* fiction, and, second, how the tale extends our understanding of it. The narrator here makes no bones about establishing an unbreakable link between the 'belleza' of Art, moral *hermosura*, angelic annunciation and perception of the divine. We can really speak here of 'the religion of Art'. The narrator may not have found its Archangel Gabriel in this instance but he remains a true believer. In one sense, then, these few pages illustrate the essence of *Modernismo*. Ayora, however, makes a different and even more valid point. 'El hombre que parecía un caballo' has been clearly recognized as linking *Modernista* prose to that of the avant-garde, to surrealism, to expressionism and even to the Absurd. In relation to this last, Ayora lays emphasis on the story as illustrating aspects of Wolfgang Kayser's theory of the Grotesque. 'El autor', he writes, 'ha evocado en el lector la presencia de un mundo ajeno a lo cotidiano . . . El mundo se ha vuelto inquietante.'[34] Fantasy can have more than one function. While it can often be merely entertaining and reassuring, in the case of grotesque fantasy it can turn into a disturbing metaphor of reality. What prevents 'El hombre que parecía un caballo' from suggesting a Borges-type threat to our complacent acceptance of the way things are is, of course, the fact that the story is in the last resort morally disturbing. It reminds us, as Ayora, puts it, that human nature is highly ambiguous, that 'el bien y el mal se tocan', that 'una alta espiritualidad no destierra por fuerza a la baja sensualidad' (p. 121). This is a more conventionally familiar message, and therefore less disturbing, than some of the implications of Borges's stories, or even of Felisberto Hernández's, but now the way ahead is clear.

The pattern of Spanish American fiction in the first half of the twentieth century was to be dominated by two parallel currents of writing. On the one hand the Realist tradition prolonged itself in the Novel of the Mexican Revolution, Regionalist or *criollista* fiction, the Anti-imperialist Novel, and in novelists like José Revueltas, David Viñas, Mario Benedetti, Manuel Cofiño and others who passed it on in a modified form to the Post-Boom. On the other hand, however, the 'artistic' novel of *modernismo* can be seen as pre-

[34] Jorge Ayora, 'Psicología de lo grotesco en "El hombre que parecía un caballo" ', *Explicación de Textos Literarios* 11.2 (1974), 117–22.

figuring what is sometimes called the *vanguardista* novel of the 1920s and 1930s which, as we shall see, may be regarded as early Modernist in the Anglo-Saxon sense and which culminated in the Boom.

Further Reading

Foster, David W., *The Argentine Generation of 1880: Ideology and Cultural Texts* (Columbia, Missouri U.P., 1990). Incisive and enlightening by a leading critic.

García Barragán, María G., *El naturalismo literario en México*, 2nd edn (Mexico City, UNAM, 1993).

Schade, George D., 'El arte narrativo en *Sin rumbo*', *Revista Iberoamericana* 44 (1978), 17–29.

Anderson Imbert, Enrique, 'La prosa poética de José Martí. A propósito de *Amistad funesta*', *Antología crítica de José Martí*, ed. Manuel Pedro González (Mexico City, Cultura, 1960), pp. 93–101. Early but often quoted.

González, Aníbal, *La novela modernista hispanoamericana* (Madrid, Gredos, 1987).

Jiménez, José Olivio, *Estudios críticos sobre la prosa modernista hispanoamericana* (New York, Eliseo Torres, 1975).

Mayer-Minnemann, Klaus, 'La novela modernista hispanoamericana y la literatura europea de fin de siglo: puntos de contacto y diferencias', *Nueva Revista de Filología Hispánica* 33.2 (1984), 431–45. A useful comparative overview.

Loveluck, Juan, '*De sobremesa*, novela desconocida del modernismo', *Revista Iberoamericana* 31 (1965), 17–32. The pioneering article on this vital text.

Orjuela, Héctor, *'De sobremesa' y otros estudios sobre José Asunción Silva* (Bogotá, Instituto Caro y Cuervo, 1976).

Villanuevo-Collado, Alfredo, '*De sobremesa* de José Asunción Silva y las doctrinas esotéricas en la Francia del fin de siglo', *Revista de Estudios Hispánicos* 21 (1987), 9–21. Good on background.

Villanuevo-Collado, Alfredo, 'José Asunción Silva y Karl-Joris Huysmans: estudio de una lectura', *Revista Iberoamericana* 55 (1989), 273–86.

Ibieta, Gabriela, *Tradition and Renewal in 'La gloria de don Ramiro'* (Potomac [Maryland], Scripta Humanistica, 1986). Attempts to re-evaluate this now neglected novel.

Foster, David William, *Gay and Lesbian Themes in Latin American Writing* (Austin, Texas U.P., 1991). Queer Criticism at its best.

Chapter 3

INDIGENISM, REGIONALISM AND THE AFTERMATH OF *MODERNISMO*

Despite the impact of Realism in the 1860s and later, the romance was a long time a-dying. Of special interest among examples of the genre are Avellaneda's *Guatemozín* (1846) and *Enriquillo* (1882) by Manuel de Jesús Galván (Dominican Republic, 1834–1910). Since they deal with the situation of the Indians at the beginning of the Colonial period, they represent the confluence of the historical romance and *Indianismo*. *Indianismo* is usually distinguished from Indigenism proper by reference to the fact that the (earlier) Indianist writers tended to romanticize and idealize the Spanish American Indians in the Romantic tradition of the Noble Savage, whereas the (later) Indigenists presented them more realistically, usually with some sort of denunciatory social agenda. It is important to recognize, however, that Indigenism itself falls into two phases. The first, which includes, for example *Raza de bronce* (1919) by Alcides Arguedas (Bolivia, 1879–1946), *Husasipungo* (1934) by Jorge Icaza (Ecuador, 1906–78) and *El mundo es ancho y ajeno* (1941) by Ciro Alegría (Peru, 1909–67) is now regarded as unsophisticated. The second phase, represented above all by the work of Miguel Angel Asturias and José María Arguedas, on the other hand, enjoys high critical esteem.

The link between *Indianismo* and Indigenism can be seen in *Aves sin nido* (1889) by Clorinda Matto de Turner (Peru, 1854–1909). Clorinda Matto is in every way a transitional writer. She evolves from the backward-looking *costumbrismo* of *Tradiciones cuzqueños* (1886), with a prologue by Palma himself, by whom they were inspired, to the modified *costumbrismo* of *Aves sin nido*, her most famous work, and then in 1895 to a form of Naturalism. This is a quite remarkable parabola, and one which deserves closer attention than it has received. *Aves sin nido* is set in the remote, imaginary Peruvian town of Kíllac in the early 1870s. Its theme, reminiscent of Sarmiento's *Facundo*, is the barbarism (here called *salvajismo*) of life in the interior of Peru, compared with the (very relative) civilization of life in the capital. The central fact of *salvajismo* is the exploitation and ill-treatment of the Indians by the local authorities (especially the priest – Matto was so fiercely anti-clerical that her novel was burned, she was excommunicated, her property was destroyed and she was driven into exile largely as a result). This barbarity is focused on the Indian family of Juan and Marcela Yupanqui, who appeal to a recently arrived white family, the Maríns, for help. In consequence the Maríns' house is attacked, Juan is killed and Marcela receives a wound from which she later dies. The Yupanqui daughters (the 'aves sin nido' of the title) are taken in by the Maríns who eventually leave the town and return to Lima. There they are joined by Manuel, believed to be the son of one of those town notables chiefly responsible for the deaths of the Yupanquis. He falls in love with one of the daughters, Margarita, only to discover that both she and he are the children of the former village priest, since promoted to the rank of bishop.

A problem connected with late *costumbrismo* is that its practitioners often persuaded themselves that they were writing realistically. In the prologue to *Aves sin nido*, Matto insists that she is 'copying' reality. Brushwood, however, points out that in the novel 'the combination of romanticism and realism indicates a rather hazy notion of the latter'.[1] Rodríguez-Luis accurately compares Matto to the Spanish pre-realist Fernán Caballero, whose work is similarly rooted in romantic-type *costumbrismo*. Two factors, apart from the shift into *folletín*-type melodrama at the climax of *Aves sin nido*, inhibit us from taking Matto seriously as a Realist. One is the obtrusive moralism informing Matto's radical social criticism. She attacks the corruption and oppressiveness of the local authorities (especially the clergy) and the lack of care in their selection and supervision from the centre, the celibacy of the clergy, more honoured in the breach than otherwise, the financial, sexual and economic exploitation of the Indians and the frequent severe ill-treatment to which they are subjected, their undernourishment and enforced illiteracy and ignorance, all observed at first hand. But ultimately these evils are seen less in a genuinely economico-social and political context than in a moral one, that of 'la sangrienta batalla de los buenos contra los malos'.[2] The answer to the problems she reports is to be found, for Matto, more in nobility of soul and compassion (here strongly associated with the women characters) rather than in radical politico-social action. The other factor which marks Matto as a pre-realist is her equally obtrusive sentimentalism, of which Rodríguez-Luis writes: 'un sentimentalismo incluso anterior al costumbrismo termina imponiéndose en la obra de Matto al costumbrismo y al propósito reformista.'[3] This having been said, and in spite of the evident failure of Matto, for all her courage, to think through the implications of her social criticism, this is the novel which broke the mold of Indianism and established the pattern for the future Indigenist novel. Three more points of importance for that future Indigenist narrative merit mention. One is the idealization of the

[1] John S. Brushwood, *Genteel Barbarism* (Lincoln, Nebraska U.P., 1981), p. 144.

[2] Clorinda Matto de Turner, *Aves sin nido* (Buenos Aires, Solar/Hachette, 1968), p. 59.

[3] Julio Rodríguez-Luis, *Hermenéutica y praxis del indigenismo* (Mexico City, Fondo de Cultura Económica, 1980), p. 22.

Indians involved. The second is the fact that Matto never envisages self-liberation of the Indians by their own efforts. The third, which should never be lost sight of, is that both Indianist and Indigenist novels were always written by white middle- and upper-class urban writers for the same category of readers. They were neither written nor read by Indians themselves, even in the case of the novels of José María Arguedas. They attempt to perform one of the functions of the intelligentsia (which includes creative writers): to explain one sector of society to other sectors. But they do so from the outside. This is not like Black writing in the United States, for instance. There is a sense in which it is always inauthentic.

The essential contribution of Alcides Arguedas's *Raza de bronce* is the shift away from idealizing and sentimentalizing the Indians. As Rodríguez-Luis puts it, this 'representa la absorción de la lección realista por la novela indigenista' (p. 60). At the same time it places the question of land-tenure squarely at the centre of interest of the novel. Icaza's *Huasipungo* shares both these features. The sufferings of the oppressed Indians and their exploitation by the landowner class offered a fertile terrain for writers influenced by the Socialist Realism in vogue between the two World Wars. *Huasipungo* is a case in point. 'Los jóvenes de Sudamerica', Icaza said in an interview, 'éramos profundamente revolucionarios, profundamente socialistas. Por tanto mi libro tenía que reflejar esa influencia.'[4] The theme of the novel is once again the gross ill-treatment, virtual enslavement and in the end seizure of the land on which the Indians depend.

The narrative technique is simple and schematic. The outer frame of the plot is provided by the near-bancruptcy of the absentee landowner, Alfonso Pereira, and the threat to the family's honour by the fact that his unmarried daughter is pregnant. There is no attempt to complicate the character presentation with psychological commentary or insight into their inner lives. Selfishness, shiftlessness, stupidity and self-indulgence are the characteristics attributed to this representative family of the landlord class. To these are quickly added greed and readiness to sell out to a North American company when it becomes apparent that salvation lies that way ('Los gringos. Buena gente. ¡Oh! Siempre nos salvan . . . Vienen a educarnos. Nos traen el progreso').[5] The decision to remove the Indians from the land they till, so that the Americans can set up their living quarters on it, is put into effect at the other end of the novel with the aid of a massacre carried out by the Army. Inside this frame, whose function is to illustrate the power and corruption of the rural upper class, is set the story of Andrés Chiliquinga, whose wife is conscripted to nurse the Pereira's new grandson, while he is sent off to cut

4 Enrique Ojeda, 'Entrevista a Jorge Icaza', *Ensayos sobre la obra de Jorge Icaza* (Quito, Casa de Cultura Ecuatoriana, 1991), p. 120.

5 Jorge Icaza, *Huasipungo* in *Obras escogidas* (Mexico City, Aguilar, 1961), pp. 82 and 86.

timber for the gringos. From this point until the climax, in which, after a brief rebellion, Andrés and his son are shot down, the plot is simply a piling up of incidents of greed and lust on the part of Pereira and the village priest, mixed in with others which illustrate the forced labour, starvation and cruel punishments which are the lot of the Indians, both collectively, when they are forced to build a road with little more than their bare hands and farm implements, and individually, as when Andrés's wife dies from eating rotting meat and he is barbarously punished for stealing a cow in order to pay for her burial.

The Indians here are quite unlike those of José María Arguedas's *Yawar fiesta*, published less than a decade later, who also collectively build a road, or those of his *Los ríos profundos*, who successfully defy the army, despite its modern fire-power. They are even more unlike those of Ciro Alegría in *El mundo es ancho y ajeno*. The indigenist novelist had two choices. One was to present the Indians in a positive light, so that we sympathize and identify ourselves easily with them. The other was to picture them in all the squalor, ignorance and animality of their lives, but to attribute these characteristics to the brutality of the conditions in which the landowner class forces them to live. Matto, Alegría and to a certain extent José María Arguedas chose the former tactic; Alcides Arguedas and Icaza, the latter. In *Huasipungo* there are residual elements of *costumbrismo*, for example in the description of the cock-fight in chapter fifteen, but they are in no sense picturesque. Rather, like other episodes implacably utilized to enhance the novel's ideological impact, they are there not to show us something pleasingly exotic but to ram home the message that the blood-sport and the gambling that goes with it are part and parcel of a degraded life-style for which the landowner class is ultimately answerable.

Among the most significant features of Matto's *Aves sin nido* was her implication that the Indians were socially, but not racially, inferior. In the preface she refers to the 'rectitud y nobleza' of the Incas as having survived in their modern descendents. Plainly this was in part a throw-back from Romantic Indianism and was not destined to survive in the Indigenist novels of Alcides Arguedas or Icaza. They protest against the degradation of the Indians but make little attempt to incorporate redeeming features into the way they present them. Both writers appear to assume that the more they can show the Indian as bestialized, the harsher will be the judgement passed by the reader on the landowning class. Even in Matto, however, emphasis on social oppression and recognition of finer qualities in the Indians do not preclude extreme pessimism. Deliberately removed from the English translation of *Aves sin nido* was her wish, expressed in the prologue, that God would mercifully destroy the Indian race, since it had no possibility of recovering its dignity or exercising its rights. Pessimism also prevails in Alcides Arguedas and Icaza. Their novels served to keep interest in the problem alive, but they offer no solutions. Indeed, if we look closely at *Huasipungo*, we see that the Indians, in trying to retain their subsistence landholdings in the face of a threat from foreign developers, are in a sense resisting the forces of change and economic progress. Kristal has shown that Matto came to regard such progress as their only, albeit faint, hope.[6] How faint it was is revealed by the novel *El Tungsteno* (1931) by the great poet César Vallejo (Peru, 1892–1938), the theme of which is how development (in this case mining operations) inevitably destroys what remains of Indian communal life.

The outlook of Ciro Alegría (Peru, 1909–67) in *El mundo es ancho y ajeno* (1941) is quite different from that of Alcides Arguedas or Icaza. His early novels, *La serpiente de oro* (1935) and *Los perros hambrientos* (1939) established him as a belated Regionalist, the theme in each case being the struggle of man against Nature. In the former we see life on the great Marañón river, just as previously life on the pampas, on the *llano* or in the Amazonian jungle had been depicted in novels by Güiraldes, Gallegos and Rivera. In *Los perros hambrientos* we are closer to a consecrated theme of Indigenism when the starving Indians attack the house of the local landowner, don Cipriano. But the blame is laid not on the feudal pattern of rural landholding but on Nature. It is the terrible drought which reduces the Indians to desperation, not ill-treatment or theft of their land. When the rains come, things settle back into acceptable normality. By contrast, in *El mundo es ancho y ajeno* Alegría returns to the now standard pattern of presenting the Indian problem in terms of a conflict with the *gamonal* (landowning) class. In the preface to the tenth edition of the novel (1948), he takes issue with those critics who had accused him of an excess of *pintoresquismo*, as well as with those who objected to any attempt to criticize prevailing conditions. He insists flatly that the problem of the Indians has always been and remains a social and economic one, and that the only possible answer is the gradual assimilation of them into a society in which there are already more mestizos than 'whites'. Significantly, the preface ends with an explicit reference to the novel's 'message'. According to Escajadillo that message basically is that the Indians manage best when living in agricultural *comunidades*.[7] If that is the case, it is not clear how they can be assimilated into a modern economy.

The treatment of Nature in the Indigenist novel is always of great interest. In *Aves sin nido*, for example, the natural surroundings of Kíllac are presented as beautiful and fertile. Their function is to contrast ironically with the ugliness and sterility of life in the township. In *Huasipungo* the hostility of nature, manifested especially when the Indians are conscripted to build the road, adds to their sufferings. In *El mundo es ancho y ajeno*, on the other hand, the majestic beauty of the Andes and the smiling fields of wheat and maize are used at the beginning to convey the almost bucolic lives of the *comuneros* before their best land is stolen by the local *gamonal*, Don Alvaro

6 Efraín Kristal, *The Andes Viewed from the City* (New York, Lang, 1987), p. 154.
7 Tomás Escajadillo, *Alegría y El mundo es ancho y ajeno* (Lima, San Marcos U.P., 1983).

Amenábar, with the aid of his legal minions and the connivance of the local authorities. Interestingly the symbol which announces this impending catastrophe is also a natural symbol, a snake. The counter-symbol, however, is man-made: the school which the *comuneros* begin to build, recognizing that one possible defensive strategy is to spread literacy and education among the members of the younger generation. Again, if we look at José María Arguedas's *Yawar fiesta*, published at the same time as *El mundo es ancho y ajeno*, and its unsympathetic presentation of the more evolved *serranos*, whose first immediate action is to desert the highlands for Lima, we may well doubt whether schooling is a major factor in the answer to the *comuneros*' problem. But the experiment is never tried since Amenábar drives the Indians away from their village before the school is completed.

Rumi, the Indian community, is clearly a symbolic place. It and its mayor, the patriarchal Rosendo Maqui, represent in spatial and human terms a rather idealized, though essentially static, way of life, protected initially by its remoteness, but in the early decades of the twentieth century threatened by changing economic conditions and the greed of the landowner class. Led at first by Rosendo and then by the more experienced Benito Castro, the Indians struggle to preserve their community and its values. At the same time, Alegría introduces a wide range of subordinate episodes, in the case of Benito and the bandit Vásquez, attaining the status of sub-plots, to illustrate his conviction that to uproot the Indians from their agricultural communities is to accelerate the process of reducing them to abjection. Work in the mines, in the jungle collecting rubber, or on the coca plantations is presented as an even worse option for the Indians than struggling, as the community has to do after losing its good land, with marginal land and unfavourable climatic conditions. The law is shown as providing no redress, so that whether the Indians stay in the community or leave, accept their fate or rebel, their lot is always to be despoiled and exploited or worse. *El mundo es ancho y ajeno* ends, like *Huasipungo*, with a massacre of the Indians.

Technically, the novel illustrates, because of its length and pronounced tendency to grow arborescently, constantly branching out in new directions as Alegría incorporates more and more incidents to create an all-inclusive picture of oppression and degradation, what Cornejo Polar calls 'una cierta aptitud para abrir la estructura de la obra en busca de insertar dentro de ella formas originariamente propias de otros géneros'[8] (myth, epic, history, folk-tales, *testimonio*, protest and so on). Characteristically, for example, Alegría introduces a footnote in chapter sixteen, rather naively explaining that the reference to the newspaper *La autonomía* was to an actual newspaper

[8] Antonio Cornejo Polar, *La novela peruana,* 2nd edn (Lima, Horizonte, 1989), p. 56.

and that he was using them to 'mostrar episodios corrientes y típicos'.[9] Not surprisingly, therefore, given this almost reportage-type, old-style realist approach to the protest part of the novel, which is after all its dominant aspect, the plot is linear and chronological, the narrative stance third-person omniscient and the pattern of causality on which the plot depends is simple and taken for granted. There are three consecutive phases: the opening one, in which 'Los comuneros de Rumi estaban contentos de su vida' (p. 342) until Amenábar forces them off their best land; the middle phase, in which they cultivate marginal land in misery, Rosendo, unjustly imprisoned, dies in jail, and we learn that leaving the community leads only to worse suffering; and the final phase of rebellion under Benito bringing about the final catastrophe. Of these the central one is the most important since it sets the pattern of communal existence in contrast to the Indian experience in a whole range of other sectors of Peru's society and economy. The tragedy of the final section is that in it the *comuneros* begin to achieve a certain awareness of the historical and economic process in which they are caught up, only to be massacred before they can attempt to adapt to it. The fact that *Huasipungo*, *El mundo es ancho y ajeno* and *Todas las sangres* (1964) by José María Arguedas all end with the Indians being shot down seems to indicate that the Indigenist novel found itself in a no-win situation. It is not clear that Arguedas's last novel, *El zorro de arriba y el zorro de abajo* (1971), in which the emigration of the Indians from the highlands to the coast is the central fact, offers a solution either. All that remains is Alegría's grim remark in the preface already mentioned: 'a pesar de la aparente derrota, queda en estas páginas, inconmoviblemente en pie, el hombre indio' (p. 333). Before leaving Indigenism, we should mention the last significant writer of the cycle, Manuel Scorza (Peru, 1928–83) whose five social-realist novels are based on the struggle in the 1950s and 1960s of the Indian communities in the Pasco area. With Scorza, whose work for a time enjoyed international popularity, the Indigenist novel seemed to take on a new lease of life because of his ability to link the old problem of local *gamonal* power and landholding injustices with techniques borrowed from non-realist fiction. But with hindsight we can see that Scorza was an end-product.

Alongside Indigenism which, as we have seen, grew in the end out of Romanticism and *costumbrismo*, we see the development of three patterns of narrative which can also be related to *Modernismo*. One, for lack of a better term, might be called Vanguardism in prose, which in some ways emerged directly from the earlier movement. Pedro Lastra writes: 'la vanguardia que emerge en la década del veinte no desdeña del todo el proyecto modernista,

[9] Ciro Alegría, *El mundo es ancho y ajeno*, in *Novelas completas* (Madrid, Aguilar, 1959), p. 848.

que no puede dejar de sentir como una antecedencia productiva.'[10] The other two were the Novel of the Mexican Revolution and what we now call Regionalism, which used to be called 'La Novela de la Tierra', the 'Telluric' novel, the 'Novela Criollista' and so on. Related to *Mundonovismo* in poetry, the Regionalist novel reacted against *Modernista*, city-bred aestheticism and cosmopolitanism, and looked for inspiration towards the great rural interior of the continent, the plains, the jungle, the great rivers, and man's struggle against the natural environment. In line with the *mundonovistas*, the Regionalists were interested in Spanish American man and in Spanish American settings, problems and values where they most differed from European models.

As both the Boom critic Emir Rodríguez Monegal and the Chilean novelist José Donoso have pointed out, Ciro Alegría was born in the same year as the author of the first great Boom novel, Juan Carlos Onetti. The significance of that fact can hardly be exaggerated. Alegría represents the end of a creative cycle, that of what we now tend to call the 'traditional' novel, while Onetti, as we shall see, represents the beginning of the new one, which we call the Boom. Despite the strident defence of the former by Escajadillo in his book on Alegría, and despite the fact that 'traditional'-type novels continued to be written during the Boom and influenced the 'reader-friendliness' of many Post-Boom novels, the fact remains that a major shift took place. It is simply not true that novels like *Doña Bárbara* and *El mundo es ancho y ajeno* have retained their huge popularity. After their first appearance, both continued to be frequently republished (in the case of *Doña Bárbara* at the astounding rate of a new printing every six months or so) for many years. But during the 1970s, when new best-selling writers, like García Márquez, Sábato, Rulfo, Puig and Isabel Allende had emerged, they rapidly faded from view, though they remained in print.

Although its roots go back to Romantic *costumbrismo* and *pintoresquismo*, Regionalism represented a reaction against the Realist/ Naturalist tendency to privilege the city, as we saw in *Martín Rivas*, *La gran aldea* and *Santa*, for example, and against the influence of foreign models of fiction. It has been suggested that part of the impulse behind Regionalism came from the example of Bret Harte, whose stories set in the outback of California began to be translated in the 1860s. In 1955, looking back forty-odd years, Mariano Latorre (Chile, 1886–1955) insisted: 'Ahondar en el rincón es la única manera de ser entendido por el mundo.' What he thought this meant in practice was to develop the theme of the struggle against conditions in the undeveloped interior of the continent or what he called 'la lucha del hombre con el medio': 'la lucha del hombre de la tierra por crear civilización en

[10] Pedro Lastra, 'Concepción y función de la literatura en Chile, 1920–1970', *Relecturas hispanoamericanas* (Santiago de Chile, Universitaria, 1987), p. 124.

territorios salvajes lejos de las ciudades.'[11] He particularly praised *Doña Bárbara*, *La vorágine* and *Don Segundo Sombra* as examples of the genre.

Before turning to them, however, we must pause to glance at a couple of examples of the Novel of the Mexican Revolution. Writing in January 1914, when the Revolution was raging, Gamboa lamented the fact that the cataclysm which had overtaken his country seemed to have blotted fiction out: 'Hoy por hoy, la novela apenas si se permite levantar la voz. Muda y sobrecogida de espanto, contempla la tragedia nacional.'[12] He could not have foreseen that the very next year, the national tragedy would produce, with *Los de abajo* (1915) by Mariano Azuela (Mexico, 1873–1952), a classic Mexican novel, which would be followed by a cycle of others. The theme of *Los de abajo* is disenchantment with the Revolution. It was destined to become one of the major themes of Mexican narrative and theatre during much of the rest of the century. The plot, to which the theme gives direction and meaning, concerns an Indian *ranchero*, or small farmer, Demetrio Macías, who, after a quarrel with the local landowner, Don Mónico, and the burning of his house by Huertista (governmental) troops, collects a band of followers and joins the revolution, eventually becoming part of the forces of Pánfilo Natera and Pancho Villa which captured Zacatecas in June 1914. Demetrio, a natural leader, distinguishes himself in the battle, but subsequently leaves the main area of fighting and leads his men in a broadly circular movement which brings him back to Aguascalientes, where the revolutionaries split irrevocably. This falling out led, after sundry ups and downs, to the dominance of Carranza and the defeat of Villa. Meanwhile Demetrio has led his increasingly demoralized irregular cavalry back towards his home area where they are ambushed and massacred by the *carrancistas*.

Azuela was writing in the Realist/Naturalist tradition represented by Gamboa and stated that he was influenced by the group of French authors whom we associate with it: Balzac, Flaubert, Zola, the Goncourts and Daudet. Like so many of the writers of his time, he was convinced that he was being faithful to observed reality: 'Como escritor independiente', he wrote, 'mi norma ha sido la verdad, mi verdad si así se quiere, pero de todos modos lo que yo he creído que es . . . sin otra intención que la de dar con la mayor fidelidad posible una imagen fiel de nuestro pueblo y de lo que somos. Descubrir nuestros males y señalarlos ha sido mi tendencia como novelista.'[13] We notice at once how, like a typical Realist, he is utterly confi-

[11] Mariano Latorre, *Autobiografía de una vocación. Algunas preguntas que no me han hecho sobre el criollismo* (Santiago, Ediciones de los Anales de la Universidad de Chile, 1955), pp. 75, 80, 92.

[12] Federico Gamboa, *La novela mexicana* (Mexico, Universidad de Colima, 1988), p. 46.

[13] Mariano Azuela, *Obras completas* (Mexico City, Fondo de Cultura Económica, [1958–60]), III, p. 1287.

dent of his ability, not merely to observe and reproduce reality, but also, and above all, to interpret what he observed. *Los de abajo* is first and foremost a novel of (simplified) interpretation. The infinitely complex historical, social, economic and innumerable other forces involved in the Mexican Revolution are brushed aside in favour of a basic monocausal explanation: the Revolution is an outburst of that inherent barbarism which Sarmiento had discovered in Argentines and which was no less a feature of Mexicans (Gallegos was presently to discover it in Venezuelans). The myth of national character (which, astonishingly, survives even in Octavio Paz's famous *El laberinto de la soledad* as late as 1950) is invoked to explain the failure of the revolutionaries to cleave to the ideals which Azuela believed underlay the struggle.

We do not nowadays accept such (inherently racial) explanations. If there is such a thing as national character (as distinct from cultural differences), we do not know where it comes from or how it operates. Is it prior to a nation's history, is it a product of history, does it interact with historical and other forces, and if so how? There are no satisfactory answers to such questions.

The statements by Solís, who quite plainly speaks for Azuela, that the Revolution amounts to 'una mueca pavorosa y grotesca a la vez de una raza . . . ¡De una raza irredenta!' (*Obras*, I, p. 362) and that it can be best understood as a manifestation of 'la psicología de nuestra raza, condensada en dos palabras: ¡robar, matar!' (p. 368) are mere oracular assertions, not susceptible of any kind of convincing proof. They illustrate the well-attested but usually forgotten fact that major works of literature have been constructed around old, creaky morals, patently foolish assertions, absurd prejudices and even gross distorsions of fact, without for that reason necessarily being dropped from the canon. Like Sarmiento's *Facundo* itself, *Los de abajo* is historically and sociologically quite misleading, but novelistically brilliant. Its superbly symmetrical plot, its exciting episodes, its rapid pace, its effective symbolism and its picture of the moral degeneration of Demetrio and his followers as they are enveloped in the toils of the Revolution are brilliantly adapted to luring the reader to take its ideology on trust; while the ideology itself is so uncomplicated and easy to accept until one thinks about it, that one tends to lower one's guard.

Its formal arrangement presents certain problems. It was written at great speed under difficult circumstances after Azuela had been involved in the consequences of Villa's defeat at Celaya in April 1915. Some critics see it as a jumble of episodes held together only by the presence of Demetrio, others argue that it has organic unity. What is undeniable is that Part I, with twenty-one chapters, accounts for half of the novel; Part II, with fourteen chapters, accounts for thirty-five per cent of it; while Part III, with only seven chapters contains only fifteen per cent of the printed pages. Two deductions are possible. One is that this arrangement is intentionally designed to represent the running down of the Revolution; the other is that the 'pressure in the tap' gradually lessened. Whichever deduction we accept, Demetrio is a brilliantly drawn and convincing character and his evolution does hold the novel together. Secondly, the circularity in the novel imposes a meaningful pattern on the episodes, in the sense that it symbolizes the inevitability with which the Revolution devours its own children. There is little variation in the lengths of the chapters and the novel marches forward briskly with only one flashback (and that put in later by Azuela): the story of how Cervantes came to join Demetrio's band. The episodes are presented scenically, with very little summary and no attempt to paint in a broader picture of the fighting. Dialogue occupies more than fifty per cent of the text. This was Azuela's sixth novel and he had learned his craft.

Part I, chapter twenty-one (the Battle of Zacatecas) is the pivotal point of the novel. In it Demetrio's fortunes reach their zenith; Solís the most aware and attractive figure after his leader on the revolutionaries' side is killed, while Cervantes, the demagogue and turncoat, reveals his cowardice and symbolically survives to betray the Revolution and to profit from it. Beginning with his desertion, in *Los de abajo* negative elements accumulate and the novel spirals downward. Episodes of dramatic action give way to those of primitive barbarism with occasional moments of pathos. This shift in the plot is in itself a form of commentary. Elsewhere the thoughts and speeches of the characters themselves underline the meaning. Finally one must mention the very prominent symbolic commentary. It takes the place of psychological commentary, which would have held back the pace of the narrative. Physical features are often used to express moral defects and, as Daydí has shown,[14] drinking is used effectively to underline Demetrio's downward evolution. While it seems clear that *Los de abajo* was not written to a consciously elaborated artistic plan it reveals Azuela's instinctive ability to impose a shape on the narrative and to incorporate technical devices, such as copious dialogue and varied symbolism, to enliven and unify the work. It is worth noticing that *Los de abajo* had no success until 1927, when it attracted critical attention in Spain. After that it seemed to trigger an outpouring of novels of the Revolution, with more than a dozen appearing in the next decade. The parallel development of the Novel of the Mexican Revolution and the Regionalist Novel, both manifestations of *americanismo*, is the most important fictional phenomenon of the first part of the twentieth century. It signalled the long-awaited break with the European tradition. However much it has been repudiated by later writers it was an indispensible step forward.

Azuela's disenchantment with the Revolution found an echo in 1928 with the publication of *El águila y la serpiente* by Martín Luis Guzmán (Mexico, 1887–1976). In keeping with the hybrid nature of the novel in Spanish America, this is a piece of novelized autobiographical memoir about the

14 Santiago Daydí, 'Drinking: A Narrative Structural Pattern in Mariano Azuela's *Los de abajo*', *Kentucky Romance Quarterly* 27 (1980), 57–67.

author's contact with some of the major figures in the Revolution between 1913 and 1915. Guzmán belongs to what Rutherford calls the 'ethical' group among the novelists of the Mexican Revolution. Even more than Azuela he sees the struggle as one between the Idealists, characterized by 'nobles aspiraciones', 'fuerza moral', 'altruísmo patriótico' and belief in 'la idea creadora de la Revolución', and the betrayers of the Ideal, characterized by 'servilismo y cobardía', 'descivilización' and 'pobreza moral y cultural', that is, between civilization and barbarism (once more). The 'Constitutionalists' are consistently portrayed positively, while the leaders of the congery of opposing factions and their henchmen present the Caliban face of the Revolution ('Villa, salvaje . . . Zapata, apóstol de la barbarie, hecha idea' etc.).[15] Guzmán presents a first-hand picture of some of the principal actors in the drama as they play out their leading roles. Instead of being seen from underneath and largely from the periphery, as in *Los de abajo*, the Revolution is here seen from the top and from the centre.

Guzmán, like Azuela, perceived the Revolution not in terms of political, social or economic forces but in terms of the personalities and outlooks of its leaders and their willingness or otherwise to accept what he calls 'el problema moral de la Revolución' (p. 254) or 'el sentido espiritual de la Revolución' (p. 262), which he identifies with 'los fines regeneradores que la justificaban' (p. 284). Once more it is necessary to stress that Guzmán not only presents a causal explanation of the failure of the Revolution, based on betrayal of morality and idealism, but that it is an essentially simplified, monocausal explanation. The relevance of the insistence of the writers in the Realist tradition on their ability to interpret causally events of vast complexity does not become apparent until the Boom, when one of the first things to break down is confidence in simple causal explanations. Part of the importance of Borges, as we shall see, is that he more than any other single figure put younger writers on their guard against the kind of confident interpretations of extremely complicated problems which we nowadays criticize in Azuela, Guzmán, Gallegos and other novelists both before and after them.

El águila y la serpiente is clearly not a well-made novel. It is held together chiefly by the presence of the personal narrator and enlivened by sensational subject-matter and documental realism. Guzmán does not approach his subject analytically or deal historically with the military campaigns. His strategy is to use juxtapositions of contrasting personalities and episodes to illustrate his black and white vision of events. The opening episode, that of the *Morro Castle*, seems to be designed to lull us into thinking that we are not going to be plunged into another tale of blood, destruction and terror. But it is balanced at the end of Part I by just that: the hideous massacre of hundreds of

[15] Martín Luis Guzmán, *El águila y la serpiente* in *La novela de la Revolución Mexicana*, ed. Antonio Castro Leal I (Madrid, Mexico City, Buenos Aires, Aguilar, 1967), p. 370.

helpless prisoners by Fierro. Meantime we are introduced to the contrasting personalities of the scholarly Vasconcelos in his charming house in San Antonio, and the brutal Villa, looking like a wild beast, living in a filthy Mexican shack. These, according to Guzmán are the two poles of the Revolution, 'dos mundos distintos y aun inconciliables' (p. 231). This contrast is followed in turn by that which Guzmán establishes between Villa, the fighting general, and the wily and ambiguous Carranza, and then between both of these and the idealized General Angeles. All this brings us to the first turning point of the story: the narrator's verbal rebellion against Carranza which leads to his imprisonment and the eventual decision to turn him over to the butcher Nafarrete.

Alongside contrasting episodes and personalities, we have contrasting symbolic scenes, such as when the narrator encounters Carrasco and his band of drunken ruffians amid mud, filth and pitch darkness, against which we can set the narrator's visit to the chapel outside Culiacán. Nor do we have to look further than Villa's pistol, in the famous chapter of Part II ('La pistola de Pancho Villa') to find a counter-symbol to the little church. In Part II, the triumph of Carranza's petty intrigues over Obregón's 'probity' leads to a direct threat to the narrator, who now moves to centre stage, and a sharp rise in suspense. The narrator is now the representative man of the Revolution, his fortunes mirroring its betrayal. He moves with the course of the struggle to Mexico City, where we come to the ideological core of the narrative: the envelopment of Gutiérrez's presidency by Villa's arbitrary power and the bitterly drawn contrast between Zapata's barbarism and the idealized figure of Don Valentín Gama, the 'ejemplo simbólico' of the defeat of all that Guzmán hoped for. With a supreme concluding irony, the narrator is eventually forced to seek refuge with Villa. Guzmán's ineffectual idealism provided him with a mental framework to which he could relate his vision of the Revolution as a struggle between the forces of light and darkness. By employing this contrastive pattern systematically to set the emphasis squarely on the behaviour of *people* rather than abstract forces he greatly increases the impact of his narrative. Nor should the narrator's description of his own evolution from idealism to something much more like the outlook of the revolutionaries whom he criticizes escape our notice. He is no olympian observer, protected by his moral superiority. He is contaminated too, which makes his account all the more humanly credible. At the same time Guzmán makes full use of the techniques of the novelist: conflict of personalities, suspense, symbolism, striking juxtapositions, invented speeches and the like to draw a compelling picture of one phase of the Revolution.

What links the novel of the Mexican Revolution to Regionalism is the assumption common to writers in both movements that their work reflects a crisis of national values. Such a crisis is a basic postulate of *Los de abajo* and *El agúila y la serpiente*, both of which primarily embrace a concept of cultural reformism (that is, advocate the need for a change in mentality and value patterns, rather than a political or socio-economic approach to the problem posed by the conflict). According to Alonso, if I have understood his contorted English, it is also the basic postulate of *La vorágine* (1924) by José Eustasio Rivera (Colombia, 1888–1928), *Don Segundo Sombra* (1926) by Ricardo Güiraldes (Argentina, 1886–1927) and *Doña Bárbara* (1929) by Rómulo Gallegos (Venezuela, 1884–1969). Alonso argues that an ongoing sense of crisis from generation to generation (after Sarmiento) has led to what he calls 'Latin America's obsession with the determination of its cultural specificity'.[16] That is to say, it has given rise to an obsession with discovering its 'indigenous cultural essence' (or what used to be called its *modo de ser* or *alma de la raza*) perceived as being under some sort of threat. This seems to be a more portentous way of suggesting that Latin American writers have repeatedly tried to describe or define what makes them Latin American and/or Argentine, Mexican, Peruvian or whichever their nationality is, and then to defend it against some implicit or explicit counter-force. A problem with Alonso's approach is that he does not deal with the novels in question in chronological order. In that way he can first apply his ideas to the novels by Güiraldes and Gallegos, where Nature assists in repelling the threat, and then back-track to *La vorágine* where Nature itself is part of the threat.

At the most obvious surface level, however, *La vorágine* is a novel intended to denounce the inhuman situation prevailing in the Amazon jungle rubber industry. During World War II the Roosevelt administration looked into the question of obtaining rubber from the region. It was found then that at any one time, because of the working conditions, about a third of the registered rubber collectors had recently died, another third were too ill to work and only one third of the workers under contract were actually fit enough to operate – this, more than twenty years later than the period Rivera depicts. He himself insisted that protest was the novel's primary theme. But the function of theme in narrative is to give direction and meaning to the plot, and by this criterion the novel is not fully satisfactory. Far from being the straight-jacket that it usually is in novels of protest, the denunciatory theme here does not even emerge until after the protagonists have entered the jungle and, when it comes into prominence, it does not hold the plot together all that well. Sommer rightly notes that *La vorágine* constantly picks away at thematic and other constraints: 'it continually transgresses the norms of gender; it deconstructs notions of heroism and ownership; and it disorganizes the traditional straight line of narrative until we feel as lost as the protagonist.'[17]

If protest is not the central theme, what is? It is commonplace to propose that the answer is the struggle of man against Nature, the jungle in this case. A problem here is that Nature at the beginning of the novel is quite attractive

[16] Carlos J. Alonso, *The Spanish American Regional Novel* (Cambridge, Cambridge U.P., 1990), p. 18.

[17] Doris Sommer, *Foundational Fictions* (Berkeley, California U.P., 1991), p. 272.

and benign and only changes when Cova, the hero, joins the rubber workers. But this change may be as much due to his growing unbalance as to the difference between the plains and the forest. Walker points out that 'Cova's view of nature is coloured by his psychological evolution, which itself is a product of the influence of this very nature'.[18] Even so this is a very important thematic element for two reasons. On the one hand we are far away from the idyllic picture of the Colombian jungle in Isaacs's *María*; and almost as far, as Alonso has indicated, from Nature as a loyal antagonist, a testing ground capable of bringing out hidden qualities which may be of value in combating the crisis of nationality. On the other hand, Nature here can be held to symbolize adverse fate, or a negative view of the human condition. Given Cova's highly romantic traits and self-image, such an interpretation becomes highly plausible. The reason why Nature is benign on the plains and terrifyingly hostile in the jungle is that Cova associates the plains with freedom and limitless aspiration, while in the jungle he is forced to recognize the 'desequilibrio entre la realidad y el alma incolmable'.[19] This interconnection between the presentation of the plains and the jungle on the one hand, and Cova's magniloquent self-dramatization on the other, is the novel's most original contribution to the Spanish American fiction of its time. Nothing remotely like Cova, as character and narrator, had been seen before. Utterly self-centred, manic-depressive, violent and impulsive, when not lost in self-compensatory fantasies, he is none the less partially aware of his own unbalance as well as being endowed with the writer's combination of observation and power of expression. This not only breaks new ground in terms of characterization, but also causes the narrative to shift radically away from previously accepted patterns of psychological cause and effect and to lurch from one unexpected event to the next as dictated by Cova's mood-swings. For the first significant time we have, instead of a pseudo-objective vision of reality by an omniscient narrator, a quite subjective, even distorted, account from the point of view of a hysterical personality. In consequence, above all, *La vorágine* has atmosphere; but it lacks systematic structure. Rivera seems to have written it without a clearly defined conception of where it was going.

Both Carpentier's *Los pasos perdidos* and Vargas Llosa's *La casa verde* were clearly influenced by the evocation of the jungle in *La vorágine*. But it is the break with logical and reasonable behaviour, rather than the nightmarish jungle and the horrors it hides, that links *La vorágine* with the next phase of narrative (the next memorable unbalanced narrator being, of course, Sábato's Castel in *El túnel,* on the eve of the beginning of the Boom). This is

[18] John Walker, *Rivera: La vorágine* (London, Grant & Cutler, 1988), p. 19.

[19] José Eustasio Rivera, *La vorágine*, 4th edn (Santiago de Chile, Zig-Zag, 1965), p. 191.

not to say that *La vorágine* does not contain backward-looking elements, both stylistically (its self-consciously poetic prose has its origins in *Modernista* narrative) and in terms of content (Cova's self-image and bombast reflect a debased Romantic view of the satanic–titanic hero). But in retrospect it is by far the most original of the 'seis de la fama' (*Los de abajo, La vorágine, Don Segundo Sombra, Doña Bárbara, La Gloria de Don Ramiro* and *El hermano asno*). Not least this is because of the underlying existential metaphor, reinforced by Alicia's pregnancy: the triumph of life is negated by the triumph of death when Cova and his companios are swallowed up by the jungle. The novel adapts to a new symbolic context the old Romantic theme of love and aspiration, crossed by fate, ending in death, and the equally Romantic notion of a struggle between action and insight as the basis of character development.

Walker (p. 33) points out the 'many references to nationality and patriotism' and the 'sense of *colombianidad*' which provides Cova with 'one of his life-giving ideals'. This is what brings *La vorágine* close at times to the pattern postulated by Alonso, which is more clearly visible in *Don Segundo Sombra* and *Doña Bárbara*. The year in which the former was published, 1926, marks a turning point in modern Spanish American narrative. For in the same year appeared Arlt's *El juguete rabioso*, one of the great predecessors of the Boom novel. *Don Segundo Sombra* is essentially Americanist, rural in setting and unambiguous in its approach to reality, whether external or psychological. *El juguete rabioso*, on the other hand, is much more existential and cosmopolitan, urban in setting and ambiguous. We should also notice that 1926 was the year of Horacio Quiroga's *Los desterrados* which contains some of his best stories about life in the jungle of Misiones. Güiraldes and Quiroga, that is, stand for the *criollista* tradition, while Arlt announces Onetti and the Boom a quarter century later.

Don Segundo Sombra is a *Bildungsroman*, a novel of apprenticeship to life, in which Fabio Cáceres, the illegitimate son of a member of the Argentine landowning elite runs away from home to become a cattle-drover on the pampas. There he finds a mentor in an old gaucho, Sombra, who teaches him first the tricks of the trade and then, far more importantly, its underlying values. When, later, Fabio is recognized by his father and inherits the latter's wealth and position in the national oligarchy, it is specifically stated that his education in the outback will fit him superbly for his new social responsibilities. It is as important to notice that Güiraldes was not a gaucho as it is to remember that the Indigenist novelists were not Indians. The author of *Don Segundo Sombra* was a minor member of the landowning class, a well-educated and highly sophisticated writer and poet in the avant-garde idiom (which is clearly apparent in the style of the novel itself, supposedly written by an ex-drover) and part of the text was written in Paris. At one level, the continuing attraction of *Don Segundo Sombra* is its evocation of life on the old pampas (as it never actually was, of course), a kind of *menosprecio de corte* narrative, full of freedom, adventure and male camaraderie in contrast to the banality of modern life, domesticity and daily drudgery. Thus much early criticism focused on the nostalgic reflection of the world of the gaucho and on *Don Segundo Sombra* as the last great monument to gauchesque literature. But its relevance to Alonso's theory of cultural crisis lies in the fact that it is plainly (too plainly) an ideological construct. As Francisco Ayala long ago pointed out, this is a preceptive novel, and Don Segundo personifies, not so much a social group on the point of disappearing, as 'una suma de valores' and a symbolic national archetype.[20] From here it is but a step to recognizing that the values in question are less national than those of the landed oligarchy, values which present no threat to their power and prestige. In that sense, Alonso argues, the novel is partly concerned with the legitimation of a privileged social group. The proof of this is that the values represented and transmitted by Sombra – courage, strength, stoicism, honour, freedom and indifference to money (as well as obvious machismo) – are individualistic and anachronistic in modern society, where team-work and technological know-how are all-important. These are the old values of a rural society, under threat in the 1920s from industrialization, the growth of cities, the ploughing up and enclosure of the pampas and perhaps above all by the huge influx of immigrants in previous decades, which destabilized the traditional social hierarchy and the outlook on which it was based, while creating a urban proletariat with new ideas and aspirations. We are, in other words, in the presence of a 'pastoral myth' which (in North America as well as in Argentina) exalted a set of values which had ceased to be useful because it offered no intellectual apparatus for coping with modernity.

The pattern of the novel is the familiar one of separation from one environment, initiation into another with subsequent learning experiences, and then return to the place of origin with greater insight and abilities. We notice that five years pass between chapters nine and ten, so that the first nine chapters express the first stage of Sombra's teachings: the need for physical and moral strength, and competence at the job. The next stage is more abstract and existential: 'Por él supe de la vida, la resistencia y la entereza en la lucha, el fatalismo en aceptar sin rezongos lo sucedido, la fuerza moral ante las aventuras sentimentales, la desconfianza para con las mujeres y la bebida, la prudencia entre los forasteros, la fe en los amigos.'[21] Not, we notice, human solidarity, compassion, civic endeavour, self-sacrifice, far less love and family values. There is a third stage, often overlooked by critics: resistence to Fate. But here we begin to notice the least recognized aspect of Fabio's

20 Francisco Ayala, 'El gaucho como símbolo nacional', *Recopilación de textos sobre tres novelas ejemplares*, ed. Trinidad Pérez (Havana, Casa de las Américas, 1971), pp. 211–18.

21 Ricardo Güiraldes, *Don Segundo Sombra*, *Obras completas* (Buenos Aires, Emecé, 1962), p. 390.

development. This is his growing awareness that Sombra is unique; there is something in his superiority to Destiny which verges on the superhuman and cannot be learned or imitated. Along with this goes Fabio's parallel recognition, after the *cangrejal* and Don Sixto episodes in chapter fifteen, that Nature (here as so often a symbol of life), though often providing a fine school of character, can also be a disloyal antagonist. Thirdly we must pay special attention to the episode in chapter twenty-three in which Antenor kills his adversary in a knife fight over a woman. It gives rise to a series of reflections by Fabio in which he seems to be questioning Sombra's values, at least as far as they affect others. Fabio concludes that for all but his mentor, man in relation to his experiences is a mystery. Significantly, it is at this point that Fabio is plucked out of his roving life and compelled to accept a broader pattern of social responsibility. The key quotation is inserted into chapter eighteen and, repeated for emphasis in chapter twenty-six: 'El que sabe de las males de esta tierra, por haberlos vivido, se ha templado para domarlos' (p. 492). It implies that Fabio's apprenticeship on the pampas prepares him in some special way for his later social role. The whole thrust of the novel, in which there is no counter-force to Sombra, so that Fabio only has one model to follow, is in this direction. But, as is the case with *Doña Bárbara* also, *Don Segundo Sombra*, despite its literary qualities, seems to misrepresent the nature of the crisis of national values it was partly intended to address.

In Holy Week of 1927, Rómulo Gallegos, at that time a teacher in Caracas, made a brief trip to the great plains, the *llanos*, in the interior of Venezuela. Allowing for the journey time he was there for about four days. But it was enough to fire his imagination to write his third full-scale novel, the hugely successful *Doña Bárbara* (1929). Gallegos had always been a novelist and essayist of ideas and his earlier works reveal a curiously ambivalent attitude towards his central preoccupation, borrowed from Sarmiento, that of the struggle between civilization and barbarism, as he saw it, in his native country. He presupposed the existence in Venezuela of a specific *modo de ser/alma de la raza* and made the by now traditional mistake of regarding it as a kind of epiphenomenon existing separately from economic and social conditions and in some way determining their development. Chiefly he regarded it as barbaric, but at the same time full of the energy and potential of a new, young nation in contrast to what, in the tradition of Bello, he, Vasconcelos in Mexico, Mallea in Argentina and others were pleased to regard as the decadence of Western Europe. *Doña Bárbara* is a classic example of what Fredric Jameson calls Third World 'national allegories' designed to identify and explore some sort of national essence, in this case, as in that of *Don Segundo Sombra*, seen as overtaken by a crisis in which once more barbarism seems to be about to overwhelm civilized values. Unlike Güiraldes, however, Gallegos submits the traditional values of the *llaneros*, the Venezuelan equivalent of the gauchos, to a somewhat positivistic critique, calling for them to be adapted to the new realities of barbed wire enclosure, clearly defined property rights, reorganization and modernization of the *llano* ranching economy and the possibility of a transport system which would revolutionize life on the plains.

Gallegos handles his theme in three main ways. First, the conflict between barbarism and civilization is presented in practical, material terms of the need to bring law and order, to fence off property and end rustling, and to put the ranches on a proper business footing. Gallegos is quite unequivocally opposed to rural underdevelopment and resistance to change. Second, the theme is reinterpreted into human and at the same time symbolic terms as the hero, Santos Luzardo, the young lawyer from Caracas with his new-fangled ideas, confronts Doña Bárbara, the incarnation of the bad old ways. Thirdly the theme is seen in terms of Santos's struggle with his own attraction to barbarism and violence. The socio-economic problem is centred on the founding of a cottage-industry cheese-making concern and the enclosure of the grazing areas. Both are presented as civilizing activities; one civilizes the wild cattle, the other the land itself. But no sooner does the process begin than Gallegos hurries on to the more fictionally rewarding question of Santos's need to 'luchar contra Doña Bárbara, creatura y personificación de los tiempos que corrían'[22] (the action takes place around 1910). Cultural reformism, that is, changing mentality, as so often in literature, elbows aside the real task, which is to change conditions. Santos decides to try to break the vicious circle of bad conditions producing barbarism which in turn perpetuates bad conditions at the human point, because it turns the novel into the story of a clash of personalities and hence makes it more interesting. But inexplicably Gallegos fails to follow through. Santos and Doña Bárbara meet only six times, are (briefly) alone only three times and have only one significant dialogue (in Part II, chapter five). If Bárbara personifies the barbarism of the plains, and if that is what Santos is attracted to, and has to overcome the attraction, why does he not feel drawn to her? Gallegos baulks at the logical consequence of shifting the presentation of the theme into human terms. In an important essay, Millington points out that what Santos is attracted to when he returns to the plains from Caracas is really 'hegemonic masculinity', and thus: 'Even in carrying out the new, Santos is reaffirming the values of the old.'[23] In the same way, we cannot overlook the fact that, even if Santos's changes were successful, he would only be replacing an unenlightened landholding class with a more progressive one. There is no suggestion of the need for a more fundamental remedy: agrarian reform. Similarly, the logic of Santos's position should have led him to civilize and marry one of the grand-daughters

[22] Rómulo Gallegos, *Doña Bárbara*, *Obras completas* (Madrid, Aguilar, 1959), I, p. 511.

[23] Mark Millington, 'As if by Magic: The Power of Masculine Discourse in *Doña Bárbara*', *New Hispanisms*, eds. Mark Millington and Paul Julian Smith (Ottowa, Dovehouse, 1994), pp. 150–75, p. 153.

of Melesio, the plainsman, but in fact the semi-symbolic figure he 'tames' and marries is his cousin Marisela. In each case Gallegos stops short of completing the novel's ideological pattern, no doubt in consideration of the outlook of his readership in 1929.

Of central importance to the understanding of *Doña Bárbara* is the extremely obtrusive symbolic commentary spawned by the novel's allegorical conception. The setting (the *llano*), the main characters, many of the episodes, the names of Santos Luzardo, Bárbara, Danger and the two ranches Altamira and El Miedo, light and darkness, sundry animals – the old crocodile El Tuerto, the horse Cabos Negros, the water snake at the end, as well as many other elements in the narrative, all possess symbolic meaning. But the key symbol is the centaur: half-man, half-beast, which is intended to express the conflict within Santos and supposedly within the Venezuelan national character. As we have suggested, it is not a wholly negative symbol, since the animality also implies strength, free self-assertion and dynamic power, as Santos recognizes when he begins to fall under the spell of the barbarism of the plains. But, as in Azuela's *Los de abajo* the attribution of an element of barbarism to the 'national essence' is not really a helpful move in interpreting and attempting to solve the problems of a collectivity.

Structurally, *Doña Bárbara* has only one chain of incidents. The love interest provided by Santos's affair with Marisela is so closely woven into the main plot that it can hardly be regarded as a sub-plot. Marisela's symbolism is inextricably connected to that of the novel as a whole; she is the only other major female figure and hence the main foil to Bárbara; finally she is the agent who liberates Santos from the barbarism into which he seems to have slipped at the end of the novel. This concentration of effect is mitigated by Gallegos's avoidance of the risk of staking everything on one single central character. Both Santos and Bárbara are fully developed figures, which allows Gallegos to deflect the reader's attention from one to the other at will without losing any of the interest. A comparison of the first edition of *Doña Bárbara* with the second confirms the care which Gallegos took to improve the balance both in regard to the arrangement of the plot and the development of the two main characters.[24] His whole aim in the changes introduced with regard to Santos was to tone down the initially crude presentation of his character in terms of over-simple conflict. As a result Santos's streak of barbarity does not lose its glamour, but its preponderance is no longer seriously implied. His ideal of civilization is shown as less of a dream; his inner barbarism as less of a reality. In the case of Bárbara, in the first edition Apolinar,

[24] See pp. 17–18 of my *Critical Guide* to *Doña Bárbara* (London, Grant & Cutler, 1972) and my articles 'Gallegos's Revision of *Doña Bárbara*, 1928–29', *Hispanic Review* 42 (1974), 265–78 and 'More about the Making of *Doña Bárbara*', *Nine essays on Rómulo Gallegos*, ed. Hugo Rodríguez Alcalá (Riverside, California U.P., 1979), pp. 198–215.

whom she murders, was her husband; in the second only her lover. Other suppressions indicate a similar intention to attenuate the darker side of her presentation. The attenuating features he introduced into the first edition – a certain grandeur of personality, a repressed capacity for 'sentimiento puro', a hint that she was capable of redemption through love, and the identification of her with the *llano* itself, which is only semibarbarous, and with its more attractive wild birds – were not quite enough. In the second edition she gains further in dignity and force of character. Very significantly (for its time) Gallegos removed the reference to her rather squalid sexual life after the murder of Apolinar which had graced the first edition. Her witch-like qualities become much more ambiguous and more of her behaviour is attributed to improvisation than to calculatedly evil premeditation. This heightened emphasis on the ambiguity of both the major characters, and the careful re-arrangement of the episodes in the second edition to underline the parallelism between Santos and Bárbara which is the novel's basic structural principle, combine to produce Gallegos's most carefully crafted work of fiction. Tautly patterned, suspenseful and pleasingly symmetrical, it is one of the finest examples of the well-made novel to emerge in Spanish America before the Boom. González Echevarría has even attempted a modern, Boom-type, reading of it, with dubious success.

The famous short stories of Horacio Quiroga (Uruguay, 1878–1937) set in the outback provinces of Chaco and Misiones form a kind of pendant to Regionalist narrative. Beardsell writes that they 'have been considered an important contribution to *criollo* literature. They help in the exploration of Argentinian territory, they are rural, they exalt *criollo* values such as virility and endurance, and they are narrated in a language that is functional rather than ornamental'.[25] However, not all Quiroga's stories illustrate this pattern. It is easy to forget that his most creative period began as early as 1906, well before the rise of Regionalism/Indigenism or the Novel of the Mexican Revolution. Not only did he dabble briefly in *Modernismo* and Decadentism, but in an early story like 'La gallina degollada' (1909) we have a paradigmatic example of Naturalism in its most obtrusive form. A horror-story of a group of retarded children who murder their normal sister, it attempts to show that this act of unconscious violence is the direct result of defective heredity operating through both of their parents, as well as of a defective environment created by the rejection of the idiot-boys by the latter, who concentrate all their love on their daughter. Their moral inadequacy is seen as connected to the mental inadequacy of the boys. Seen from that angle, the story is cast in the form of a crime and punishment process in which the parents pay for their 'inferiority' (they are described as having 'corazones inferiores') by the death

[25] Peter R. Beardsell, *Quiroga, Cuentos de amor de locura y de muerte* (London, Grant & Cutler, 1986), pp. 19–20.

of their normal child at the hands of the abnormal ones. As a metaphor of human experience the story makes sombre reading. That which represents renewal of life, which symbolizes hope and confidence – having children – turns into a doubly ironic nightmare: the abnormal children first 'kill' the love of the parents. Then they kill their sister. This intense existential pessimism persists in Quiroga's work. But just as important are two other features of the story. One is Quiroga's pseudo-scientific assumptions about cause and effect. The causes, developed in the flashback which occupies the centre of the tale, 'explain' the effect: the dreadful ending. Borges never uses explanatory flashbacks of this kind. He knew that human behaviour is a mystery. Quiroga still believes in a comprehensible world. He and Borges are on different sides of a cultural watershed.

The other feature is the *dispositio*: the logical structure of the tale. Quiroga is famous for his 'Decálogo del perfecto cuentista', ten rules for short-story writing. They are indispensible for analysing his stories. But when we look closely at them we notice a startling absence. The first four concern the writer's attitude, and are of minor importance. The remaining six emphasize the importance of the opening in individual stories, economy of language, character development, and detachment. But what about narrative strategy and internal arrangement? Obviously all Quiroga's most memorable tales are carefully structured, but he does not seem to have thought it necessary to allude to the need to address this aspect in the *decálogo*. No doubt he took it for granted. But there is another explanation. It is instructive to examine a comment on the short story made by the Mexican poet and short-story writer, Amado Nervo, in 1906 just as Quiroga's career was getting started. 'Es cierto', Nervo wrote, 'que para escribir un cuento suele no necesitarse la imaginación; se ve correr la vida, se sorprende una escena, un rasgo, se toman de aquí y ahí los elementos reales y palpitantes que ofrecen los seres y las cosas que pasan, y se tiene lo esencial. Lo demás es cosa de poquísimo asunto: coordinar aquellos datos y ensamblear con ellos una historia.'[26] Observation, content, these are the essentials; the rest is straightforward. This cavalier attitude towards interior organization is partly shared by Quiroga himself. He too stressed content. 'La idea es naturalmente lo esencial en el arte', he wrote, 'Al acto de sentirlas suele llamársele "Tener algo que decir". De aquí que el tener ideas primero y la suerte luego de hallar las palabras que las expresen definitivamente son las dos facultades maestras del escritor.'[27] Once more, as in the *decálogo*, we go straight from content to style. Tech-

[26] Amado Nervo, *Almas que pasan*, cited in Antonio Muñoz, 'Notas sobre los rasgos formales del cuento modernista', *El cuento hispanoamericano ante la crítica*, ed. Enrique Pupo-Walker (Madrid, Castalia, 1973), 50–63, p. 59.

[27] Horacio Quiroga, cited in José Enrique Etcheverry, 'La retórica del cuento', *Aproximaciones a Horacio Quiroga*, ed. Angel Flores (Caracas, Monte Avila, 1976), p. 180.

nique seems unimportant. Why? Because Quiroga (and Nervo), in the Realist tradition, did not question reality or the notion that comprehension of it was achieved by thinking in terms of linear sequences of causes and effects (which is what Nervo meant by *ensamblear*). Reality is 'straightforward'; so the basic technique is juxtaposition: one incident following on from another. This is what we find in 'La gallina degollada', heavily underlined by the idea of hereditary and environmental determinism. José Pereira Rodríguez interestingly has shown that, although Quiroga often revised his stories before republishing them in book form, he normally only made stylistic changes, not alterations to the narrative arrangement.[28] This is a matter of key importance to the twentieth-century short story (or novel, for that matter). Linear juxtaposition, like third-person omniscience, carries with it the comforting metaphor of a comprehensible world. Break with linear juxtaposition (as, for example, Bombal was to do in the next generation – it was to become a feature of Modernism in the Anglo-Saxon sense) and you irretrievably undermine the metaphor.

Quiroga's most famous and memorable stories, however, are set in the rural interior, in the Chaco and Misiones. As in Rivera, Güiraldes and Gallegos, whose novels they precede, Nature is man's great antagonist and becomes at bottom a metaphor for life, but is not seen as either a testing ground or a devouring Green Hell. It is seen as being, like life, dangerously unpredictable. Man can cope most of the time with its risks, but often these are so unexpected and extreme that he succumbs. Neither Borges nor Quiroga believed in a 'Fatherly World according to Design'. But whereas Borges thought that we are not programmed to understand its mysteries, Quiroga thought that we are not equipped to handle its risks. He had no strong religious convictions, and behind the apparent objectivity of his narrative stance lies a deep pessimism. Death is his most fundamental theme. Beardsell points out that of the eighteen stories originally published in *Cuentos de amor de locura y de muerte*, no fewer than fifteen involve death in some way or other. The key idea is that of inevitability, but based on what? Mere chance. Beardsell also indicates that in the original version of 'A la deriva' for example, the snake whose bite kills the protagonist is a common yarará. But in the final version it becomes the much more uncommon yararacusú. In other words this is not just an everyday risk; it is a blow of fate. Once the man, Paulino, is bitten, suspense is created. But as he slowly dies, suspense is converted into illusion on his part, but ironic awareness of his impending death in us the readers. Saúl Yurkievich in *Aproximaciones* carefully analyses the tale into five scenes and two descriptive interludes. We notice how impressively Quiroga manages the parallelism between the gradually increasing grip of the poison and Paulino's gradually decreasing reac-

[28] José Pereira Rodríguez, 'El estilo', *Ibid.*, pp. 183–206.

tions, as well as the symbolism of the setting sun (over an impassively beautiful Nature) and Paulino's illusion of an improvement just before he dies. But once more everything is reduced to a chronological series of effects following from an arbitrary cause. What happens is dreadful and inevitable, but comprehensible.

In a much later story 'El hombre muerto', the theme is once more, not so much death, as the process of dying. Again a chance event in which a man stabs himself inadvertently with his own machete is the triggering-device. Not a creature this time, but something familiar and reliable, turns in a flash into a mortal enemy. The metaphor is the same: no benevolent Providence is there to protect us (nor was there for Quiroga in reality – attacked by cancer, he killed himself). The story is also almost symbolic technically. On the one hand, we have, beginning in the fifth paragraph, a characteristic example of old-style authorial intervention for the sake of commentary. On the other we notice in this story how close we are to stream of thought, not really naturalized into mainstream Spanish American narrative until Asturias's *El Señor Presidente* sixteen years later. One step back; one step forward. We notice too the unadorned language: almost no metaphors, only one simile, the emphasis on the triviality of the event, and the cruel pathos of the child's approach.

These, then, are highly condensed, dramatic stories, often of human beings living under extreme conditions. They do not exhibit Hemingway's 'grace under pressure'; neither they nor the natural surroundings are idealized. Often they make almost superhuman efforts, and as often are crushed inexorably by unforeseeable circumstances which we can sometimes recognize as arbitrary adverse fate. They do not inhabit, that is, a harmonious universe, but one which is inherently conflictive. At times, as in 'Van-Houten' (1919), 'Tacuara-Mansión' (1920) or 'Los destiladores de naranja' (1923), characters collaborate with their own fate or are ironically punished for their own mistakes. But a careful reading of his tales suggests that for all his pessimism, Quiroga thought of the human condition as risky and at times tragic, but not absurd. In the light of future developments, the distinction is significant.

A final offshoot of the Realist novel, nowadays all but forgotten, was the anti-imperialist novel directed against the United States. Characteristic of this sub-genre were *Canal Zone* (1935) by Demetrio Aguilera Malta (Ecuador, 1909–81) on the effects of the ceding of the zone by Panama, *Mamita Yunay* (1941) by Carlos Luis Fallas (Costa Rica, 1911–66), protesting against the banana monopoly and *Mancha de aceite* (1935) by César Urbe Piedrahita (Colombia, 1897–1951) against the oil companies. We should not overlook the fact that this was where part of Miguel Angel Asturias's fictional career fits in, with his famous Banana Trilogy, *Viento fuerte* (1949), *El papa verde* (1954) and *Weekend in Guatemala* (1956) or that he and Fallas hover behind the story of the Banana Company in García Márquez's *Cien años de soledad*.

It has sometimes been suggested (by Vargas Llosa among others) that the

Indigenist and Regionalist writers against whom his generation reacted were 'primitive' in their fictional techniques. This is not wholly true. Certainly they were not as technically sophisticated or as devoted to experimentation as gradually became the case after Macedonio Fernández began advocating a radical shift in the approach to fiction with *No toda es vigilia la de los ojos abiertos* as early as 1929. But more important is the fact that, preoccupied as they were with the discovery and expression of a genuinely Spanish American reality, they tended to see that reality as unambiguous, accepting, in the Realist tradition, that what they observed on the battlefields of the Mexican Revolution, on the pampas or the *llano*, Misiones or in the Amazonian jungle was really real. In the course of his commentary on *Doña Bárbara*, González Echevarría re-states a second basic reason why it and the *novelas de la tierra* in general, together with Indigenist fiction and the whole Realist tradition from which they stem have come to seem old-hat. Underlying the *novela de la tierra*, he argues, there is a 'myth of nature and its organic coherence'; and this myth has now been radically questioned, in large measure because we can no longer accept the idea of a simple correspondence between language and nature/reality. 'This correspondence', González Echevarría writes, 'assures the close relationship between signs and things, between writing and the world. But *at the same time* modern literature is founded on a radical doubt as to whether such a correspondence exists, whether there really is a congruity between the world and the signs that presumably express it.'[29]

This is why to understand the pattern of fiction in Spanish America in the first half of the twentieth century, it is not enough to follow out the various movements which grew out of the realism of the end of the previous century. What led to the Boom was not a further process of development of Realism but a gradual break with Realism. When did this begin to manifest itself? Or, to put it in terms of a more meaningful question in a Western perspective: when was the beginning of Modernism in the Anglo-Saxon sense in Spanish America? We can all agree that it peaked in the 1960s in certain areas of the Boom. But in 1970 both Vargas Llosa and Rodríguez Monegal in *Books Abroad* asserted that the Boom had been in existence since 1950. Roa Bastos and Anderson Imbert went further, the former arguing in 1965 that the writers of his generation 'son herederos de aquellos escritores que, a partir de la segunda década del siglo, bajo el estímulo de los experimentos de la vanguardia . . . iniciaron la transformación de nuestro arte narrativo'.[30] The latter agreed that the Boom writers inherited the 'esquemas anti-realistas o

29 Roberto González Echevarría, *The Voice of the Masters* (Austin, Texas U.P., 1985), p. 44.

30 Augusto Roa Bastos, 'Imagen y perspectivas de la narrativa latinoamericana actual', *La novela hispano americana*, ed. Juan Loveluck, 3rd edn (Santiago de Chile, Universitaria, 1969), pp. 193–211, p. 210.

desrealizadores de los magos de 1930 a 1950'.[31] Writers in the Realist tradition were assumed to have (and believed that they had) some sort of privileged vision, an access to epistemological truth or a deeper, objective knowledge of how things are. Modernist authors, on the other hand, tend to privilege individual, subjective consciousness, a retreat from straight representational writing and, partly as a consequence, innovations in technique, which often require the reader to make a readjustment both to a different angle of vision on the human condition and new ways of figuring it forth.

It could be argued, therefore, that Modernism in Spanish America began to emerge timidly as the Regionalist novel passed its peak with *Doña Bárbara* in 1929. It is worth noticing that Ortega y Gasset had already published his enormously influential 'La deshumanización del arte' in 1925. Over time the term took root in Spanish America and seems to have been used on occasion as a kind of code-word to attack the movement away from Realist Regionalism. Already in an article of 1930, 'Lo cursi', Quiroga attacked the new *arte deshumanizado* as a 'pasatiempo retórico' and proclaimed his belief that 'la creación artística valía por la cantidad de vida que la empapaba'. In 1951, Ciro Alegría, criticizing the way Güiraldes presented Don Segundo Sombra as 'más una idea que un hombre' asserted: 'No es preciso deshumanizarlo para que represente algo.'[32] In a lecture in 1972, the Nobel Laureate Miguel Angel Asturias was more explicit about a split in Spanish American fiction. Having unequivocally aligned himself with Regionalist fiction, setting his own *Hombres de maíz* alongside *La vorágine* and *Don Segundo Sombra*, he went on to criticize the emergence of what he called the 'novela poética', described as 'esa novela deshumanizada, sin arraigo real, creada diríase para dar salida a bellas imágenes, a juegos de ingenio y soluciones irreales, mitológicas, caprichosas y ambiguas'.[33] It is not made clear which novels Asturias had in mind. What is evident, however, is that he realized that another pattern of narrative had come into being, and that he disapproved of it because it was not sufficiently *americanista*. Meantime, in the 1950s, Mariano Azuela too, looking back over his own writing career, had noted the shift and described how he tried to align himself with it, 'escribiendo con técnica moderna y de la última hora'. He went on: 'Estudié con detenimiento esa técnica que consiste nada menos en el truco ahora bien conocido de retorcer palabras y frases, oscurecer conceptos y expresiones, para obtener el efecto de la novedad.' But after seeing it fail in *La luciérnaga*

[31] Enrique Anderson Imbert, *El realismo mágico y otros ensayos* (Caracas, Monte Avila, 1976), p. 24.

[32] Ciro Alegría, 'Notas sobre el personaje en la novela hispanoamericana', *La novela hispanoamericana*, ed. Juan Loveluck, 3rd edn (Santiago de Chile, Universitaria, 1969), pp. 118–26, p. 120.

[33] Miguel Angel Asturias, 'Paisaje y lenguaje en la novela hispanoamericana', *Rassegna Iberistica* 54 (1995), 69–77, p. 75.

(1932), he tells us, 'hice un serio examen de conciencia y me sentí pecador'.[34] And so he abandoned the effort. The joint hostile testimony of these four major authors leaves no room for doubt that a new post-Realist mode of writing had come into being, challenging their own practice.

Who were the representatives of this other pattern which Roa Bastos and Anderson Imbert had also discerned? We can mention some obvious names: Pedro Prado (Chile 1886–1952) with *Alsino* (1920); Eduardo Barrios (Chile, 1884–1963) with *El niño que enloqueció de amor* (1915) and *El hermano asno* (1922); Eduardo Mallea (Argentina, 1903–82) with *Cuentos para una inglesa desesperada*, (1926); Jaime Torres Bodet (Mexico, 1902–74) with *Margarita de niebla* (1927); Martín Adán (Peru, 1908–85) with *La casa de cartón* (1928); Teresa de la Parra (Venezuela, 1889–1936) with *Las memorias de Mamá Blanca* (1929); Felisberto Hernández (Uruguay, 1902–64) with *Fulano de tal* (1925) and *Libro sin tapas* (1929) and María Luisa Bombal (1910–80) with *La última niebla* (1935) and *La amortajada* (1938). We can see at once that this group was contemporaneous with the Indigenist/Mexican Revolution/Regionalist group and, except for Bombal, published in the same time-period. But they belonged to a quite different sensibility. Prado, Torres Bodet and Adán were all poets. While the members of the group we have been looking at above were social novelists, concerned with collective problems, those of this group were primarily concerned with the inner world of the individual and his or her emotional, psychological and even spiritual problems, often expressed in innovative, sometimes lyrical prose. Influences were quite different also; this group were far more cosmopolitan. Barrios cultivated an acquaintance with the work of Pascal, Schopenhauer and Nietzsche; Prado with that of Bergson. Torres Bodet, and the *Contemporáneos* to whom he belonged, read Proust, Joyce and Kafka, and Torres Bodet himself was a professor of French literature. Hernández lived in France on a government scholarship and knew Supervielle. Bombal even graduated from the Sorbonne, enjoyed Virginia Woolf and was one of the very few Spanish American writers published by *Sur*, the avant-garde Argentine review run by Victoria Ocampo. All this is a far cry from Realism and its offshoots. There is a need for a fully researched book on these early Modernists.

For the moment we can only glance at the two most important of them: Barrios and Bombal. What links them closely together is their preoccupation with emotion and especially with emotional frustration. In that sense both look back, like their fellow Chilean poet, Gabriela Mistral, through *Modernismo* to Romanticism. This has not helped their reputations in recent times, though interest in Bombal has been stimulated recently by Feminism.

[34] Mariano Azuela, 'El novelista y su ambiente II', *Obras completas* (Mexico, Fondo de Cultura Económica, 1958), III, pp. 1113 and 1118.

One by one writers in later periods from Carpentier and Donoso to Skármeta have gone out of their way to repudiate the heritage of Regionalism. But novelists like Barrios and Bombal have just been allowed to fade from view as more innovative and more sophisticated Boom novelists took over. With Fray Lázaro of *El hermano asno*, we break away from 'representative' characterization (Macías the representative of the corrupting influence of the Mexican Revolution; Doña Bárbara, the representative of barbarism on the *llanos* and so on). So many 'representative' characters stand for more than what they are. They are close to being symbolic; they tend to lack interior life, the quirks, the individual reactions, the private problems of real people. Lázaro represents only himself. He is a monk who lacks confidence in his vocation. The novel is his autobiographical confession.

Lázaro believes unashamedly in emotion and states his position unequivocally: 'La emoción es la esencia virtual de las cosas. La emoción es el alma.'[35] Like Pascal he insists that there are truths which the heart can know but which the brain cannot reach. After an unsuccessful love affair he has taken refuge in a monastery in the hope that dedication to God will cure his sick soul. But emotion follows him, in the form of María Mercedes, his former fiancée's sister to whom he is deeply attracted. Meanwhile, one of his fellow monks, Fray Rufino, a saintly figure of Franciscan spiritual simplicity, is undergoing severe carnal temptations. The novel develops the evolution of the two monks in parallel until Rufino cracks under the strain and sexually attacks María Mercedes. By accepting the blame for the scandal, though innocent, Lázaro makes what may be an acceptable sacrifice to God and may be rewarded by finding his vocation at last confirmed. This is a ticklish topic to handle and Barrios came in for criticism at the time for mixing sex and sainthood, as well as for his picture of life in the monastery. But this is not a 'Catholic Novel' of the kind we associate with Mauriac or Bernanos. It deserves its place among the six best novels of its time in Spanish America because it is a sensitive study of a troubled man torn between wordly love and love of God.

This is not how the novel begins. Initially Lázaro's problem is that of Unamuno: intellectual analysis threatening simple faith. At the same time, Lázaro is unable to overcome a sense of superiority towards his fellow monks. It is only when María Mercedes suddenly appears that his struggle becomes one of emotion with emotion. Her presence acts like friction on a wound, bringing his already disturbed attitudes to a point of crisis. But before that point Lázaro has been very skilfully situated among his fellow monks: Rufino, who appears to have achieved what Lázaro desires, Elías, hard-headed and uncomplicated, and Bernardo who has come to terms with the

[35] Eduardo Barrios, *El hermano asno*, *Obras completas*, II (Santiago de Chile, Zig-Zag, 1962), p. 625.

problem more through pity than through charity towards his fellow men. There is nothing mechanical about Lázaro's evolution. He passes from a problem with his insight to a problem with his feelings, and then to a series of fluctuations. At first, though sensing the threat to his precarious spiritual equilibrium, he feels a false sense of security. But soon he is forced to flee the convent on a Mission in order to regain control of his reactions. Meanwhile, Rufino, originally a slightly ridiculous figure, begins to acquire the reputation of a saint, though not without certain elements of caricature of Franciscan *sancta simplicitas*. But now comes the difficulty. Lázaro has been playing with fire, deceiving himself about his feelings for María Mercedes. He is rather weak and vacillating. We can readily understand his position. But Rufino, however silly some of his ways appear, has been presented as genuinely in love with God, innocent and utterly self-denying. Yet he is suddenly assailed by two sharp and bitter forces of spiritual disturbance, sexual temptation and the temptation to spiritual pride as his fame increases. These forces in the end combine in his final act of deliberate self-disgrace (if that is what it is). There is a certain irony here: Lázaro longs for just enough sanctity to justify his taking his final vows but is tormented by his feelings; Rufino possesses sanctity, Franciscan simplicity, total self-abnegation but is tormented by the flesh. This is what troubles some Christian readers. Barrios seems to be questioning God's treatment of two of his elect. In fact, Barrios, as Walker cogently argues,[36] is not quite orthodox. Deeply influenced by Schopenhauer, Barrios (like Unamuno, on occasion) seems to have believed not so much that God moves in a mysterious way, but that 'There is an evil force in life that causes pain and suffering' (Walker, p. 72), perhaps independently of God himself. But we cannot overlook the fact that, although Lázaro perceives the final episode to have been 'absurdo, trágico y grotesco', it none the less may have resolved his problem, albeit by a pious fraud. Scandal is avoided; Rufino's saintly reputation is preserved and Lázaro seems set to take his final vows. The whole situation may be seen (if we so wish) as a test of Lázaro's faith. But it remains ambiguous and in this ambiguity resides much of the greater modernity of *El hermano asno* over other novels in the 'seis de la fama'.

The novel is superbly structured. After the exposition, establishing the initial spiritual positions of Lázaro and Rufino, the arrival of María Mercedes creates the first articulation of the plot, followed by an upward development in the evolution of the two monks. The central section, with its main episode: the fourth meeting of Lázaro and María Mercedes outside the monastery, shows the former vacillating, falling into crisis, but finally bringing his feelings under control. The final section, announced by the reference to Rufino's

[36] John Walker, *Metaphysics and Aesthetics in the Works of Eduardo Barrios* (London, Tamesis, 1983).

'penas sucias' and the explanation of the novel's title ('El hermano asno' is the body), presents the two men symmetrically: Rufino's saintliness leading him to harm an innocent girl; Lázaro's vacillations and temptations culminating in heroic self-sacrifice for the Church. The prose style is, as Henríquez Ureña long ago pointed out,[37] heavily indebted to *Modernista* colourism and emphasis on visual and other sensations, but is more functional than is the case in some of the *Modernista* novels we have mentioned. It stands indeed interestingly between their style and the more surrealist style of Asturias's *El Señor Presidente* for instance. However, we lack sound studies on the evolution of prose style in modern Spanish American fiction.

If in his last novel *Los hombres del hombre* (1950) Barrios returned to psychological self-portrayal, previously in his best-seller *Gran señor y rajadiablos* (1948) he had written one of the last major old-style *criollista* novels. For this reason Alone was correct when he asserted that Bombal was 'la que inauguró con más derechos que nadie la nueva etapa de nuestra literatura posterior al criollismo'[38] and certainly one of the first genuinely Modernist writers, in the Anglo-Saxon sense, in Spanish America. For in breaking with *criollismo*, she also broke, and radically, with old-style Realism, writing that the truths of the creative imagination are as true as those of everyday reality, or even truer: 'el sentimiento de las realidades esenciales, encarnadas en símbolos y descifradas a través del arte son tanto o más verdaderas que las realidades cotidianas.'[39] With this we are in a new phase of fiction. A further sign of this is that Bombal's two first-person narratives are not quite psychological novels in the sense of being *romans d'analyse*. They do not use conventional psychological commentary to delve into reasons for the protagonists' frustrated unhappiness; they simply voice it, and do so explicitly and exclusively from a woman's point of view. Bombal was more of a feminine than a Feminist writer, in the sense that she accepted, with regret, an essentialist view of womanhood. According to it men were creatures of the intellect and women of the emotions ('puro corazón') and in which women were condemned by their very nature to a psychologically and emotionally dependent role. '¿Por qué, por qué la naturaleza de la mujer ha de ser tal que tenga que ser siempre un hombre el eje de su vida?' the narrator asks in *La amortajada*.[40] Bombal's heroines do not rebel against their nature. They are, as Boyle says, 'complicit' with their

[37] Max Henríquez Ureña, *Breve historia del modernismo*, 2nd edn (Mexico City, Fondo de Cultura Económica, 1962), p. 362.

[38] Alone (Hernán Díaz Arrieta), introduction to *La amortajada*, cited by Catherine Boyle, 'The Fragile Perfection of the Shrouded Rebellion (Re-reading Passivity in María Luisa Bombal)', in her edition of *Women Writers in Twentieth Century Spain and Spanish America* (Lewiston, Edwin Mellen Press, 1993), pp. 27–42, p. 31.

[39] María Luisa Bombal, cited by Agata Gligo in *María Luisa (Sobre la vida de María Luisa Bombal)* (Santiago de Chile, Andrés Bello, 1985), pp. 20–21.

[40] María Luisa Bombal, *La amortajada* (Santiago de Chile, Orbe, 1968), p. 99.

situation. But they yearn to find within it a level of emotional and sexual fulfilment which their respective marriages deny them.

The narrator of *La última niebla* is described by Kostopoulos-Cooperman as 'an individual who progressively withdraws from a conventional reality that is not only hostile but also insensitive to her innermost needs'.[41] It is hostile in the sense that she has married a widower who judges her by the standard set by his dead wife and who has carried her off into the countryside where she can find no fulfilling activities to offset her dreary marriage. It is insensitive in the sense that it frustrates her intense desire for love and physical togetherness: '¡Oh, echar los brazos alrededor de un cuerpo ardiente y rodar con él, enlazada, por una pendiende sin fin!'[42] She retreats into silence and a compensatory daydream of a mysterious lover with whom she spends a night of passion. Thereafter this obsessional fantasy becomes the central feature of her life. Her ironically paradoxical position, having lost her fantasy lover, without being able to displace her husband's memory of his former wife, is re-emphasized by the presence in her house of her sister-in-law, Regina, who is carrying on an adulterous affair, but one which is nevertheless 'un verdadero amor'. When the latter attempts to kill herself, the narrator also makes a suicidal gesture, but is restrained by her husband, with whom she is now condemned to live for the rest of her life surrounded by the mist, which symbolizes all that which swallows up love and vitality and surrounds everything with an immobilizing, suffocating greyness. At the same time, according to Adams, 'its function is to externalize her interior state of withdrawal, confusion and fantasy'.[43] Nature, as we see, has radically changed its role. In line with the subjectivism of Modernism, it has ceased to be an external force testing or threatening the central character. Instead, it now supplies symbols through which the narrator can express her inner feelings and desires. Water-imagery, birds, visual, sound and tactile effects are all exploited in subtly rhythmical prose not to tell a story but to convey an *état d'âme*. Time, similarly, moves forward and backward following the memories, the nostalgias and the sad sense of ongoing experience and aging of the narrator. Logic, chronological linearity and causality, the mainstays of Realist fiction, are undermined as the novelette follows the vagaries of the narrator's mind. As Borges never failed to point out, the introduction of dreams into reality contaminates it with fantasy.

La última niebla ends with a dreary realization: the mist, with all its negative connotations, now envelops the life of the narrator for ever. The last word of the text is 'definitiva'. From now on nothing can change. Only death,

[41] Celeste Kostopoulos-Cooperman, *The Lyrical Vision of María Luisa Bombal* (London, Tamesis, 1988), p. 8.

[42] María Luisa Bombal, *La última niebla* (Santiago de Chile, Nascimento, 1962), p. 49.

[43] M. Ian Adams, *Three Authors of Alienation* (Austin, Texas U.P., 1975), p. 24.

implicitly, will bring release. This is the theme of *La amortajada*. For the purposes of the narrative, Bombal invites the reader to accept that the mind can go on functioning briefly after physical death. The story, which is once more that of a woman's emotional frustration, is told retrospectively from the coffin of the dead woman before she finally accepts the (in this case positive) reality of death. Thus, as Guerra-Cunningham reminds us, there are two 'realities' present: that of Ana María's memories and the more fantastic reality of her brief phase of consciousness after death: 'La yuxtaposición de una realidad concreta y una realidad maravillosa expresa una cosmovisión típicamente vanguardista.'[44] Once more we perceive the radical break with old-style Realism; once more the prefiguration of the movement of the Boom writers away from observed towards created reality. It is not irrelevant that Fuentes in *La muerte de Artemio Cruz* uses a variant of the same technique and that the finest scene of that novel, between Artemio and Catalina, uses the themes of pride and rejection, where there could have been love, just as Bombal had done in her second novel.

The underlying metaphor is that only death can bring relief and final understanding of the obstacles which stand inexorably in the way of feminine fulfilment. Failure to overcome them means *incomunicación*, constant, painful awareness of the 'otherness' of the other person, spouse or lover. This too is to be, with Mallea, Gálvez, Sábato, Onetti, Cortázar, and even Rulfo and Fuentes, one of the great themes of fiction in much of the rest of the century. As different mourners stand by her coffin and in a sense confess or reveal themselves, or are revealed by her memories of them, otherness is finally overcome and Ana María can accept death and dissolution into the great Earth-Mother. There is a measure of forgiveness and reconciliation not present in the earlier novel. Three narrators are finally present: Ana María herself, another woman bystander who observes her with compassion and understanding and, in a new section added in 1968, her confessor Padre Carlos. If in one sense *La amortajada* brings to mind Fuentes's *La muerte de Artemio Cruz*, this added scene is inevitably reminiscent of the death-scene of Susana in *Pedro Páramo*, in which Padre Rentería in vain seeks to bring her to what he regards as a proper frame of mind for death. Few features of Bombal's work are more enlightening than this belated addition to *La amortajada*. It reminds us, as does Lázaro's longing for confirmation of his vocation in *El hermano asno* and Silvio's anguished outcry in *El juguete rabioso* that, behind the emotional and psychological problems of the Modernist characters, there lies, half-hidden, a spiritual void. It reappears in Mallea, Sábato and Rulfo among others, and lends additional significance to the overtly religious motifs in the fiction of Marechal, Roa Bastos and

[44] Lucía Guerra-Cunningham, *La narrativa de María Luisa Bombal: una visión de la existencia femenina* (Madrid, Playor, 1980), p. 76.

Lezama Lima and even the prayer of the librarian at the end of Borges's 'La Biblioteca de Babel'. There is a pattern here, which the ongoing search for some form of 'order' in a chaotic reality attests to in the Boom and beyond. Once more Bombal is among the forerunners. The 'horrible irony' to which Boyle correctly draws our attention in *La amortajada*, consists precisely in the fact that Ana María perceives this order underlying her relationships with her family and her confident, Fernando, only when the mysterious 'Alguien, algo' leads her away to her tomb.

If the year 1926 was crucial because it saw the publication of Güiraldes's *Don Segundo Sombra*, Larreta's *Zogoibi*, Quiroga's *Los desterrados* and Mallea's *Cuentos para una inglesa desesperada* (that is to say, the peak of Regionalism and a clear sign of the beginning of Modernism), it was even more crucial because it saw the publication of *El juguete rabioso* by Roberto Arlt (Argentina, 1900–42). Arlt saw with complete clarity that the epoch of Regionalism was over. The denizens of the cities were not in the least interested in going out to civilize the outback. '¿Sabe Vd lo que es el proletariado . . . de nuestras ciudades?', a character asks in *Los lanzallamas* (1929). 'Un rebaño de cobardes. En vez de irse a romper el alma a la montaña o a los campos, prefieren las comodidades y los divertimientos a la heroica soledad de los desiertos.'[45] It was time to come back from the great interior of the continent to the cities, in his case to Buenos Aires, Argentina's Great Wen. Onetti is sometimes credited with being the first urban novelist in modern times in Spanish America; but this is mere ignorance. The modern novel of the city begins with Arlt, though this was not his greatest originality. Three other features of his work are fundamental. The main one is the shift from preoccupation with the specific condition of Spanish American man to preoccupation with the human condition generally. Both Mallea and Sábato (in *El sayal y la púrpura* and *El escritor y sus fantasmas*) are at one in stressing the importance of the modern existential crisis for fiction in their time. It has been pointed out already that we can trace a strong sense of spiritual malaise back through Bombal and Barrios to the *Modernistas* at the end of the nineteenth century. This was not the 'crisis' which Alonso postulates with respect to the Regionalists; it was something far more universal, and it is with Arlt that we begin to see it clearly. Sábato comments: 'Roberto Arlt escribía sus novelas que algunos creen costumbristas, pero que en realidad son mágicas y desaforadas fantasías de un ser desgarrado por el mal metafísico.'[46] This is what most of all reveals in Arlt the great precursor of so much more recent fiction, not just in Argentina but in Spanish America as a whole, in which existential disquiet, in different forms, is almost omnipresent.

The second feature of modernity in Arlt's writing is the importance of sex-

[45] Roberto Arlt, *Obra completa* (Buenos Aires, Carlos Lohlé, 1981), I, p. 234.

[46] Ernesto Sábato, *El escritor y sus fantasmas*, 3rd edn (Buenos Aires, Aguilar, 1967), pp. 187–88.

uality, once more inherited from *Modernismo*. Eroticism was not a major component of regionalist narrative. In *Los de abajo* references to sexuality are part of the moral commentary: Demetrio's downward spiral is illustrated by his treatment of Camila and the moral degradation of Anastasio and La Codorniz is suggested by coy references to outward signs of venereal desease. There is no room for sexual relationships in *Don Segundo Sombra*, where prudence in dealing with the other sex is specifically included in Sombra's teaching. We have seen that in *Doña Bárbara*, Gallegos toned down Bárbara's sexuality. Santos's redemption of Marisela has no overtly sexual overtones, while in *La vorágine* Cova's sexual behaviour is implicitly contrasted negatively with his dream of an 'amor ideal'. Arlt not only brings Spanish American fiction back from *criollismo* and ruralism to serious interest in the human condition and urban settings, but also reintroduces sexuality, in the wake of *Modernismo* and a novel like Pedro César Dominici's *La tristeza voluptuosa* (1899). More particularly, he does so once more in an existential context. To quote Sábato on modern fiction yet again: 'El sexo, por primera vez en la historia de las letras, adquiere una dimensión metafísica' (*El escritor* p. 84). Once more Arlt is first in the field (though soon to be followed by Bombal, whose *La amortajada* contains the first evocation of a female orgasm in Spanish American fiction, characteristically in a context of *incomunicación*). The third original feature of Arlt's fiction is his use of humour, in contrast to the solemnity of so much of Spanish American fiction after Lizardi. We have to wait for Borges, with his background in English literature, to begin to restore humour to the place of prestige it now has, after *Cien años de soledad*, *Tres tristes tigres* and *Pantaleón y las visitadoras*, for example (and even he had reservations). All these factors give Arlt a unique and all too rarely acknowledged place in the history of Spanish American fiction.

El juguete rabioso, then, represents a turning point in modern Spanish American fiction. It is the story of a bright young boy, Silvio Astier, from a poor immigrant district in Buenos Aires who, after a brief foray into juvenile delinquency, undergoes a couple of humiliating and frustrating experiences trying to earn a living and attempts suicide. Later, however, he manages to become a reasonably successful salesman, but, when propositioned by a friend to join in a burglary, betrays him to the victim in return for the latter's help in getting a job in the south of Argentina. As we can see, on the one hand the novel is about *la lucha por la vida* in a hostile society; but on the other it is about Silvio's acute sense of *orfandad espiritual*, his anguish in the face, not of social obstacles, but of life.

A persuasive case can be made out for interpreting Silvio's anguish in social terms, as Rita Gnutzman, for example, shows in the introduction to her 1985, Madrid, Cátedra, edition (though she rightly rejects Raúl Larra's tendentiously Marxist approach). But we should also take into account literary influences, such as those of Baroja (and even more Dostoyevsky) and more especially that of the contemporary Western *Weltanschauung*, which was deeply pessimistic.

Like Sábato later, Arlt was obsessed with human evil. In dedicating *El amor brujo* to his wife in 1932, he wrote: 'Los seres humanos son más parecidos a monstruos chapoteando en la tinieblas que a los luminosos ángeles de las historias antiguas.' But he did not adopt a social explanation; instead he argued, a propos of his characters: 'Estos individuos, canallas y tristes, viles y soñadores simultáneamente, están atados o ligados entre sí por la desesperación. La desesperación en ellos está originada, más que por la pobreza material, por otro factor: la desorientación que, después de la gran guerra, ha revolucionado la conciencia de los hombres, dejándolos vacíos de ideales y esperanzas.'[47] This helps us to recognize that the deep theme of *El juguete rabioso* (which was originally called *La vida puerca*), frustration, operates at three levels: social (the poverty of Silvio's family, leading to his delinquency in chapter one); emotional (his unfulfilled yearning for love, leading to daydreams and sentimentality); and spiritual (his sense of the absence of God, leading to his attempted suicide, his anguish, and finally to his decision to seek self-understanding through exploration of his own degradation). Critics have tended to emphasize one or another of these levels, but it is clear that his problems arise from all three acting together. However, the fact that the spiritual frustration is placed last in the narrative seems crucial.

El juguete rabioso consists of four autobiographical vignettes designed to express Arlt's view of life as horrible and absurd and of Silvio as a frustrated idealist who wavers manic-depressively between affirmation of life and happiness, despite the odds, and a masochistic acceptance of self-abasement as a means of self-enquiry and self-affirmation or what Arlt calls, in a chapter-heading of *Los siete locos* (1929), ' "Ser" a través de un crimen'. In chapter one, a version of which was written when Arlt was only nineteen, what prevails is the triumph of reality (petty theft) over the illusion of overturning all accepted moral values. The young gang-members surrounding Silvio try to act out what they have read in blood-and-thunder crime novels, but the technique is one of anti-climax, symbolized by the fact that their pad is opposite a lavatory, amid dirt and rubbish. Anti-climax in literature is a metaphor: it tells us that our hopes and dreams will not be fulfilled. At the same time, Silvio's hopeless dream of pure, tender love with Eleanora only makes him more aware of the horror of life. Near the end of chapter one, the image of Silvio hearing the strains of a waltz wafting over the toilet says it all.

In chapter two Silvio is forced to abandon adolescent rebelliousness and conform, that is, find a job. When he does so his boss is the repulsive Don

[47] Cit. Aden W. Hayes, *Roberto Arlt, la estrategia de su ficción* (London, Tamesis, 1981), p. 51.

Gaetano, a shopkeeper. Like Céline in France, with whom he shares numerous affinities, Arlt saw in this class the quintessence of all that is odious in bourgeois society. Silvio reacts to the humiliations heaped upon him by Gaetano in three ways: by dreaming (which only leads to masturbation); by attempting to burn down the shop (which fails miserably); and by embracing self-abasement. In Arlt's world not only external reality is horrible, but so too is the internal reality of the individual. Silvio reacts to the first by attempting, in chapter three after more failure, to set fire to a street dosser; he reacts to the second by inflicting psychological pain on himself. But as yet he does not understand the full significance of this last. In the last chapter he hears from one of his former gang companions, now a private detective, that another of the gang is in prison. Silvio stands in between them: he can neither reconcile himself to society and become one of its minions, nor can he rebel and accept a life of crime. Instead, at the climax of the novel, he betrays his best friend, Rengo. This is in no sense an 'acte gratuit'. It stems from the realization (that reaches back through Dostoyevsky to Baudelaire) that an act of infamy both creates a link with others, who are all just as infamous, and at the same time allows the individual to reach down to his 'raíces oscuras'. By betraying Rengo, Silvio brings himself consciously face to face with his own evil and guilt in what he clearly regards as an act of self-discovery and even self-liberation. He touches bottom, and his move to the south (as in Sábato's *Sobre héroes y tumbas* a symbol of cold purity) is implicitly the beginning of a possible self-redemption.

The rest of Arlt's fiction leaves us not very optimistic about that possibility. Flint, in one of the most level-headed books on Arlt, suggests that the weakness of his characters is that 'They are anguished beyond hope of redemption and therefore, in the literary sense, incapable of further development. . . . They live and die in anguish.'[48] One of the most revealing passages in all of Arlt's work contains the reflections of Erdosaín, the central character of *Los siete locos* and *Los lanzallamas* (1931) shortly before he proposes to El Astrólogo that they should kidnap Barsut, a relative of his wife, in order to extort money from him, and the discussion that follows. Erdosaín is anguished about his own sense of nullity and feels the temptation to observe himself while committing a murder in order to discover what he believes he and those like him are seeking: 'la verdad de nosotros mismos' (p. 176). El Astrólogo, who is planning a violent social revolution in order to save his fellow countrymen from discovering the meaninglessness of life without God, is more interested in the collective problem of a directionless society. The thoughts and ideas of the two men fit together to confirm that at the deepest level what interests Arlt is the dilemma of modern Western man, and that his novels are examples of what Sábato was to call for when he advo-

[48] Jack M. Flint, *The Prose Works of Roberto Arlt* (Durham U.P., 1985), p. 30.

cated 'una novela novelesca y metafísica.' At the opposite extreme from the Americanist, Regionalist novel, Arlt's fiction, with its themes of despair and solitude, antedates, as Flint points out, the direction later taken by a central current of the French Existentialist novel. More specifically, in Argentina, it begins an unbroken pattern of development via the writing of Raúl Scalabrini Ortiz, Manuel Gálvez and Eduardo Mallea to that of Onetti, Sábato and Cortázar in the Boom. With Arlt, that is, we turn the corner into the new fiction.

Further reading

Miller, Martin C., 'Clorinda Matto de Turner and Mercedes Cabello de Carbonera: Societal Criticism and Morality', *Latin American Women Writers: Today and Yeserday*, eds. Yvette E. Miller and Charles M. Tatum (Pittsburgh, The Review Press, 1977), pp. 25–32.

Sackett, Theodore A., *El arte en la novelística de Jorge Icaza* (Quito, Casa de la Cultura, 1974). Tries to get beyond content-analysis.

Early, Eileen, *Joy in Exile. Ciro Alegría's Narrative Art* (Washington, University Press of America, 1980). A useful overview of Alegría as a writer rather than just as a social critic.

Taylor, Lewis, 'Literature as History: Ciro Alegría's View of Rural Society in the Northern Peruvian Andes', *Iberoamerikanisches Archiv* 10 (1984), 349–78.

Langford, Walter M., *The Mexican Novel Comes of Age* (Notre Dame U.P., 1971).

Portal, Marta, *Proceso narrativo de la revolución mexicana* (Madrid, Cultura Hispánica, 1977). A well-known classic.

Rutherford, John David, *Mexican Society during the Revolution: A Literary Approach* (Oxford U.P., 1971). Uses fiction as a source for social commentary.

Leal, Luis, *Mariano Azuela* (New York, Twayne, 1971).

Franco, Jean, 'Image and Experience in *La vorágine*', *Bulletin of Hispanic Studies* 41 (1964), 101–10. The best early article.

Leland, Cristopher Towne, 'The Failure of Myth: Ricardo Güiraldes and *Don Segundo Sombra*', *The Last Happy Men: The Generation of 1922. Fiction and the Argentine Reality* (Syracuse U.P., 1986). Sees through some of the nationalistic critical interpretations.

Michalski, André S., '*Doña Bárbara*: un cuento de hadas', *Publications of the Modern Language Society of America* 85 (1970), 1115–22. An original approach.

Martínez Morales, José L., *Horacio Quiroga: teoría y práctica del cuento* (Xalapa, Vera Cruz U.P., 1982). Tries to come to terms with the technique of this foundational writer.

Davison, Ned J., *Eduardo Barrios* (New York, Twayne, 1970).

Rodríguez Peralta, Phyllis, 'María Luisa Bombal's Poetic Novels of Female Estrangement', *Modern Latin American Fiction*, ed. Harold Bloom (New York, Chelsea House, 1990), pp. 111–21. A good modern re-evaluation.

Zubieta, Ana M., *El discurso narrativo arltiano, intertextualidad, grotesco y utopía* (Buenos Aires, Hachette, 1987). Less tendentious than much Arlt criticism.

Chapter 4

THE 1940s, THE PRE-BOOM
THE CHANGING VIEW OF THE WRITER'S TASK

The 1930s saw a diminution of creative output in Spanish American narrative, almost as if there needed to be a pause between the peak of Regionalism, with *Don Segundo Sombra* (1926) together with *Doña Bárbara* (1929), and the shift towards the Boom which characterizes the fiction of the 1940s. The 1930s represent a trough in which the novel largely marked time or moved in directions which with hindsight we can now see as dead-ends. Azuela, still writing, though past his best work, tries to reinvent himself as a more sophisticated writer in *La luciérnaga* (1932), moving consciously towards the later idea of the novel as a 'verbal exploit' but gives it up as a bad job. Gallegos publishes another Regionalist classic, *Cantaclaro* (1934), and then *Pobre negro* (1937) in which he follows the old pattern of simplistic protest writing, which Icaza transfers to the Indigenist novel with *Huasipungo* (1934) as does Alegría, with *Los perros hambrientos* (1938). The anti-Imperialist novels of Uribe Piedrahita and Aguilera Malta look like starting a new trend, but it does not take off. The outstanding figure of the decade is unquestionably Roberto Arlt, whose later novels (after the key *El juguete rabioso* in 1926) continue to contrast with and subvert old-style Realism and Regionalism, producing the enthusiasm of Onetti, whose *La vida breve* (1950) was to mark the advent of the Boom itself.

Timid signs of a potential renovation were not lacking in the 1930s. Asturias began his career with *Leyendas de Guatemala* (1930) and Carpentier made something of a false start, which he was later to criticize, with *Ecue-Yamba-O* (1933), an attempt to re-vitalize the Regionalist novel by taking it in a new direction, towards the culture and life-style of the blacks in Cuba. The earliest fiction of Mallea and Borges began to appear, and with it the two remarkable novels of Bombal, *La última niebla* (1935) and *La amortajada* (1938) which contain eerie prefigurations of themes: Time's mystery, lack of communication, female experience of marginalization, love's failure to reconcile the lover to life, among others, which look forward to the Boom and beyond. In their separate (and disparate) ways, Arlt and Bombal break away both from Regionalism and the prose of the avant-garde in their time.

If the thirties was on the whole a negative period for fiction in Spanish America, this was not so in the case of the next decade. The forties was the crucial decade of the century, for with it comes the run-up to the Boom and the consolidation of what was beginning to take shape as Modernism, in the Anglo-American sense (always to be carefully distinguished from Hispanic *Modernismo*). For proof, we can mention one of the writers who failed to recognize or rejected what was happening in the forties and as a consequence forfeited their chance to belong to the Boom: Mario Benedetti. Sadly, left-wing writers and critics have all along tended to associate Modernism (and with it, in the Spanish American context, the Boom) with a turning away from analysis and criticism of Spanish American society, from preoccupation with collective issues from a progressive standpoint, towards repression of 'reality', elitism, pseudo-universalism, emphasis on the autonomy of works of art, on the creative imagination and its expression by means of experimental techniques and non-referential language, combined with a generally negative outlook on life. Benedetti is no exception. He has stuck in principle to mimetic realism and has strongly criticized writers who fell prey to what he calls their 'horror a la realidad circundante'.[1] Although he and others like him represent a certain underground continuity between the old realistic novel and the neo-Realism of some aspects of Post-Boom writing, they have been heavily, and perhaps permanently, overshadowed by the success of the Boom writers.

Carlos Fuentes has asserted that the four founders of modern fiction in Spanish America are Quiroga, Arlt, Felisberto Hernández and Macedonio Fernández.[2] Quiroga's claim to such a title is dubious. But there is no denying the foundational status of the other three. Nor can we avoid noticing that they all belong to the river Plate region. Of Arlt mention has already been made. Like Quiroga, Hernández (Uruguay, 1902–64) was a short-story writer and not a novelist, but it is impossible to ignore his work in any treatment of modern Spanish American fiction. One might even begin by noticing that a leading novelist in the Post-Boom, Rosario Ferré, wrote a short study of Hernández as a university thesis, later to be published.

The story of Modernism, in Spanish American as well as in European and North American fiction, is the story of an increasingly radical break with old-style Realism, usually with the aim of telling a truer truth, or at least a different kind of truth about human behaviour or about the human condition. In the short story in Spanish America that break became evident most of all with the advent of fantasy. The three best-known practitioners of the fantastic short story (in which fantasy is usually not gratuitous, but important for what it tells us, or implies to us, about reality) are probably Hernández, Borges and Cortázar. Hernández began publishing his tales as early as 1925 with the collection *Fulano de tal* and continued to bring them out in book form until

[1] Mario Benedetti, 'El escritor y la crítica en el contexto del desarrollo', *Casa de las Américas* 107 (1978), 7.

[2] Carlos Fuentes, *La nueva novela hispanoamericana* (Mexico, Mortiz, 1969), p. 24.

1960, after which two posthumous collections appeared. This makes him contemporaneous with Borges, and, as with the latter, the crucial decade for his work was that of the forties, with the collections *Por los tiempos de Clemente Colling* (1942), *El caballo perdido* (1943) and *Nadie encendía las lámparas* (1947). However he has been consistently overshadowed by the great Argentine.

Perhaps the crucial difference between Hernández's stories and those of Borges lies in the fact that Borges's tales are exquisitely organic artefacts. That is, they are meticulously written so that everything fits. There are no loose ends. Yet here we have a paradox: Borges is writing about a world which may be one of pure flux of events: 'un infinito juego de azares', a chaotic universe in which any 'order' may simply be artificially imposed by our minds. Yet his stories are so carefully crafted that their formal arrangement, like the regular shelving in the identical rooms of the Library of Babel, partially conceals the significance of the chaos inside the texts that are on them and of the worrying absence of any central catalogue. Hernández's stories are often not organic in that sense. The are apt to present us with strange inexplicabilities which mirror the sometimes disturbing and disconcerting illogicalities of reality. Merrim has described their author as 'a writer poised on the brink of the void', whose tales 'give rise to both forced interpretations and frustrated incomprehension'.[3] She quotes him as writing around 1940 in 'Buenos Días': 'me seduce cierto desorden que encuentro en la realidad y en los aspectos de su misterio.'[4] Disparate elements, deliberately unresolved discontinuities and bizarre, unexplained events, tend to characterize his most memorable stories. By making them short-circuit our assumptions and expectations derived from realist writing, which presumed to make sense of reality through the author's privileged insight, Hernández at his best communicates an impression of strangeness which is designed to undermine our complacent acceptance of the intelligibility of the way things are. The unpredictable, the incongruous, the unexpected, the apparently unmotivated are his typical stock in trade.

It cannot be by mere chance that the great Italian master of fantasy, Italo Calvino, recognizing in Hernández a kindred spirit, associates, like Merrim, the Uruguayan's ability to unite 'the quasi oneiric automatism of his imagination' and 'traditional narrative structure' with his impulse to 'venture on to footbridges cast over the void'.[5] It is not enough simply to register the uncanniness of Hernández's best stories; that uncanniness has to be seen as a meta-

[3] Stephanie Merrim, 'Felisberto Hernández's Aesthetic of "Lo otro": The Writing of Indeterminacy', *Revista Canadiense de Estudios Hispánicos* 11 (1987), 521–40, p. 525.

[4] Felisberto Hernández, *Diario de un sinvergüenza y últimas invenciones* (Montevideo, Arca, 1974), p. 147.

[5] Italo Calvino, 'Introduction' to *Piano Stories* by Hernández (New York, Marsilio Publishers, 1993), p. ix.

phor for a reality which we often think we understand, but which might turn out to be deceitfully ungraspable. Before Macedonio Fernández, before Borges, before Cortázar, Hernández was already an established Modernist. 'Mis cuentos no tienen estructuras lógicas', he wrote in his famous essay 'Explicación falsa de mis cuentos' (1955). But this statement needs interpretation. The disturbing thing about the tales is precisely the discrepancy between their often relatively straightforward initial setting and chronological development, which at first lull us with a sense of familiarity, and the weird episodes that follow, which are often unrelated to normal conceptions of causality, but which are usually narrated with a straight face as if they were everyday occurrences. Thus, in 'La casa inundada', a young man is hired as a companion by a rich widow, stays for a time at her mansion and then is sent away. But his main job is to row her around the interior of the house and the garden, both of which she has had artificially flooded. Clearly the water bears a symbolic meaning related to her widowhood, but it remains baffling. In 'Las hortensias', Hernández's longest and most complex story, the wealthy husband of an affectionate, childless woman organizes strange charades with life-sized, female dolls. His obsession with them ultimately destroys his marriage and thrusts him into madness. Barrenechea writes: 'Todo el relato . . . (con la rebelión de los objetos inanimados, los dobles, los espejos, los espectáculos, las amenazas de la locura y la muerte) es un constante juego de seres humanas y muñecas que se relacionan, se rechazan, se sustituyen y también invierten sus naturalezas.'[6] In 'El balcón' a woman falls in love with a balcony. In 'El cocodrilo' an improvised stocking-salesman learns to earn his living by crying. In these and the other most famous Hernández stories ('Menos Julia', 'El caballo perdido', 'El acomodador', 'Casa de Irene' etc.), inanimate objects, feelings, abstractions like silence, and sense-impressions like perfume, acquire human characteristics, while humans are often caricatured. We are constantly tempted to try to make out a symbolic message. Why is there so much emphasis on odd rituals, on innocence and guilt, on suppressed eroticism, forbidden pleasures, deceit, timidity, nostalgia and even anguish? We look in vain for Borgesian 'inlaid details' which contain clues, or Cortazarian 'figuras' which imply meaning behind apparent randomness. The tales have a dream-like (or nightmarish) quality which defies interpretation. For Rosario Ferré, this is because Hernández simply enjoyed an almost impersonal contemplation of the mysterious episodes he created for their own sake. There was no longing for meaning. Although at the end of *Por los tiempos de Clemente Colling*, he refers (mysteriously) to 'el alma del misterio', there is no indication in his work that it can ever be reached. In the only full-scale treatment of

[6] Ana María Barrenechea, 'Ex-centricidad, di-vergencias y con-vergencias en Felisberto Hernández', *Modern Language Notes* 91 (1976), 311–36.

Hernández in English, the author writes: 'The salvation of Hernández's protagonists is in an inward retreat to the fantastic beings who they are, insulated by their private realities and protected by the masks melded to their faces. These protagonists espouse an existential perception of reality as meaningful only because it lacks an inherent meaning; it is reorganizable by whatever design one wishes to impose.'[7]

Macedonio Fernández (Argentina, 1874–1952) is in a quite different category from Hernández. A cult figure among the intelligentsia in Argentina in the sixties, he has been the subject of an increasing number of critical studies and is the central character in *La ciudad ausente* (1992) by the prominent and innovative contemporary novelist Ricardo Piglia. The key to understanding his importance is to recognize that he was, on the one hand, a man of ideas, fully cognisant of the ontological and epistemological insecurities which underlie Modernism, and at the same time uniquely radical for his period in his break with the Realist tradition. In 1905, he wrote in a letter: 'I want to know whether the reality which surrounds us has a key that can explain it, or whether it is totally and definitively impenetrable.'[8] Clearly this was one of the two main preoccupations which he passed on to, or confirmed in, Borges, who regarded the beginning of his friendship with Macedonio as the major event connected with his return from Europe in 1921. The other, as Borges remarked in a graveside address at Macedonio's funeral, was the non-existence or the illusion of the self.[9] Similarly Macedonio shared the view later expressed by Miguel Angel Asturias that there was no fundamental difference between dreaming and being awake or, if there is, we are not equipped to know it. As we shall see, this is but a step from asserting that imaginary reality and the reality which we take for granted as really real are in fact one and the same. This step would be taken by Onetti in *La vida breve* in 1950 and would prove to be of crucial importance both for the writers involved with Magical Realism and for the Boom writers in general. In other words, with his slogan 'Let reality be that which is questioned', we can see Macedonio as having made a significant contribution to the process of diminishing confidence in the writer's ability to observe, report and interpret reality, which reached a climax in the fiction of the 1960s.

Macedonio's literary theory is much more important than his work as a novelist. But both challenge our ideas about fiction, just as his philosophical stances challenge our conventional notions of the 'reality' to which fiction is often supposed to refer. His novel *Museo de la novela de la eterna*, published

7 Frank Graziano, *The Lust of Seeing. Themes of the Gaze and Sexual Rituals in the Fiction of Felisberto Hernández* (Lewisburg, Bucknell, U.P., 1997), p. 25.

8 Cited by Jo Anne Engelbert, *Macedonio Fernández and the Spanish American New Novel* (New York, New York U.P., 1978), p. 19.

9 The address is reproduced in *Sur* 209–10 (1952), 145–57.

posthumously in 1967 is specifically designed to undermine what we normally expect of a narrative. We 'trap' reality by imputing to our experiences a set of causes which lead chronologically to effects in such a way that they appear to provide us with explanations. *Museo* deliberately sets out to break both with causality and with time-sequence, partly by using a technique of constant digression. Realism, appealing to our sense of what things are like and encouraging us to identify ourselves with characters and situations evoked in familiar ways, is what Macedonio calls 'culinary' art (because it substitutes sensory for artistic pleasure), and art aimed at 'hallucination'. His aim in *Museo* is something quite different and novel. It is to call into question our easy acceptance of our own existence and that of our surroundings, producing instead a shake-up of our comfortable presuppositions about ourselves, or what he called 'la conmoción de la certeza del ser'. At the same time, in order to make his aims that much more unmistakable, Macedonio wrote, in *Museo*, the first great, genuinely metanovelistic work of fiction in Latin America: a novel which constantly contemplates itself and the processes of its creation. Preceded by fifty-six prologues, in several of which he re-elaborates his attack on realism, it takes place on a Ranch called 'La Novela', where El Presidente plays host to La Eterna, to whom he is emotionally attached, and to a series of other guests including Quizagenio, Dulcepersona, Deunamor and El Viajero, as they – for the most part – converse on topics of interest to the author, who, together with the reader, occasionally intervenes. The object is, through discontinuity and incongruence, to compel the reader not merely to do without a plot, but to focus on Macedonio's strategies for avoiding both emplotment and 'rounded' characterization. *Museo* exemplifies his theory of *Belarte*: art which is essentially, in the case of literature, writerly, rather than being based on reader-appeal, an art which is dependent on originality and supremacy of technique, utterly opposed to realism, communication of feelings or what Macedonio contemptuously called 'information'. Instead it is designed in the last analysis to startle the reader into a liberating flash of insight into the substantiality or otherwise of the self.

Had *Museo* not been published posthumously at the height of the Boom, Macedonio would probably now be seen with Borges as one of the two great progenitors of the movement. As it is he is much less well known than the Nobel Laureate Miguel Angel Asturias (Guatemala, 1899–1974) whose work also demands attention in this connection. The key event in Asturias's life was the fall of the then dictator of Guatemala Manuel Estrada Cabrera in 1920 when the future writer was a young student political activist. To his disgust, another dictator soon took over. Asturias liked to maintain that as a consequence of his political activities he had to flee Guatemala in 1923. At all events, he (like Carpentier) soon found himself in Paris, where Surrealism was the big new literary force. It rapidly caused him to reconsider his attitude both towards the outlook and 'primitive' vision of the Central

American Indians, whose culture he began to study, and towards the old-style Realist orientation of much of the Regionalist novel. This led his work in two related directions. One of these is represented by his masterpiece, *El Señor Presidente* (1946) and to a lesser extent by his 'Banana Trilogy': *Viento fuerte* (1946), *El papa verde* (1954) and *Weekend in Guatemala* (1956). The other gave rise to *Hombres de maíz* (1949) and *Mulata de Tal* (1963).

El Señor Presidente, re-written seven times between 1924 and 1932 and not published for another fourteen years, is the novel which marks the watershed between the old Spanish American novel and the new-style fiction which began at the mid-century. The story of the President's henchman, Cara de Angel, who is redeemed by love only to be destroyed along with many others by his evil master, is at first sight an outstanding example of the hundred or so novels extant on the theme of dictatorship, a subgenre of the novel of protest in Latin America. Its treatment of the love plot between Cara de Angel and Camila, whom the former marries when she is at the point of death, today seems almost unbearably melodramatic and sentimental. By contrast the novel's innovative characteristics seem to be the extraordinary verbal fireworks of the opening page and the compelling surrealist style of descriptions in later chapters, alternating with 'straight' referential language, together with the use, for the first time in an important Spanish American novel, of Stream of Thought. The terrifying evocation of nightmarish life under a cruel dictatorship, identifying the President with the bloodthirsty local God of the Indians, Tohil, signifies the incorporation of mythical reality into the new novel, a technique which was to be prominent in the Boom.

There is nothing really new in the use of the theme of dictatorship apart from the intensity of the presentation. But we cannot ignore one important feature of Asturias's approach: his emphasis on the responsibility of the people themselves. This is not just the case of one of the President's other victims, Canales, a powerful army general, who is forced into exile. During his flight he reflects bitterly on his short-sightedness (and by implication that of the Spanish American military generally) in lending support to a dictatorial regime. But in the same chapter we find a strangely revealing reference to the savage natural background through which he is escaping: 'aquella naturaleza fatídica, inabordable y destructora como el alma de su raza'. What this seems to imply harks back to Sarmiento and the old-fashioned racist/determinist notion of the inborn barbarism of Latin Americans. It is backed up by the President's description of his fellow countrymen (primarily the middle-classes) as 'gente de voy', that is, people who are always 'going to do' this or that, but in the end leave everything to him. Worse still, the figure in the novel who represents student activism (in which Asturias had participated against Estrada Cabrera without in the end any lasting results) describes his compatriots as 'un pueblo maldito' and as '¡Viles! ¡Inmundos! ¡Cómplices de iniquidad!' Certainly the novel leaves us with an unanswered question: are the people as corrupt and grovelling as they are because of the President's tyranny, or is the tyranny the result of the corruption? Not to be overlooked is the figure of the Puppeteer, who discovers that even the children seem instinctively to enjoy scenes of cruelty and acute suffering more than joyful farce.

At this point, a closer inspection of the text reveals the presence of an inverted Christian myth which threatens to change the whole interpretation. Instead of Lucifer rebelling against a loving God from pride, and being cast into hell, Cara de Angel, as a redeemed Lucifer, rebels against an evil God (the President: all-powerful, all-knowing) on behalf of love, and is also cast into hell, dying in an underground dungeon believing, through the President's cynical cunning, that Camila has betrayed his love. This inverted mythical sub-text lifts the novel to a level of universality, making it possible to read it as an allegory of the human condition, with life seen as hellish, God as the opposite of benevolent, Christ as 'INRI-idiota', and man as victim, sometimes actively collaborating, through greed and self-degradation, with his own fate. As was to be the case in the next decade with Rulfo's *Pedro Páramo*, and subsequently with García Márquez's *Cien años de soledad* and Donoso's *El lugar sin límites* (to take only obvious examples) the Spanish American 'specificity' of the texts, so typical of the Regionalist novels, is overtaken by the possibility of a much more universal relevance. Instead of writing, that is, about the condition of man (and woman) specifically in Spanish America, writers now were increasingly to write about the human condition in general, as it just happens to manifest itself in a Spanish American setting. Finally, in this connection, we cannot overlook the narrator's comment in chapter twenty-six: 'Entre la realidad y el sueño la diferencia es puramente mecánica', which undercuts the whole notion of realism and aligns Asturias with Macedonio Fernández and Borges. Not surprisingly in the inaugural novel of the Boom, Onetti's *La vida breve* (1950) we find the first-person narrator, at a key point in the plot, remarking: 'Sentí que despertaba – no de este sueño, sino de otro incomparablemente más largo, otro que incluía a éste y en el que yo había soñado que soñaba este sueño.' If writers do not know for sure the difference between reality and dreaming, how can they confidently interpret the world around us? Here we see the first steps being taken towards the Postmodern notion that fiction cannot, by its very nature, be cognitive.

The other vital contribution of Asturias to modern Spanish American fiction was his launching in 1949, along with Carpentier, of Magical Realism. Carpentier was a major theorist of the movement in Spanish America as well as a participant, but Asturias was its most authentic practitioner. Magical Realism arises in part out of the astonishment which certain aspects of reality in Latin America, both historical and contemporary, can at times produce. It differs from 'the fantastic' in that it is also rooted in what Asturias called 'una realidad que surge de una determinada imaginación mágica'.[10] Whether or not it is a Western phenomenon, in Spanish American narrative it is non-eurocentric and mythico-magical in outlook, its characters tend towards the grotesque, it sees historical change allegorically, it often uses hyperbolic and baroque language and it is inseparable from a certain primitivism derived from a re-evaluation of the Indian world-view. While both represent a reaction against old-style mimetic realism, Magical Realism is quite different from the fantasies of Borges or Cortázar and should not be confused with them, because of its tendency to see actual reality 'out there' as in some sense magical, rather than creating a fantastic reality. We note García Márquez's remark: 'La realidad diaria es mágica, pero la gente ha perdido su ingenuidad y ya no le hace caso.'[11] The Magical Realist novels of Asturias *par excellence* are *Hombres de maiz* (1949) and *Mulata de tal* (1963). While it should never be forgotten that Asturias always insisted on the primacy of sociopolitical protest in his work, insisting even in his Nobel Prizewinning oration on the need for writers to 'dar testimonio', critics other than those on the left have tended to see this nowadays as increasingly anacronistic and to emphasize his Magical Realism.

Hombres de maíz deals in mythico-legendary and magical terms, instead of realistic, documental terms, with a very real social problem: the conflict between the traditionalist mentality of the Indians, for which the cultivation of maize is a sacred activity which should not be undertaken for profit, and the *ladinos*, or mixed race Indians, who see it as a cash crop. Beneath this conflict, however, exists a much wider one: that of the conflict between the First World, cut off from its roots in Nature, alienated, greedy and destructive, and the Third World, peripheral, economically colonialized, yet still open to the possibility of conciliating man with the earth on which he depends. Structurally, as Gerald Martin makes clear, *Hombres de maiz*, despite its six parts and and twenty 'chapters', falls into two halves, since the sixth part is as long as the first five put together. The two halves figure forth two worlds or two cultures, the modern and the traditional, the historical and the myth-dominated, so that the novel 'contrapone a la vez las dos grandes cosmovisiones contrapuestas: indios y ladinos, América y Europa, naturaleza y cultura, *mythos* y *logos*, presencias y ausencias, femenino y masculino, sombra y luz, oído y ojo etc.'.[12] Once more we see an example of the universalization of *americanismo*; once more a break with conventional notions of logic, causality and chronology; once more an alternative vision of reality.

The vision of *Hombres de maíz* is in the end a positive one. When the

10 Gunter W. Lorenz, 'Dialogo con Miguel Angel Asturias', *Mundo Nuevo* 43 (1970), 49.

11 Raphael Sorin, 'Entrevista con García Márquez', *Review* 70 (New York, Center for Inter-American Relations, 1971), 175.

12 Gerald Martin, 'Estudio general', preface to his edition of *Hombres de maíz* (Paris, Klincksieck, 1981), p. cl.

curse of the wizards provoked by the *ladinos* is worked out, man is received back into the fruitful bosom of Nature. Not so in *Mulata de tal*. '*Hombres de maíz*', Prieto writes, 'was conceived as an outburst of hope; *Mulata* – a direct confrontation with historical truths – as its antithesis.'[13] In the novel, Celestino Yumí, a peasant, sells his wife Catalina to the Maize Devil Tazol. Like the cultivation of maize for profit, this is a triggering act of greed which unleashes the forces of evil, and Celestino quickly finds that he has the worst of the bargain. After much trouble he recovers Catalina but, since they are no longer integrated into the peasant community, they have lost part of their identity. They set out to empower themselves by becoming sorcerers, only to find themselves at the center of a struggle between devilish forces, both Christian and Mayan in origin, at the end of which Celestino is crushed to death and Catalina buried alive. *Mulata* is no more mimetic than *Hombres de maíz*. The characters are symbolic of human shortcomings or terrible forces, and the plot is largely allegorical. Both these novels are in a sense nostalgic laments for the conquest of a harmonious, communal pattern of life by destructive capitalistic and selfish values which deny those of love and sharing. They illustrate the tendency of Magical Realism to allegorize historical processes; but we should realize that they do so purposively. They have an ideological agenda. Although they approach reality differently from the Regionalists, though their setting is still Spanish American and rural, they still contain the assumption that the writer has a privileged access to a form of truth.

The link between Magical Realist fiction and Indigenist fiction, that is to say, fiction which deals specifically with the culture and problems of the Spanish American Indians, lies of course in the fact that both deal, in different ways, with the outlook of the native races. We can perceive the link at once when we read the work of José María Arguedas (Peru 1911–69). Commenting on the influence of left-wing ideology on his work, he declared in 1968: '¿Hasta dónde entendí el socialismo? No lo sé bien. Pero no mató en mí lo mágico.'[14] But whereas in Magical Realism the important thing is precisely the 'magical' vision borrowed from the Indians, in Indigenist fiction it may even not be consistently present. Arguedas incorporates elements of it, especially in *Los ríos profundos*, but only sporadically, as an essential part of the presentation of the young central character, Ernesto. In his two most significant novels, *Yawar fiesta* (1941) and *Los ríos profundos* (1958) his aim is not simply to explore and express the Indian world-view, but rather to try to set the record straight, as he saw it, after earlier attempts to use the situation of the Andean Indians as fictional material. Arguedas, whose father was a

[13] René Prieto, *Miguel Angel Asturias's Archaeology of Return* (Cambridge U.P., 1993), p. 173.

[14] José María Arguedas, 'No soy un aculturado', *Recopilación de textos sobre José María Arguedas*, ed. Juan Larco (Havana, Casa de las Américas, 1976), p. 432.

rural lawyer compelled to move about the High Andes in search of clients, had spent his early youth living among the Indians working the land of his step-mother, speaking Quechua almost exclusively, and sharing their tasks. He was thus in a position to criticize earlier Indigenist novelists in Peru, like Enrique López Albújar (1872–1966), Ventura García Calderón (1886–1959) or even Ciro Alegría (1909–67), either on the grounds that they belonged to the white urban intelligentsia and were out of touch with the real reality of Indian life up in the Andes, or because (in the case of Alegría) the Indians described were untypical. 'Me sentí', he wrote, 'tan indignado, tan extraño, tan defraudado, que consideré que era indispensable hacer un esfuerzo por describir al hombre andino tal como era y tal como yo lo había conocido a través de una convivencia muy directa.'[15]

In another kind of writer, this would have meant producing documentary, 'testimonial' novels, denouncing the exploitation of the Indian masses and calling for land reform and radical social change. That is, it would have meant seeing the problem essentially in economic terms and envisaging the solution, to some degree at least, in terms of assimilation of the Indians into modern society much as had been the case with Ciro Alegría. Mario Vargas Llosa, in his excellent book on his fellow Peruvian novelist, reminds us of the tremendous pressure to which creative writers were subjected in Arguedas's day to protest against prevailing social and economic injustices from an explicitly left-wing position. At times, Arguedas did in fact adopt this stance and his work has been interpreted from this angle. Nor are materials for such an interpretation lacking. But it has to be recognized that Arguedas himself was not temperamentally a man of the militant left and he did not see the problem in simplistic terms of class struggle. Struggle, yes: but with forces in play which were not just economic. He thought in terms of cultural issues which involved other, deeper and more intractable factors. 'Las clases sociales tienen también un fundamento cultural especialmente grave en el Peru andino', he wrote in 1950, 'cuando ellas luchan, y lo hacen bárbaramente, la lucha no es sólo impulsada por el interés económico, otras fuerzas espirituales profundas y violentas enardecen a los bandos; los agitan con implacable fuerza, con incesante e ineludible exigencia.'[16] What makes Arguedas the figure that he is within Indigenism is precisely his awareness of the almost irreconcilable 'otherness' of the Indians, whom he deeply loved and admired, but for whose problems he saw no easy solution.

This makes *Yawar fiesta*, for example, problematic to some readers and critics. Set in Puquio in the High Andes of Southern Peru, it deals with the different social and ethnic groups in the town, and with the influence of those former inhabitants who had emigrated to Lima and joined together in a Social

15 José María Arguedas, 'La narrativa en el Peru contemporáneo', *ibid.*, p. 412.

16 José María Arguedas, 'La novela y el problema de la expresión literaria en el Peru', *ibid.*, p. 398.

Club. They key-episodes are: the construction of a road by the Indians of the locality as a concrete example of their ability and tenacity; their capture of a legendary wild bull, previously regarded as an impossibility, and the organization of a special kind of bull-fight in which representatives of the Indians take terrible risks, using small sticks of dynamite to excite and eventually kill the bull. These are clearly semi-symbolic events specifically designed to create a new, much more positive, image of the Indians based on their ethnic solidarity, their potential for collective endeavour and their almost insane courage in certain situations. The presentation of the municipal authorities, the landowning groups, the mixed-race inhabitants and the urbanized members of the Social Club makes no bones about the greed, cruelty and blind arrogance of most of the former and the ambiguous situation and often falsified, acquired values of the latter. Similarly, the differences among the various groups of Indians (some being much more pauperized and submissive than others) and the negative aspects of their behaviour (drunkenness, superstition and sometimes ill-treatment of their womenfolk and children) are clearly brought out. But the overwhelming message of the novel is 'Nu'hay empusible para ayllu'.[17] Even the landowner group, grudgingly or otherwise, recognize this and are capable on occasion of taking the Indian side against the wilful incomprehension of the *Subprefecto*, sent from Lima to administer the town. Perhaps even more significantly, Arguedas slightly ridicules the Social Club members, who regard themselves as emancipated and advanced because they have acquired left-wing ideas, while at the same time losing touch with their roots. This has led to bitter attacks on Arguedas and *Yawar fiesta* on the grounds that the author substitutes a private 'Cultural' mystique, based on notions derived from his work as an anthropologist, for open socio-economic protest and testimony. Academic critics, such as Cornejo Polar and Castro Klarén, on the other hand, tend to emphasize Arguedas's avoidance of the crude antitheses of earlier *Indigenista* fiction, his deeper and more complex insight into the clash and attraction of the two races in Peru, the enduring literary quality of his work, and above all his unique ability to express the mentality of the (Quechua-speaking) Indians, through a re-working of Spanish oral expression, one of his major achievements in his own view.

In 1924 Arguedas was removed from Puquio by his father and sent to a Catholic boarding school in the town of Abancay, run by the Mercedarian order. His experiences there were to inspire *Los ríos profundos*. The story is therefore that of a sensitive, 'white' boy, separated from his family and his acquired Indian roots, growing up in a religious environment which he feels is partly alien. The themes, on the other hand, are: the personal one of the conflict of innocence and experience in the young Ernesto, centred primarily

17 José María Arguedas, *Yawar fiesta* (Santiago de Chile, Universitaria, 1968), p. 35.

on the episodes connected with sexuality and with his friendship for another boy, Antero, together with the social theme of oppression of the Indians, notably the *pongo* in chapter one, representing the poorest and most downtrodden of them, and the *Opa*, the retarded girl at the school who is used by the pupils as a sexual object. Whereas in *Yawar fiesta*, it was the landowners and the *Subprefecto*, the government representative, who were the targets of criticism, here it is the Church and the Army, while the reaction of the Indians is seen in the Salt Riot and the occupation of the town by the rural Indians during an outbreak of plague. Arguedas seems to be trying to do three things: to describe in the first person the life of a confused adolescent 'outsider', especially in regard to his experiences of evil, to portray his sense of a semi-magical reality, derived from his upbringing among Indians, and to convey social criticism. The critical question is whether these aims are always compatible with each other.

At the beginning of the novel Ernesto's first serious act is to take an oath. We are not told what it is; but clearly it is an oath of fidelity to his Indian roots, which later are symbolized in the *zumbayllu*, the spinning top which has magical qualities. Shortly afterwards his father observes: 'Tu ves, como niño, algunas cosas que los mayores no vemos. La armonía de Dios existe en la tierra.'[18] This explains both why Arguedas chose a youthful, 'innocent-eye' narrator and what he hoped against hope would prove to be true in Peru. Ernesto himself is a symbol, since the two cultures of his country meet in him. There are others, notably the famous wall in Cuzco of which the Inca-built base merges into the Spanish upper section, and the equally famous church bell in which Inca gold was used by the Spanish bell-makers as part of the metal from which it was formed. But this aspect of the novel's symbolism is always somewhat ambiguous, as if Arguedas could not quite bring himself to accept it fully. Far less ambiguous is the presentation of Ernesto's developing awareness of suffering and evil. An early symbol of the former is the small, sweet-scented cedar tree which Ernesto finds vandalized and which is associated both with Nature and with the oppressed *pongo* in Cuzco. The latter is associated with the role of the priests in the school in Abancay, but even more with the sexuality of the pupils. Both religion and sexuality are seen as natural and good things which (in a 'white' context) have been corrupted and perverted. The whole lesson of the novel is implicit in Ernesto's evolution from sunshine to shadow. This is, indeed, a genuine *Bildungsroman*, a novel of apprenticeship to life. Ernesto and his schoolmates, Padre Linares, and other major characters are fully rounded, believable individuals, in some contrast to the socially defined figures of *Yawar fiesta*.

[18] José María Arguedas, *Los ríos profundos*, ed. William Rowe (Oxford, Pergamon, 1973), p. 9.

At the social level, the turning point in Ernesto's developing insight is the failure of the Salt Riot and the arrival of troops to reassure the landowning group and its supporters. This is quickly followed by Ernesto's discovery of the role of the college headmaster, Padre Linares, in quelling the riot and restoring the rioting women to submission. Inside the college, although Ernesto finds friendship and a measure of understanding of his emotional and spiritual situation, he is forced to recognize that his friend Antero will run true to type as an oppresive landowner and that one of the priests, who happens to be black (and thus like himself the meeting place of two cultures) suffers similar humiliation, despite his cloth. Worst of all, Ernesto is exposed to the degraded and machistic sexuality of some of his companions and their abuse of the retarded girl. All of this is seen in implicit contrast to the more natural and human behaviour of the Indians among whom Ernesto had been living. In line with Arguedas's pusuit of balance in his approach to the racial situation in Peru, we expect that Ernesto will reveal a certain disenchantment with his Indian heritage too; but this does not happen. The key event at the end of the novel is the peaceful occupation of Abancay by large numbers of the neighbouring Indians, despite their being fired on by the army. They have come to demand a mass, which they believe will stop an outbreak of plague. Arguedas repeatedly insisted that this was a symbolic episode, like the road-building in *Yawar fiesta*. Whether anyone benefited, or the wrong people benefited, was simply not the point. The episodes showed what the Indians collectively could do; they revealed their hidden strength and courage. What was needed was not a policy of forced assimilation and Westernization, which would fail, because the Indians accept nothing from white culture without subtly changing it to fit their own, but a policy which took account of their mentality and traditions. Arguedas recognized that these were in many respects obstacles to the full incorporation of the Indians into the national family; nevertheless, they provided a form of defence and preservation of the Indian identity which the Indians would stubbornly defend. Understanding of this had to form part of any aspiration to bring about a more integrated society.

In the rest of his fiction: *El Sexto* (1961), *Todas las sangres* (1964) and *El zorro de arriba y el zorro de abajo* (posthumous, 1971) Arguedas continues to use places as microcosms of Peru, as he had done in Puquio and Abancay. In *El Sexto*, it is a terrible prison in Lima where both the most criminal and degraded convicts mingle with the most committed and self-sacrificing political prisoners. In *Todas las sangres*, it is San Pedro, another mountain town, dominated by landowners with differing outlooks and with an Indian leader who is shot down by the army. In *El zorro de arriba y el zorro de abajo* it is the great fishing port and social/racial melting pot, Chimbote, the symbol for Arguedas of the 'hervidero que es el Peru actual'. In each case his concern is to deepen understanding, to explain as well as to criticize, to break out of the simplifications and black and white dualities of the earlier Indigenist novel and explore in greater depth the complexity of what he saw as the 'inquietante y confusa realidad' of his country. In a wider sense, his aim was to remind readers in the rest of the world that ideological simplifications do not necessarily produce short cuts to the solution of social and racial problems.

Indigenism is an off-shoot of Regionalism and, like the latter, tends as we saw to be rather traditional in its narrative methods. Arguedas was well aware of the shift towards the Boom which was taking place and indeed carried on a significant polemic with Cortázar about the role of the novelist in Spanish America. He himself was more innovative in his approach to his material and, as we have seen, in his creation of a 'language' to express Quechua speech, than in, for example, narrative technique. Both *Yawar fiesta* and *Los ríos profundos* are linear and rather episodic in structure and to that extent backward-looking towards old-style Realism.

Jorge Luis Borges (Argentina 1899–1986) detested Regionalism and all its offshoots, Indigenist, Testimonial or whatever. He did not believe in the social role of literature, or any kind of truth-claims on its behalf. Though, like Felisberto Hernández he never wrote a novel and affected to despise the genre, novelist after novelist (Fuentes, Cabrera Infante, Donoso) has recognized his work as crucial to the development of the novel in Spanish America. Cabrera Infante, indeed, is on record as stating categorically: 'No hay un solo escritor hispanoamericano que escriba ahora y que pueda echar a un lado la influencia de Borges en su escritura.'[19] Nor can there be much doubt about it. For this reason non-Argentines are regularly surprised by the virulence with which Borges has been (and is) attacked in his own country by writers and critics on the Left who regard his private political stance as deplorable, his exploration of fantasy as dehumanized and a betrayal of the need to face politico-social reality, and from those on the Right who condemn him for not being sufficiently nationalistic. It is equally sad to see one of the foremost English critics of Spanish American fiction describing him as an 'imperialist', a man who 'only played with philosophical ideas' and as begging 'virtually all of the important questions about the moral relation of an author to reality and to his readers'.[20] If these accusations were true, it would be hard to explain Borges's vast and continuing influence both inside and outside Spanish America. 'He is', Geoffrey Green has written, 'everywhere present in contemporary fiction.'[21]

A number of his own statements are useful in understanding his outlook. In *Otras inquisiciones* (1952) he wrote of 'la imposibilidad de penetrar el

[19] Guillermo Cabrera Infante, interviewed by Rita Guibert, *Revista Iberoamericana* 76–7 (1971), 552.

[20] Gerald Martin, *Journeys through the Labyrinth* (London, Verso, 1989), pp. 155–7.

[21] Geoffrey Green, 'Postmodern Precursor. The Borgesian Image in Innovative American Fiction', *Borges and his Successors*, ed. Edna Aizenberg (Columbia, Missouri U.P., 1990), pp. 200–13, p. 201.

esquema divino del universo' (*Obras completas 1923–1972*, p. 708) and concluded: 'Es dudoso que el mundo tenga sentido' (p. 722). We notice that neither of these affirmations is altogether categoric. There may be a divine pattern in the cosmos, even if we are not programmed to be able to perceive it; the proposition that the world is meaningful is not denied, but merely questioned. Pressed by Reina Roffé to confirm the implication of his story 'La Biblioteca de Babel' that the world is mere chaos, Borges replied: 'Es lo que siento desgraciadamente, pero quizás sea secretamente un cosmos, quizás haya un orden que no podemos percibir; en todo caso debemos pensar eso para seguir viviendo. Yo preferiría pensar que, a pesar de tanto horror, hay un fin ético en el universo, que el universo propende al bien, en ese argumento pongo mis esperanzas.'[22] This resigned, only minimally hopeful, extreme scepticism is central to all his work. It extends to ourselves. Also in *Otras inquisiciones* he remarks: 'Los hombres gozan de poca información acerca de los móviles profundos de su conducta' (*O. C.* p. 727). We probably do not understand reality and we probably do not understand ourselves. But even if we did, we should not necessarily be much better off. For language is inadequate to express any understanding we might achieve. Not only is it simply 'un mecanismo arbitrario de gruñidos y chillidos' (p. 672) (and how could that tell us anything about anything?), but by its very nature it is successive: it has to describe phenomena one after another, when in fact they often occur simultaneously. Few concepts mark the difference between the novel as it was before Borges and the novel after his influence was felt more than the changed concept of language. José María Arguedas, like Mario Benedetti still within the mentality of realism in that respect, insisted on the simple referentiality of language: 'la palabra es nombre de cosas o de pensamientos o de reflexiones que provienen de las cosas: lo que es realidad verbal es realidad-realidad.'[23]

If Borges's notions are accepted, it is no longer possible to go on taking reality, social, psychological or of any other kind, for granted. It is, to use one of Borges's favourite adjectives, 'inasible': 'No sabemos que cosa es el universo' (p. 708). Time is a mystery (one which fascinated Borges all his life) and causality at the deepest level probably hidden from us. What we call the real is most likely to be a construct. We select from the flux of experience what we can live with. We build it around ourselves like an Eskimo building an igloo, to protect ourselves, to keep out awareness of what it is like outside.

22 Reina Roffé, 'Jorge Luis Borges el memorioso', in her *Espejo de escritores* (Hanover [New Hampshire], Ediciones del Norte, 1985), pp. 3–20, p. 11.

23 José María Arguedas replying to Sebastián Salazar Bondy in *Primer encuentro de narradores peruanos* (Lima, Casa de la Cultura del Perú, 1969), p. 140. Compare Benedetti's similar insistence that language is purely instrumental and that any other view represents cultural imperialism in his essay, 'Subdesarrollo y letras de osadía', in *El escritor latinoamericano y la revolución posible* (Buenos Aires, Alfa, 1974).

The best of Borges's stories invite us to question our constructs. He does not deny our need of them; all he asks is that we should be aware of them for what they are. His tales are designed to induce us to reassess our complacency and assurance, but no more than that. Borges is not in the business of knocking down one igloo to drive us into another of his own making. He is only too well aware of our longing to recognize some sort of 'order' in things, and where it leads to: 'bastaba cualquier simetría con apariencia de orden – el materialismo dialéctico, el antisemitismo, el nazismo – para embelesar a los hombres', he wrote (referring, of course, to us) in 'Tlön, Uqbar, Orbis Tertius'. Similarly, in 'La lotería en Babilonia' the Babilonians prefer to believe in the existence of 'La Compañía' (God), managing things, however mysteriously, rather than to accept that the world is nothing more than 'un infinito juego de azares'. Not for nothing does the climax of 'La Biblioteca de Babel' contain a prayer. Borges, however, had no religious beliefs. He divided people chiefly into those who believe in religious absolutes, but are not interested in them, and those who are interested but do not believe. He belonged to the latter.

Borges's favourite metaphor for the human condition is a labyrinth, Why a labyrinth? And what kind of labyrinth? Seen from above, a maze can be perceived to combine both order and chaos. Tidily symmetrical in appearance, its walks appear to lead progressively to the centre and then allow a return to the outside. But once one is inside the maze, direction is rapidly lost, the turnings may be regular, but they bear no relation to the objective. In addition, a Borgesian labyrinth must be thought of as circular (symbolizing futility) and with no entrance or exit. We are born already inside it. At its centre is death, though in a few cases (like that of Tzinacán in 'La escritura del Dios', or the Borges of 'El Aleph') characters are accorded some terrible vision, or at best the discovery of who they really are. What matters is less the centre, which is seldom reached, but the maze itself, the symbol of existence. It has the appearance of predictability, but then turns out to be baffling; or, seen from the other perspective, it presents us with a series of baffling experiences, which neverleless contain teasing hints of design. Borges's best stories – chiefly those of the forties – are in the main, parables or fables which explore the possibilities of his conception of a world in which 'toda estrafalaria cosa es posible'. His standard response to such a world is that it is perplexing, but interesting, and that there is no need for outcries of existential anguish. On the contrary, the appropriate response is one of detachment and humour, as far as we can manage it.

But we must be clear that underlying his apparently tranquil stance, as we saw above, is a deeply unhappy vision. Significantly, one of Borges's favourite adjectives is 'atroz'. We have a strong hint of why this is, when we remember that he confessed to a French interviewer: 'Dans tous mes contes, il y a une partie intellectuelle et une autre partie – plus importante je pense – le sentiment de la solitude, de l'angoisse, de l'inutilité, du caractère mystérieux de l'univers, du temps, ce qui est plus important: de nous-mêmes, je dirais: de moi-même' ('In all my stories, there is an intellectual part and another part – a more important one, I think – the feeling of loneliness, of anguish, of uselessness, of the mysteriousness of the universe and of time, what is more important still: of ourselves, I should say: of myself' [Charbonnier, p. 20]). Such confessions are rare, but precious. They establish up to a point the way we should read Borges's stories. They also establish a link between Borges's outlook and the generally pessimistic outlook of the Boom writers. However, we should notice that, despite his scepticism, Borges never lost sight of one value, physical courage, and more than that, moral courage, as we see from his early, much misunderstood 'Hombre de la esquina rosada' and the sequel he wrote partly to explain its real theme: 'Historia de Rosendo Juárez'.

Another link which connects Borges (as so often) with Macedonio Fernández on one side and with the Boom writers on the other is his mastery of technique. If reality is an enigma, then the figuring-forth of that enigma must in turn reflect it, not just in terms of theme but also in terms of form. New wine cannot be put into old bottles; a new disturbing vision of life cannot be adequately expressed in the old reassuring ways of Realist fiction. Borges was a meticulous writer, who sometimes carried stories around in his head for years, slowly piecing them together and trying them out on friends or his mother. When he wrote them down they often contain traps for unwary readers. We have not understood a Borges story properly until all the details fit. Nothing is there by chance; everything has meaning. A Borges story is a mechanism like a watch: each element is functional. Sometimes the form of the tale is significant in itself, as, for example, when he writes 'El acercamiento a Almotásim' in the form of a book review, or refers to 'Tlön, Uqbar, Orbis Tertius' in the *posdata* as an 'article', thus deliberately blurring the distinction between fiction and non-fiction. At other times the form gives a clue to a story's meaning(s), or when examined, confirms that we are on the right track. Such a mode of writing often demands a new kind of reader-response. We enjoy fiction in the Realist tradition chiefly through self-identification with the episodes and characters, But we can hardly identify ourselves with Yu Tsun or the Funes of 'Funes el memorioso', any more than we can with Deunamor or Quizagenio of Macedonio Fernández; they have too little interior life. How then do Borges's stories appeal? Often the analogy is with detective stories or even crossword puzzles, that is, from problem-solving. Many of Borges's best stories are deliberately puzzling and demand to be 'cracked'. At the end of the first reading we tend to jump to a conclusion about the meaning and (hopefully) to check it by re-reading. The result is an increase in reader-satisfaction, especially if, as is frequently the case, we then come to recognize several levels of meaning coexisting in the same tale.

Before Borges (even in most of Quiroga's stories, despite Fuentes's praise of them), Spanish American short stories worked primarily by simple juxtaposition of episodes, each one leading on causally to the next until the climax is reached. Borges's stories are much more technically complex and require very attentive analysis. At its best his method is not that of mere juxtaposition (which implies an intelligible, predictable world in which one thing follows from another), but rather of interaction. In 'El jardín de senderos que se bifurcan', for example, the central part of the story is set within a frame which presents it as a (highly ingenious) spy story. The frame has several functions. It stimulates our interest (especially as it is told by the spy, Yu Tsun, who is just about to be executed); it lulls us into thinking that we are reading something familiar; but also, since Yu Tsun's message to his control in Germany is quite useless – it contains information which readers of Liddel Hart, who is specifically mentioned in the text, know the Germans already had – it interacts ironically with the core of the tale. Secondly, when Yu Tsun gets off the train to make his way to meet his eventual victim, Albert, he enters a static, terrestrial labyrinth: the lanes leading to Albert's house. This interacts with the theme of the labyrinth in the lost novel by his ancestor which Albert alone has found and understood, to prepare us for the most difficult part of the story to grasp: that which postulates a non-static, constantly evolving labyrinth of lines of time surrounding us like a web, but of which we only recognize one strand.

Another example might be that of 'El Aleph'. In the story there are two frames, each interacting with the core of the tale: 'Borges's' encounter with a (possible) Aleph. The outer frame alludes to the love 'Borges' felt for the dead Beatriz Viterbo. It calls into question that which we long to think of as eternal and time-defying. It also alludes to Dante's Beatrice; but whereas she in the end guided the poet to the beatific vision of the *Paradiso*, Beatriz Viterbo brings 'Borges' into contact with the anti-beatific vision afforded by the Aleph. The inner frame introduces us to Daneri's hideous and grotesque poem, which offers us an apallingly trivial and passively realistic vision of the world, seen from the outside in terms of mere appearances. It interacts with the implicit reference to the *Divina Comedia*, with its evocation of a God-ordained cosmos, on one side, and the frightful Aleph-vision on the other. In the centre of the tale, the Aleph reveals, in all its meaningless, atrocious unbearableness, the chaos and horror of reality and thereby contrasts both with Dante's divinely inspired order and Daneri's neutral, documentary observation. We are led by the narrator through the first frame into the second and then down to the underground Aleph. Subsequently we are led in reverse order up to the second frame and through it to the first frame once more, the story ending with the name Beatriz. Seen as a metaphor, it tells us that we have to pass through veils of illusion to reach insight (but woe to us if we do, unless we can rapidly forget!). Clearly all this goes far beyond Magical Realism.

It is worth mentioning, however, that not all critics have been willing to see that in Borges fantasy is important for what it suggests about 'reality'. There is a critical faction which holds that his stories are not about the enigmatic nature of the supposedly real at all, but are much more about the act of writing. This is a possible way of reading at least some of the tales. But it is at best reductive, since it narrows their range of themes. At worst it is misguided, because it can lead to interpretations of individual stories which are unpersuasive. However, it does focus our attention on the fact that, with *Ficciones*, Spanish American imaginative writing suddenly became more aware of its own fictive nature, more ready to display and foreground its own devices. It thus compels the reader to recognize what is being read for what it is: fiction. To this extent *Ficciones* helped to open the way to forms of literature, some of which we now think of as Postmodernist, which allude to their own limitations or parody themselves. Sklodowska writes: 'El papel fundamental en la transformación del concepto de literatura en Hispanoamérica a través de la burla, el juego lingüístico, la autoironía, la parodia y la autoparodia corresponde, por cierto a Borges', and goes on to affirm what is now generally accepted, that 'el escritor argentino es, sin duda alguna, el precursor más inmediato e importante de la nueva novela hispanoamericana'.[24]

One of the most lucid writers to have attained wide recognition in the 1940s, though now rather neglected, is Eduardo Mallea (Argentina 1903–82). To understand the intellectual and spiritual position of many of the Spanish American intelligentsia at the time, few works are more relevant than his *El sayal y la púrpura* (1941). It antedates Sábato's much more famous *El escritor y sus fantasmas* (1963) by more than twenty years, but the resemblance is noteworthy. From the beginning two related themes dominated Mallea's work. The first is that of the need to regenerate Argentina, reclaiming the country from intellectual sloth and moral indifference. The second theme is personal and at the same time more universal. It springs from Mallea's deep consciousness of the difficulties which lie in the way of human communication, especially between the sexes, and the waste and frustration which result. Behind both these themes lies the broader problem of forging for oneself a satisfying interpretation of existence and working out a harmonious pattern of ideas and beliefs. The section 'El invierno de las ideas' in *El sayal* contains in a few pages an acute diagnosis of the spiritual malady of mid-century Western man. The collapse of faith in any specifically religious foundation for living, in scientific and material progress, in political and social action, Mallea affirms, has left the men and women of his generation groping confusedly in the dark for a new 'order', 'un nuevo tipo de vida', a renewed sense of existential security. But unlike Borges, who, as we have just seen, shared his awareness of this human longing, Mallea thought he had

[24] Elzbieta Sklodowska, *La parodia en la nueva novela hispanoamericana* (Amsterdam, Benjamins, 1991), p. 22.

a form of therapy: active, ethical endeavour, the development of 'una moral combatiente'.

Like the writers of the Generation of 1898 in Spain, that is, he saw the problem of national regeneration in terms of cultural reformism. Instead of seeing it as arising out of concrete economico-social conditions, which can be changed, and which in turn often appear to influence collective outlook, he saw the problem almost exclusively in terms of mentality, which is notoriously much harder to change by itself. He came to believe that part of his task as a writer was to try to modify the Argentine mentality by means of non-fictional works like *Historia de una pasión argentina* (1937), in its time an enormously influential book, and via some of his novels, which incorporate to a greater or lesser extent the theme of the revitalization of his native country. The novels and essays which he published after *Historia* in the 1940s: *La bahía de silencio* (1940), *Todo verdor percerá* (1941), up to *Los enemigos del alma* (1950) represent the peak of his creative activity although he continued to publish fiction right through the Boom years, into the 1970s.

Curiously, for a culture so influenced by French writers, there are conspicuously few psychological novels by Spanish American writers. The great tradition of the *roman d'analyse* did not cross the South Atlantic. Mallea is an exception. *La bahía del silencio* exhibits the typical predominance of a single central character, Tregua, with a group of conversational partners designed to draw him out, an inner circle composed of his 'familia espiritual', who contribute to his development, and an outer ring of bit-part players, chiefly representative of social and other outlooks which Mallea opposes. Tregua's psychological evolution, which is the book's theme, is seen inevitably in spiritual terms, that is, in terms of his quest for a set of life-directing values. Typical also is the relative absence of exciting incidents; what the novel depicts is Tregua's inward flowering of consciousness. His innermost difficulty, the need to 'creer en la vida' and his inability to do so, grows as the story progresses and gives the novel its main outward form: that of a three-part downward spiral determined by Tregua's gradually diminishing confidence. In Book I he comes to realize that his activities are merely 'huídas intelectuales', alibis for avoiding life's interrogations. In Book II, set in pre-World War II Europe, Tregua meets a set of interlocutors who represent what he wished to see as the decadence of the Old World and act as new foils for the central figure. On his return to Argentina he undertakes a symbolic task, the redemption of Gloria Bambil, with undertones of the redemption of Argentina. It fails, and Tregua is thrown back on literary activities which also prove unsatisfactory. But like the protagonist of Carpentier's *Los pasos perdidos*, Tregua is finally able to write the novel as a memoir intended to warn and assist others in a similar situation. This positive fact and the sporadic affirmations of faith in the new generation in Argentina to which Tregua belongs, prevent the novel from recording a collapse into total despair.

Todo verdor perecerá portends Mallea's secondary evolution towards the novel of psychological observation divorced from preoccupation with the national situation (*Los enemigos del alma* [1950], *Chavez* [1953]). The story is that of Agata, one of Mallea's 'mujeres híspidas', the breakdown of her marriage and death of her husband, Nicanor, the process of her ripening solitude, physical, emotional and spiritual sterility and her descent into madness. Mallea uses symbolic descriptions, flash-backs and interior monologues with great effect to get her distress across. He was, as he wrote later, trying to 'burst the seams' of the traditional, well-made novel. Mallea viewed solitude, his favourite theme, ambivalently. In the case of certain psychologically strong people, it tempers their personalities and encourages the development of their authentic selves (sometimes so that they can become part of 'La Argentina invisible', the hidden Argentina out of which regeneration will come). But in others, like Agata, it is destructive. It implacably reveals the inadequacies which human contact and loving solidarity, for instance in a reasonably successful marriage (something Mallea never describes) can help the individual to overcome.

The themes of solitude, the otherness of other people, the failure of love to bring reconciliation with life, anguished pessimism and the spiritual quest were all destined to undergo massive development in the fiction of the Boom. Equally we should not forget that the author of *Historia de una pasión argentina* and *Todo verdor perecerá* was also the author of *Notas de un novelista* (1954), reflections on the art of the novel which stand between those of Macedonio Fernández and those of Sábato, Vargas Llosa and other Boom writers and mark another stage in the evolution of ideas about fiction writing.

When the break with the old pattern of Realism in Spain came, with the fiction of the Generation of 1898, one of the directions which the novel took, especially in the case of Unamuno, the Giant of the Generation, was metaphysical. We think immediately of the latter's *Niebla* (1914) with its theme of the struggle of the protagonist to authenticate his own existence. In the case of Spanish American fiction, movements like the Novel of the Mexican Revolution and Regionalism intervened before the legacy of the 'Existential' novel could be taken up. Felisberto Hernández planned to write, but never completed, a 'novela metafísica' called *Tal vez un movimiento*. Some of Mallea's novels straddle the psychological and the metaphysical, but, as we have seen, it is really in his non-fictional works, like *El sayal y la púrpura*, that he comes directly to grips with the crisis of modern man. The shift actually takes place with Onetti's *El pozo* (1939), further developed in *La vida breve* (1950), the foundational novel of the Boom. But it was left to Ernesto Sábato (Argentina, 1911–) in his essay, 'Para una novela novelesca y metafísica', and in *El escritor y sus fantasmas* (1963), to enunciate clearly the implications for fiction of the modern metaphysical malaise.

In 1977 he wrote: 'Mala o buena, mi narrativa se propone el examen de los dilemas últimos de la condición humana: la soledad y la muerte, la esperanza y la desesperación, el ansia de poder, la búsqueda de lo absoluto, el sentido o sinsentido de la existencia, la presencia o ausencia de Dios. No sé si he logrado expresar cabalmente esos dramas metafísicos, pero en todo caso es lo que me propuse.'[25] The explanation is to be found in *El escritor y sus fantasmas*. For Sábato there are really only two kinds of novel: those of pure entertainment and those which explore the human condition, which is one of spiritual crisis. Like Carpentier at the beginning of *Los pasos perdidos*, Sábato sees modern man as enslaved and dehumanized by modern technology and capitalistic greed. The writer is ideally the repository of the humanistic values which science, technology and rationalism have tried to ignore or crush. His ideal role is to liberate his readers from servitude to those forces. Hence the novel of today must be first and foremost psychological and metaphysical (rather than, say, Regionalist, Testimonial, Magical Realist or whatever). Its basic theme must be modern man's spiritual degradation and misery and thus will involve as major sub-themes, sexuality, solitude and lack of communication with others, and, in particular, evil.

But what kind of novel does Sábato advocate (apart from what it should be about)? He suggests that his sort of novel will have little actual plot, in terms of events and episodes, and concern itself primarily with psychological and metaphysical exploration. It will foreground subconscious and unconscious (i.e. non-rational) aspects of personality: dreams, obsessions, hallucinations and the like, in an attempt to reflect the irrationality and ambiguity both of reality and of human character and behaviour. It will try to present them from different human viewpoints (aiming, that is, at *intersubjetividad*). It will not hesitate to abandon chronological presentation of time. Its tone will be basically sad and its language and style simple and direct. It is not clear quite how, by investigating irrationality, the writer can come up with a message of hope (what Sábato has called 'una absurda metafísica de la esperanza') or how this would relate to man's spiritual dilemma in the face of transcendental problems. All the same, it clarifies Sábato's approach to fiction and suggests how we should read his three novels.

The first of these is *El túnel* (1948) written in the first person, from confinement, by an unbalanced painter, Castel, who has murdered his lover, María, in a fit of irrational jealousy. We see at once that it exemplifies Sábato's aim of exploring the human condition through the presentation of individuals caught up in extreme situations. The title refers to Castel's view of life as a dark, empty, enclosing tunnel along which we are compelled to move. Sometimes two tunnels merge and the individuals in them can meet, communicate and perhaps fall in love, which, as Sábato explained in his non-fictional *Hombres y engranajes* (1951), may give our lives meaning. But

[25] Ernesto Sábato, 'Entrevista', *Cuadernos para el Diálogo* 195 (22–28 January, 1977), 52.

in Castel's case this does not happen. The tunnel-wall becomes, as it were, sporadically transparent; he can see María but not make life-enhancing contact with her. By making a figure like Castel the narrator, Sábato is taking a calculated risk. The reader is clearly intended both to see Castel's alienated outlook and actions as in some way related to the crisis of contemporary humanity and, up to a point, to identify with him and understand him. The danger is that we shall dismiss him as simply neurotic or deranged.

When we meet him he has just painted a symbolic cry for help. Having by this means met María, who understands his painting, he begins an affair with her which intensifies, rather than attenuating, his problems of insecurity, suspicion, self-pity and above all excessive analysis of his own and others' behaviour (which only serves to rationalize his own inadequacy). Still, although it is never made clear by Sábato how human love can fulfil a spiritual, 'metaphysical' need, Castel is momentarily able to escape his loneliness and his sense that 'nada tiene sentido'. The problem from this point is posed by the character and actions of María. Critics are divided about how to interpret her personality and role. Why is she constantly evasive, enigmatic, secretive and sad? By any standards she is not the sort of woman Castel desperately needs; Sábato seems to be stacking the cards against him, despite her other characteristics of tenderness and self-control, which might have tempered his selfish sexual demands and *atolondramiento.* As his mania intensifies, he demands total possession of her while at the same time endowing her with an impossible moral perfection. Once he decides that she falls short of this ideal, and indeed has surrendered to evil, he feels impelled to kill her (and himself). The actual stabbing can be interpreted in several different ways: as the ultimate penetration, as a crime of frustrated passion and as an act of rebellion against the absurdity of an existence which operates by imbuing us with deep spiritual aspirations, but prevents their fulfilment.

Sábato's other major novel, *Sobre héroes y tumbas* (1961), equally fulfils the author's desire to join with Mallea in writing (in different ways) fiction which reflects what the latter called the 'anormalidad terrible' of our time. Once more its themes are solitude and irrational perversity versus hope, this dichotomy being again associated, perhaps rather arbitrarily, with the modern Western crisis. The central strand of the book is concerned with the extremely painful evolution of Martín from his crippling obsession with his upbringing by dysfunctional parents, through his tragic involvement with Alejandra, who in turn is incestuously involved with her semi-demonic father Fernando, to his achievement of a minimum of hope and ideal after Alejandra's murder of Fernando and her suicide. The narrative rhythm is slow, with much dense and obtrusive commentary and a plurifocal technique in which different characters narrate. Whereas in *El túnel* Sábato had incorporated references to Castel's paintings and his dreams into the commentary, as well as exploiting references to light and darkness to great effect, here he uses, apart from Fernando's nightmarish 'Informe sobre ciegos', a kind of descent into hell, which in some ways is the novel's symbolic core, a highly figurative style. At the centre of it is the image of the abyss. Each individual is surrounded by an abyss of solitude and lack of communication separating him or her from others. Martín and Alejandra are desperately seeking to bridge the abyss between them chiefly through love and sexuality. These here assume their typical Boom-novel role as the chief means of overcoming the 'otherness' of other people, usually only sporadically. But inside each of the characters there is also an interior abyss, full of horror and of the demons by which they are possessed. Another major pattern of imagery is concerned with warfare. Here the central image, developed from an episode in the history of nineteenth-century Argentina, is of the soldier, condemned to inevitable defeat but to whom is granted an awareness of the absolute value of human courage, loyalty to the ideal and human solidarity in the midst of hostile circumstances. Alejandra and Fernando are swallowed up by their own abysses. Martín enjoys only a dream of love and a few moments of supportiveness on the part of certain minor characters, before leaving at the end of the novel for the symbolic cold purity of Patagonia to try to rebuild his life. The theme of individuals struggling against forces of cosmic evil is again central in Sábato's last novel *Abbadón el exterminador* (1974).

Summing up, we can see how, by the end of the 1940s, Spanish American fiction had begun to reach beyond realism and Americanist themes towards a greater universalism, a much more sophisticated view of reality (magical, mysterious, often deeply disturbing) and of ourselves, and the need for new types of narrative to do justice to it. In one short but intense decade the Spanish American novel had begun to gear up for the 'salto de calidad' which was to come with the Boom.

Further Reading

Franco, Jean, *Society and the Artist: The Modern Culture of Latin America* (London, Pall Mall, 1967). A very famous work in its time.

Lindstrom, Naomi, *Twentieth Century Spanish American Fiction* (Austin, Texas U.P., 1994). Informative rather than critical.

Rama, Angel, *La novela latinoamericana, panoramas 1920–1980* (Bogotá, Instituto Colombiano de Cultura, 1982). Too many names, but good categories.

Swanson, Philip, ed., *Landmarks in Latin American Fiction* (London and New York, Routledge, 1990). Background to the Boom, Asturias, Borges. An outstanding compilation.

Echevarren, Roberto, *El espacio de la verdad. Práctica del texto en Felisberto Hernández* (Buenos Aires, Sudamericana, 1981).

Lasarte, Francisco, *Felisberto Hernández y la escritura de "lo otro"* (Madrid, Insula, 1981).

(There is no fully satisfactory book on this mysterious and elusive writer.)

Lindstrom, Naomi, *Macedonio Fernández* (Lincoln, Nebraska, Society for Spanish and Spanish American Studies, 1981).

Callan, Richard, *Miguel Angel Asturias* (New York, Twayne, 1970).
Calviño, Julio, *La novela del dictador en Hispanoamérica* (Madrid, Cultura Hispánica, 1985). A useful overview of this hugely important theme.

Castro Klarén, Sara, *El mundo mágico de José María Arguedas* (Lima, Instituto de Estudios Peruanos, 1973). The first really good critical work on Arguedas.
Vargas Llosa, Mario, *La utopía arcaica. José María Arguedas y las ficciones del indigenismo* (Mexico City, Fondo de Cultura Económica, 1996). Insightful, by a major fellow Peruvian novelist.

Barrenechea, Ana María, *Borges, The Labyrinth Maker* (New York U.P., 1965). The foundation of much future criticism of Borges.
Bloom, Harold, ed., *Jorge Luis Borges* (New York, Chelsea House, 1986). Many good essays.
Charbonnier, Georges, *Entretiens avec Jorge Luis Borges* (Paris, Gallimard, 1967). With useful remarks by Borges.
McMurray, George R., *Jorge Luis Borges* (New York, Ungar, 1980).
Shaw, Donald L., *Borges' Narrative Strategies* (Liverpool, Cairns, 1992).

Lewald, H. Ernest, *Eduardo Mallea* (Boston, Twayne, 1977).
Lichtblau, Myron I., *Mallea ante la crítica* (Miami, Universal, 1985).

Giacoman, Helmy E., *Homenaje a Ernesto Sábato* (New York, Anaya/Las Américas, 1973). Like all Giacoman's *homenajes*, it collects the best earlier essays.
Oberhelman, Harley D., *Ernesto Sábato* (Boston, Twayne, 1970).

Chapter 5

THE BOOM

Which was the inaugural novel of the Boom? There is no agreement. Everyone recognizes that the sixties was the Boom's crucial decade, and there is a growing consensus that the movement was running out of steam by the mid-seventies. But when did it begin: with Cortázar's *Rayuela* and Vargas Llosa's *La ciudad y los perros* in 1963, as is sometimes asserted, or much earlier? The problem is: if the starting date is put too far forward, a number of major figures have to be presented merely as precursors; if it is put too far back, writers who are really transitional have to be accepted as fully fledged members of the movement. What seems obvious is that we cannot exclude from the central group of Boom writers men like Carpentier, Cortázar, Onetti, Rulfo, Roa Bastos and possibly Marechal, all of whom were well established before the sixties. On the other hand, as we have argued, the forties was a decade of shift, of lead-up to the Boom. That leaves us with a date in the fifties, and the evidence seems to suggest: the earlier, the better.

The choice depends on how we attempt to define the Boom. In 1981 I tried to list the movement's major characteristics as follows: the replacement of the old Regionalist novel with the new Indigenism of Asturias and Arguedas; a turning away from the 'Americanista' civic novel of protest, to a more universalist or cosmopolitan novel of exploration of the human condition generally; a tendency away from 'observed' reality, towards 'created' reality and myth; absence of love as a source of existential support and emphasis on sexual activity as a means to overcome solitude and the 'otherness' of the partner; a strong element of pessimism; and emphasis on the mystery, irrationality and ambiguity of the personality and the absurdity of life. At the technical level, we observe a tendency to abandon linear plot-structure, and chronological arrangement, both of which suggest intelligibility and predictable causality; the decline of the omniscient third-person narrator; the more frequent incorporation of humour, satire and parody; and a more prominent use of symbolic elements. To these we must add a visible shift in the presentation of fictional characters with greater stress on the mystery of the human personality and its many-facetedness. What all of this adds up is a further questioning of what we think of as 'reality' and a continuing reassessment of the writer's task, extending what had got under way in the forties and even in some earlier avant-garde novels.[1]

Is there a major writer, and more especially a key-novel, which seems to mark the shift? Adolfo Bioy Casares's *La invención de Morel* (1940) has to be mentioned because of the extraordinary originality of its conception, its total rejection of observable reality, its use of fiction within fiction, its incorporation of not one but three unreliable narrators, in brief, because of its striking experimentalism. But Bioy is not a major figure and his first work remained isolated for another decade. Sábato's *El túnel* (1948) and Leopoldo Marechal's *Adán Buenosayres* (1948) are much stronger candidates, since both illustrate the shift away from *Americanismo* towards the *novela metafísica*. But this began after all with Arlt. Without in any way minimizing their relevance, it can be argued that there is a still more obvious turning point in 1950, with the publication of *La vida breve* by Juan Carlos Onetti (Uruguay, 1909–94).

Onetti's first novel, the brief and fragmented *El pozo* (1939) marks an important step between Arlt and Sábato in terms of the rise of the 'Existential' novel (i.e. which criticizes life, not just life in Spanish America).[2] The central character, Linacero, is an out-of-work journalist, whose wife is about to divorce him, living in a squalid slum. His first-person narrative is divided between what he regards as 'el mundo de los hechos reales' and what he calls 'aventuras', which are in fact pathetically melodramatic compensatory daydreams based on stories for boys about Alaska, about pirates in the Caribbean or about gun-running in Europe. These fantasies clearly have a double function. On the one hand they emphasize, by their very immaturity, the intensity of Linacero's frustration with real life (while at the same time hinting that one of its real causes lies inside the narrator himself). On the other hand, they serve to illustrate a quite different cause: Linacero's inability to establish communication, at the deep personal level they represent, with other people to whom he tries to recount them. There is a curious *mise en abîme* here: Onetti uses Linacero's first-person narrative to describe how the latter also uses first-person narratives to try to establish empathy with others. He fails with them; but does his description of the process fail with us, the readers?

[1] For a more extensive discussion of the characteristics of Boom fiction see chapter 7 of my *Nueva narrativa hispanoamericana*, 6th edn (Madrid, Cátedra, 1999), pp. 237–51. Subsequently J. Ann Duncan in *Voices, Visions and a New Reality. Mexican Fiction Since 1970* (Pittsburgh U.P., 1986), p. 9, and Elzbieta Sklodowska in *La parodia en la nueva novela hispanoamericana* (Amsterdam, Benjamins, 1991), pp. xii–xiii, have dealt with the issue, reaching similar conclusions.

[2] See, in this connection, Paul Jordan, 'But my writing has nothing to do with Arlt's: Trace and Silence of Arlt in Onetti', in *Onetti and Others*, ed. Gustavo San Román (Albany, State University of New York Press, 1999), pp. 65–81, and Hugo Méndez-Ramírez, 'El narrador alienado en dos obras clave de la narrativa latinoamericana moderna', *Hispanic Journal* 16 (1995), 83–93.

Clearly not. It is because of the sympathy with Linacero's failures which the narration evokes in us that we are able to do what his interlocutors do not do: identify ourselves with his problem and relate it to our own sense of solitude and the lack of understanding we at times experience when we take others into our deepest confidence.

Linacero, like Sábato's Castel in *El túnel* (the *pozo* is a symbol of the darkness and oppression surrounding human existence, just like the *túnel*) is a deeply alienated individual. The key word for his attitude to life, people and surroundings in the text is 'asco': utter disgust. He shares a filthy room with a man whose dreams of revolution he despises, amid neighbours whom he finds repugnant. Neither political ideology, nor the idea of human solidarity, that is, offer him any comfort or hope. From his youth he has believed himself to have little in common with the rest of humanity. Basically, this is because he has convinced himself that no-one else is capable of understanding, much less sharing, his aspiration to beauty and especially to high ethical standards. 'No hay nadie', he writes, 'que tenga el alma limpia.'[3] The collectivity offers no refuge. In contrast to the Regionalist novel, which, in *Don Segundo Sombra* and *Doña Bárbara*, for example, optimistically explores sets of proposed national values, *El pozo* contemptuously dismisses the will to 'hacer patria': '¿qué se puede hacer en este país? Nada, ni dejarse engañar' (p. 53). There are only two possible answers to Linacero's problem: love and *comprensión*. But he is destined to enjoy neither. The central episode of the novella shows him trying to make his wife help him to re-enact a happy episode from their past, only to find that she uses what happens as evidence for the divorce. In the Boom, as we have suggested, love never brings reconciliation with life. Here we have an early example of its failure. Sex, in Linacero's case, is not a possibility either. He longs for it, as the Alaska 'aventura' reveals, but only in the context of a relationship with a partner who is uncontaminated by the hatefulness of most other people. While they are 'bestias sucias', his dreamed-of woman has 'la mirada abierta, franca' and 'La bondad y la inocencia de una animal'. Again like Castel, Linacero subjects love to a strain which it normally cannot bear. Meantime he makes bids for understanding by describing his daydreams on the one hand to a cheap whore and on the other to a talented poet. Both confirm his view of others by being utterly incapable of empathizing with his fantasies. At the end of the narrative he is totally despairing: 'Todo en la vida es mierda y ahora estamos ciegos en la noche, atentos y sin comprender' (p. 60). Published a year after Sartre's *La Nausée* and two years before Camus's *L'Etranger*, *El pozo* challenges us in a similar way to reassess our comfortable view of the human condition.

[3] Juan Carlos Onetti, *El Pozo. Para una tumba sin nombre* (Barcelona, Seix Barral, 1979), p. 27.

La vida breve has much in common with *El pozo*. Once more the central character, Brausen, is a deeply frustrated figure whose marriage has collapsed, who loses his job and who takes refuge in daydreams, this time of an imaginary town in Uruguay called Santa María. Once more we are confronted with *mise en abîme*: as Onetti imagines Brausen, so Brausen imagines an alter ego, Díaz Grey, a doctor in Santa María. So far, so good; but now the fundamental shift that establishes *La vida breve* as the inaugural novel of the Boom takes place. Brausen takes a leaf out of Arlt's *El juguete rabioso* and seeks to re-invent himself as Arce, the cynical, violent, abject lover of a prostitute, La Queca. That is, to seek self-regeneration through self-degradation. This leads him to contemplate murdering the woman. When in fact she is murdered by another occasional partner, Ernesto, Brausen decides to help the latter to escape justice and together they flee Montevideo. But where do they go? To Santa María! There they meet Díaz Grey who is present at their arrest. The created reality of Santa María is treated as if it were on all fours with the 'real' reality of Montevideo. This is what marks the collapse of old-style, mimetic Realism. Bendetti comments: 'El protagonista crea un ser imaginario que se confunde con su existencia y en cuya vida puede confundirse. La solución irreal, ya en el dominio de lo fantástico, admite la insuficiencia de ese mismo realismo que parece la ruta preferida del novelista y traduce el convencimiento de que tal realismo era, a fin de cuentas, un callejón sin salida.'[4] We can go further in linking *La vida breve* to later developments in the Boom. Brausen's two self-projections, Arce and Díaz Grey, engage in creative interplay with him, to the point that in Part II, chapter five, the narrator can refer to himself as 'Yo, el puente entre Brausen y Arce'.[5] He is now neither, but an intermediate figure, soon to be sporadically replaced as the first-person narrator by Díaz Grey. These two levels of interior reduplication function to cast doubt, not just on the comprehensibility of the self, but on its very reality. And, as if to underline the effect, Onetti introduces himself as a character in the novel. Finally we must refer to the novel's self-referentiality. The writing of it becomes part of the action, during which Díaz Grey intuits the existence of his creator, his dreamer (Brausen) and converts him into a species of divinity, who thereafter in future novels presides over the destinies of Santa María. Where can we find any equivalent of this in Spanish American fiction before 1950?

The idea of 'salvation' recurs almost obsessively throughout *La vida breve*. It has sometimes been suggested that writing was Onetti's personal means of salvation, though it is questionable whether it ever offered more than an attenuation of his deep-seated feelings of nihilism. The two master-

[4] Mario Benedetti, 'La aventura del hombre', *Juan Carlos Onetti*, ed. Jorge Ruffinelli (Montevideo, Marcha, 1973), pp. 21–47, pp. 22–23.

[5] Juan Carlos Onetti, *La vida breve*, ed. Sonia Mattalía (Madrid, Anaya & Mario Muchnik, 1994), p. 208.

pieces of the 'Saga of Santa María', *El astillero* (1961) and *Juntacadáveres* (1964), deal, in reverse order, with the last period in the life of 'Junta' Larsen, a small-time pimp and book-keeper from Montevideo. Larsen is the archetypal Onettian major character, a man who pursues an illusion, knowing it to be an illusion, and what is more an absurd illusion; an individual who attempts to give meaning to his futile existence by embracing an activity which is condemned from the outset to total failure. Larsen seeks a form of salvation first by trying to establish in Santa María a perfect brothel, and then by trying to regenerate a derelict shipyard owned by a lunatic. The story of *Junta- cadáveres* is told from different viewpoints by several narrators but is dominated by Díaz Grey whose detached, sarcastic view of himself is paralleled by his cold, unsentimental, bored view of his fellow inhabitants of the small town, in part intended to be a microcosm of Uruguay (and even of Western society). Behind him we discern Onetti, compelled by his creative impulse to contemplate an ugly and absurd reality which he would rather not observe but which is a source of inspiration. The brothel image is recurrent in modern Spanish American fiction (e.g. in Vargas Llosa's *La casa verde* or Donoso's *El lugar sin límites*) with various symbolic meanings. It stands, of course, at the opposite pole from Catholicism's emphasis on the family unit as the nucleus of society and can be used to criticize the moral rottenness of bourgeois society, its hypocrisy, oppression of women and so on. Here, with typical irony, Onetti converts it into an anti-ideal, an anti-vocation to which Larsen devotes himself. His dream of creating the perfect whorehouse is a parody of man's eternal search for a self-transcending goal. The use of religious vocabulary: 'vocación', 'fe', 'predestinación' etc. leaves the reader in no doubt. But the short-lived attempt to realize the ideal in Santa María is also a parody, not only because it fails but because it is not the fulfilment of Larsen's dream, and in any case he is too old, already too defeated and embittered, to enjoy it. All the major characters in *Juntacadáveres* are either incurably stupid and hypocritical or oppressed with a degraded self-image, as weak, without faith in anything, unable to bear life's solitude. Larsen's persistent self-identification with a hopeless dream near the end of his life is parallelled by the young Jorge Malabia's discovery of himself in late adolescence as 'desleal como siempre', a role-player, cold, detached, ironic and on the way to becoming another Díaz Grey. We close this and all Onetti's novels both attracted and repelled by Onetti's wryly humourous, disgusted fascination with his fictional world.

Alejo Carpentier (Cuba 1904–80) began publishing even earlier than Onetti and his work spans the whole chronological range of modern Spanish American fiction from Regionalism, through the shift in the forties to the Boom and the Post-Boom. He started his career in 1933, after fleeing from the Machado regime in Cuba to Paris, with *Ecue-Yamba-O*, an example of Afro-Cuban Regionalism which he afterwards considered unsatisfactory. Its theme is the degeneracy of white society in Cuba, dominated by Yankee commercialism and exploitation, and the greater human authenticity of the black central character, Menegildo, seen as a kind of cultural hero, closer to nature and 'natural values', and to a magical vision of reality. Although its attempt to explore black reality from inside an inescapably non-black frame of reference fails, its obtrusive use of a highly innovative style to subvert the pre-existing literary code of old-style Realism marks it as a transitional work. In Paris, along with Asturias, Carpentier came under the direct influence of Surrealism and, like his fellow novelist, made the discovery that what was 'marvellous' in European eyes, was everyday reality in Latin America. This led him to the conception of 'lo real maravilloso', just as intrinsically Latin American as Asturias's brand of Magical Realism, but slightly different in the sense that whereas in the latter's case (as in that of Arguedas) the 'magical' element is closely associated with the Indian mentality, Carpentier insisted that in Latin America the 'magical' was actually out there in reality itself for all to see. It is very important always to distinguish this Magical Realist approach, almost always restricted to Latin American reality and to what has been called 'una preponderante visión "primitiva" de la realidad',[6] from the kind of fantasy which we find in the short stories of Borges or Cortázar which has to do with a highly sophisticated subversion of all 'reality' as we conventionally perceive it. Failure to make this distinction has long dogged writing about Magical Realism.

Carpentier in fact practised both approaches. In his very famous short story 'Viaje a la semilla' (1944) the gesture of a wizard causes time to go into reverse, breaking with everyday notions of cause and effect and subverting the notion of a rationally intelligible world, very much in line with what Cortázar states about his stories in 'Algunos aspectos del cuento' mentioned below. Had Carpentier developed this approach he would have been a writer of fantasy, but not of 'lo real maravilloso'. In 1949 he published *El reino de este mundo*, set in Haiti during the period of the French Revolution, and again, like *Ecue-Yamba-O* with a black protagonist. The prologue contains the classic definition of 'lo real maravilloso' as an American phenomenon, which is probably Carpentier's most famous piece of writing. The novel itself proves ambiguous. The choice of a black central character enables Carpentier to present certain 'magical' events as if they were factual, the magic residing in Ti Noel's outlook, in line with Asturias's practice. But this is not consistently the case, and in addition Haiti and the Caribbean islands are seen as lands full of prodigies, far more magical than anything European. Richard Young has subjected this double vision of American 'magical' reality to a

[6] Erik Camayd-Freixas, *Realismo mágico y primitivismo* (Lanham, University Press of America, 1998), p. 4. This book should be read in conjunction with Seymour Menton's *Historia verdadera del realismo mágico* (Mexico, Fondo de Cultura Económica, 1998), which takes a much more eclectic and universalist line. The two books represent polar opposite views of the movement.

crushing critique, concluding that there is nothing inherently marvellous about the real in Latin America, but that it simply appears marvellous to someone who judges it from the perspective of his belief about how reality should be constituted.[7]

El reino de este mundo contains a strong political statement, though one which has not always been clearly understood. Carpentier was always a (timidly) progressive writer, in principle in favour of revolutionary change. But he knew better than some of his critics that such change was slow to come about. In fact, in *El reino de este mundo*, revolution fails disastrously, as it was to do also in *El siglo de las luces*. Carpentier was simply recognizing historical fact. What is important is the author's concluding assertion in the novel that the grandeur of man lies in struggling forward despite historical setbacks. In Carpentier's probably best-known novel, *Los pasos perdidos* (1953), this takes the form of repeated references to the myth of Sisyphus, endlessly rolling his stone up the hill, only to see it roll back again. Carpentier explained that this did not mean that he despaired; only that the task was never completed. The stone rolled back but not necessarily as far back as before. Carpentier's famous vision of cyclic progress is the most (often deliberately) misunderstood aspect of his outlook. He did not embrace a circular, futile, vision of history. For him history proceeded in a terribly long, slow, but upward spiral. Men's lives were commonly not long enough to see this clearly and the sillier kind of revolutionaries could not allow themselves to see the inevitability of gradualness. But progress was inevitable and might be thrust on by revolution. This is the key to understanding his work.

In *Los pasos perdidos*, the unnamed central character is the son of a Swiss-German Protestant father and a Cuban Catholic mother. He is born in Latin America, emigrates to the United States and makes two extensive visits to Europe. He clearly represents Western man, and the novel is in one sense an extended allegory of the latter's situation. At the beginning of the novel, the first-person narrator is trapped in New York in a frustrating job, which prostitutes his musical talent, and an unsuccessful marriage. The great showpiece city of Capitalism is shown here (quite falsely, of course) as imposing on its inhabitants a robot-like life of falsehood and repetition leading to complete alienation and self-degradation. The symbol of this is the narrator's affair with his mistress Mouche, the result of which is that he succumbs to her suggestion that he should embark with her on a phoney expedition to Latin America, supposedly to look for primitive instruments, but actually to swindle the University which finances the trip into paying for a pleasant get-away. Technically what is memorable about *Los pasos perdidos* is the brilliant evocation of a journey into the Amazonian jungle as a series of steps

7 Richard A. Young, *Carpentier. El reino de este mundo* (London, Grant & Cutler, 1983), p. 45.

backward in time from New York (the present), through Caracas (the nineteenth century) to Los Altos (the Colonial period) and so on back to the Stone Age in the jungle itself. As the journey progresses, the narrator gradually recovers his sense of authenticity, his power to love (he sheds Mouche and takes up with Rosario, a Latin American woman of mixed race, representing Latin America as a highly successful racial melting-pot) and his ability to compose. In a tiny jungle village, Santa Mónica, he finds momentarily his Shangri-La. But he fails a series of tests which would justify his staying there and is eventually 'rescued' and taken back to New York, where he finds himself plunged back into deceit and eventual humiliation.

In most of Carpentier's fiction, theme tends to be rather obtrusive and to over-influence both the choice of episodes and the presentation of character. Here we see the latter effect typically in the women. Ruth, the narrator's wife, is an actress who is incapable of anything except role-playing. When her husband seems to be lost in the jungle, she plays her part of anxious wife to perfection, but she quickly shows her true colours when he comes home. Mouche too is completely sacrificed. An astrologer, she, like Ruth, earns her living by providing commercialized illusion. They are both too relentlessly phoney to be fully convincing. Mouche has three functions in the plot. First, she is there to underline the narrator's evolution by the contrast which she presents. They are the only characters in the novel who actually do evolve. Her slide from mere charlatanism in New York to moral and physical collapse in the jungle is used to point up the opposite development in the narrator. Her second function, when she turns up again at the end, is to destroy the imposture built up around the narrator by his wife and thus prevent him from returning to Santa Mónica, as he had intended, until it is too late. Her third function is to contrast with Rosario. The latter's simple fortitude in adversity, her innate dignity, her acceptance of her role vis-à-vis the narrator as her man, her uncomplicated sexuality, all mark her as a male fantasy. She is the woman who creates no complications, who is not clever enough to see through her partner, who is carnal enough to satisfy him without demanding emotional support in return, with none of the possessiveness, the insecurity, the vanity, jealousy and exasperating obliqueness that so often characterize her sex. The narrator himself largely escapes the charge of existing simply in relation to the plot, without real autonomy. He is able to step out of his symbolic role and act like a convincing human being. The beginning of his diffident and rather insecure courtship of Rosario in sub-chapter eleven, for example, strikes a chord of immediate sympathy in every reader (particularly male ones) and brings him fully alive. Alive, that is, as a typical anti-hero of modern fiction.

What makes such figures attractive and original (Onetti's Brausen, Fuentes's Artemio Cruz and Skármeta's Papst also belong to the category, and there are plenty of others) is their contrast to the typical nineteenth-century fictional hero. The narrator here has that touch of ignobility that makes us all kin; that repressed, betrayed, better nature; that insecurity, that sneaking self-contempt, just too easily placated, that minimum of aspiration hidden behind layers of not-too-successful self-deception, in which we immediately recognize ourselves. What above all is part of his bedrock character, and what survives his experiences in the jungle, is his weakness, his characteristic and all-too-human inability not just to make sacrifices, but to make enough sacrifices. At first sight, he is, on his return to New York, simply where he was before, though if anything worse off. However, we have to take two things into account. The first is that the allegory of the story carries with it the clear message that there is no escape from modern man's alienation back into the past. The narrator's ill-advised trip represented 'las vacaciones de Sísifo'. Now he must return to rolling the stone uphill (making his contribution to the slow upward spiral of progress) instead of trying to avoid the task. The second thing which we must notice is that he writes the account which we are now reading. He does not simply sink back into his previous alienation; he warns us that the road is forward.

This is also the lesson of *El siglo de las luces* (1962). Again set mainly in the Antilles during the period of the French Revolution it follows the fortunes of three young people, Carlos, his sister Sophia and his cousin Esteban who fall under the spell of Victor Hugues who has come to spread the revolution. He represents the corruption of its ideals. Contemplation of his self-serving opportunism leaves Esteban wary of historical change without apparent progress. But at the end, he is dragged back into the struggle by Sophia, who incarnates Carpentier's faith in progress despite all inevitable setbacks. The Student in his *El recurso del método* (1974) plays a similar but more minor role. This satirical novel belongs to a group of three, the others being Roa Bastos's *Yo, el supremo* (1974) and García Marquez's *El otoño del Patriarca* (1975), all of which explore the well-known theme of dictatorship which Asturias had already thrown into such terrifying relief in *El Señor Presidente.* The authoritarian regimes which came to power in the southern cone of Latin America, bringing with them the sinister figures of Videla in Argentina and especially Pinochet in Chile, remind us that this trio of novels was by no means irrelevant to its times.

Carpentier accepted a place in the Boom, at least to the extent of recognizing that there was what he called a family resemblance linking him to a number of the other writers whom we associate with the movement. But at the end of his career, after his return to Castro's Cuba, his work entered a final phase visible in his penultimate novel *La consagración de la primavera* (1978). It tells of Vera and her husband Enrique, bourgeois intellectuals who gradually evolve through a series of significant experiences to acceptance of the Castro revolution. It portends the return to *Americanismo*, reader-friendliness and commitment which, as we shall see, are characteristics of the Post-Boom. But the critical question is: does it work as a novel? The answer is: not quite. It has in generous measure some of the great qualities of its author's best writing: human insight, historical vision, superb descriptive purple passages and confident handling of the narrative voices and the story line. But the ideology is too near the surface, the adulation of Castro is distasteful and the ending is melodramatic. Above all *La consagración de la primavera* conspicuously lacks two of the greatest qualities of Carpentier's earlier work: ambiguity and irony, and without them its view of social and historical reality seems simplified and reductive.

One of the major differences between modern literary works and those (say) of the nineteenth century becomes visible when we recall that all or most of such works contain a metaphor of reality. So long as works seemed to reflect an intelligible reality, even if it were a violent, sordid or even tragic one, the metaphor was reassuring. We may not like the world we live in but we understand it, or, at least, writers with their power of insight understand it, and can communicate that understanding to us. But modern works increasingly contain disturbing metaphors of a world which is unintelligible, chaotic, absurd, without Providential design. We have mentioned this in regard to Borges, and it is equally a part of Onetti's deepest *Weltanschauung*. Linacero is trapped in *El pozo* 'sin comprender'; Brausen complains of his 'vergüenza de estar vivo y no saber lo que esto quiere decir' (p. 231). In the same way Cortázar, in *Rayuela*, his best-known novel, writes 'somos como las comedias cuando uno llega al teatro en el segundo acto. Todo es muy bonito pero no se entiende nada' (Havana, 1969, ed. p. 194). This led him in a famous article, to attack what he called 'ese falso realismo que consiste en creer que todas las cosas pueden describirse y explicarse como lo daba por sentado el optimismo filosófico y científico del siglo XVIII, es decir, dentro de un mundo regido más o menos armoniosamente por un sistema de leyes, de principios, de relaciones de causa a efecto'.[8] He had earlier declared that this awareness came to him in 1959 while writing his novella, *El persiguidor*, about a jazz-trumpeter (inspired by Charlie Parker) who finds a kind of visionary transcendence through his music. 'En ese cuento', Cortázar told Harss, 'dejé de sentirme seguro. Abordé un problema de tipo existencial, de tipo humano, que luego se amplificó en *Los premios*, y sobre todo en *Rayuela*.'[9] At the level of the creative imagination this led him to the notion that there may be 'otro orden más secreto' which the writer may discover, and which sometimes seems to manifest itself in the form of 'figuras', unexpected but apparently meaningful juxtapositions of events or people which imply a mysterious pattern amid the randomness of reality. These in turn may be connected with the existence of a 'Yonder' or 'Kibbutz del deseo' to which privileged people may achieve access and which may represent either

[8] Julio Cortázar, 'Algunos aspectos del cuento', *Casa de las Américas* 15/16 (1962/3), 3–14, pp. 3–4.

[9] Julio Cortázar in Luis Harss, *Los nuestros* (Buenos Aires, Sudamericana, 1968), p. 274.

an escape from life and time as we know them, or a space of insight from which we can make sense of things. At the public level, Cortázar's metaphysical malaise seems to have been to some degree offset by a gradually increasing commitment to left-wing politics which led him to go on supporting the Castro revolution in Cuba long after it was fashionable among the intelligentsia to do so. In the main however, he tended to consider that the progressive writer's primary task was to revolutionize literature rather than to write revolutionary literature.[10] While this has produced irritation in some critical quarters, it has not altered the fact that Cortázar is unquestionably the Boom novelist who has had the greatest influence on the next generation. Skármeta wrote a thesis on him for Columbia University (New York); Ferré wrote a book about him; Sainz refers to him repeatedly. This cannot be overlooked.

Cortázar's first novel *Los premios* (1960) is about a group of eighteen passengers, representing a cross-section of the inhabitants of Buenos Aires, who have won a cruise as a prize in a lottery. Collective means of transport (ships, trains, trams), fascinate Cortázar and tend to take on symbolic importance in his novels. This is the case here. The cruise-ship *Malcolm* becomes on the one hand a sort of symbolic microcosm of Argentina (particularly because it is not on course for anywhere) but also on the other hand takes on certain characteristics which have to do with life in general. It is not clear who is on the bridge (=God); the crew speak an incomprehensible language. In particular the passengers are forbidden to visit the ship's stern. Thus, as Boldy points out, 'the divided vessel becomes an image of the dualism inherent in their lives'.[11] Reaching the stern becomes an imperative, a quest, with two related goals. One is to overcome the kind of national crisis that had preoccupied Mallea in *Historia de una pasión argentina*, and Ezequiel Martínez Estrada in *Radiografía de la pampa* (1933). The other is to establish bonds of human solidarity and to come to terms with the modern Western crisis. Reaching the 'taboo zone' implies rediscovering some form of national and/or personal authenticity. In the opening chapters Cortázar adopts a somewhat satirical stance with regard to the cross-section of Argentines which he has assembled. But soon the tone changes and it becomes clear that they are in a test-situation. As long as they ask no questions and obey the prohibition, they can have all the fun they like. But when in a medical emergency they try to storm the taboo zone, one of them is shot down. The ship has become the symbol of an authoritarian society. At a deeper level, the illness of the young child, Jorge, forces the older passengers to recognize the futility of their lives, their self-deception and their surrender to comfortable passivity and acceptance, so that their rebellion also implies a break with their former selves and

10 See in this connection his contribution to the debate printed by Oscar Collazos in *Literatura en la revolución y revolución en la literatura*, 2nd edn (Mexico City, Siglo XXI, 1971).

11 Steven Boldy, *The Novels of Julio Cortázar* (Cambridge U.P., 1980), p. 12.

a quest for self-regeneration. All of this is presided over by a kind of philosophical onlooker, Persio, who in a series of soliloquies voices the deep themes of the novel from a different perspective.

Borges noticed that nowadays 'agrada misteriosamente el concepto de una busca infinita'.[12] This is, of course, because life seems to have lost its centre. *Rayuela* (1963), like Marechal's *Adán Buenosayres* (1948) and Carpentier's *Los pasos perdidos* (1953), is a quest novel. In each case (and those of many others in contemporary fiction) the quest is for a means of coming to terms with life when religious and rational/scientific cosmic explanations have ceased to seem persuasive to the quester. The novel is divided into two halves, one set in Paris and the other in Buenos Aires. In each half, the central character, Oliveira, undergoes a series of experiences, some of them symbolic, in the course of an attempt to reach the 'Paradise' with which the game of *rayuela* (hopscotch) ends in Spanish-speaking countries. He is, Cortázar has asserted, 'un hombre que se golpea contra la pared, la pared del amor, la pared de la vida cotidiana, la pared de los sistemas filosóficos, la pared de la política . . . porque él cree que un día . . . esa pared va a caer y del otro lado está el kibbutz del deseo'.[13] In Paris two of his companions are especially important. One, La Maga, a not very cultured woman from Montevideo, represents a simpler, more intuitively harmonious, vision of life than he can achieve (though he would sometimes like to) and the body as distinct from the mind. She stands in part for Cortázar's realization that the old idea of *civilización* versus *barbarie* was a false dichotomy (in fact he rejects all such dichotomies – body/mind, truth/error, primitive/civilized, authentic/inauthentic etc. as misleading), and that part of his problem is the need to reconcile or transcend them. When her baby, Rocamadour, dies while Oliveira and his cronies are partying, he loses her and, after wandering around Paris trying to find her again, he is arrested and compelled to return to Buenos Aires. The other companion, Gregorovius, is a rootless European pseudo-intellectual, who in part shares Oliveira's search for a hidden side of reality. In certain respects he is Oliveira's double, so that in him the latter can see reflected the negative side of his own intellectual, moral and even emotional situation. The function of Gregorovius in the novel is to make it clear to Oliveira that, like Tregua in Mallea's *La bahía de silencio*, he is not going to find in European culture the answers he is looking for.

On his return to Buenos Aires, Oliveira falls in with his old friend Traveler, who is in many ways the opposite of Gregorovius, and his wife Talita who, mysteriously, is to take on some of the personality of La Maga. As so often in books like this, the diagnosis of the ills of modern man, the Parisian

[12] Cit. Frank Dauster in 'Notes on Borges' Labyrinths', *Hispanic Review* 30 (1962), 142–48, p. 145.

[13] Evelyn Picón Garfield, *Cortázar por Cortázar* (Xalapa, Veracruz U.P., 1978), p. 22.

chapters, are more persuasive than the therapy, explored in the Buenos Aires chapters. No critic has been able to give a fully satisfying account of this last. At one level of reading, Oliveira fails in his quest and commits suicide. At another, his final experiences in Europe are not wholly negative but represent the paradoxical beginning of his success in the quest, which culminates in an ineffable moment with Talita, when something 'unnameable' happens, after which his apparent suicide can be seen instead as a final leap into authenticity. The problem with Cortázar's thoughts about the modern human situation is that, like Sábato, but unlike Borges, he was unable to stand back from it and view it as perplexing, but interesting, and not something to become wrought up about. Instead, just as Sábato had postulated an 'absurda metafísica de la esperanza' which he was never fully able to justify, so Cortázar oracularly posits the existence of a 'Yonder' he is never able to situate or define, and of 'figures' which only he could see.

From our point of view the interest of his fiction is twofold. On the one hand it is very closely linked with the pattern of 'Existential' fiction which begins with works by Arlt and includes others by Sábato, Onetti and Marechal, but to which he brings, especially in some of his best short stories, a level of symbolic fantasy which reminds us of Borges, by whom he was discovered. On the other hand, the complexity of his fictional techniques and strategies, which, in the case of a later novel, *62. Modelo para armar* (1968), have baffled many critics, place him at the forefront of the experimentalism which is a major Boom characteristic. *Rayuela* is especially significant in this respect because of its relatively early date. It is the archetypal example of the 'splintered mirror' technique. When the reader has put it together like the broken pieces of a mirror, it still reflects reality, though not in a conventional way, and the effort involved in putting it together repels the superficial reader, but gives additional satisfaction to the committed one. *Rayuela* is also a characteristic example of the *metanovela*, the novel which incorporates awareness of its own processes of creation.

Cortázar's next novel, *62. Modelo para armar* (1968), actually begins with a brief prologue which promises that it will break with all the standard conventions of earlier fiction. The pattern of transgression is continued in *Libro de Manuel* (1973) and *Los autonautas de la cosmopista* (1984). All three of these novels evidence a ludic approach to fundamentally serious problems, alienation in *62*, political activism in *Libro de Manuel* and the problem of appearances and reality in *Los autonautas*, in so far as this work can be regarded as a novel at all, since like other works of Cortázar it is an assemblage of different elements not all of which are wholly fictional. What we find in these novels is what we find in the Boom as a whole: a constant pushing back of the frontiers of fiction, a systematic exploration of new techniques, especially those leading to greater reader involvement. But what is chiefly characteristic of them is their extreme development of one of the three forms of humour which prevail in the Boom. Up to the middle of the twentieth century, mainstream fiction in Spanish America had been solemn and civic. Humour, which in reality marks the achievement of maturity in much Western writing outside Europe, was considered frivolous. With the Boom come very notable developments in satirical humour (for example in García Marquez's 'Los funerales de la Mamá Grande'), purely ludic humour (such as we often find in Cabrera Infante) and, in Cortázar above all, what Unamuno called 'lo bufotrágico', humour with a deadly serious content, which the Argentine had recognized as the essence of 'la patafísica' borrowed in part from the French serio-comic writer Alfred Jarry. This is one of the great contributions of Cortázar to the Boom.

If any more evidence were needed that we cannot restrict the period of the Boom to the sixties, it would be provided by the fact that both the principal works of Juan Rulfo (Mexico, 1918–86), *El llano en llamas* (1953) and *Pedro Páramo* (1955) date from the previous decade. Most of the features of the Boom listed earlier are clearly present in them: the shift away from Regionalism, the subversion of 'observed reality' accompanied by a move towards mythification and creation of an imaginary reality, absence of love, pessimism, obtrusive use of symbolism and the abandonment of chronology and linearity in the structuring of the plot. In appearance both the short stories of *El llano en llamas*, and the plot of Rulfo's only novel, *Pedro Páramo*, reflect the reality of rural life in Mexico. But, as all his best critics have recognized, they really present a view of the human condition, and one which is deeply despairing. It is often forgotten that the Mexican Revolution, which occupied most of the second decade of the twentieth century, was followed by a series of revolts, including the *Cristero* rebellion (1926–8), one of the last openly religious civil wars in our time. Rulfo's early life was deeply scarred by what was happening around him. Like the World War I in Europe at the same time, the Revolution (and its aftermath) produced a dislocation of sensibility in Mexico, of which he was a prominent victim. Thomas Lyon was one of the first critics to assert that the starting point for reading Rulfo properly is to understand his 'visión del mundo'. Lyon identifies four repeated motifs in Rulfo's stories, which point us in the right direction. They are: constant movement, the attempt to escape from the past, the futility of effort and the prevalence of symbolic darkness.[14] The characters in these tales struggle painfully forward but generally in vain and as they do so, they are assailed by bitter memories from the past. A standard pattern is for the tale to begin in the present, only to show the past inexorably catching up with the characters, turning their current situation into one in which time remembered blocks any path to the future. Hence futility, solitude and frustration underlie all Rulfo's plots; life becomes a fruitless journey through a sterile

[14] Thomas E, Lyon, 'Motivos ontológicos en los cuentos de Juan Rulfo', *Anales de Literatura Hispanoamericana* 4 (1975), 305–12.

landscape. 'Los hombres creados por Rulfo', Lyon writes, 'se esfuerzan por adquirir justicia, dignidad y una vida completa, pero todos son frustrados por su propio pasado (memoria), por otros seres humanos y por la misma tierra hostil' (310). Finally, eleven of the fifteen stories in *El llano en llamas* take place in darkness, the symbolic importance of which hardly needs to be stressed. Man's life is a blind journey with no happy arrival. We often seem to be in the presence of a kind of hostile fatality with which the characters actively or passively collaborate. Rulfo once asserted that all a short-story writer needs to do is to create characters and their surroundings and make them speak convincingly. But this is a complete simplification. All great writing implies an attitude to life. This is why Yvette Jiménez is able to link Rulfo with other Boom writers like Arguedas, García Márquez, Carpentier and Roa Bastos, all of them Modernists in the sense that their work incorporates an epistemology, a 'knowledge' or 'truth' about life. In this case a terribly negative one: 'una perspectiva existencial límite que denuncia la pérdida de un sistema de valores añorados y no reemplazados.'[15]

Like Cortázar, Rulfo recognized that life cannot always be organized into a sequential chain of recognizable causes and effects. He once declared: 'La vida es caótica. No tiene una secuencia lógica. Cualquier de nosotros sabemos (sic) que nuestras vidas . . . jamás siguen una línea lógica, una secuencia. . . . La narrativa actual no es consecuencial.'[16] His stories tend to illustrate this. Like Borges's, they tend to feature interaction of elements rather than simple juxtaposition and to avoid dramatic climaxes. A standard example is 'No oyes ladrar los perros', in which a father is discovered carrying his mortally wounded son on his shoulders to a village where he hopes to find help. He struggles on along a symbolic stony road, beside a dried-up stream in the darkness. He longs for light to be able to see ahead and for the sound of the village dogs barking which will announce the end of his quest. But the moon, the story's central symbol, plays a cruelly ironic role, both shining down on the dying son's bloodless face, portending his death, and illuminating the old man's inner feelings; while, instead of being broken positively by the dogs, the sinister silence is reinforced by the son's stubborn refusal to participate in his father's task by encouraging him, or broken only by the younger man's coldly laconic 'bájame'. Even the imminence of death cannot establish an affective link between the two men. The central part of the tale contradicts the implications of the opening. Pathos gives way to antagonism. In the very act of trying to save his son, the father rejects him, cursing him as a murderer. The harshness of the natural background stands

[15] Yvette Jiménez, '*El llano en llamas*', *La Torre* 2. 5 (1988), 139–59, p. 158.

[16] Cited in Marcelo Coddou, 'Fundamentos para la valoración de la obra de Juan Rulfo', *Nueva Narrativa Hispanoamericana*, 1. 2 (1971), 139–58, p. 141. This important article is also available in Helmy F. Giacoman, *Homenaje a Juan Rulfo* (New York, Anaya / las Américas, 1974), pp. 61–89.

for the harshness of the human condition, in which evil is inborn. The story goes to the root of the incomprehensibility of the human condition. The father seems bewildered by the fate which has condemned him to carry a weight of evil for which he is not responsible. With implacable irony, Rulfo makes the last word of the tale 'esperanza', but by then the old man is alone and defeated.

Another archetypal Rulfo story, which in some ways looks forward to *Pedro Páramo*, is the famous 'Luvina'. Once more the terrible desolation of the uplands of Jalisco comes to represent the human condition. The narrator and the narratee in the story are teachers, representatives of culture. The old narrator is about to retire and be replaced by the younger one. His monologue makes it clear that in the village of Luvina nothing is to be achieved through the medium of ideas. Nor is anything to be gained through faith. Luvina's church, like the one in 'El día del derrumbe', is a tumbledown ruin offering neither protection nor serenity. Once more the theme is hope betrayed by experience (as in 'Es que somos muy pobres', where in the past two of the young narrator's sisters have had to resort to prostitution to survive, and now their fate is about to overtake another, despite her father's futile attempt to save her). The presentation of Luvina's inhabitants portends the death-in-life we find in Rulfo's novel. The dead govern the fate of the living, with the passive consent of the latter. In response, the narrator's wife symbolically shrugs her shoulders three times. She seems to think it not worth the effort to understand. The narrator tries to interest the villagers in a better life somewhere else, but his suggestion is rejected. In the end the silence that symbolizes the lifelessness of Luvina crushes him. Now, as he contemplates his replacement, he realizes that his destiny is about to be repeated.

It is possible to argue that the stories of *El llano en llamas* are only about life in rural Mexico and not about life in general. If so, it is difficult to understand why they have generated so much more interest than other Mexican stories and novels which are simply Regionalist. The brilliance of their technique is not a complete answer. But in any case, the criticism of life latent in them becomes fully apparent in *Pedro Páramo*. At the surface level this is a biographical narrative, seen retrospectively, composed predominantly of episodes dealing with Pedro's youth, his return in manhood to the village of Comala where he kills most of the people involved in the death of his father, his activities as a despotic local landowner and those of his son Miguel, his marriage to the deranged Susana San Juan, his strangulation of the life of the village after her death and his own death at the hands of one of his many illegitimate sons. In essence, a melodramatic and overdrawn picture of the familiar *cacique*-figure, in which Pedro is less original than Azuela's Andrade in *Esa sangre* (1956) and less memorable than Barrios's Valverde in *Gran señor y rajadiablos* (1948). With a little goodwill we can see these episodes, in Deborah Cohn's words, as 'emblematic of the fate of Mexico and the legacy of *caciquismo*' in the context of a nation in which revolution had failed to bring fundamental change to society. But if this is what the novel is about, why does it begin with another of Pedro's sons, Juan Preciado, arriving in Comala to seek out his father, only to find that Pedro and everyone else in the village has left or is dead? In turn Juan dies and the story is in fact told by him (and to him) from the grave. Why does the story appear to contain references to universal myths, above all to the Greek myth of Telemachus, whose search for his father in this case clearly alludes to man's search for God? Why is this search initially perceived as a journey to paradise, but turns out to be a descent into hell? Above all, why does Juan, in the exact centre of the novel, happen on an incestuous couple, whose life parodies that of Adam and Eve after the Fall? None of these questions can be answered satisfactorily unless we are willing to see, as Cohn recognizes (albeit reluctantly), that *Pedro Páramo* is, like Asturias's *El Señor Presidente* which inverts biblical motifs in a similar way, 'an allegory of the human condition'.[17]

The novel actually contains three strands of narrative. One is centred on Pedro; a second tells the story of Juan Preciado; while a third blends in the figure of Padre Rentería, the village priest. These strands are interlaced together in what at first reading seems a confusing way, which is made more confounded by two other highly significant techniques. One is connected with the narrative voice which shifts nimbly and without warning from that of an omniscient narrator, to interpolations by Juan and other characters in the form of monologues, reported monologues, dialogues, reported dialogues and stream of thought. This is one of the great discoveries of Rulfo. It gives him enormous flexibility, so that he can have all the advantages of first-person narration and all those of third-person narration, while at the same time vivifying the novel with dialogue, changing the angle of vision and shifting effortlessly from outside to inside the characters' minds. We should note, however, that (significantly) we never get inside Pedro's mind. The other technique is the use of flashbacks and sudden alterations of time-order, with the object (as in the apparent jumbling of episodes in Cortázar's *Rayuela*) of challenging our assumptions about causal sequence and forcing us to read the novel actively. When we do so, what we find are two interlocking allegories, with the story of Padre Rentería relevant to both. In the first Juan (Man) seeks his father (a just God), residing in a kind of paradise, expecting from him a reward for his mother's acceptable sacrifice. He finds an evil, vengeful God who, after a period of omnipotence, has died at the hands of man (another of his sons, Abundio, who kills him without understanding what he is doing),

[17] Deborah Cohn, 'A Wrinkle in Time: Time as Structure and Meaning in *Pedro Páramo*', *Revista Hispánica Moderna* 48 (1996), 261–2. Indispensible to the understanding of the universal, mythical and biblical elements in *Pedro Páramo* are the essays by Julio Ortega, 'La novela de Juan Rulfo: *summa* de arquetipos', and above all George Freeman, 'La caída de la gracia; clave arquetípica de *Pedro Páramo*', both in *La narrativa de Juan Rulfo*, ed. Joseph Sommers (Mexico City, Sepsetentas, 1974), pp. 76–87 and 67–75.

having turned Comala from a supposed Eden into an earthly hell, populated by tormented souls. In the second, Pedro (a despotic, cruel God, who has begotten a son only too much in his own image, who dies unredeemed and unredeeming) longs for the love of one of his creatures (Susana) but is denied it, since she prefers earthly, sexual love. Rentería (and the bishop who condemns the incestuous couple) represents a perverted, dogmatic and unforgiving vision of the Church's role in a hellish world, which is brushed aside by the dying Susana. Her longing on her deathbed for the carnal, fulfilling love of her dead husband rather than for the absolution Rentería offers her (after he himself has been refused it by one of his fellow-priests) is the only positive motif in this novel of living death.

Here we see that, given the presence of powerful elements of existential malaise among Boom writers, conventional religion is not a prominent theme in their work. Instead we find a tendency to invert or parody Christian motifs, imagery and symbolism.[18] Borges repeatedly exemplifies it, notably in 'Tres versiones de Judas' in *Ficciones*. The classic example occurs in the final chapter of García Márquez's *Cien años de soledad*, when the village priest of Macondo, whose normal role would be to strengthen people's confidence in their God-ordained existence as his children, says to the last Aureliano 'Ay hijo. A mí me bastaría con estar seguro de que tú y yo existimos en este momento'. We have already seen that Asturias's *El Señor Presidente* contains an obvious inversion of the story of the fall of Satan, with Christ parodied as INRI-idiota. Roa Bastos's *Hijo de hombre* from the title on inverts the idea of Christ as the son of God. We have just seen a parody of the story of Adam and Eve in Rulfo's *Pedro Páramo* and we shall meet another equally obvious caricature of Christian belief in a loving and merciful God in Donoso's *El lugar sin límites*. There is a bitter parody of popular religious belief in Vargas Llosa's *Pantaleón y las visitadoras*. The list could easily be continued. Curiously enough, Carpentier, with the great insight which he shows in his most mature writing, reveals in *El siglo de las luces* his conviction that revolutionary endeavour is founded on faith. Inside revolutionary ideology there is a hidden desire, common to most men, to give life meaning through effort and self-sacrifice, a semi-religious dynamic. The revoltionaries 'yearn for the crucifix'. The weakness of the revolution, Esteban concludes, is its lack of valid Gods.

To the extent, then, that religious themes figure prominently in his work, José Lezama Lima (Cuba 1910–76), like Marechal, stands in a slightly excentric relationship to the rest of the Boom. An important poet, he wrote only two novels, *Paradiso* (1966) and *Oppiano Licario* (incomplete, 1977). As we read them what is most striking is the 'family resemblance' which

[18] See my 'Inverted Christian Imagery and Symbolism in Modern Spanish American Fiction', *Romance Studies* 10 (1987), 71–82.

Carpentier perceived, linking different Boom writers together. Like the latter's *Los pasos perdidos* and Marechal's *Adán Buenosayres*, but most of all like Cortázar's *Rayuela*, Lezama's are quest-novels. Along with Arlt, Borges and others, he and the other novelists are seeking a means of recognizing a cosmos, an order, amid the chaos of reality. The collapse of Christian belief among the intellectual minority had left writers without a 'cosmic explanation'. All critics realize that Lezama had a deeply religious temperament, but one which orthodox Catholicism could not satisfy. The hero of his two novels, José Cemí, having suffered the traumatic loss of his father at an early age, is brought up by his mother Rialta to fulfil what she conceives as a high destiny. The two novels, which describe his childhood and youth, are once more novels of apprenticeship to life and follow a three-stage pattern: first, early formation by his mother; second, adolescence and friendship with two young men, Fronesis and Foción, in contact which whom his personality develops rapidly; third, discovery of his mentor, Oppiano Licario, who leads him to understand that his creative gift as a poet is what opens the gates of perception and brings final positive insight. As with Octavio Paz, Cemí comes to believe that his poetic, creative imagination can in some sense be cognitive, that it can overcome what for Paz is a symbolic barrier-wall, and for Cemí life as an endless flat plain, and yield insight into 'la vida más vida' (Paz) or for Cemí/Lezama the possibility of 'Resurrection'. Alvaro de Villa and José Sanchez Boudy comment: 'Aquí la poesía parece ir mucho más allá de la creación de belleza, busca una finalidad sobrenatural, se torna magia, hechizamiento, medio para alcanzar un fin que según parece es la resurrección.'[19] The link with Cortázar, who in 1967 published a famous essay 'Para llegar a Lezama Lima', lies in Lezama's notion that poetry could somehow reveal mysterious connections, similar to Cortázar's 'figuras', and that behind these lay a divine pattern. The origin of this notion, both in Paz and Lezama is (it is usually forgotten), the Symbolist belief of the great Nicaraguan poet Rubén Darío that

> toda forma es un gesto, una cifra, un enigma . . .
> cada hoja de cada árbol canta un propio cantar
> ('Coloquio de los centauros', *Prosas profanas*)

which only poets and visionaries can hear. Lezama's 'región dorada', towards which the connections point, corresponds to Cortázar's 'kibbutz del deseo'.

Paradiso begins as a family chronicle, painting in Cemí's background and schooldays, culminating in the famous chapter eight with its heavy emphasis on the sexuality of two of his companions. It raises one of the critical prob-

19 Alvaro de Villa and José Sánchez Boudy, *Lezama Lima: peregrino inmóvil* (Miami, Universal, 1974), p. 182.

lems of the text, in which there is never a case of simple, loving, fulfilling sexuality, nor does love itself or even friendship with women play any role. It is clear that sexual awareness (Cemí is not directly involved in sexual activity in the novel) and poetic experience are inseparable for Lezama and both are involved in his quest. Pellón explains the role of (aberrant) sexuality in *Paradiso* as follows: 'homosexuality and other sexual deviations offer Cemí the knowledge of good and evil and a form of immortality which is understood as an eternal cycle of destruction and creation. Cemí sees this type of immortality as a false *telos* whose true nature is revealed in the *dromomania*, the ceaseless wandering of all the sexual psychotics in the novel.'[20] In its central section, Cemí finds himself situated between Fronesis, representing, practical good sense, prudence and thoughtfulness, on the one hand, and the somewhat older figure of Foción, the homosexual, on the other. One might think that they represent options facing Cemí, but this would be a simplification. In a sense he has no options as such. One of the deep themes of the novel is that of Free Will and Determinism. Doña Augusta, Cemí's grandmother, speaking to the Protestant Florita, makes one of the basic assertions in the novel when she remarks that every Catholic knows that each action forms part of a mysterious divine plan the ends of which are mysterious. It follows that resisting the apparent chaos of reality consists in understanding that human will cannot impose a pattern on it. The pattern comes from God and is visible, through a form of Grace, to people endowed (as Cemí perhaps ultimately is) with conscious poetic insight. Thus any final epiphany is both religious and poetic, and is not necessarily governed by logic and causality. This realization is one of the rewards of Cemí's quest.

It can at times be difficult for those too young to remember the early impact of Boom fiction to understand the widespread disorientation it produced among critics who had internalized the idea of mimesis as the primary criterion of value. Pellón mentions cases related to *Paradiso* but there are many others. The classic (and scariest) example is that of Manuel Pedro González, at that time a respected figure, who in *Coloquio sobre la novela hispanoamericana* (1967), at the peak of the Boom, published a furious tirade against the movement, accusing it of 'bizantinismo de temas y formas', and holding up Mariano Azuela as an example of what a novelist should be like. He does not in fact deal with *Paradiso*, which only appeared as he was writing his memorable philippic, but it is not difficult to imagine what he would have thought. A dozen years later, the smoke had cleared and Noé Jitrik was able to write that '*Paradiso* trata de poner en crisis toda una concepción todavía vigente de la narración',[21] thus aligning it with Cortázar's

[20] Gustavo Pellón, *José Lezama Lima's Joyful Vision* (Austin, Texas U.P., 1989), p. 43. The whole of Pellón's third chapter is illuminating for the difficult question of eroticism and homosexuality in *Paradiso*.

[21] Noé Jitrik, '*Paradiso* entre desborde y ruptura', *Texto Crítico* 13 (1979), 89.

Rayuela, Fuentes's *La muerte de Artemio Cruz*, Rulfo's *Pedro Páramo*, Donoso's *El obsceno pájaro de la noche* and a big group of other experimental Boom novels which undermine the whole notion of Realism. *Paradiso* is not a reader-friendly novel. Its basic structure is relatively straightforward, beginning, as we saw, as a family chronicle and then revealing itself as a *Bildungsroman*. But this structure is buried under a proliferation of fragments and digressions which illustrate Lezama's famous 'barroquismo'. Jitrik writes: '*Paradiso* se presenta como un conjunto bastante bien articulado, regularizado, y también como un mosaico de fragmentos' (p. 72). It is a 'torrente verbal' and even a 'tejido canceroso' in which different descriptive codes, borrowed from medicine, gastronomy or whatever are pillaged by Lezama and used as raw material for his richly poetic but often highly elliptic style. 'Para Lezama', Ada Teja reminds us, 'la realidad es un sistema de vasos comunicantes; la capta con la intuición poética, la "distracción", el meandro que caracolea asistemáticamente a través de símiles e imágenes y acarrea todas las irradiaciones en un recorrido de vía unitiva.'[22]

The key episode in *Paradiso* is Cemí's meeting with Oppiano Licario, which is when the 'vía unitiva' begins to emerge. In *Paradiso*, his semi-symbolic friends, Fronesis and Foción at length disappear, leaving the narrative wholly centred on Cemí. Now in *Oppiano Licario*, the sequel, they reappear but are ultimately replaced by the (now dead) 'maestro', Oppiano, and his visionary sister Ynaca Eco, whose role is to help Cemí to complete his evolution. Once more, as in *Paradiso*, all the major characters function in relation to him. Each of them is a 'fragment' which contributes to his search for totality; each of them conveys some kind of message or lesson. This is especially the case with those who belong to one of the sundry trios in the two novels: Cemí and his parents, Cemí and his two friends; Cemí, Oppiano and Ynaca. The sign of three is always significant. Oppiano, according to Lezama himself, stands for infinite wisdom. It is he who understands the 'true causality' which lies behind the invisible connections which the poetic imagination can perceive, so that the 'imagen', which we are repeatedly told is Cemí's goal ('penetrar en la imagen', 'vivir en la imagen') becomes an 'imagen cognoscente'. Despite the various calamities and test situations which occur in the narrative, and which affect his progess, Cemí, after a symbolic sexual union with Ynaca Eco, discovers his destiny and perhaps achieves a final epiphany, though not all critics are in agreement about this. It is certainly promised on several occasions in the uncompleted novel, for example to Fronesis by the prophetess Editabunda and implicitly by Ynaca Eco to Cemí himself. But, apart from being incomplete, the novel was clearly designed to

22 Ada María Teja, '*Paradiso* y la cuestión del destino: tragedia, comedia, epifanía', *Revista Hispánica Moderna* 52 (1999), pp. 151–79, 153.

be open-ended and the quest therefore perhaps infinite. The emphasis is on the quest itself rather than on its fulfilment.

Before we pass to other Boom writers, it is important to underline afresh three features of Lezama's fictional work. The first is its probable happy ending, in contrast to the pessimism of the Boom. Cemí seems to come within reach of a state of final poetico-religious insight. But as in the case of Cortázar, we have to take it on trust. It is a purely oracular mystique. However it exemplifies R. L. Williams's contention that, in the early part of the Boom, literature's 'truth claims' still survive, in contrast to their collapse with the advent of Postmodernism. Second, we should note once more the predominance of sexuality over love, and its new function of often leading to greater existential and self-awareness.[23] Third, we may henceforth keep in mind that *Paradiso* and the other highly experimental novels mentioned above represent the high point of Modernism (in the Anglo-Saxon sense) in Spanish America. Postmodernism there, as we shall see, carries the process of formal experimentation to a further extreme, while, as we shall argue, Post-Boom fiction in contrast represents a cautious return to a kind of realism and reader-friendliness.

Further Reading

(Some general works on the Boom writers and their period):

Bacarisse, Salvador, ed., *Contemporary Spanish American Fiction* (Edinburgh, Scottish Academic Press, 1980). Excellent essays by British critics on major Boom texts.

Donoso, José, *The 'Boom' in Spanish American Literature: A Personal History* (New York, Columbia U.P., 1977). Testimony by a major Boom writer.

Gazarian Gautier, Marie-Lise, *Interviews with Latin American Writers* (Elmwood Park, Illinois, Dalkey Archive Press, 1989). Very helpful remarks by leading Boom writers.

Guibert, Rita, *Seven Voices* (New York, Knopf, 1973). Often quoted interviews.

Harss, Luis, *Into the Mainstream* (London, Harper and Row, 1967). The best early book on the Boom. Full of sound doctrine.

Latin American Literary Review 15. 29 (1987). A special number on the Boom.

Rodríguez Monegal, Emir, *El boom de la novela latinoamericana* (Caracas, Tiempo Nuevo, 1972). By the great champion of Boom criticism.

(On this chapter)

Mattalia, Sonia, *La figura en el tapiz* (London, Books, 1991).

[23] See in this connection my articles 'Notes on the Presentation of Sexuality in the Modern Spanish American Novel', *Bulletin of Hispanic Studies* 59 (1982), 275–82 and 'More Notes on the Presentation of Sexuality in the Modern Spanish American Novel', *Carnal Knowledge*, ed. Pamela Bacarisse (Pittsburgh, Tres Ríos, 1993), pp. 113–27.

Millington, Mark, *Reading Onetti: Language, Narrative and the Subject* (Liverpool, Cairns, 1985). The best book in English.

González Echevarría, Roberto, *Alejo Carpentier. The Pilgrim at Home* (Austin, Texas U.P., 1990). Probably the best all-round book in English.

Shaw, Donald, *Alejo Carpentier* (Boston, Twayne, 1985).

Smith, Verity, *Carpentier. Los pasos perdidos* (London, Grant & Cutler/Tamesis, 1983). Very concise and cogent.

Ivask, Ivan and Alazraki, Jaime, eds., *The Final Island: The Fiction of Cortázar* (Norman, Oklahoma U.P., 1978). Early but helpful essays by leading critics.

Moran, Dominie, *Questions of the Liminal in the Fiction of Julio Cortázar* (Oxford, Legenda, 2000). A closely argued Deconstructive Approach.

Yovanovich, Gordana, *Julio Cortázar's Character Mosaic. Reading the Longer Fiction* (Toronto U.P., 1991).

Leal, Luis, *Juan Rulfo* (Boston, Twayne, 1983).

Recopilación de textos sobre Juan Rulfo (Havana, Casa de las Américas, 1969). Many of the best early critical essays and other valuable material. All the *Recopilación* series are excellent.

Souza, Raymond D., *The Poetic Fiction of José Lezama Lima* (Columbia, Missouri U.P., 1983). Along with Pellón's, very helpful to English speakers on this complex novelist.

Chapter 6

THE BOOM CONTINUED

With the publication of *Cien años de soledad* in 1967, the Boom peaked. Those who are old enough can remember how news began to circulate of an extraordinary novel by a Colombian writer and how its success set the seal on the Boom as a new movement which for the first time brought Spanish American narrative into the mainstream of Western fiction. Gabriel García Márquez (Colombia, 1927 or 1928, the date is uncertain) began his career as a journalist writing features and editorials for a paper in Cartagena where he came to realize something of fundamental importance for much of his later work: that Latin American and Caribbean reality was in itself full of extraordinary, incredible events. His early journalism contains the seeds of his future outlook and has been profitably analysed by critics for that reason. He read modern fiction voraciously and great emphasis has been placed on the influence on him of Faulkner, an influence which he himself downplays in favour of Kafka, whose 'Metamorphosis' dazzled him and led directly to the writing of his first story, and later Rulfo's *Pedro Páramo*. His first novel, *La hojarasca* (1955) is already set in the Macondo where the events of *Cien años de soledad* were also to take place. It is already a highly original work both in terms of form and content. García Márquez himself has pointed out that it includes what he regards as the most basic theme of his work, solitude. In this case it is the solitude of a former doctor who, having refused to assist some wounded villagers, is hated and shunned by the rest of the inhabitants. After his suicide, his only friend, an old Colonel, defies them and organizes his burial. The title of the novel refers to a large section of the villagers, 'desperdicios humanos', who had arrived to get rich quick in the wake of the North American Banana Company which had exploited the area for a while and then moved away leaving it to rot. Their ferocious hatred of the doctor reappears throughout García Márquez's work in the form of a deeply pessimistic presentation of his fellow Colombians (and by extension, since Macondo is a microcosm of Spanish America, of his fellow Spanish Americans and perhaps of mankind generally). In chapter eight the doctor's solitude is explained in terms of his (Man's?) inability to come to terms with the idea of the existence of God, a theme which goes back through the anguished prayer uttered by the Librarian in Borges's 'La Biblioteca de Babel' to the outcry of Silvio in Arlt's *El juguete rabioso*. This is one way in which *La hojarasca* reaches out towards the universal. Another way is visible in its technique. The story is modelled on Sophocles's tragedy *Antigone* in which Antigone defies Creon in order to bury her brother Polyneices. The use of the source alludes to the unchanging nature of man's inhumanity to man and to the need for moral courage, such as the Colonel's. The novel contains twelve chapters made up of twenty-eight monologues divided between the Colonel, his daughter Isabel and his ten-year-old grandson: an example of perspectivism which, breaking with the tradition of the omniscient third-person narrator, in turn alludes to the complexity of reality.

We have referred already, à propos of Vargas Llosa's book on Arguedas, to the heavy pressure on Spanish American writers of the Boom generation to write works of militant left-wing protest. García Márquez, himself a declared Socialist, surrendered to this pressure in his next works. 'Mis amigos militantes', he told Plinio Mendoza, 'me crearon un terrible complejo de culpa', by reproaching him for the lack of reference in *La hojarasca* to the terrible civil war then raging in Colombia which left more than 200,000 dead. It was the same reproach that was to be levelled at the Boom writers as a whole and which contributed to a fresh wave of denunciatory writing in the Post-Boom on the part of writers like Allende and Skármeta. 'Me llevó a pensar', García Márquez went on, 'que yo debía ocuparme de la realidad inmediata del país, apartándome un poco de mis ideas literarias iniciales, que por fortuna acabé por recuperar.'[1] This led to *El coronel no tiene quien le escriba* (1957), and *La mala hora* (1962) and some short stories. The first is a small masterpiece; but García Márquez, while not repenting of having written them, came to see them as too narrow in scope. In 'Los funerales de la Mamá Grande' (1959, in book form 1962), he moved from cold anger and head-on opposition to the reactionaries in Colombia to comic satire of the old landowning oligarchy and its political minions, using popular, mythicizing fantasy and caricaturesque exaggeration. The story occupies the same pivotal position in his work as 'El persiguidor' does in Cortázar's. After it nothing would be quite the same, especially because of the presence of humour instead of indignation. But behind it there is unmistakable ambiguity. The story ends positively in the sense that an obsolete, feudal pattern of power, seems to have come to an end. But we notice, if we are reading alertly, that the rubbish left behind by the funeral of the representative of the old order will take an endless length of time to clear up (and the history of Colombia in the last half century has proved García Márquez correct). The circularities within the tale, which prefigure those of *Cien años de soledad*, similarly undercut any simple optimistic message the events appear at first reading to proclaim.

This prepares us for *Cien años de soledad* itself which is the opposite of an

[1] Gabriel García Márquez, in Plinio A. Mendoza, *El olor de la guayaba. Conversaciones con Gabriel García Márquez*, 2nd edn (Barcelona, Bruguera, 1983), p. 82.

optimistic work. In the meantime García Márquez had discovered Rulfo who, he was to write generously, 'me dió por fin el camino que buscaba para continuar mis libros'.[2] Critical debate about the novel's meaning has reached no consensus. Thematically, it appears to function on three different levels. One is concerned with the nature of reality itself. It is possible, though not all critics agree, that what we are reading is in fact the manuscript written by Melquíades, a visionary friend of the Buendía family, which the last of the Aurelianos deciphers near the end. It is a long prophecy of the family's history written in Sanskrit, in poetry and in code. This has been interpreted as implying first, that all reality is fictional, and second, that it is perplexingly difficult to understand. We have already alluded to the village priest's uncertainty about the reality of his own existence or that of anyone else. But if all reality (including our own) is possibly fictional, how can a fiction have any meaning or convey any message other than that all reality is possibly fictional? A second level of meaning seems to have to do with universal human destiny, while a third is plainly connected with the problems of Latin America past and present. But are these last two levels of meaning compatible with the first? Critics have tended to stress one of these levels at the expense of the other two, but this will not do. Let us take an example: time. Like Borges, García Márquez is obsessed with time. In one respect, since *Cien años de soledad* is a family chronicle covering several generations of the Buendías, time is conventionally ongoing. But already in 'Monólogo de Isabel viendo llover en Macondo' (1955) time stops, as it does in Aurelio Buendía's laboratory, where it is always Monday.

Meanwhile we are repeatedly informed in the novel that time in Macondo is circular. This has led critics into contradictions. For, on the one hand, if we accept that time is ultimately circular, then there can be no progress. That is why Carpentier postulates spirals. Some critics have accepted this, noting the obvious biblical subtext in *Cien años de soledad* (there is a Genesis myth, an edenic period, then a Fall and an Exodus towards a promised land, plagues, like those in the Old Testament, etc.). But there is no Redemption. Latin America/Mankind seems condemned to Eternal Return. This is not a new idea and provides a perfectly acceptable approach to certain aspects of the novel. But this is a novel written by an avowed Socialist! Those unable to swallow this interpretation sometimes argue that the Rushing Mighty Wind which blows Macondo away for ever at the end represents the Revolution, after which reconstruction can begin along left-wing lines. The problem is that there is no evidence of such a possibility in the text. It is true, however,

[2] Gabriel Gárcía Márquez, 'Nostalgias sobre Rulfo', in *Los murmullos: antología periodística en torno a la muerte de Juan Rulfo*, ed. Alejandro Sandoval (Mexico City, Katún, 1986), p. 177. It is worth noting that José María Arguedas in Peru was another fellow writer who immensely admired Rulfo, as did Mempo Giardinelli in the next generation.

that the episode of the Banana Company massacre, which the government succeeds in passing off as a popular myth, actually happened in Colombia in 1928. It forms part of the close similarity of various events described in the novel to events in nineteenth- and twentieth-century Colombian history. These events are presented critically, as a commentary on how things went wrong. They are clearly intended to provoke indignation and to raise the level of awareness of the reader (and not only in Latin America: oppression and injustice combined with governmental hypocrisy are practically universal phenomena). But what then becomes of the fictionality of reality? It is clear that a deep ambiguity in García Márquez's outlook surfaces in *Cien años de soledad*.

What is wrong with the *macondinos*? What does the prominent theme of incest symbolize? Why does Macondo simply rot after the Banana Company leaves? Again there is no consensus. García Márquez has stated that *soledad* is the opposite of *solidaridad*, and some critics have stressed lack of social cohesion and lack of love among the villagers. We notice an incapacity to modernize, a passive acceptance of the Buendías as an oligarchy and alternations of violence and political stagnation. All of this presents a terribly negative picture of Latin America (and perhaps of mankind) afflicted by a kind of moral gangrene or a curse like Original Sin. The technique of the novel, in which many of the chapters show a certain circularity of structure in conflict with the chronological development, mirrors the ambiguity of the thematics. Similarly the curious arrangement of the plot in which everything either mirrors some other element or contrasts with it, in sets of two, which produces a ludic effect, like a game, and above all the humour, which contrasts with the deeply serious content, leave us with the recognition that this novel, immensely popular and influential as it has been, is a critical minefield.

El otoño del Patriarca (1975) belongs, as we saw, with Carpentier's *El recurso del método* (1974) and Roa Bastos's *Yo el Supremo* (1974) forming the Boom's trio of novels on the topic of dictatorship. All of them follow the lead of Asturias in *El Señor Presidente*, in that they avoid straight denunciation and handle the theme in a disconcerting and ambiguous way. Nowhere more than in this case, where the basic theme is power, but in this case power as expressed in language.[3] On the one hand language is the substance of the dictator's power, the means by which he exercises it, via commands issued to subordinates. In the long run this undermines his position, since, as an unseen despot, he gradually turns into a myth, while at the same time becoming more and more cut off from the people and reality. On the other hand, the story of his decline and (presumed) death, told as a long flashback from the discovery of what seems to be his corpse, is recounted by a bewildering array of narra-

3 See especially Jo Labanyi, 'Language and Power in *The Autumn of the Patriarch*', *Gabriel García Márquez. New Readings*, eds. Bernard McGuirk and Richard Cardwell (Cambridge U.P., 1987), pp. 135–49.

tors, none of whom can be regarded as reliable. This turns the tables on the reader since, at the very moment when the narrative appears to be deconstructing the reality of absolute power, it undermines its own credibility. Swanson puts it in a nutshell: 'la complejidad narrativa de esta novela o refleja una realidad percibida como enrevesada y multiforme o implica que la ficción no puede funcionar como equivalente de la realidad.'[4] We can now see why left-wing critics became impatient of the Boom's cult of ambiguity and complexity in the face of the often terrible reality of oppression in Latin America. *El otoño de Patriarca* is at the opposite pole from testimonial writing or from novels like Isabel Allende's *De amor y de sombra*, or Skármeta's *La insurrección*. It raises questions about the view shared by García Márquez and Cortázar that the most revolutionary thing a writer can do is to revolutionize literature. A novel like Diamela Eltit's *Lumpérica* (1983) can be seen in retrospect as an attempt to combine highly innovative modes of writing with *compromiso* in a way the Boom writers sometimes failed to do adequately.

García Márquez's fiction turned another corner in 1985 with *El amor en los tiempos del cólera*. Before that he had published another very innovative novel *Crónica de una muerte anunciada* (1981), in which the foretold death is systematically emptied of intelligibility and significance, except in so far as the bystanders refuse to assume any civic or human responsibility for what is going on in front of them.[5] *Cronica* is a murder mystery stood on its head. We know how it happened and who did it; we never learn the central facts. Once more reality fights back at us. After *El amor en los tiempos del cólera* came *El general en su laberinto* (1989), García Márquez's primary contribution to the 'New Historical Novel' in Spanish America, a centrally important genre which cuts across both Boom, Post-Boom and Postmodernist fiction, creating difficulties and upsetting categorizations in each case. In broad terms New Historical Novels tend either to re-tell historical events from an unconventional perspective but one which preserves their intelligibility, or to question the very possibility of making sense of the past at all. *El general en su laberinto* belongs to the first category. It picks up the story of Bolívar on his final journey down the Magdalena river and presents him, like Colonel Aureliano Buendía in *Cien años de soledad,* as having fought his wars in vain. *El amor en los tiempos de cólera* is in one sense more interesting than the novels on either side of it, because it seems to reveal that García Márquez had taken note of the shift in fiction after about 1975, in which one of the new

[4] Philip Swanson, *Cómo leer a Gabriel García Márquez* (Madrid, Jucar, 1991), p. 137.

[5] See my '*Chronicle of a Death Foretold*. Narrative Function and Interpretation', in *Critical Perspectives on Gabriel García Márquez*, eds. Bradley Shaw and Nora Vera-Godwin (Lincoln, Nebraska, Society of Spanish and Spanish American Studies, 1986), pp. 91–104.

factors was a return to the theme of love as a life-directing force. Whether or not the love affair(s) of Florentino and Fermina are treated sarcastically, and once more critics do not agree, there is no doubt that aspects of the novel represent a significant turning away from the mainstream of Boom fiction. *Del amor y otros demonios* (1994), on the other hand, returns to the Boom's anti-romantic conception of love, which in this case is seen as a demonic force destroying its victims, one of whom is a priest. Set in late Colonial times, the novel necessarily comments on the religious mind-set of the period; but it would be a mistake to see Sierva María and Cayetano simply as victims of it. Religion, scepticism, love and demonic possession are all presented ambiguously. As with all García Márquez's fiction, even if it is true, as he insisted to Plinio Mendoza, that everything he has written is based on reality, we have to avoid jumping to conclusions about his treatment of it.

The religious theme which re-surfaced in the mythic sub-plot in Asturias's *El Señor Presidente* and in García Márquez (we recall the notice set up in Macondo stating 'Dios existe') comes to the fore again in *Hijo de hombre* (1960) by Augusto Roa Bastos (Paraguay, 1917). The novel clearly belongs to the category of 'national allegories' which Fredric Jameson regards as characteristic of Third World literature. It contains references which go back to the regime of Dr Francia, the dictator of Paraguay from 1814 to 1840, to the War of the Triple Alliance (1864–70) which devastated the country, and to the Chaco War (1932–6) and its aftermath. Roa Bastos needs this historical sweep to develop a view of historical change which is similar to Carpentier's: one in which history slowly advances, thrust along by human effort and sacrifice, despite dispiriting setbacks. The image of the Cristo de Itapé (which never enters a Church) dominates the first part of the novel. It symbolizes the crucifixion, not of Christ as the son of God, but of Christ as the Son of Man, a role eventually adopted by Cristóbal Jara, whose local name, Kiritó, is the phonetic equivalent of Christ in Guaraní. The novel is highly allegorical: Cristóbal (=Christ), who is loved by Salu'i (=Mary Magdalene, a reformed sinner), is betrayed and killed by Miguel Vera (=Judas), while attempting to save his fellow men by bringing them water (=the Water of Life). But again, as with Carpentier, we are firmly within the kingdom of *this* world. Salvation comes from man himself, heroically carrying out tasks on behalf of others, not from God: 'Lo que no puede hacer el hombre', Cristóbal affirms, 'nadie más puede hacer.'[6] Cristóbal is born when his parents are in semi-slavery on a *yerba mate* plantation. After their escape he grows up with them in an abandoned railway carriage which they gradually push away from the line. This is another important symbol in the novel, standing for patient, unremitting human effort. As a young man Cristóbal joins a group of anti-government

6 Augusto Roa Bastos, *Hijo de hombre* (Buenos Aires, Losada, 1976), p. 245.

guerrillas until these are betrayed by Vera and he barely escapes with his life. His final Christ-like mission takes place during the Chaco War.

Clearly this is a novel of political protest. What marks it as a boom novel is its technique: the allegorization of history, the presence of prominent symbolism, the inverted Christian motifs, the contrast between Cristóbal and Vera (hero and anti-hero), but above all the interaction of four story lines, which gives rise to different focalizations, and the complex alternation (not obvious at first reading) of the narrative voices. Only half of the novel is in fact narrated directly by Vera, while the rest seems to be told by another voice or even voices, which, when recognized, produces a contrapuntal effect. In addition, the source of the entire novel is a manuscript which may have been 'edited' by his girl-friend, which, as Foster points out, may 'reduce all statements and interpretations in the novel to a level of conjecture'.[7]

If *Hijo de hombre* is a novel which lends itself to multiple readings, this is even more the case with *Yo el Supremo* (1974), the story of the nineteenth-century dictator, Dr Francia, told autobiographically, 'from within'. Ultimately Roa Bastos is a humanist commenting on inhuman regimes in Paraguay and by extension in the world generally. In this case his humanism emerges in his avoidance of the temptation to denigrate this figure who was at once the tyrant, the founder and the defender of his country. The novel hangs between two threads. On the one hand, as the French tell us, to understand everything is to forgive everything. Roa Bastos has to use Francia's own voice to allow the dictator to defend himself, without making that defence too convincing. On the other hand the text itself emphasizes problems of accuracy in terms of memory and of knowledge itself as well as the impossibilty of achieving real communication through words. At one point Francia compares himself to a man imprisoned inside a tree, desperately trying to make himself heard over the noise made by the tree itself (and failing). So that even if he could defend himself and his regime, the message would become distorted in transmission. The ambiguities already present in *Hijo de hombre* are carried to an extreme in *Yo el Supremo*, as Francia compiles his private journal and dictates to his secretary Patiño, while the latter in turn plays fast and loose with what he is supposed to record, and the compiler of the text includes notes of his own which contradict some of Francia's assertions. The novel illustrates what was remarked earlier about the New Historical Novel in Spanish America. While García Márquez's *El general en su laberinto* presents an alternative account of Bolívar's achievement from the standpoint of his last weeks of life, it does still contain an interpretation, as does Fuentes's *La campaña* or Del Paso's *Noticias del imperio*. Whereas *Yo el Supremo*, Elmore points out, 'sirve para interpelar a fondo las

[7] David W. Foster, *Augusto Roa Bastos* (Boston, Twayne, 1978), p. 43.

categorías que fundamentan la autoridad de los discursos sobre el pasado nacional'.[8]

As in the case of García Márquez's Patriarch, one fundamental ambiguity in the novel relates to the personality of the dictator himself. As he finds himself late in life reduced from action to mere dictation, his frustrated aspiration to total power reveals itself in alternating outbursts of paranoid self-apotheosis and the haunting sensation that he himself is no more than an insubstantial shadow. He comes over as an almost Unamunesque figure, split between his private personality and his public image, between his 'querer ser' as the semi-mythic incarnation of the nation he leads, and his sensation of inner nothingness. The other major ambiguity relates to his regime, which in a banal sense could be seen as the antithesis of the Stroessner regime in Paraguay (1954–89). While this last was one of simple oppression under the mask of anti-Communism, which left the country poverty-stricken and debased, Francia's rule, despotic as it was, thwarted the designs of other powers on the independence of Paraguay, checked those of the Church and the landed oligarchy and, according to Roa Bastos, effectively brought about genuine material and cultural progress. But it did so at the cost of stifling libertarian movements, like authoritarian regimes of both the Left and the Right in Latin America and the rest of the world. Paradoxically, Francia achieved what the movements which threw off Spanish colonial domination generally failed to achieve: an increase in order, national prestige and economic development. The challenge implicit in his self-defence is the challenge facing democratic countries: can freely elected governments do as much in conditions of liberty? Alternatively, can there be what the text calls a 'verdadera revolución' which does not devour its children and betray its own ideals?

Unlike some Post-Boom writers and writers of Testimonial fiction, the Boom writers tend to be sceptical about political and social progress. Roa Bastos is not an exception. In *El fiscal* (1993), which completes his trilogy on the theme of power and *Contravida* (1994), what strikes us is the implacability with which both novels progress towards horror at the end. The first deals with a grotesque attempt to assassinate Stroessner and ends with imprisonment and torture; the second deals with the escape of a political prisoner and ends with his murder just as he seems to have reached safety. Both novels include elements of fantasy and metafiction and, in the first especially, a further critique of the intelligibility of history and the reliability of historians. This had already reappeared in *La vigilia del Almirante* (1992) on the theme (like Carpentier's *El arpa y la sombra* [1979]) of Columbus and the Discovery. *Madama Sui* (1995) combines a curiously romanticized portrait of one of

[8] Peter Elmore, *La fábrica de la memoria. La crisis de la representación en la novela histórica latinoamericana* (Mexico City, Fondo de Cultura Económica, 1977), p. 78.

Stroessner's mistresses, seen partly as a symbolic victim of the process of national degeneration under the dictator's tyranny, and a strangely disenchanted vision of the people of Paraguay, in complete contrast to Roa Bastos's earlier exaltation of their stoicism and dignity. None of these later novels, however, can compete in literary quality with the first two.

Writers both of his own generation and of the next have paid tribute to Carlos Fuentes (Mexico, 1928) as the novelist who opened the way for them to follow. Donoso, in his interesting *Historia personal del Boom* (1971), writes that Fuentes's first novel, *La región más transparente* (1958), challenged young writers like himself at that time to equal its audacious innovations. Gustavo Sainz in Mexico itself tells us that he was dazzled by this novel, which rendered obsolete the Novel of the Mexican Revolution and what had followed it.[9] In contrast to the 'novela de la tierra' of Regionalism, Fuentes inaugurates in Mexico the modern novel of the city as Arlt had done in Argentina and Onetti in Uruguay. But with this difference: one of the central themes of Mexican literature in the twentieth century (popularized by Azuela) is the failure of the Mexican Revolution. For Fuentes, Mexico City, which saw the rise of a newly enriched middle and upper class after the Revolution, is the symbol of that failure. The difference between *La región más transparente* and *Las buenas conciencias* (1959), on the one hand, and Fuentes's third and greatest full-scale novel *La muerte de Artemio Cruz* (1962) on the other, is that the first two are more Mexico-centred, while the third reaches out successfully towards the universal.

The action of *La región más transparente* is framed between two monologues by Ixca Cienfuegos, a magical figure, who stands for Mexico and its capital city. Both end with the phrases 'Aquí nos tocó. Qué le vamos a hacer. En la región más transparente del aire'. The second phrase sets the tone of (not quite) resigned fatalism in the face of the problems of this society split by racial differences, haunted by the Conquest and crippled by successive defeats of the national ideal since Independence. The novel is both contemporary and historical, a great freize-like structure covering the period 1951–4 but stretching backwards to the Revolution and earlier, in an attempt to explore the enigma of Mexican identity and its influence on the nation's destiny. The attempt centres on two families, that of the tycoon, Federico Robles (who portends Artemio Cruz, surviving the Revolution and acquiring great wealth, but losing his son), and that of Gervasio Pola, a popular agitator who dies in the Revolution, but who leaves a son to take his place. *La región más transparente* is a characteristically hybrid novel, full of discussion and historical allusion. It is designed to try to make sense of the recent history of

9 Gustavo Sainz, 'Carlos Fuentes. A Permanent Bedazzlement', *World Literature Today* 57.4 (1983), 568–72.

Mexico, as Sarmiento had tried to make sense of Argentine history a hundred years before, by using archetypal figures. Such 'cultural' approaches to national problems, as we see from the *regeneracionismo* of the Generation of 1898 in Spain, always fail, and in this case the failure is visible in the absence of any suggested way forward in the novel. But, both because of its urban setting and its audacious experimentalism of technique, it remains a turning point in modern Mexican fiction. Fuentes receded from technical innovation in *Las buenas conciencias,* which is a much more conventional, realist-type novel of adolescence and early youth which partly reflects a personal crisis of ideas and beliefs in the author himself.

La muerte de Artemio Cruz (1962) is once more an attempt to depict through the life of an individual (Federico Robles, Artemio Cruz) the failure of a historical process. But this time, behind the social symbol, we find a man with whom we can identify: partly responsible for his actions, partly conditioned by circumstances; weak, as we all are, ashamed of his weakness, and overcompensating for it by bluster; emotionally frustrated but machistic; haunted by the sense of his own guilt; constantly seeking and failing to find a satisfying self-excuse. Born of a liason between the son of a once-rich landowning family and a mulatto servant girl, Artemio survives an incident of shameful cowardice and the loss of his first love during the Revolution, marries into the old landed class, and becomes a successful representative of the new Mexican plutocracy of exploiters and *vendepatrias*. The opening of the novel finds him on his deathbed recalling his life through a series of twelve apparently disconnected flashbacks. Some of these are related to the events of his public career: his oligarchic life-style and that of his family, his betrayal of comrades during the Revolution, his political turncoat-behaviour afterwards, his disenchantment in old age with wealth, power and success. We, of course, reject him, not for what he does, but for what he is; not because he betrays his country, but because he betrays himself. He is a man who, faced with moral choices, makes the wrong ones. This comes out in the flashbacks which deal with his private, emotional and sexual life. Here his weakness is balanced by pride; the pride which prevents him from breaking the barrier of lack of loving, honest communication with his wife. With pride go fear and guilt; the fear which stops him from starting afresh with another woman, the guilt stemming from his encouragment of his son to do what he could not do: fight and die for a cause. There is a mysterious reference to a 'secret'. We presume that it refers to the requirement in life to sacrifice: to 'darlo todo a cambio de nada'.

Technically *La muerte de Artemio Cruz* breaks away from the old plot+sub-plot+commentary pattern. It is told in a new way which is both subjective (the 'Yo' sequences), objective (the 'El' sequences) and in a sense moral (the 'Tú' sequences in which Artemio faces his better self). In addition the twelve flashbacks dealing with different periods of Artemio's life are not arranged chronologically but in a non-chronological pattern which reveals itself to be a subtly articulated set of contrasts and transitions, each interrelating functionally with the rest to produce the maximum effect.[10]

La muerte de Artemio Cruz requires a high degree of reader-competence, but it is basically a referential text dealing with modern Mexico. *Aura* (1962) published shortly before it is quite different, though it too makes heavy demands on the reader. It is a fantastic, 'Gothic' tale of a young man lured into a strange house by a witch-figure, Consuelo, who attempts to reconstruct with him, by means of a ghostly double, her relationship with her long-dead husband. The themes of time and personal identity, of another reality behind the apparent one, of reincarnation and of the strange influence of the past on the present, will surface afresh in Fuentes's later works, such as *Cumpleaños* (1969) and *Una familia lejana* (1980) which deal in mystery rather than history. From this point on, in other words (though portended by magical elements in *La región más transparente*), there is a bifurcation in Fuentes's fiction, which now deals with two separate kinds of reality, one involving normal notions of causality, the other not. One of his basic themes is power. In *Zona sagrada* (1967) one of the two major figures, Claudia, a top-rank film star and business woman, combines the kind of power Robles and Cruz have previously represented with a different, Circe-like, power of magical domination, which comes from the other side of Fuentes's outlook. At one level, *Zona sagrada* is a peculiar kind of psychological study, centred on the destructive relationship between Guillermo (Mito) and his overpowering mother and one of her lovers, Giancarlo. With increasing desperation, Mito attempts to establish an emotionally satisfying relationship with Claudia, expressing his frustration in a variety of ways involving fetishism and even dressing in her clothes. But he ultimately fails disastrously and begins to hallucinate that he has become a dog, in this case a symbol of abjection. At this level the theme of the novel is Mito's search for identity which was lost when he was rejected as a small child and which he hopes to rediscover through recovery of his mother's love, symbolized by a return to her womb. But his conversion into an animal underlines the presence of another level of meaning, here made manifest in one of the mythical sub-texts of the novel, which is freely adapted from the story of Ulysses, Penelope, Circe, Telemachus and Telegonus. Another one is adapted from the Oedipus myth. The role of a mythical subtext, as we have seen in the cases of Asturias's *El Señor Presidente* and García Márquez's *La hojarasca* is often to confer wider significance on the plot, whether at a national or a universal level. Several attempts have been made to interpret the Circe myth in this way, including seeing Claudia also as Coatlicue, the man-eating Aztec goddess. But none of

10 This has often been studied. But see my 'Narrative Arrangement in *La muerte de Artemio Cruz*', *Forum for Modern Language Studies* 15 (1979), 130–43, reprinted in *Contemporary Latin American Fiction*, ed. Salvador Bacarisse (Edinburgh, Scottish Academic Press, 1980), pp. 34–47.

them has so far proved fully convincing, mainly because the references are so complicated and ambiguous.

It seems as though, once he had managed to entwine the social, the psychological, the magical and the mythical in *Zona sagrada*, Fuentes was encouraged to push complication to an extreme. This allows us to posit another bifurcation in his work. Published in the same year (1967) as *Zona sagrada*, *Cambio de piel* belongs with Cortázar's *62. Modelo para armar* and Donoso's *El obsceno pájaro de la noche* as one of the three most baffling novels of the Boom. While they provide plenty of work for critics, their historical importance is less connected with them as novels in themselves, than as representing the high-water mark of all that anti-Boom writers and critics like David Viñas, Mario Benedetti, Hernán Vidal and Juan Manuel Marcos complain about when they accuse Boom writers of contempt for the common reader. In fact any discussion of the return to reader-friendliness in the Post-Boom could well begin from these three Boom novels. After 1967 Fuentes went on to write another couple of ambitious, block-buster novels which present the reader with serious difficulties: *Terra nostra* (1975) and *Cristóbal nonato* (1989). But, in the meantime, he confirmed his extraordinary versatility by using/spoofing the popular format of the spy-story in *La cabeza de la hidra* (1978) and by producing a couple of reasonably straightforward historical novels in *Gringo viejo* (1985) and *La campaña* (1990). One is tempted to suggest that, like García Márquez, Vargas Llosa and Donoso, whose remarks will be reported in the next chapter, he had seen which way the wind was blowing after the mid-1970s and modified his stance accordingly.

Durán explains why *Terra nostra* involves the reader in 'guessing games' by remarking that 'The characters move or swim through a world of intermingling time and space with no apparent boundaries' and that the narrative is conveyed by 'multiple narrators and multiple viewpoints'.[11] It is what Fuentes himself has called a 'novela de polivalencias'. In one sense its fundamental theme is space-time, which its central figure, who is based on Philip II of Spain, wishes to believe is somehow static, a closed circle in which everything is already included and accounted for. But the discovery of the New World has skewed this idea of the way things are and introduced a notion of change and flux, represented in the novel by three mysterious youths who are wrecked on the southern coast of Spain and whose function seems to be to set in motion events which will destabilize the king's world view. Historically speaking, the era of Philip II is set in the novel between that of the post-Augustan age of the Roman Empire and the end of the twentieth century. Each era involved the making of historical choices which might

[11] Gloria Durán, *The Archetypes of Carlos Fuentes* (Hamden, Connecticut, Archon Books, 1980), p. 152.

have led to significant human progress (*Terra nostra* is not without a certain utopian aspiration). But it does not become clear whether such choices were actually made successfully; critics differ about whether the thrust of the novel is positive or negative.

If we were to read backwards from *Cristóbal nonato* (1987) we should have to conclude that Fuentes's vision of history, at least so far as it relates to Mexico, is profoundly pessimistic. At the end of it, the narrator's (Cristóbal's) voice is subsumed in Fuentes's when he tells us that the aim of the novel has been to communicate to the reader his nightmares and dreams. What we get are chiefly the former. The novel begins with Cristóbal's being conceived in 1992 (almost five years after the novel was published) on a beach at Acapulco under a shower of excrement. It ends in Acapulco just before his birth, and hence is narrated from inside his mother's womb. In the intervening months Acapulco is washed away in a surge of filth, to make room for more speculation by political insiders. Mexico has lost another major slice of its territory, but the populace is temporarily distracted by the President's creation of an archetypal Mexican virgin-mother out of a young typist, until a horde of lorry-drivers with a rival virgin protectress invade the capital and are shot down in a bloodbath, while the slum shacks surrounding the capital begin to burn down, poisoning what breathable air remains. Amid these events the behaviour of Cristóbal's parents, his uncles and aunts and grandparents and their hangers on, representing different groups in Mexican society (with heavy emphasis on the upper class and the political hierarchy) is manipulated to provide a black-humour satire of the greed, self-indulgence, power hunger and violence of Mexican society, not unlike what we think of in relation to Gustavo Sainz's *Obsesivos días circulares* and *La Princesa del Palacio de Hierro*, both published much earlier. Perhaps, like García Márquez in *El amor en los tiempos del cólera*, Fuentes had indeed recognized which way the new wind in fiction was blowing.

More evidence of this is provided by the fact that the novel, despite everything, ends on a positive note, with a general reconciliation of Cristóbal's parents, who have been separated, with the family and a couple of associated figures, one Mexican, one Asiatic, who turn out to be symbolically related. The curtain scene invokes a new Pacific Rim international community replacing Canada, North America and Mexico which will reverse the Spenglerian notion of civilizations moving from East to West and which will be orientated to the Pacific and the Orient instead of the Atlantic and Western Europe. This is the dream, after the preceeding nightmares. What is important, in regard to Fuentes's development, is that it is there at all, and that it contrasts with the pessimism of the Boom.

Already in *La cabeza de la hidra* (1978) Fuentes had moved away from the Boom's normally uncompromising 'high-literature' stance, adopting the strategy, which some critics hasten to call Postmodernist, of adapting a popular form (in this case the spy-story thriller) to carry levels of meaning not usually found in this sub-genre. Borges, had already done it in his short story 'El jardín de senderos que se bifurcan', where what is important is the interaction between the spy story itself and philosophical core of the tale. So too in this case: unlike detective stories, which Borges had also used in the same way, what matters in a modern spy story is not solving a puzzle (which is why detective stories appealed to Borges), but creating unforeseen complications. To unravel those of *La cabeza de la hidra* is too daunting a task to undertake here. The themes are what matter. Two of them are familiar: that of personal/national identity and that of criticism of Mexico, still as a country dominated by poverty, corruption and ineptitude, but this time as possessing enormous oil resources, which, properly managed, could solve all her problems. The third theme is that which spawns the labyrinthine plot: both Arabs and Israelis are desperately anxious to discover the extent of Mexican oil reserves, which could be decisive in a future crisis. Behind them are the CIA and the KGB, each protecting the interests of the superpowers at the expense of the oil-producers. Drama (as distinct from complexity and intrigue) is injected by means of a plot to assassinate the President of Mexico.

The message of the novel, frequently repeated, is that power politics rule. Small nations are manipulated by the superpowers and have no genuinely independent national identity. Similarly the experience of the central character, Maldonado/Velázquez, who experiences 'ese paso insensible de la realidad a la pesadilla, esa rendija por la que se cuela cuanto parece cierto y seguro en tu vida para volverse incierto, inseguro y fantasmagórico',[12] symbolizes yet again the Boom's vision of reality as 'inasible'. A further twist is added when we realize that the identity of the real narrator only becomes apparent late in the narrative, thus indirectly tying the plot and the narrative strategy together.

Fuentes's last big novel in the twentieth century was *Los años con Laura Díaz* (1999). As he makes clear, its intention was to use the life-story of Laura, with 'toda su experiencia vital, su origen provinciano, su vida de joven casada, su doble maternidad, sus amores y lo que sus amores trajeron',[13] to present another long freize-like account of Mexican life and history in the twentieth century. In that sense the novel harks back to *La región más transparente*. But in another sense it bears comparison with *La muerte de Artemio Cruz* (in fact Artemio and his mistress Laura have walk-on parts, as if to drop us a hint). Laura is intended to provide the focus here as Artemio was earlier. But this time, instead of being presented with a successful male tycoon, whose private life is disastrous because of his own character defects, we encounter a woman who is striving to find herself through love, marriage, motherhood and eventually a successful career. In the case of the earlier novel it is much easier to relate the story of Artemio to

[12] Carlos Fuentes, *La cabeza de la hidra* (Barcelona, Argos, 1978), p. 237.
[13] Carlos Fuentes, *Los años con Laura Díaz* (Mexico City, Alfaguara, 1999), p. 510.

the double theme (public success/private failure) and to the historical theme of the failure of the Revolution which his evolution symbolizes. *Los años con Laura Díaz* is in appearance a more sprawling, episodic work, though the technique of selecting incidents taken from individual years of Laura's life to discuss, is superficially similar. The immediately noticeable feature is that this time the time notations are chronological (running, between the introductory chapter set in 1999 and the conclusion in 2000) from 1905 to 1972, with a concentration in the 1930s. We do not have to put together the pieces of the splintered mirror. What this implies, is, of course, that in the interval since the early 1960s Fuentes's attitude to reality may have undergone a change, one (as we have suggested) that was perhaps already visible in his historical novel *La campaña* (1990) and more typical of the Post-Boom than of Postmodernism. This is to say, there seems to have come about a recovery of confidence in the comprehensibility of reality and thus a return to a more realistic approach.

To view *Los años con Laura Díaz* as in some sense a companion novel to *La muerte de Artemio Cruz*, as Fuentes has suggested to interviewers, raises problems. This is chiefly because it is much less easy to recognize a deep theme in the book. In one sense this is a political novel with emphasis on the Revolution, the Spanish Civil War, the Macarthy period in the USA, the massacre in Tlatelolco in 1968 and so on. Here Fuentes seems to be calling for an end to ideological fanaticism and acceptance of a plurality of attitudes. In another sense the novel illustrates Laura's quest for some kind of non-traditional (i.e. non-Christian) vision of human progress based on positive values of love, rebelliousness and sexual freedom, rather than on acceptance of the fall and human sinfulness. The ending of the novel suggests that towards the end of his creative career Fuentes, with however many reservations about the mystery of individual human destinies and about the ongoing prevalence of violence and injustice in Mexico and elsewhere, had achieved a more harmonious and hopeful outlook than earlier.

As we have seen, a conspicious sector of Spanish American fiction has been critical of the upper class and the national leadership. In the Indigenist novel or a work like 'Los funerales de la Mamá Grande', the critique was directed at the feudal-minded landowning oligarchy. In the Dictatorship Novels of Asturias, Roa Bastos, Carpentier, García Márquez and others it was directed at presidential power. Fuentes attacked Artemio Cruz as an example of post-revolutionary tycoonery. José Donoso (Chile, 1924–96) fits into this pattern, but with a difference. Even when, as in *El lugar sin límites* (1966) or *Casa de campo* (1978), he deals with the oligarchy, it is in terms of disintegration. This is in fact the central theme of his work as novels like *Coronación* (1957) and *Este domingo* (1966), with their picture of a decaying middle class clearly illustrate. To perceive it afresh, we need only compare Don Alejo, the rural landowner in *El lugar sin límites* with his counterpart, Valverde, in Eduardo Barrios's *Gran señor y rajadiablos* published less than twenty years earlier in 1948. But Donoso is equally interested in the disintegration of his own class, the Chilean bourgeoisie. What Blest Gana had earlier perceived as a dynamic, expansive class on the way to playing a hegemonic part in the life of the nation, Donoso seems to see as a class which had lost confidence in its values and social role. The paradigmatic work in this respect is his long short story 'Los habitantes de una ruina inconclusa' in *Cuatro para Delfina* (1982), in which a middle-aged, middle-class couple allow themselves to fall under the spell of the life style of a group of beggars and street-people, a fascination which leads them to their death.

But Donoso is not primarily a social novelist, and he has complained about criticism which categorizes him in that way. Indeed, if one wanted to choose a short novel which illustrates the way the Boom writers were able to engraft more universal levels of meaning onto the traditional social novel, *El lugar sin límites* would provide an excellent example. For that reason it it proposed to glance at it here. Plainly, one of its primary themes is social: that of class mobility in early mid-twentieth-century Chile and the shift of social allegiances in the countryside. But equally clearly the novel is about human (sexual) identity and ambiguity, and in addition offers grounds for a religious/metaphysical interpretation, in terms of man's rebellion against God. The critical question is how the social observation and the symbolic vision mesh together.

The specifically Chilean aspect of the novel is concerned with how the myth of a benevolent landowning oligarchy (with political connections), already wearing thin, is challenged by the outlook of a new managerial class. Don Alejo, the local landowner and former politician, old and ill, is associated with the railway, now obsolete and in decay, which he had had built in order to facilitate the marketing of his wine. The new commercial middle class is represented by Octavio, who owns a service station on the nearby highway, which is not under Alejo's control or influence and does not traverse his land. Symbolically, the future (road transport) does not pass through the old oligarchy's power base. Octavio owes Alejo nothing and is quite prepared and able to defy his wishes. Between Octavio and Alejo is positioned Pancho, Octavio's brother-in-law, a lorry owner-driver, who stands in a client relationship with Alejo. The latter has provided him with a humiliatingly unsecured loan to buy his lorry. At the beginning of chapter eight Octavio unsuccessfully tries to convince Pancho that his dependency on Alejo is purely economic. We recognize that in fact it is psychological; he experiences a kind of mental servitude, based on his social inferiority and acceptance of the Alejo myth, which he is unable to cast off. Even more dependent is Alejo's semi-feudal serf, Don Céspedes, while only slightly less subject to his apparent all-powerfulness are La Japonesita, the local brothel madame, and her father, a homosexual entertainer who lives with her in the whorehouse. At this level, what we have is a quite clear-cut class-conflict situation, in which a new commercial bourgeoisie is emerging in competition with the old landed proprietors. Any interpretation of *El lugar sin límites* in these terms (which are foregrounded, for example, by Achugar and Vidal)[14] is, of course, completely valid.

However, if this is the basic interpretation, why is the principal character the homosexual Manuela? And what about the novel's mythical sub-structure, which, as Moreno Turner points out in a valuable article,[15] is based (from the epigraph onwards) on the notion of rebellion against God, man's pact with the devil and earthly reality as hell? We should also notice that *El lugar sin límites* was based on a section of *El obsceno pájaro de la noche* (1970), which is far from being a social novel. Manuela's homosexuality is the central symbol here of ambiguity, both of human identity and, up to a point, of reality as a whole. Manuela does not know who s/he is. Is 'she' a woman who has generated a child by another woman? Is 'he' a man, merely because he has male genitalia even though in every other important respect 'he' is feminine? This is much more than mere social ambivalence, as Achugar would have it. It is reinforced by the fact that La Japonesita is described in chapter two as 'pura ambigüedad' (a virgin who runs a brothel!), while Pancho evolves from ostentatious *machismo* to the gradual manifestation of his latent attraction to Manuela. All this implies, in Quinteros's view, a reflection of a lack of unity in the human personality and even, as McMurray argues, the total ambiguity of the human condition.[16] A possible objection is that this last is subject to Donoso's presentation of it as hellish. To call the world hellish is not to make an ambiguous statement. Yet, on the one hand, we view reality through the personality and, on the other, that reality may be seen as hellish precisely because it is ambiguous; lacking that order which Donoso, along with so many other writers mentioned here, from Borges to Valenzuela, longs for. It is this shift from social considerations to preoccupation with the wider human condition which marks this novel as a typical Boom narrative.

The main setting of *El lugar sin límites* is La Japonesita's squalid brothel. As in Onetti's *Juntacadáveres* and Vargas Llosa's *La casa verde*, and elsewhere, the brothel symbolizes a degraded reality: exploitation of the weak, self-indulgence and immediate gratification, at the opposite extreme from the family home, the traditional repository of stable values. It implies a world

[14] See Hugo Achugar, *Ideología y estructuras narrativas en José Donoso* (Caracas, Centro de Estudios Rómulo Gallegos, 1979) and Hernán Vidal, *José Donoso: surrealismo y rebelión de los instintos* (San Antonio de Calonge, Aubí, 1972).

[15] Fernando Moreno Turner, '*El lugar sin límites*, la inversión como forma', in *José Donoso. La destrucción de un mundo*, ed. Antonio Cornejo Polar (Buenos Aires, García Cambeiro, 1975), pp. 73–100. Previously in *Cuadernos Hispanoamericanos* 295 (1975), 19–42.

[16] See Isis Quintero, *José Donoso: una insurrección contra la realidad* (Madrid, Hispanova, 1978), chapter 5, pp. 139–85, and George McMurray, *José Donoso* (New York, Twayne, 1979), chapter 4, pp. 89–107.

without an accepted moral order; in fact a world of inverted moral values. The orgasm of Manuela, in bed with La Japonesa: a woman acting like a man becoming pregnant by a man acting more like a woman, without love, in a brothel, for reward, symbolizes the overturning of all values, which are reduced to absurdity by this central episode. Moreno Turner rightly sees that the values in question are in the end Christian values. So that if the brothel symbol links *El lugar sin límites* to novels by Onetti and Vargas Llosa, the inverted Christian symbolism links it with Asturias's *El Señor Presidente* and with Rulfo's *Pedro Páramo*.[17] The weight of it rests on Alejo as a God-figure, who, however, is evil and not good; who creates only to destroy; who grants his favours capriciously and with a deliberately cruel irony, and who is losing his powers and is about to die. Pancho's rebellion, by paying off his debt and by breaking Alejo's prohibition of any further visit to the brothel, symbolizes man's rebellion against God, with Octavio in the role of the tempter. Pancho's last meeting with Alejo represents the expulsion from Paradise. But it is treated with irony. It seems clear that, in contrast to the view of Moreno Turner and Swanson,[18] who connect Pancho with the Devil, that he really represents Man. His rebellion is not a liberation; it leads him deeper into Hell. He tries to think of it as finding his identity, but the thought of Alejo's death terrifies him. If at the social level his rebellion only signifies a change of masters (since he is now in debt to Octavio), at the mythical level he has only exchanged metaphysical servitude for metaphysical solitude. Nothing in this novel is positive.

The second part of Magnarelli's chapter on *El lugar sin límites* reminds us that its technique illustrates the Boom's reaction against the traditional *criollista* or Regionalist novel. The way in which much of the plot is narrated through flashbacks within flashbacks by a shifting narrative voice, the method of 'mixing time, place and the words of one character with those of another', the lack of 'ultimate authority and reliability',[19] convert the narrative method into a metaphor by means of which the reader's comfortable illusion of an orderly reality is constantly challenged. Once more we see the Boom altering the vision of the writer's task and substituting a disturbing metaphor for a reassuring one. Even so, we can still readily discern a symmetrical structure in *El lugar sin límites* around a centre in chapters six and seven, which are situated in the brothel twenty years earlier. The narrative organization is clear and logical, with Manuela at the centre of the main plot

17 See my article 'Inverted Christian Imagery and Symbolism in Modern Spanish American Fiction', *Romance Studies* 10 (1987), 71–82.

18 Philip Swanson, *José Donoso: the "Boom" and Beyond* (Liverpool, Cairns, 1988), p. 51. This is at present the best book in English on Donoso's novels up to and including *El jardín de al lado*.

19 Sharon Magnarelli, *Understanding José Donoso* (Columbia, South Carolina U.P., 1993), chapter 5 esp. pp. 77–78.

and the Pancho/Octavio/Alejo sequence functioning as a sub-plot. The flash-backs are clearly signposted and create a pattern of intelligible causation underlying the events. Such reader-friendliness is abandoned in *El obsceno pájaro de la noche* (1970), widely regarded as Donoso's masterpiece. No justice to its baffling complexities could be done here. The reader is referred to Swanson and Magnarelli among others. The latter in particular shows convincingly how masking and artifice, the threat of the irrational, loss of narrative reliability and the undermining of the authority of the word, all latent in *El lugar sin límites*, become explicit in *El obsceno pájaro de la noche* creating a novel which is full of conflicting discourses and has several possible readings. It, and a small number of other baffling novels, including Cortázar's *62. Modelo para armar* (1968) and Fuentes's *Cambio de piel* (1967), as we recently saw, constitute the high-water mark of the Boom's deconstruction of traditional mimetic narrative. They point the way to further radical experimentation, which R. L.Williams amongst others sees as characteristic of Spanish American Postmodernism. But at the same time, as Donoso himself and others were to indicate (see p. 167 below), the strain they impose on the readership may well have been a factor which contributed to the rise of more plot-centred, more easily readable fiction in the Post-Boom.

Casa de campo (1978) has been seen as illustrating the end of the Boom. The date of publication is important, since the boom is often supposed to have run out of steam by the mid-1970s. Donoso has described it as his first political novel, and it can be read as another allegory of the rise and fall of the Allende regime. Hence, since it deals, like Skármeta's *La insurrección* or Vargas Llosa's *Historia de Mayta* (albeit less directly) with a contemporary Spanish American political situation, and since it is largely plot-centred and deals predominantly with young people, one could argue that it points towards the Post-Boom. But it is not yet mainstream Post-Boom because of the way Donoso here combines allegory with self-reflexivity, so that, for the careful reader, the latter threatens to deconstruct the former. But it only threatens to do so. The main impact of *Casa de campo* is produced by its political dimension.

The story is that of a group of plutocratic adults of the extended Ventura y Ventura family who, with a horde of their children and an army of servants move for the summer to their country mansion and then go off on a picnic leaving the children behind. The main juvenile character, Wenceslao, releases his supposedly insane father, Adriano Gomara, who had been under restraint in the mansion and, in the absence of the other adults, the latter leads the youngsters in what amounts to a social revolution. The process lasts a year, but only a day in the lives of the absent adults. When they return, with a group of foreigners, they restore 'order' but ultimately it is the foreigners who benefit. It requires no effort to see that all this could reflect what happened in Chile between 1970 and 1973. The adults would represent the oligarchy; the children, the middle class; the servants, the armed forces; the butler, Pinochet; Gomara, Allende; the local inhabitants whose work supports the family, the proletariat, and the foreigners, the North Americans or the International Companies. At this level *Casa de campo* clearly represents a reaction to Pinochet's seizure of power.

But, as Lucille Kerr and others have pointed out, and as Donoso himself made clear in his 1978 interview with Martínez,[20] we cannot leave it at that. For we have in the novel a persona of Donoso, who masquerades as the author–narrator at two different levels. At the internal level, this narratorial voice intervenes at frequent intervals to comment on the way the story is being told, in an attempt to manipulate the reader's reactions. Here Donoso is criticizing Boom-type experimentalism and calling for a return to the older realist convention, from which he believes the contemporary novelist can still get some mileage. In this he prefigures the neo-realism of some areas of the Post-Boom. But even as the 'fictive-author' here looks over his shoulder to the usable past, he continues to remind us that what we are reading is a fiction and not to be taken as referential to any possible 'reality' in a simplistic sense. This kind of deliberate ambiguity is deeply rooted in the outlook of the Boom writers and does not carry over into that of Post-Boomers like Isabel Allende. They write 'as if' fiction could be directly referential, often without troubling to remind us of their full awareness that old-style Realism is irretrievably a thing of the past. Donoso, in other words, here both uses a 'referential' approach (since the allegorical elements clearly reflect Chilean reality) and puts us on our guard against it at the same time. To make sure we get the point, he introduces a sequence in which the author–narrator steps out of the narrative and, with the novel under his arm, engages in an imaginary encounter with an interlocutor 'outside' the plot. This facing both ways technique is what situates *Casa de campo*, with Vargas Llosa's *La tía Julia y el escribidor*, as a novel of transition between the Boom and the Post-Boom.

Balancing the theme of disintegration in much of Donoso's work is that of the search for some kind of 'order' in reality, which will allow us to make sense of our experiences. This quest emerges strongly in the later fiction, notably in *La misteriosa desaparición de la marquesita de Loria* (1980) which, in Postmodernist fashion, takes a 'popular' genre, the erotic novelette, and converts it into a 'high literature' product (as Vargas Llosa was also to try to do less successfully in *Elogio de la madrastra* [1988]). The key element in the conversion is the introduction of the dog, Luna, who symbolizes the possibility of transcending the series of banal sexual adventures of the marquesita, which only lead to the frustrated question '¿para qué?', and reaching a world of meaningful 'essences', or, alternatively, to conscious acceptance of a world of chaos. As we have seen in the cases of García

[20] Lucille Kerr, 'Conventions of Authorial Design: José Donoso's *Cara de campo*', *Symposium* 42 (1988), 133–52. Z. Nelly Martínez, 'Entrevista: José Donoso', *Hispamérica* 21 (1978), 53–74.

Márquez and Fuentes, the leading Boom novelists, after the mid 1970s seem to oscillate between continuing the pattern of experimentalism and innovation of the Boom itself, which critics like R. L. Williams interpret as moving in the direction of Postmodernism, and moving in a more realistic direction, which is here regarded as characteristic of the Post-Boom. Donoso is no exception. After *La misteriosa desaparición de la marquesita de Loria*, which seems to belong to the first category, in his last major novel, *La desesperanza* (1986), he uses an overtly referential, realistic approach to deal with the return to Pinochet's Chile of Mañungo, an exile singer who has made a career out of committed pop music. The novel attacks the false order imposed on Chile by the military regime. But its title is explained by the fact that Mañungo and his eventual partner, Judit, can neither accept the authoritarian solution, nor continue to lend credence to the left-wing alternatives they had hitherto accepted (and in the case of Mañungo, exploited). Boom-type scepticism goes on prevailing. At the end of his career, in his posthumous *El Mocho* (1997), Donoso seems to conclude: 'nada queda. Todo se disuelve. Los proyectos fracasan.'[21] We can see why, by contrast, Cortázar, with his intensifying political commitment and emphasis on the positive role of the writer (in at least some of his later work and statements) was the Boom writer who seems most to have enjoyed the respect of the younger novelists.

'Si no hay una voluntad de lenguaje en una novela en América Latina', Fuentes once stated, 'para mí esa novela no existe.'[22] Repeatedly in the Boom period, beginning with Asturias's surrealist descriptions in *El Señor Presidente* and continuing through Carpentier's 'baroque' purple passages and García Márquez's linguistic *tour de force* in *El otoño del Patriarca*, we see language paradoxically playing an obtrusive role in fiction. Paradoxically because, after Borges, there is a growing awareness, culminating in the early Sarduy, that language is simply a system of signs capable of constructing its own 'reality', which may bear no direct relationship to the signified ('reality' out there). Yet linguistic experimentation goes hand in hand with formal innovation in the Boom and even beyond, as we see in the early work of Skármeta. The great monument to it in the Boom is the comic novel *Tres tristes tigres* (1965) by Guillermo Cabrera Infante (Cuba, 1929–). Set in Havana in 1958, that is, in the year before the triumph of the Castro revolution, it is a collage chiefly of reported monologues, the main 'speakers' being Códac (a photographer), Arsenio Cué (an actor), Eribó (a drummer) and Silvestre (a writer). They are all young and more or less hard up, scraping a living but more intent on partying, frequenting bars and nightclubs, making it with local girls and above all amusing themselves and one another, and sometimes mystifying the uninitiated, with verbal play of a very creative and

[21] José Donoso, *El mocho* (Madrid, Alfaguara, 1997), p. 152.

[22] Carlos Fuentes, interviewed by Emir Rodríguez Monegal in *Homenaje a Carlos Fuentes*, ed. Helmy F. Giacoman (New York, Las Américas, 1971), p. 54.

sustained kind. It peaks when we are presented with a series of brilliant parodies of well-known Cuban writers (Martí, Lezama Lima, Piñera, Lydia Cabrera, Novás Calvo, Carpentier and Guillén) describing the murder of Trotsky. These are attributed to their friend, Bustrófedon, a kind of linguistic *éminence grise,* who never speaks with his own voice in the novel, but who inspires their word games.

The critical problem with *TTT* is how to read it. Cabrera Infante himself was adamant that it is purely ludic. 'Literature', he writes, 'can *never* be experimental. Literature can and must be a game.'[23] Realism and referentiality are out. In fact, he disowned his own first book, *Así en la paz como en la guerra* (1960), for a time, because of its realistic elements. He insisted that, although the incidents described are based on ones that actually took place, and the characters are borrowed from life, *TTT* is in no sense documental. It is simply nostalgic: a comic recreation of the world of Havana nightlife and pop/youth culture which the Revolution attempted to sweep away. And yet, and yet . . . The *tigres* are, after all, *tristes*. Why so? There are a number of possibilities. Cabrera Infante himself has asserted that *TTT* is about friendship, which breeds betrayal, and that 'betrayal is the name of the game in *TTT*'.[24] This may relate to the fact that Silvestre and Arsenio both love the same woman, whom the former proposes to marry. Equally, the sadness of the main characters may reflect Cabrera Infante's personal depressiveness and deep pessimism about mankind, which has led him to declare that men are 'evil without redemption' and 'the cancer of the planet' (MacAdam, pp. 159–60). Peavler argues that 'the entire novel takes place under the shadow of fear cast in 1962', when Cuba could have been the site of a nuclear attack, and points to mentions of nuclear conflagrations in the text.[25] Swanson, despite the author's insistence that *TTT* is absolutely unpolitical, suggests that it 'can be read as an actively political text' in the sense that it reflects a society rotted by the Batista regime which Castro overthrew, but which his regime only made worse. Several critics emphasize the quiet desperation of Silvestre in the vitally important section 'Bachata' at the end, after the novel has been largely composed of failed quests and incidents which end on a melancholy or even tragic note. While the very last section of all is a monlogue by a madwoman whose vision is of a world falling apart. *TTT* implicitly criticizes both society and human existence. Like Cortázar's *Rayuela*, with which it has other elements in common, *TTT* appears at first

[23] Guillermo Cabrera Infante, 'Cain by Himself: Guillermo Cabrera Infante, Man of Three Islands', *Review* 28 (1981), 8–11, p. 9.

[24] Guillermo Cabrera Infante interviewed by Alfred MacAdam in 'The Art of Fiction LXXV. Guillermo Cabrera Infante', *Paris Review* 25 (1983), 154–95, pp. 170–71.

[25] Terry J. Peavler, 'Cabrera Infante's Undertow', *Structures of Power, Essays on Twentieth Century Spanish-American Fiction*, eds. Terry J. Peavler and Peter Standish (Albany, State University of New York Press, 1996), pp. 125–43, p. 129.

reading to be scrappy and fragmentary. But Julio Matas has shown conclusively that the novel's prologue, epilogue and seven sections are carefully linked together and interrelated, so that they form a coherent whole.[26]

Cabrera Infante is, unfortunately, a *mononovelista*. None of his other works approaches the quality of *TTT*. The only one worthy of mention here is *La Habana para un infante difunto* (1979). Linked to the earlier novel by similar qualities of humour and nostalgia, *La Habana* evokes, in a linear, autobiographical narrative, the adolescence of the writer, who explores a city, slightly mythicized by memory, and plunges into a series of erotic experiences in which he hopes to find, as Cabrera Infante suggested to Rodríguez Monegal, 'una consolación por el erotismo – o una salvación por el erotismo'. 'Se trata de una persona, en este caso el autor, colocado en una serie de situaciones peligrosas, no tanto para la vida como para el ser', Cabrera Infante went on, 'y que siempre es salvado de una manera o de otra por la intervención del amor.'[27] This, at least was the original intention in this curious *Bildungsroman*. But, in the end, the theme which the author seems to allude to when he speaks in the novel of 'mi via crucis sexual' is less optimistic. Later he was to confess: 'the main theme of *La Habana* is not simply love but the pursuit of happiness across the empty space of loneliness' (MacAdam, p. 171). Many of the spaces of loneliness in *La Habana* are cinemas. As in *TTT*, 'pop' films and music figure prominently. This again places Cabrera Infante on the outer edge of the Boom and in close proximity, not only to Puig but, as we shall see, to Skármeta, who shares Cabrera Infante's joint interest in youth culture and salvation through sex. We should notice already, however, that it is not quite the same thing to incorporate 'pop' elements into fiction, as it is to fuse 'Low' literature with 'High' literature in a new synthesis, often regarded as Postmodernist.

Mario Vargas Llosa (Peru, 1963–), the youngest of the central group of Boom writers, was also its youthful prodigy, since his very first work *Los jefes* (1959), a collection of short stories about young upper-class Peruvians, won the Alas Prize in Spain, the first of a long series of literary prizes he has since carried off. Four years later his first novel *La ciudad y los perros* (1963) won the Biblioteca Breve Prize and at once gave rise to a number of differing interpretations. Essentially these turn on the question of whether the novel should be read simply as a critique of Peruvian society, of which the military school where the action takes place is a kind of symbolic microcosm, or whether we should see behind this interpretation the wider problem of social determinism. The two approaches are not mutually exclusive. The view taken

26 Julio Matas, 'Orden y visión de *Tres tristes tigres*', *Guillermo Cabrera Infante*, ed. Julián Ríos (Madrid, Fundamentos, 1974), pp. 157–86.

27 Emir Rodríguez Monegal, 'Las fuentes de la narración', *Mundo Nuevo* 25 (1968), 41–58, p. 54. Reprinted as 'Guillermo Cabrera Infante' in his *El arte de narrar* (Caracas, Monte Avila, 1968), pp. 49–80, p. 79.

here is that the emphasis should be placed primarily on the social criticism. What links Vargas Llosa to the Boom is his technical virtuosity, the innovative ways he finds to tell his stories. What to some extent distances him from other Boom writers is his almost exclusive preoccupation with the shortcomings of strictly Peruvian reality. By this means he largely escapes facing us with the dilemma we mentioned in regard to García Márquez's *Cien años de soledad*: if we are uncertain about the reality outside ourselves, or about our own reality, how can we justify social criticism? Vargas Llosa has frequently referred in essays and interviews to the indeterminacy of reality, but, right up to *Pantaleón y las visitadoras* and even beyond, his fictional work has been firmly anchored to referentiality. This is the case with *La ciudad y los perros*. The novel deals with a group of cadets at a military school in Lima. A set of exam questions is stolen; one of the cadets reveals the name of the culprit to the authorities and is murdered by the central character, el Jaguar, who is not brought to book. The real victim, apart from the murdered cadet, is one of the Instructors, Gamboa, who tries to do the decent thing and suffers accordingly. In essence a group of cadets who have no conception of a personal or collective honour code and set out to beat the system at any price are confronted by a cynical, hypocritical, authoritarian group of officers who run the school. It is not difficult to extend the pattern to Peruvian society as a whole.What brought *La ciudad y los perros* huge critical success, and caused it to be hailed by Donoso as one of the first novels to put the Boom on the map, four years before the furore surrounding *Cien años de soledad*, was the strikingly original narrative technique. Abandoning linear plot-structure, Vargas Llosa rotates the narrative voice among sundry characters, interweaves past and present, and shifts the scene from inside to outside the Academy. The reader cannot be passive. S/he has to be alert and ready to work at making connections. This is crucial to much of Boom fiction, in contrast to some Post-Boom fiction, which has returned to greater reader-friendliness. But the point to be borne in mind is that the narrative technique here is designed to bring out different and sometimes confusing aspects of reality, but not to question whether we are programmed to understand it at all.

One of the problems with respect to Vargas Llosa's early narrative strategies is how far they are congruent with the plots. In *La cuidad y los perros* there is a good fit. The world of the cadets and their superiors is complex, much is hidden from view, motivations are not always clear and in the novel an effort is being made to solve a mystery: that of the death of the cadet who squealed on the others. The complexity of the technique reflects the reality which Vargas Llosa is exploring. In *La casa verde* (1966), which won the prestigious Gallegos Prize in Venezuela, the situation is different. Once more, Vargas Llosa is writing fully within the realist tradition. A sentence in *Historia secreta de una novela*, a lecture which explains how the novel came to be written, gives the game away: 'La "verdad real" es una cosa y la "verdad literaria" otra y no hay nada tan difícil como querer que ambas coincidan.'[28] The 'literary truth' which Vargas Llosa wants to get across to us, corresponds to the 'real truth' of conditions in the provincial Peruvian town of Piura, where he spent time as a boy, and those in the jungle on the other side of the Andes as he encountered them on a later journey. There is no issue here of questioning the writer's ability to observe and report such truth. As Gerdes argues, the technique which Vargas Llosa employs is designed to make 'a significant comment on the nature of reality', to be (as he quotes from Hirsch) 'an instrument of knowledge'.[29] Vargas Llosa's confidence, at this stage in his career, in the ability of literature to function in this way, is in significant contrast to the trend of the Boom in general, which was towards the Postmodernist view that 'reality' cannot really be 'known'.

The novel centres on life in Piura, a northern provincial township in Peru where Vargas Llosa had lived briefly as a boy, and in the jungle region of the upper reaches of the river Marañón. In both areas it reflects a cruel, squalid, violent, repressive and morally corrupt reality, with only rare redeeming features, in which the characters find themselves trapped (enclosure and imprisonment of different kinds form an important series of motifs in the text). Almost all the major figures are degraded or destroyed either by themselves or by a kind of mysterious evil determinism which Vargas Llosa seems to see as inherent in existence. Characters make choices; but they tend (as in *La ciudad y los perros*) to make the wrong choices, and are savagely and sometimes arbitrarily punished by life. Expressing this vision of the Peruvian (and perhaps the human) condition, are two major symbols, the 'Green House' itself and the river. Many contradictory interpretations of what the Green House symbolizes are in circulation. But what is it? It is a bar, a dance-hall and a brothel, hated by the right-thinking people of Piura, burned down by them, with the local priest egging them on, but quickly resurgent. It surely cannot be other than a moral symbol. Like the brothel-symbol elsewhere in modern Spanish American fiction, it stands for self-indulgence and immediate gratification, and as such it reappears in *Pantaleón y las visitadoras*. It is the central, judgemental, symbol here of Vargas Llosa's ongoing critique of his fellow-countrymen. The river, as is common, stands for the river of time, down which the morally contrasting figures of Aquilino and Fushía drift towards death as the end of love, hatred, evil, goodness, all: an existential symbol alongside a moral symbol.

This set of five interwoven stories, with plenty of plot (in terms of action), exotic background, suspense, heroism, villainy, sex, violence and sensationalism is written with an extreme attention to narrative method. In most novels

[28] Mario Vargas Llosa, *Historia secreta de una novela* (Barcelona, Tusquets, 1971), p. 66.

[29] Dick Gerdes, *Mario Vargas Llosa* (Boston, Twayne, 1985), p. 63. The reference to Marianne Hirsch is to her *Beyond the Single Vision* (York [S. Carolina], French Literature Publications, 1981), p .4.

we are conscious of 'dead ground' filling in between major episodes. Vargas Llosa has often said that he would like us to be able to read his novels as if we were reading Dumas's *The Three Musketeers*, with no dead ground to skip. The systematic interweaving of strands of narrative, separated in time and place, is designed to switch our attention from one to another before we have time to become bored. The critical question, however, is not so much whether we can see behind this technique a commentary on the nature of reality itself and on our understanding of it, as whether there is a functional relationship between one strand and another. Is the distribution of the episodes 'inevitable'? Would it make a difference if they were distributed another way? In fact, what we see in much of the novel is not relevance (of the episodes to one another) but regularity: the strands following one another in a given order. Reality is certainly not as regular as that. What we discern is a certain comparativeness, an effect of intensification of the same themes of squalor, self-destruction and degradation.

These themes recur in the short *Los cachorros* (1967), which deals with the cruelty and *machismo* of Peruvian society, which come to the surface when a boy is accidentally castrated, and in Vargas Llosa's next block-buster novel *Conversación en la catedral* (1969), whose theme is the creeping degradation of Peruvian society under the dictatorship of Odría (1948–56). The starting point of the novel is a four-hour conversation in a bar between Santiago Zavala, a downwardly mobile middle-class journalist, alienated specifically from the world of his father, a wealthy businessman, and more generally from the society which his job compels him to observe, and Ambrosio Pardo, one of the black underclass. In a series of flashbacks, the two men evoke the financial, political and moral corruption of Peruvian society under Odría from top to bottom. One of the most crucial symbolic patterns of this corruption is created by the sexual lives and fantasies of sundry characters. The relevant episodes include the traumatic discovery by Zavalita that his father is a passive homosexual whose lover was Ambrosio, symbolizing the utilization and corruption of the lower class by the upper one, for its own selfish and degrading gratification. Another important aspect of the novel is the contrast between the futile rebellion of Zavalita against his class-background and privileges, which merely pushes him down into the amorphous, powerless white-collar category, and the rise of the cynical and voyeuristic Cayo Bermúdez from humble beginnings to ministerial rank. Once more the narrative technique is that of a highly complex collage of voices and incidents working outwards from the initial conversation, which, as Oviedo has shown, produces a pyramidal effect of which the conversation itself is in a sense the tip. Martín, for his part, has shown how, inside the frame of the conversation, there are two main foci of narrative: one centred on Don Fermín, Zavalita's father, and the other on the life-story of la Musa, whose murder, in the exact centre of the novel, provides a source of dramatic interest which prevents the plot from flagging.[30] Interestingly, Antonio Skármeta, a leading Post-Boom novelist and commentator, made *Conversación en la catedral* the target of criticism, suggesting that Zavalita offered the wrong model. 'En general,' he wrote in 1975, 'los jóvenes [escritores] que vibran en tonalidades políticas, han encontrado en la inutilidad, escepticismo, cobardía, superintelectualización del Zavalita de *Conversación en la catedral* de Vargas Llosa el modelo paradigmático del personaje en *affaires* políticos'.[31] The remark illustrates the difference between the political scepticism of most of the Boom writers and the greater sense of politico-social commitment we find in the Post-Boom.

A curious feature of modern Spanish American fiction is the almost total absence of humour. Where is the great comic novel of the nineteenth century (or the first half of the twentieth) in Spanish America? Even Borges, who helped to break the grip of excessive solemnity, had doubts about the role of humour in fiction. Vargas Llosa changed his mind on the subject around the beginning of the 1970s. The result was the hilarious *Pantaleón y las visitadoras* (1973) which is about how a rather ingenuous young army officer is ordered to set up a peripatetic brothel for the use of troops stationed out in the wilds, and turns it into the most efficient unit in the Peruvian armed services. McMurray makes a certain amount of play with the notion of metaphysical absurdity underlying Panta's ludicrous activities.[32] But there is no need for this. The key to Panta's character is his admission: 'Yo necesito tener jefes. Si no tuviera, no sabría qué hacer, el mundo se me vendría abajo.'[33] The object of the humour and irony in *Pantaleón y las visitadoras* is primarily to satirize the blind, roboticized dedication of Panta to carrying out his orders without stopping to think where that might lead. The source of the comedy is the discrepancy between his maniacal efficiency and the aim in view. The first theme of the novel is thus the danger to society implicit in the empowering of hyper-efficient but morally irresponsible figures like Panta. The second theme towards which the satire is directed is the hypocrisy of the three great institutions on which Peruvian society rests, the church, the army and the media. The novel reaches a superb climax in which, as Panta pays the price of his folly, all those involved in censuring him are in bed with his collection of whores.

The most basic irony in *Pantaleón y las visitadoras*, however, derives

[30] Cf. José Miguel Oviedo, *Mario Vargas Llosa, la invención de una realidad*, 3rd edn (Barcelona, Seix Barral, 1982), esp. chapter 5. José Luis Martín, *La narrativa de Vargas Llosa* (Madrid, Gredos, 1974), esp. chapter 6.

[31] Antonio Skármeta, 'Tendencias en la más nueva narrativa hispanoamericana', *Avances del saber*, Enciclopedia Labor, vol. 11 (1975), pp. 751–71, p. 756.

[32] George McMurray, 'The Absurd, Irony and the Grotesque in *Pantaleón y las vistadoras*', *World Literature Today* 52 (1978), 44–53.

[33] Mario Vargas Llosa, *Pantaleón y las visitadoras* (Barcelona, Seix Barral, 1978), p. 294.

from the obvious parallel between the ever-more-proliferating brothel service and the equally ever-growing sect of el Hermano Francisco, a grotesque parody of popular religiosity in which the devotees begin by crucifying animals and end by crucifying the founder of the movement. With this, Vargas Llosa has found a new theme, that of religious fanaticism. It was to surface again in *La guerra del fin del mundo* (1981) and even in *Lituma en los Andes* (1991), while in *Historia de Mayta* (1984) it emerges in a different guise, that of ideological fanaticism. What is worrying is the way Vargas Llosa seems to present different forms of fanaticism as constituting a kind of mysterious epiphenomenon built into the Latin American mentality, much as Sarmiento thought that barbarism was. We find a similar notion in García Márquez's *El general en su laberinto*.

Prior to the often forgotten uprising of the *Cristeros* in Mexico in the 1920s, religious fanaticism broke surface in Brazil in the Guerra de Canudos in 1897 which figures in the famous *Os sertões* (1902) by Euclides da Cunha. Inspired by this work, Vargas Llosa revisits the historical episode, in which thousands of fanaticized peasants, behind their leader Antonio Conselheiro, held off the Brazilian army for months until they were overrun and massacred. In an interesting essay, the left-wing critic Angel Rama argues that Vargas Llosa reveals himself to be incapable of understanding the objective, class-based, cultural and economic conditions which gave rise to the rebellion.[34] But this is open to question. *La guerra del fin del mundo* is Vargas Llosa's main contribution to the new historical novel in Spanish America. As we have seen already, running through the genre is the theme of the comprehensibility or otherwise of history. Vargas Llosa is surely not unaware of the basis on which Rama's criticism rests. He simply does not accept that historical interpretation is that simple. For that reason, the journalist, who in the novel corresponds to da Cunha, is symbolically short-sighted to begin with, and subsequently breaks his glasses, which deprives him of any (in)sight at all. In an interview on the novel, Vargas Llosa asserted: 'I've been trying for a long time to show the limitations of ideas and reason. . . . Reality is always richer than the ideas which try to express it; that's what I am trying to show here.'[35]

In the same interview, Vargas Llosa asserted that he had mixed techniques which hark back to the mainstream of nineteenth-century fiction to describe the characters of the religious insurgents and their activities with others

[34] Angel Rama, '*La guerra del fin del mundo*. Vargas Llosa y el fanatismo por la literatura', *Antípodas* 1 (1988, Special Number on Vargas Llosa), 88–104.

[35] Mario Vargas Llosa in 'Mario Vargas Llosa le cannibale' (an interview with Albert Bensoussan), *Magazine Littéraire* (Paris, 197, July/August, 1983), pp. 76–81. The original French (p. 80) reads: 'J'essaie despuis longtemps de montrer les limites des idées et de la raison. . . . La réalité est toujours plus riche que les idées qui essaient de l'exprimer, c'est ce que je tente de montrer ici.'

which are closer to his own earlier innovations to handle the parts of the novel which take place in more urban and civilized surroundings. Enkvist and Gerdes[36] have both shown that, while the narrative strategies here are less obtrusive than in Vargas Llosa's earlier fiction, they are none the less highly sophisticated and functional. What is crucial, however, is to distinguish the explicit commentary from that which is implicit in the horrifying and fantastic episodes. Much of the explicit commentary revolves around el barón de Cañabrava, an intelligent and educated onlooker whom the author shows as the most lucid figure in the novel and whose words and actions (even when he rapes his deranged wife's servant under her very eyes) are designed to reveal much of the novel's message, both in terms of the inexplicability of events and of the triumph of passion, instinct and imagination over rationality.

Vargas Llosa insisted that the Canudos rebellion taught him to understand much that was still relevant to modern Latin America. The proof of this came with his next novel *Historia de Mayta* (1984), once more the story of a failed crusade, but this time very contemporary. One of the best ways to understand a major difference between the Boom and the Post-Boom is to contrast *Historia de Mayta* with Antonio Skármeta's *La insurrección* (1982). The latter, one of the few genuinely revolutionary novels in Spanish American fiction (in the sense that it applauds the success of the Sandienista uprising against the Somoza regime in Nicaragua), illustrates Skármeta's clear-cut commitment at that time to violence as the necessary midwife of historical change and his unquestioning confidence in his ability to explain why and how it operated in this case. Whereas Vargas Llosa, just as he had contradicted Da Cunha's rational, 'scientific-positivistic' (and racist) approach to the Canudos rebellion, now sets out to undermine once more any confidence we may have in the ability of the intellectual (the narrator) to make sense of what happened when Mayta attempted his abortive rebellion in Peru. What Skármeta asserts, Vargas Llosa, in true Boom fashion, problematizes. Mayta's attempted rebellion is based on a real-life incident which occurred in 1962, but Vargas Llosa puts it back to 1958 so that it takes place before the impact of the Cuban Revolution. On the one hand it is thus presented as the triggering episode of recent Peruvian history, which portended the horrific irrationality and violence of the *Sendero Luminoso* insurrectionaries. On the other hand, the pattern of investigating Mayta's past and motivation through a series of contradictory interviews conducted by the narrator is intended to repeat the message of the previous novel: any attempt to explain historical events rationally is simply a construct, created by selecting the evidence. But

36 Inger Enkvist, *La técnica narrativa de Vargas Llosa* (Gothenburg U.P., 1987), pp. 203–43; Dick Gerdes, *op. cit.* note 30 above, pp. 170–81.

this is only one – abstract – aspect of the novel, The other, explored by Boland,[37] is more concrete: the link between Mayta himself, a pathetic, ugly, flat-footed homosexual, and his tragically absurd political escapade. The fact that Mayta embarks on it partly because of his homosexual attraction to a young revolutionary-minded army officer, Vallejos, once more underlines Vargas Llosa's idea that the dynamics of human behaviour are not primarily rational and ideological. At the same time, by openly associating revolutionary endeavour with the polar opposite of what we might think of as the archetype of the revolutionary hero, Vargas Llosa is to some extent deliberately parodying the revolutionary impulse. For this reason he has been sharply criticized by left-wing critics who see him as having moved to the Right.

It has been argued that beginning with *Pantaleón y las visitadoras*, Vargas Llosa's novels in the 1970s began to show strongly parodic elements which were not present at the beginning of his writing and which indicate an ideological shift. An early sign of that shift was *La tía Julia y el escribidor* (1977) of which, in an illuminating chapter, Swanson writes that 'The political significance of the novel may therefore be precisely that it is not a political novel'.[38] The duality present in Vargas Llosa's fiction up to this point (microcosm/macrocosm in *La ciudad y los perros*, Piura and the jungle in *La casa verde*, the pair Zavalita/Ambrosio in *Conversación en la catedral*, etc.) reappears here as the duality Vargas Llosa, the established literary novelist and the *escribidor* Pedro Camacho, the churner-out of popular fiction for broadcasting. The novel contains ten such scripts by Camacho, each more deliriously melodramatic and incredible than the last, among which are interspersed chapters which purport to tell the 'real-life' story of the meeting of the young aspiring writer Vargas Llosa with his 'aunt' Julia (who later published her own account of the affair) and their marriage. *La tía Julia y el escribidor* is not only not a political novel, but even the social context is downplayed. What is important in the novel itself is the way the story of Varguitas's love affair evolves in parallel with Camacho's scripts and to some extent shares their larger than life features, so that the difference between 'real life' and fiction is deliberately blurred. Secondly, there is the theme of Varguitas's self-discovery as a writer, in part by differentiating himself from Camacho, though we can see a certain similarity in the former's tendency to introduce extreme situations into his novels. But of greater significance is the way in which *La tía Julia y el escribidor* once more shows a certain evolution on the part of a Boom writer towards the inclusion of Post-Boom features. Prominent among these is the incorporation of 'pop' elements in references to radio shows, the cinema and popular music,

[37] Roy Boland, *Oedipus and the Papa State* (Madrid, Voz, 1988), chapter 7.
[38] Philip Swanson, *The New Novel in Latin America* (Manchester U.P., 1995), p. 59.

together with 'low literature' borrowings, such as we saw already in, for example, Donoso's *La misteriosa desaparición de la marquesita de Loria*. But equally noteworthy are the foregrounding of love, with an apparently happy ending when Varguitas and Julia succeed in marrying, the plot-centredness and reader-friendliness of the novel as a whole, the use of an adolescent hero, the light-hearted humour and sexuality which permeate the text, and its urban setting. Coming as it does in the mid-seventies, right at the beginning of the Post-Boom, this is clearly in some respects a transitional work.

Vargas Llosa's fiction since *Historia de Mayta* has not provoked the degree of critical interest that his earlier work did. There have been two novels using Lituma, from *La casa verde*, as protagonist: *¿Quién mató a Palomino Molero?* (1986) and *Lituma en los Andes* (1993), both crime-stories in which the main link with the author's previous work is the way in which the crimes reveal, not just the mystery of human behaviour, but the mysterious nature of reality. Another pair of novels, *Elogio de la madrastra* (1988) and *Los cuadernos de Don Rigoberto* (1997), venture into the world of soft pornography. In the first a young teenager, Fonchito, seduces his stepmother, Lucrecia, and wrecks her marriage to his father, Rigoberto, while in the second he brings them back together by fabricating a series of anonymous letters from each to the other. They remind us of the role often attributed to pornography in Postmodernism, and at the same time can readily be related to the theme of son versus father, so insightfully explored in Vargas Llosa's work by Boland. The problem they present to critics is the lack of a convincing psychological dimension in the characters. In the second novel Fonchito shows a sick insight far beyond his years, while the author rings the changes on a series of erotic situations, real or imaginary, involving Rigoberto and Lucrecia. The key, so far as there is one, is to be found in chapter eight of *Los cuadernos de Don Rigoberto* in which Rigoberto attempts to rationalize his carnal obsessions without convincing us that his outlook is anything but immature. The importance of these two novels has to do chiefly with the way in which they illustrate afresh the tendency of the Boom to privilege sex over love.

More important was *El hablador* (1987) which tells the story of Saúl Zuratas, 'Mascarita', a Peruvian of partly Jewish origin, who was marginalized by a disfiguring birth-mark. In the novel he goes to live with the Machiguenga Indians and becomes their tribal storyteller and in a sense the repository and transmitter of their oral culture. The novel functions at the literary level as a kind of allegory of the role of the literary artist in society, his/her cultural importance and the shift of identity (and discovery of a truer identity) that goes with storytelling. At the same time the novel reproposes the problem of the relation of 'real' and 'literary' reality as Mascarita both re-tells and modifies through his own culture the stories which are the tribe's heritage. Nor, as Geddes reminds us, must we ever overlook the fact that the stories in question are in fact constructs created by the narrator of the novel, that is, ultimately by Vargas Llosa.[39] Once more we notice the typical dualism of Vargas Llosa's novels. In this case the fact that the novel is narrated from one of the centres of Western culture, Florence, but deals with an aboriginal community in America. At another level, the novel deals with the preservation of cultural identity in the modern global village, a problem shared by all Western countries, but one which is particularly relevant to the Third World and to marginalized cultures like those of native tribes.

In 2000 Vargas Llosa published what may turn out to be the last of the major 'Dictatorship Novels' by Boom writers, *La fiesta del chivo*, on the final phase of the regime of Rafael Trujillo in the Dominican Republic and his assassination in 1961. The novel descends directly from Asturias's *El Señor Presidente*, with Trujillo as the omnipotent tyrant, a cynical hypocrite, suspicious and implacable, convinced that he alone has lifted the country from 'African' backwardness and the threat of infiltration by the Haitian blacks. He is supported by Johnny Abbes, the disgustingly ugly and sadistic head of his Intelligence Service, by the 'clan privilegiado e intocable'[40] composed of his corrupt, selfish and greedily irresponsible family members, and by a shifting group of utterly servile (and, worse still, adoring) politicos who blindly carry out his bidding. The novel begins with the return to Ciudad Trujillo of Urania Cabral, the daughter of the President of the Senate under Trujillo, several decades later to visit her dying father. Now a highly successful lawyer and financial expert in New York, she would prefer to obliterate from her memory the fact that her father had offered her virginity to the dictator after falling into disgrace. Her recollections and those of others, including his assassins, blend into a series of scenic evocations of the last days of Trujillo and the failure of the coup intended to follow his death. A key figure is one of his killers, Tony Imbert, originally an uncritical admirer of Trujillo's achievements on behalf of the Dominican Republic. But now:

> Ya no recordaba cómo empezó aquello, las primeras dudas, conjeturas, discrepancias, que lo llevaron a preguntarse si en verdad todo iba tan bien, o si, detrás de esa fachada de un país, que bajo la severa pero inspirada conducción de un estadista fuera de lo común progresaba a marchas forzadas, no había un tétrico espectáculo de gentes destruidas, maltratadas y engañadas, la entronización por la propaganda y la violencia de una descomunal mentira. (p. 186)

The Dominican people do not figure in the novel except when they pillage the houses of those arrested after the assassination and queue up to pay

[39] Jennifer L. Geddes, 'A Fascination for Stories, the Call to Community and Conversion in Mario Vargas Llosa's *The Storyteller*', *Literature and Theology* 10 (1996), 370–77.

[40] Mario Vargas Llosa, *La fiesta del chivo* (Madrid, Alfaguara, 2000), p. 400.

hysterical homage to the dead tyrant. On the one hand the plot revolves around the already ailing dictator, his problems with the Church and the U.S.A., and his pathetic sexual adventures. On the other, it emphasizes the servility, cowardice and moral corruption of his immediate aides. To complete the picture we are compelled to contemplate the ineptitude of the plotters, the appalling tortures inflicted on them after their arrest and the failure of the military leaders to grip the situation after Trujillo's death. Worst of all, Urania discovers, decades later, that 'debido a los desastrosos gobiernos posteriores, muchos dominicanos añoraban ahora a Trujillo. Habían olvidado los abusos, los asesinatos, la corrupción, el espionaje, el aislamiento, el miedo: vuelto mito el horror' (p. 128). Thematically, this is an unexpected throw-back to an earlier pattern of fiction, which we associate with Asturias, Carpentier, García Márquez and Roa Bastos. But it serves to remind us of an important truth: the political tradition in Spanish America is not a democratic tradition; it is an authoritarian tradition.

In retrospect, it is clear that the Boom marked the coming of age of Spanish American fiction, characterized above all by the rejection of old-style Realism, by a new vision of the writer's task and by the exploration of new narrative strategies to convey that vision. 'Created' and/or 'mythic' reality tended to displace observed reality as writers lost confidence in their ability to report it. Ambiguity and fragmentation tended to displace 'straight' mimesis. Many taboos disappeared. Sexuality, long repressed in Spanish American fiction, overshadowed the old love-ideal. Universalism prevailed over the aim of conveying the here-and-now of Spanish America, even as novels continued to use Spanish American settings. While humour came to play an important role in fiction, the movement was imbued with deep pessimism about human nature and the human condition. The characteristic of Boom fiction have been widely discussed and there is now a consensus about them. The critical question at present is whether the Boom corresponds to Modernism, in the Anglo-Saxon sense, and subsequent fiction to Postmodernism, or whether there is a fault-line running through the Boom such that certain works mark the peak of Modernism, while others set the scene for Postmodernism. To what degree are such borrowed terms relevant to Third World literature at all? Ought we to think rather in terms of Postcolonialism? Do we need another category specific to Spanish America? In the last part of this book we shall attempt to address, all too briefly, some of the implications of these questions.

Further Reading

(On the New Historical Novel, along with Peter Elmore's *La fábrica de la memoria*)
Balderston, Daniel, ed., *The Historical Novel in Latin America* (Gaithersburg, Hispamérica, 1986). A fine symposium.
Menton, Seymour, *Latin America's New Historical Novel* (Austin, Texas U.P., 1993). At present, the main reference work.

(On this chapter)
Bell-Villada, Gene H., *Gabriel García Márquez: The Man and his Work* (Chapel Hill, North Carolina U.P., 1990).
Fiddian, Robin, *Gabriel García Márquez* (London, Longman, 1995).
McMurray, George R., ed., *Critical Essays on Gabriel García Márquez* (Boston, G. K. Hall, 1987).
(The bibliography on Gabriel García Márquez is vast. These are good recent books in English. For an overview of criticism of *Cien años de soledad* up to 1990 see Shaw, Donald L., 'Concerning the Interpretation of *Cien años de soledad*', *Antípodas* 14 (1992), 121–38.)
Vargas Llosa, Mario, *García Márquez. Historia de un deicidio* (Barcelona, Barral, 1971). Another insightful work by this fellow Boom novelist.

Burgos, Fernando, ed., *Las voces del kirai: estudios sobre Augusto Roa Bastos* (Madrid, Edelsa, 1988).
Sosnowski, Saúl, ed., *Augusto Roa Bastos y la producción cultural americana* (Buenos Aires, Ediciones de la Flor, 1986).

Brody, Robert and Rossman, Charles, eds., *Carlos Fuentes. A Critical View* (Austin, Texas U.P., 1982).
Giacoman, Helmy F., *Homenaje a Carlos Fuentes* (New York, Las Américas, 1971). Once more, with most of the best early essays.
Faris, Wendy, *Carlos Fuentes* (New York, Ungar, 1983).
Ibsen, Kristine, *Author, Text and Reader in the Novels of Carlos Fuentes* (New York, Lang, 1993). A competent, recent, well-documented approach.

Adelstein, Miriam, ed., *Studies on the Works of José Donoso* (Lampeter, Edwin Mellen Press, 1990). Valid, but read Swanson and Magnarelli first.

Feal, Rosemany Geisdorfer, *Novel Lives. The Fictional Autobiographies of Guillermo Cabrera Infante and Mario Vargas Llosa* (Chapel Hill, North Carolina U.P., 1986). An original comparative approach.
Nelson, Ardis L., *Cabrera Infante in the Menippean Tradition* (Newark, Delaware, Juan de la Cuesta, 1983). Puts him in the tradition of Petronius and Sterne.

Booker, M. Keith, *Vargas Llosa among the Postmodernists* (Gainesvilles University Presses of Florida, 1994). Useful for the Postmodernist debate.
Gerdes, Dick, *Mario Vargas Llosa* (Boston Twayne, 1985).
Rossman, Charles and Friedman Allen W., *Mario Vargas Llosa: a Collection of Critical Essays* (Austin, Texas U.P., 1978). Some first-class contributions.

Chapter 7

THE POST-BOOM

By the mid-1970s the Boom was beginning to run out of steam. A sign of this was that several of the writers associated with it began to have second thoughts about the experimentalism we think of as an integral part of the movement. The first to voice them was Carpentier in two essays, 'Problemática del tiempo y del idioma en la moderna novela latinoamericana' (1975), and more bluntly in 'La novela latinoamericana en vísperas de un nuevo siglo' (1979). His call for a more politically involved, popular, even melodramatic kind of fiction was to some extent self-serving, for, after his return to Cuba he had moved in that direction in *La consagración de la primavera*. But over time other voices chimed in. Donoso in 1982 asked 'hasn't the time come to turn back a little bit' and, in fact, as we have seen, had openly changed to a more direct mode of writing in *Casa de campo* (1978). Four years later, in an interview with Raymond Williams, Vargas Llosa commented: 'We Latin American writers discovered the technical and formal possibilities of the novel in the fifties and sixties. The idea was to experiment with form and to show it.' But now, he conceded a shift had taken place. Later still, the Mexican Salvador Elizondo, along with Sarduy one of the two most extreme experimentalists of his time in Spanish American fiction, confessed in 1991: 'He llegado a la conclusión, un poco deplorable para mí, que ya no hay campo para los experimentos', and in *Elsinore* (1988) published a much more conventional novel than any of his others. Finally, and rather late in the day, Roa Bastos in 1994, recognized the need to write 'con una escritura más llana y simple'.[1] By this time, of course, the influence of the Post-Boom, with its emphasis on reader-friendliness, had

[1] Carpentier's two essays are both in his *La novela latinoamericana en vísperas de un nuevo siglo y otros ensayos* (Mexico City, Siglo XXI, 1981). Donoso's remark is in Ronald Christ, 'Interview with José Donoso', *Partisan Review* 49 (1982), 41. Vargas Llosa was speaking to Raymond L. Williams in 'The Boom Twenty Years Later: An Interview with Mario Vargas Llosa', *Latin American Literary Review* 15.29 (1987), 201–6, p. 202. Elizondo's remark is taken from Alejandro Toledo and Daniel González Dueñas, 'Entrevista', *Universidad de México* 484 (1991), 37–41, p. 41. Roa Bastos's words are reported by Aldo Albónico in 'Roa Bastos y el "Napoleón de la Plata" ', *Revista Iberoamericana* 180 (1997), 467–84, p. 475.

long been felt: Elizondo and Roa were simply acknowledging the *fait accompli*, as Sarduy himself was to do in his last works.

What this tells us is that there was no smooth transition from the Boom to Postmodernism, as critics who use the latter label indiscriminately sometimes seem to imply. The lure of the term Postmodernism is irresistible. For a country or a culture not to be able to call its major prose writers Postmodernist seems to be regarded as a humiliation and a sign of having been left behind culturally. But it needs to be repeated that many contemporary fictional texts in Latin America cannot convincingly be reconciled with any acceptable definition of Postmodernism and that we need an alternative term to describe them. That term is Post-Boom. I have argued that the Post-Boom represents a turning away from the Boom-type 'interrogative' novel, which tends to question our earlier assumptions about reality and the writer's task, towards the 'declaratory' novel, with less complicated technique and more engagement with the here and now of Spanish America. But before rehearsing the arguments afresh, we should pause to glance at the most extreme reaction against Boom fiction, testimonial writing, because it brings into very sharp focus the fact that literary sensibility was changing.

In 1996, Adelaida López de Martínez affirmed that '*testimonio* signals the final break with the Boom'.[2] This is putting it a bit strongly, but to the extent that the most famous testimonial texts date from the late seventies and the early eighties, the timing at least is right. Mainstream testimonial writing springs from first-hand experience and normally takes the form of eye-witness accounts of events involving real people and the actual participation in them of an individual who represents people caught up in a significant historical situation. Usually written realistically in straightforward language, *testimonio* is purposive in the sense that it is designed to uncover censored realities, to strengthen the will to resist, to formulate accusations against institutionalized violence and injustice, and to raise the reader's threshold of awareness. The hope is that it represents a form of empowerment of the witness/victim and is intended to contribute to bringing about change. Hence it tends to appeal strongly to the political Left, especially since the speaker or writer is apt to belong to an underprivileged or oppressed sector of society. Such writing is not unproblematic. Viewed from the perspective of a Boom-friendly critic, it may appear reductive and simplistic. Sklodowska concedes that *testimonio* generally presents itself in non-modern terms, to the extent that it does not incorporate doubt or question the validity of its own standpoint. Testimonial writing is often melodramatic, in the sense that it appeals to heightened emotion and to shared values which the reader is not

2 Adelaida López de Martínez, 'Dynamics of Change in Latin American Literature: Contemporary Women Writers', *Studies in Twentieth Century Literature* 20.1 (1996), 13–40, p. 23.

invited to rethink. It tends to lack the ambiguity, irony and humour which we customarily associate with 'high' literature.

It can be argued, on the other hand, that we receive testimonial writing differently from the way we receive high literary fiction. We are challenged to make an effort of human sympathy rather than to apply categories of response learned from reading Modernist or Postmodernist texts. Even so, we must remain conscious of the fact that we are reading stories which are 'invented' *post-facto* with an ideological purpose in mind. The act of writing itself selects and 'arranges' reality by its very nature. We have to remain alert to possible discrepancies between what actually happened and why, and the witness's memory and explanation of it. We have to recognize that the presentation of events is necessarily affected both by the writer's intention and by the need to set forth the events in an intelligible and effective pattern.

Testimonial writing is not a new phenomenon. There are plenty of diaries, for example, of the war in Cuba in the late nineteenth century or first-hand accounts of experiences in the Mexican Revolution. But the Holocaust in World War II and life in the Russian gulags produced new models, and anthropological writing, like Oscar Lewis's *Los hijos de Sánchez*, suggested new techniques, while the Cuban Revolution, insurgency in Central America, the Tlatelolco Massacre in Mexico in 1968 and the Dirty Wars in the Southern Cone gave the genre a new vigour and relevance. The Castro regime in Cuba deliberately encouraged it. An early text is *Biografía de un cimarrón* (1966) by Miguel Barnet (Cuba, 1940–), the reported life-story of a runaway slave who even took part in the Cuban War of Independence from Spain. Quite different is *Hasta no verte, Jesús mío* (1969) by Elena Poniatowska (Mexico, 1933–), also a reported biography of a working-class woman who had been a *soldadera* in the Mexican Revolution. Different again is *Nunca estuve sola* (1988) by Nidia Díaz (El Salvador, 1953–), a first person account of this guerrilla-author's capture and detention. The two most famous examples of *testimonio* are *Si me permiten hablar* (1978) by Domitila Chúngara (Bolivia, 1937–) and *Me llamo Rigoberta Menchú* (1983) by Rigoberta Menchú (Guatemala, 1959–), who won the Nobel Peace Prize in 1992. The first is by a tin-miner's wife, writing directly to other women about the struggle, not only of the men, but of their womenfolk, to organize themselves to struggle against inhuman conditions. The second records from the inside the appalling treatment of a Quiché Indian family in Guatemala and at the same time includes a defence of the Indian culture and life-style against the threat posed by modernization of the economy. Recent criticism has tended to question some aspects of Rigoberta's narrative, but it still occupies a key-position in testimonial writing.

There are plenty of other examples of resistence-narratives, such as *La montaña es algo más que una inmensa estepa verde* (1992) by the Nicaraguan guerrilla Omar Cabezas and *Tejas verdes, diario de un campo de concentración* (1974) by the Chilean Hernán Valdés. Closer to conventional fiction are works like *Un día en la vida* (1980) by Manlio Argueta from El Salvador, *Después de las bombas* (1979) by the Guatemalan Arturo Arias and *La mujer habitada* (1988) by Gioconda Belli (Nicaragua, 1948–) which, as Linda Craft has shown,[3] exhibit more deliberate artistic elaboration. But, whatever the degree of fictionality involved, testimonial narrative wrenched Spanish American narrative violently back to its long standing and perhaps central tradition of protest, specific *americanismo*, and uncomplicated acceptance of referentiality. It stands on one side of the Post-Boom as Postmodernism, with its continuing experimentalism and scepticism about simple referentiality, stands on the other.

In an interview with Jason Wilson in the mid-1980s Cabrera Infante, distancing himself from the Boom, said: 'I've always felt more comfortable, as a reader and as a writer, with Severo Sarduy and Manuel Puig.'[4] Plainly, this is because he shared with Puig a love of 'pop' art and the cinema, and with Sarduy a strong attachment to the concept of language as play. Cabrera Infante's statement situates him towards the outer edge of the Boom and close to the transition from the Boom to subsequent developments. With these developments Puig and Sarduy were closely connected. What we hope to show is that they were connected with them in rather different ways. The difference has to do with their respective attitudes towards the relationship between literature and reality, and hence towards referentiality. It is highly instructive to glance at the attitudes of a couple of well-known novelists, Mario Benedetti (Uruguay, 1920–) and David Viñas (Argentina, 1929–) who were contemporary with the Boom but who fiercely criticized it. Both did so, primarily on the grounds that the Boom writers turned away from direct observation of, and commentary on, reality, chiefly social reality. Benedetti lashed out at their 'horror a la realidad circundante' and Viñas at their 'torpeza frente al concreto cotidiano' (specifically in the case of Cortázar, who is accused of pointing younger writers like Puig, Néstor Sánchez and Ricardo Piglia in the wrong direction). Both writers tended to see the Boom writers as belonging to an elitist movement, given to producing experimental, reader-unfriendly narratives for a limited public, culturally depended on, and imitative of, European and North American fictional models, indifferent to the problems of their nations and their continent and lacking any clearly defined ideology. This should remind us of an important fact: alongside the Boom there always existed a stream of fictional writing which harked back to mainstream realism. As the Boom came to the end of its main creative cycle this kind of

3 Linda J. Craft, *Novels of Testimony and Resistence from Central America* (Gainesville, Florida U.P., 1997).

4 Guillermo Cabrera Infante in Jason Wilson, 'Guillermo Cabrera Infante: An Interview in a Summer Manner', *Modern Latin American Fiction. A Survey*, ed. John King (London, Faber & Faber, 1987), p. 316.

writing provided a major link between the pre-Boom and the Post-Boom. Symbolic of it is the fact that Gustavo Sainz, an important Post-Boom writer, readily acknowledged his admiration for Viñas.

To put it very simplistically, Puig and Sarduy, who emerged as important novelists in the late sixties, when the Boom was passing its peak, can be usefully seen historically as representing the transition to the Post-Boom and to Postmodernism respectively. By this time the characteristics of the Boom were clearly recognizable and were soon to be more or less well codified by Vargas Llosa and Rodríguez Monegal in *Books Abroad*.[5] With Puig's first novel, *La traición de Rita Hayworth* (1968, the year after García Márquez's *Cien años de soledad* had marked the peak of the Boom), came a challenge to the Boom's hegemony and above all to its concept of 'high' literature which so annoyed Benedetti and Viñas. Tittler has pointed out perceptively that Puig's problem was to issue such a challenge without falling back into the kind of realism still being touted by Benedetti and Viñas or into 'pop' mass culture itself.[6] He succeeds by continuing, on the one hand, the Boom's tendency to foreground experimentation and to explore new possibilities of style and of different linguistic registers. But at the same time, he moves deliberately away from what Giordano calls the tendency towards 'escritura irrealista' present in many Boom writers (fantasy, myth, emphasis on the ambiguity of reality) towards what the same critic calls 'lo referencial, una forma de realismo más depurado'.[7] This is a crucial shift.

The first two novels by Manuel Puig (Argentina, 1932–90), *La traición de Rita Hayworth* and *Boquitas pintadas* (1969), deal with commonplace people living humdrum provincial lives in Coronel Vallejos.There is almost no plot. The emphasis is on the frustrations (social, emotional and sexual) of the not-so-well-off characters, the male dominance and feminine submission, and the narrowness and constrictions of belonging to this hick town, out on the pampa, more than three hundred miles from Buenos Aires. Puig has insisted that this is 'real' reality, based on his own recollections. What is missing from this small-town society? Surely three things above all: real love, human solidarity and rebelliousness against the prevailing conditions. Puig leaves them out (for the most part) because his main concern is with social criticism and with showing how illusions take their place. In *La traición de Rita Hayworth*, the symbol of a narrow oppressive society is the machismo we see personified in Héctor, the cousin of the central character, the effeminate Toto. Puig's problem in the novel is to develop the contrast

5 Mario Vargas Llosa, 'The Latin American Novel Today', *Books Abroad* 44 (1970), 7–16. Emir Rodríguez Monegal, 'The New Latin American Novel', *ibid.*, 45–50.

6 Jonathan Tittler, *Manuel Puig* (New York, Twayne, 1993), p. 8.

7 Enrique Giordano, '*Boquitas pintadas*, recontextualización de la cultura popular', in Roberto Echevarren and Enrique Giordano, *Manuel Puig, montaje y alteridad del sujeto* (Santiago de Chile, Monografías de Maitén, 1986), p. 27.

between these two youngsters, without turning them into flat representative characters. In solving the problem he is able to add a convincing psychological dimension to his social critique. The title of the novel refers to the Hollywood dream-factory and its betrayal of its audiences by providing them with compensatory fantasies to offset the dullness, pettiness and often solitude of their lives. But while male oppressiveness brutalizes the men and degrades the women, we realize that is not only the latter who fantasize. Both victims and victimizers are compelled to seek psychological relief in daydreams. By the same token, both Héctor and Toto are shown as highly ambiguous. Puig's moral categories are there, but they do not make him simplify or distort character. Toto represents intelligence, sensitivity and insight, but also, as he grows up, malice, subservience, jealousy and feelings of self-rejection. Héctor, the young stud, has apparently adapted better to the environment, but in fact is depressive, emotionally repressed and afraid of any relationship he cannot dominate.

The bitter vision, unrelieved by humour, and the deep pessimism about human behaviour, which emerge in *La traición de Rita Hayworth*, are equally present in *Boquitas pintadas*. Once more this is a highly original novel both in content and in formal arrangement. Like its predecessor, it is emphatically not a satire, but an exposure of the banal lives of provincial young people. A major theme is the contrast between their acceptance of what Puig called the 'rhetoric' of love and passion, and their lack of the real thing: tenderness, mutual comprehension, self-sacrifice. The plot, which is much more complex and developed than in Puig's first novel, concerns the town's young Casanova, Juan Carlos, and his relationships with various female partners before he dies of tuberculosis. Alongside this strand of narrative there is another which concerns his more proletarian friend, Pancho, who in the end is rather melodramatically murdered by the servant girl, Raba, whom he has seduced and abandoned. We read *Boquitas pintadas* with the pleasure that most people get from listening to salacious gossip, though in order to get that kick, we have to work hard at unravelling the roles of the different characters.

When we do so, there is a certain temptation to read the novel as a kind of *folletín*, but Bacarisse warns us against selling Puig short. 'If [Puig] does highlight the standards of the society he is describing', she writes, 'it is in order to question them', and insists that if many of the characters put self-interest first and deny their emotions a suitable outlet 'it is the system that they live in that convinces them that this is what they have to do'.[8]

Once more, then, we have a return to direct referentiality. But the incorporation of 'pop' elements, the use of young, adolescent and post-adolescent characters, the colloquiality, the everyday semi-banality of the content and

[8] Pamela Bacarisse, *The Necessary Dream. A Study of the Novels of Manuel Puig* (Cardiff U.P., 1988), pp. 49 and 52.

the introduction of working-class characters like Pancho and Reba also point away from the Boom and towards the Post-Boom. It should be noticed that Puig does not use 'pop' material (films, radio serials, tangos etc) as, for example, Skármeta or Sainz have done, to make the young people they describe come alive in their 'youth-culture' context. Rather he purposely instrumentalizes it as a means of revealing the shallowness of their personalities and the paltriness of what they turn to in search of consolatory fantasies. This changes in *El beso de la mujer araña* (1976) which points forward to the novels of political protest by writers like Skármeta and Isabel Allende in the Post-Boom. The scene is a prison cell which a left-wing terrorist, Valentín, shares with an older passive homosexual, Molina, who has been convicted of corrupting minors and who is being forced to spy on his companion for the prison governor. We notice at once the radical difference in tone from, for example, Cortázar's *Libro de Manuel*, a Boom-type spoof of political activism, published only three years earlier. Here the tone is deadly serious. We have already seen how sexual oppression for Puig is the paradigm of all oppression. The sexual power-play which goes on between Valentín and Molina, initially corresponds to the power play outside the prison between the authoritarian regime and the people, even to the extent that the people (Molina) are partly complicitous with the authorities (the governor). But by the end we see that Puig is suggesting that it is possible to get beyond the dichotomy power/submission. As Bacarisse points out (p. 98), in the course of the novel 'the two men act as catalysts on each other' in such a way that Molina is unable to bring himself to rat on Valentín, while the latter, initially cold and unemotional, ultimately becomes more caring and involved with Molina to the point of making love to him. One of the major innovations in the novel is the way stories of 'pop' films, told by Molina to Valentín, are integrated functionally into the narrative. They both mediate the relationship and portend, through the choices certain characters have to make in them, Molina's own rebellion and decision to align himself with Valentín and his fellow urban guerrillas. At this point the two main thematic elements in the novel, insurrection and the removal of taboos about homosexuality, intersect. Both are aspects of freedom. In this openly didactic *novela comprometida* Puig is performing one of the most serious functions of the intellectual, that of explaining one or more social groups to others and raising the latters' level of consciousness, especially where the social groups in question (insurrectionaries and homosexuals, in this case) are objects of suspicion, fear and prejudice.

Morello-Frosch has described sexuality in Puig as 'oppressive',[9] and so indeed it is, in contrast to its role in the Boom where it is often seen positively

[9] Marta Morello-Frosch, 'La sexualidad opresiva en las obras de Manuel Puig', *Nueva Narrativa Hispánica* 5.1/2 (1975), 151–7.

as self-liberating and as a means of overcoming solitude and existential despair. In both *The Buenos Aires Affair* (1973) and *Pubis angelical* (1979) we see this quite clearly. The former deals with two intelligent and sophisticated members of the Buenos Aires creative intelligentsia, a woman artist, Gladys, and a critic, Leo, both of whom are intensely sexually frustrated, a state which the novel implacably explores. In each case the exploration climaxes in an unsatisfying sexual act, masturbation in the case of Gladys and forcible sodomy followed by murder in the case of Leo. The form of *The Buenos Aires Affair* is both highly original and at the same time not without banality. The novel uses a detective story format, when Galdys is abducted and sexually abused by Leo, but as in Borges and some recent 'high-literature' detective fiction (e.g. Mempo Giardinelli's *Luna caliente* [1983]), the format is manipulated. There is no detective and no real crime except the murder of Leo's victim, which is not central. In other words, what attracted Borges to the genre, its neat and tidy crime (problem)-investigation (discussion)-arrest (solution) pattern, which is a reassuring metaphor of rationality, is deliberately parodied and converted into a disquieting one. The banal aspect derives from the insertion into the plot of a happily married couple, which tends to produce a note of ingenuousness and sentimentality. *Pubis angelical* takes its title from the notion that angels are sexless. Once more the novel illustrates Puig's basic theme: a collision between aspiration and harsh reality. Ana, who appears to be suffering from a terminal illness, none the less still clings to romantic fantasies despite her situation and a previous unsuccessful marriage. A couple of contrasting interlocutors, Beatriz, an emotionally stable, intelligent feminist and Pozzi, a cynical, left-wing lawyer who attempts unsuccessfully to manipulate Ana for his own political reasons, represent positive and negative options connected with her state of mind. Alongside them two make-believe love stories within the story of the novel in a sense allegorize her deepest yearnings. For once in Puig, the novel has at first sight a happy ending. Ana recovers and at the same time discovers a new, less emotionally and sexually dominated identity. But Solotorevsky and Bacarissse both point out that, humanly, this renunciation is really a self-mutilation and that, on reflection, the novel's ending is hard to interpret in a positive way.[10]

Maldición eterna a quien lea estas páginas (1980) and *Sangre de amor correspondido* (1982) were both inspired by chance meetings, in the first case with a young North American intellectual rebel and in the second with a semi-literate Brazilian building labourer. Both are in a sense, like *Pubis angelical*, psychodramas. Larry, the intellectual, works his way through a

10 Myrna Solotorevsky, 'El cliché en *Pubis angelical* y *Boquitas pintadas*, desgaste y creatividad', *Hispamérica* 38 (1984), 3–18. Pamela Bacarisse, 'Superior Men and Inferior Reality: Manuel Puig's *Pubis angelical*', *Bulletin of Hispanic Studies* 66 (1989), 361–70.

series of sexual, emotional and even metaphysico-religious problems and achieves, like Ana, a certain degree of improved self-insight through contact with, in this case, just one interlocutor, Juan José Ramírez. But once more a close reading suggests that the ambiguities which Puig incorporates into the picture of their relationship undercut the notion that the strategies each adopts to come to terms with his problems really succeed. A key element in all Puig's fiction is frustration. It is prominent both in *Sangre de amor correspondido* and in his last novel *Cae la noche tropical* (1988). In the former, Josemar, the thirty-two year old labourer, evokes episodes from his past which have resulted in his current deep unhappiness. But, as we read, we become aware of strong elements of self-compensatory fantasy. What is perhaps most original about this novel is the social position of Josemar. Usually (and certainly in the Boom) working-class figures scarcely exist, and if they do they are normally unusually intelligent or used to illustrate social oppression. Here we have an almost unique example of an attempt by a middle-class intellectual writer to express the problems of a not-too-bright proletarian protagonist unable to come to terms with his life. To find an equivalent we should have to turn to Diamela Eltit's *Vaca sagrada*. The various interlaced stories of love, sex and frustration, covering three generations in Puig's last novel seem to confirm what is being argued here: that Puig is a transitional writer between the Boom and the Post-Boom. As we shall see, notably in the work and outlook of Allende, the Post-Boom tends to re-incorporate human love, in its fullest sexual sense, into fiction, in contrast to the relative absence of love as a possible solution to some of life's problems in the Boom. Similarly, comparing her fellow-writers to those of the Boom, Allende has remarked: 'Somos gente más esperanzada.' While some of Puig's work contains obviously forward-looking elements ('pop' and 'low-literature' material, youth-culture, *cotidianeidad*, proletarian figures, reader-friendliness), he continues the anti-romanticism of the Boom and its general pessimism.

Something of the same exuberance of language which we find in Cabrera Infante's *Tres tristes tigres* and which underlies Carpentier's advocacy of *baroquismo*, combined with a more bitter and caricaturesque vision, is to be found in *La guaracha del Macho Camacho* (1976) by Luis Rafael Sánchez (Puerto Rico, 1936–). The novel's *Advertencia* prepares us for the contradiction between the besotted obsession of the whole population of San Juan with the *guaracha*, a hit song, whose title is 'La vida es una cosa fenomenal', and the *splendeurs et misères* of the representative characters: the corrupt Senator Vicente Reinosa, his mulatto mistress La China Hereje, his wife Graciela, their wastrel son Benny and an older, proletarian friend of La China, Doña Chon, with whom she chats in the park where she has taken her hydrocephalic son, El Nene, to enjoy the sunshine. In contrast to the narcotizing, feel-good message of the *guaracha*, mindlessly belted out by the media, Doña Chon's *ritornello* is the far more realistic 'La vida es un lío de ropa sucia'.[11] All the settings of the various episodes in *La guaracha del Macho Camacho* tend to be symbolic spaces. The most important is the traffic jam in which the Senator and his son Benny find themselves separately, the Senator in his Mercedes and Benny in his Ferrari. Both cars symbolize the conspicuous expenditure of the corrupt Puerto Rican upper class (as we see in Rosario Ferré's famous short story 'Mercedes Benz'), but they are ironically immobilized in 'un tapón fenomenal como la vida made in Puerto Rico' (p. 27). The narrator, that is, hastens to explain the meaning of the symbolic traffic jam, but in such a way that his explanation, complete with its English-language label, implies the foreign origin of Puerto Rico's frustrating inability to move forward.

However, the actual beginning of the novel is in the flatlet hired by the Senator for his assignations with La China, as she waits for him. She is presented as naked and irritated by his delayed arrival. Though she despises and exploits his pathetic, middle-aged *machismo*, her own inauthenticity, symbolized in turn by her imitation jewelry, is only too apparent. A cheap tart, daydreaming of being a successful pop-star – her values and aspirations being dictated by the mass media – this 'stereotypical sensual *mulata* becomes the symbol of a colonized, even prostituted, Puerto Rico'.[12] Sadly, when La China, in one of the most erotic scenes in the novel, makes love because she wants to, there is no idealized contrast with the Reinoso assignations. The cousin who is her partner she used to masturbate as a child. He is presented by the narrator as a hairy thug, one of those 'que un pelo les falta para ser mono' (p. 87). On the one hand, the insistent references in *La guaracha del Macho Camacho* to the media are used, as in Puig's *Boquitas pintadas*, as a form of critical social commentary because of the way they impose patterns of stereotypical behaviour and outlook on a passive public living empty lives. On the other hand, the equally insistent sexual references (to prostitution, masturbation, fellatio, homosexuality and to Graciela's frigidity) are just as plainly used to carry implicit moral commentary. It emphasizes (like the brothel symbol in Vargas Llosa's *La casa verde*, repeatedly destroyed but ever resurgent) the easy surrender of some groups of Puerto Ricans to immediate self-gratification. In other cases (that of the semi-impotent Benny, his hysterical mother or the transvestite whom the Senator lusts after in the traffic jam), the stress is on the degradation of what in a different context would be a life-enhancing activity. Nowhere in *La guaracha del Macho Camacho* is sex associated with love or real fulfilment. As in Sainz's *La Princesa del Palacio de Hierro*, behind the ludic humour of many of the episodes, there is a deep negativism. As Schlau points out, only Doña Chon is

[11] Luis Rafael Sánchez, *La guaracha del Macho Camacho* (Buenos Aires, De la Flor, 16th edn 1994), p. 180.

[12] Stacey Schlau, 'Mass Media Images of the Puertorriqueña in *La guaracha del Macho Camacho*', *Modern Latin American Fiction*, ed. Harold Bloom (New York/Philadelphia, Chelsea House, 1990), p. 392.

allowed some measure of authenticity as a representative of an older, more traditional life-style and outlook, less adulterated by media pressure and self-gratification. But even she adheres to the home-kitchen-mother stereotype; her son is in prison and La China describes her implacably as 'una derrotá igual que yo' (p. 207). From her and Benny's parents, who represent two sides of the older generation, through La China, Benny and his worthless fellow adolescents, down to the children who torment El Nene in the park, the picture is of a degraded, dysfunctional society. Critics like Ortega and Perivolaris have attempted to suggest that this negativity is offset by the vitalism, eroticism and survival ability of some of the characters and by the carnavalization which accompanies the satire. It is hard to find this convincing. Parkinson Zamora is more correct when she writes that 'Sánchez clearly aims to condemn (not celebrate) a culture'.[13]

Technically *La guaracha del Macho Camacho* is highly innovative both in its intense orality and its visual and acoustical effects, its nimble shifts from third-person narration (sometimes in implicit dialogue with the reader) to a kind of stream of thought and to an openly cinematographic technique of sequences and cuts which we find further developed in Diamela Eltit's *Lumpérica* a few years later. Barradas rightly corrects those critics who regard the orality as directly reflecting Puerto Rican speech.[14] It is an essentially artificial literary elaboration not an imitation, as we can also perceive from the figurative style ('esta tarde se le enrolla en el alma como guirnalda de papel crepé' [p. 15], 'esa mujer parece que se iba a romper de tanto que se meneaba . . . como si fuera una batidora eléctrica con un ataque de nervios' [p.18] etc.) or from the fact, for example, that La China is made to paraphrase a scrap of poetry by Darío. The date of publication, just as the main creative impulse of the Boom was coming to an end, should not be overlooked. Sánchez belongs with Puig and Sarduy as a transitional writer on the edge of the Post-Boom or Post- modernism. Which of these terms applies? If we look at the combination of high literature allusions alongside the role of the pop-music *guaracha*, the fragmentary technique, and the open artificiality of the style discussed by Barradas, we might see *La guaracha del Macho Camacho* as Postmodern. Indeed Julio Ortega describes its technique as 'característicamente post-moderna'.[15] But as so often in Spanish American fiction, we are given pause by the fierce social criticism, in this case of Puerto Rico as a doubly colonized society (first by Spain, then by the USA) underlying the comic-ludic approach. Only if we are prepared to remove one of the main planks of the Postmodernist platform, the critique of ideology, can we

[13] Lois Parkinson Zamora, *The Usable Past* (Cambridge U.P., 1997), p. 191.

[14] Efraín Barradas, *Para leer en puertorriqueño, acercamiento a la obra de Luis Rafael Sánchez* (Río Piedras, Cultural, 1981), esp. the section '¿Quién canta la guaracha?', pp. 103–28.

[15] Julio Ortega, *Reapropriaciones* (Río Piedras, Puerto Rico U.P., 1991), p. 14.

regard Sánchez as a Postmodernist. On the other hand, if we are beginning to accept the term Postcolonial in regard to some aspects of modern Spanish American fiction, this would seem to be a paradigmatic example.

A good place to start for anyone who wants to understand the Post-Boom and the difference between it and Postmodernism in Spanish American fiction is 'Al fin y al cabo es su propia vida la cosa más cercana que cada escritor tiene para echar mano' (1979)[16] by Antonio Skármeta (Chile, 1940–). Along with his other essays and interviews, it offers a way in to the work of the writers to be discussed in the rest of this chapter. More than Carpentier's essays, 'Problemática del tiempo y del idioma en la moderna novela latinoamericana' (1975) and 'La novela latinoamericana en vísperas de un nuevo siglo' (1979), it spells out the need for change. It marks the desire of the younger writers to distance themselves from the Boom, without forgetting its legacy. The key here is Skármeta's criticism of the Boom writers' tendency to subvert what he calls (choosing his words carefully) 'esa realidad que por comodidad llamamos realidad'.[17] What this phrase tells us is crucial: the Post-Boomers write *as if* reality could be observed and reported, but with the realization that this is probably a convenient illusion. The whole problem of what might constitute the Post-Boom and what might be identified with Postmodernism turns on this uneasy relationship with 'reality'. The more comfortable writers appear to be with the compromise implicit in Skármeta's phrase, the more they can be regarded as Post-Boom. The more they tend towards sometimes obtrusive 'writerliness', towards prolonging and intensifying the Boom tendency to question and to deconstruct reality, often at some risk to reader-friendliness, the more they can be regarded as Postmodernist. It should be emphasized, however, that many contemporary writers (Valenzuela is a prominent example, as we shall see) are apt to zig-zag, sometimes disconcertingly, between the two. In such cases the critical question is where the main emphasis in their work lies.

It has been argued that the 'Dirty Wars' in the Southern Cone and the horrors of repression in Central America and elsewhere in the Continent forced writers away from Boom-type cosmopolitanism and back to the nitty-gritty 'here and now' of Spanish America, a move of which testimonial literature was simply the extreme illustration. At all events Skármeta highlighted politico-social commitment, alongside urban settings, emphasis on youth-culture, sexuality, exuberance and spontaneity, direct reflection of everyday life and colloquiality of speech as characteristic of his generation of writers. Interestingly, however, he also added fantasy (but with a basis in reality) and intranscendence, in the sense of deliberately turning away from

[16] In Raúl Silva Cáceres, ed., *Del cuerpo a las palabras. La narrativa de Antonio Skármeta* (Madrid, LAR, 1983), pp. 131–47.

[17] From an interview with Jorge Ruffinelli entitled 'Antonio Skármeta, la embriaguez vital' in the former's *Crítica en Marcha* (Montevideo, Premia, 1979), pp. 132–45, p. 143.

the high seriousness of theme and open preoccupation with the human condition which we often find underlying Boom fiction. He might also have added a return to love as a central theme, often hilarious humour, optimism and reader-friendliness (which tends to translate into plot-centredness, drama and even melodrama) as salient characteristics of the reaction against the Boom.

When did it take shape? A suitable date is 1975, the date of Skármeta's first novel *Soñé que la nieve ardía*. Before that he had published three collections of short stories, *El entusiasmo* (1967), *Desnudo en el tejado* (1969) and *Tiro libre* (1973). Some of the tales, notably 'La Cenicienta en San Francisco' and 'El ciclista del San Cristóbal', are good examples of early Post-Boom writing and already exemplify Skármeta's ability to bring young people alive and to mix reality and fantasy in a new way. They also tend to illustrate Skármeta's belief, which conditioned much of his work up to and including *Match Ball*, that in the right conditions of affectionate tenderness, sexual fulfilment can bring a kind of epiphany which reconciles one to the human condition. One wishes it were true. The collapse of the left-wing Allende government in Chile, which Skármeta had broadly supported, triggered a shift in his literary outlook. He later described his early stories as 'una literatura de un adolescente fascinado por el espectáculo del mundo e indeciso con repecto a su papel en él' and elsewhere as 'individualista y egocéntrica', asserting that he was shaken out of this by his experience of Chile under Allende and by the *pinochetazo* which brought it to a sudden end.[18]

Soñé que la nieve ardía is set mainly in a boarding house in Santiago under Allende and concerns a group of politically committed young people whose outlook contrasts with that of Arturo, a young provincial who comes to the capital to seek fame and fortune as a football professional. Skármeta uses the highly competitive star-player system in professional soccer as a symbol of the greedy bourgeois individualistic mentality which Arturo has to outgrow. At the same time Arturo's virginity, which he is desperate to lose, is presented as symbolizing not just his emotional immaturity but also his political immaturity. The fact that he cannot see beyond purely physical relationships with women stands for his lack of human (and, of course, class) solidarity. Arturo fails the various tests to which Skármeta submits him and finally is thrown off his team because of his selfish, primadonna, style of play. At this point he turns to his proletarian comrades for consolation and a kind of absolution. It comes when he finally scores with one of the girls, Susana, whose embrace symbolizes the warmth of worker solidarity. At the end of the novel he is not quite redeemed, but is on his way. Susana's role is extremely important. She is a strong, confident figure who breaks with the conventional presentation of women in earlier Spanish American fiction and

[18] In Carlos Rincón, 'Entrevista con Antonio Skármeta', *Caribe* (Caracas), 4 January, 1976 (the pages are unnumbered) and in Menene Gras Balaguer, 'Entrevista con Antonio Skármeta', *Insula* 478 (1986), 1 and 14.

portends other strong women figures of the Post-Boom, especially those of Isabel Allende. She reminds us that Post-Boom fiction incorporates groups (women, young people, workers, homosexuals, Jews) who hitherto had been marginalized and largely denied a voice. She also reminds us that henceforth Feminism will be a force to be reckoned with in the Post-Boom. But could such a highly ideological force easily find a place in Postmodernism?

Skármeta's next novel is the short *No pasó nada* (1980) – his contribution to the novel of exile. Set in Berlin, where Skármeta was himself now in exile, it deals with the tribulations of Lucho, a young Chilean boy who is living there with his family after they had fled from the Pinochet regime. A fight with a German boy followed by a reconciliation and the acquisition of a suitable German girlfriend figures forth one of the themes which is again that of solidarity and in this case getting past ethnic differences. In another sense the events constitute a rite of passage into full adolescence for Lucho, which gives the novel an additional dimension. Meanwhile his courage, forbearance and readiness to conciliate, are clearly intended to symbolize the moral qualities which, surviving defeat and exile, will guarantee the coutry's resurgence after the fall of the military regime. We saw, à propos of *Historia de Mayta*, that Skármeta's openly revolutionary *La insurrección* (1982) stands in sharp contrast to the sceptical and pessimistic handling of political insurrection by Boom writers from Carpentier (prior to *La consagración de la primavera*) to García Márquez, Donoso and Vargas Llosa. It deals with an uprising in the town of León in Nicaragua, against the tyranny of the Somoza regime. There is a certain schematicness about Skámeta's first two novels, due to their ideological thrust. It is still present here in the melodramatic contrast between the unspeakable sergeant Cifuentes, the representative of the worst face of the Somoza regime (he rapes the heroine, Victoria) and, for example, Leonel, her freedom-fighter boyfriend. But it is mitigated by the more ambiguous treatment of Lieutenant Flores, his superior. The main emphasis, however, is on the process of radicalization of the collective protagonist, a group of townspeople who sacrifice the integrity of their homes in order to allow a pipe to pass through them which will spray the local barracks with petrol and burn it down. Once more certain figures undergo an ideological transformation from apathy or collaboration with the military to heroism during the struggle. The novel ends happily, in contrast to so many unhappy endings in Boom fiction, with the triumph of love over adversity and of the townspeople over their oppressors. A positive metaphor of the human condition displaces the negative one characteristic of Boom writing. But, we recall that Vargas Llosa once observed that optimistic writers are usually liars.

Skármeta's most memorable novel seems likely to remain *Ardiente paciencia* (1985), now renamed *El cartero de Neruda*, after being made into a highly acclaimed film. It is at one level a kind of allegory of the destruction of love, happiness and culture by the Pinochet coup. For that reason the incidents closely follow developments leading to the latter: the run-up to the election of Salvador Allende, the election night, the award of the Nobel prize to Neruda, the crisis and fall of the Allende government and the *pinochetazo* itself. During the military take-over the hero, Mario, the young layabout who learns from Neruda how to be a poet and from love and marriage how to become a useful member of society, is 'disappeared'. At all three levels of the plot: the personal, the love-story between Mario and Beatriz, the artistic, the emergence of Mario as a poet and the political, the influence and fate of the Allende government, the underlying theme is liberation. His marriage and his poetry brings different forms of self-liberation for Mario, while Allende brings liberation from old oligarchic government to Chile. Pinochet's coup destroys them all. The novel see-saws between the exuberant fun of the first fifteen chapters, including plenty of life-enhancing sexual activity and the unravelling of it all in the remaining ones. An archetypal Post-Boom novel, *Ardiente paciencia* is plot-centred and reader-friendly, with rapid movement and non-intelligentsia-type characters, centred on youth and love. But above all it presents a tidy, ideologically explicable reality.

'*Match Ball*' [1989 now retitled *La velocidad del amor*], Binns writes, 'marca un cambio radical: el espacio y los personajes ya no son ni hispanoamericanos ni populares.'[19] This is true. We cannot overlook the fact that a number of recent Spanish American novels including this and the next by Skármeta (*La boda del poeta*, 1999), Allende's *El plan infinito* and Sainz's *A la salud del serpiente*, along with others by Donoso, Elizondo and Arenas, have been set outside Spanish America. This militates against the idea that fiction after the Boom tended to become more concerned with the here and now of the continent; but it does not entirely contradict it. What seems less true is Binns's affirmation that the novel is Postmodernist on the rather flimsy grounds that it is slightly self-reflexive and ironic. This is typical of the attempt to stick the Postmodernist label indiscriminately on contemporary Spanish American writers and works. The novel deals with the middle age crisis of a fifty-two-year-old physician, Papst, who gives up a lucrative practice in Berlin and a hitherto satisfactory marriage in order to give free rein to his sexual passion for a teenage tennis professional. As a result he undergoes humiliation and frustration and offers his account of the affair while in prison in London for wounding a younger rival. The theme is his fear of age and disgust with his daily routine, from which he escapes temporarily into the illusion that physical passion will bring him back to a more authentic form of existence. At the end of the novel he is unrepentant, but not ridiculous. He tells his story with endearing humour and flashes of self-insight, but we have the uneasy feeling that *Match Ball* illustrates a crisis in Skármeta's typically Post-Boom re-evaluation of love and joyful sexuality

[19] Niall Binns, '*Match Ball* de Antonio Skármeta: confrontaciones hispanoamericanas con la postmodernidad', *Conversación de otoño, homenaje a Mario Vargas Llosa*, ed. Victorino Polo García (Murcia, CAM, 1997), pp. 227–34, p. 228.

as the ultimately life-enhancing experiences. This crisis intensifies in *La boda del poeta.* Set in an island off the coast of Yugoslavia under Austrian domination before the First World War, its themes are love and death on the one hand, and on the other violent opposition to military occupation. Both are typical Post-Boom themes as we see from *La insurrección* or from Allende's *De amor y de sombra*. But now they are implacably parodied. The young men who rebel against the Austrians are distorted mirror images of the young, politically committed protagonists of some of Skármeta's earlier novels and tales. They are engaged in futile adventurism and commit useless atrocities. Finally they run away leaving their fellow islanders to take the heat. This is a burlesque of libertarian endeavour. Sexual liberation and the love-ideal are equally parodied, when it is revealed that the heroine, Alia Emar, is quite willing to marry for money, provided that she can lose her virginity with a young lover beforehand (it takes two tries!). *La boda del poeta* seems to mark a transition in Skámeta's work and perhaps may be seen in the future as indicating a turning point in the Post-Boom.[20]

If *Soñé que la nieve ardía* was an inaugural novel of the movement, its great popular success in the early eighties was *La casa de los espíritus* (1982) by Isabel Allende (Chile, 1942–). Like Skármeta's, her interviews and statements are full of useful data for interpreting the Post-Boom. Once more she leaves us in no doubt that she has taken on board the Boom's questioning of our ability to observe and report reality, as when in an interview she referred to 'el mundo *aparentemente* ordenadado, donde vivimos y cuyas leyes *creemos* conocer' (emphasis added).[21] A little later she referred to reality as chaos and to the artifice of imposing a fictional pattern on it: 'The first lie of fiction is that you're going to put in some order the chaos of life', and this is a lie 'because life is not that way'.[22] Yet in true Post-Boom fashion she insists that 'I'm always trying to portray reality' (p. 595), to find meaning and truth, and to communicate it in a straightforward, reader-friendly way. If, as Williams argues in *The Postmodern Novel in Latin America*, 'truth-telling' in fiction is more associated with Modernism than with Postmodernism, we clearly have to be cautious about where we situate Allende.

La casa de los espíritus deals with a long span of recent Chilean history by using it as the background to a family saga. The 'truths' it attempts to communicate have to do with the nature of reality, feminism, political oppression,

20 For a more complete account of the work of Skármeta see my *Antonio Skármeta and the Post-Boom* (Hanover, New Hampshire, Ediciones del Norte, 1994) and my article '*La boda del poeta*: Skármeta's Parody of Post-Boom Themes', *Language Quarterly* 49.1, 2001, 1–10.

21 Michael Moody, 'Interview with Isabel Allende', *Discurso Literario* 4.1 (1986), 41–53, p. 46.

22 Elyse Crystall, Jill Kuhnheim and Mary Layoun, 'An Interview with Isabel Allende', *Contemporary Literature* 33.4 (1992), 585–600, p. 598.

love and the act of writing, among others. Up to the pivotal ninth chapter there is a mingling of reality and fantasy, which is part of the heritage of the Boom and which corresponds to what we find in Skármeta's 'El ciclista del San Cristóbal', for example. Allende has explained this as reflecting the childhood vision of the narrator, who afterwards grows up and after chapter nine attains a clearer perspective on reality. But it is obvious from her later work that Allende believes that reality has a mysterious side and that she invites us to see beyond appearances and recognize the existence of hidden (usually benevolent) forces operating within it. More important is Allende's acknowledged commitment to Feminism, which shifts the balance of 'strong' characterization in her fiction from men to women. We saw an aspect of this in Skármeta's *La insurrección* in which the uprising is eventually led by a woman, Myriam. But Allende goes much farther. As Rojas puts it, the major women characters now 'constituyen centros de energía pulsores y propulsores del dinamismo narrativo, ginofuerzas que desafían el despotismo patriarcal, los prejuicios socio-sexuales, la dictadura y la represión política'.[23] With this goes a change in the depiction of some of the male characters, now seen from a woman's angle, who become more sensitive, tender and supportive. It marks a real change in conventions of characterization.

In making Esteban Trueba stand for both political and sexual patriarchy, Allende relates the women's struggle to liberate themselves with the political struggle for liberty in Chile. Until recently Allende repeatedly insisted on the duty of writers to embrace political commitment, and the second half of *La casa de los espíritus* shifts sharply in that direction. The main female figures in the novel – Nívea, Clara, Blanca and Alba – represent generational steps towards the latter's open commitment to what Swanson rightly calls 'the interlinked class, political and women's struggles'.[24] That the love stories of Clara, Blanca and Alba end unhappily does not affect the central role played by love in all Allende's work. All three committed heroines in Allende's first three novels reach commitment via collaboration with the men they love (which has brought angry comment from the radical feminist critic Gabriela Mora). Finally, *La casa de los espíritus* has to do with self-affirmation on the part of women through the medium of writing. As was to happen later with Eva Luna, Alba finds her identity and participatory role through writing, that is, by helping to raise the threshold of awareness of others, rather than through love and domesticity on the one hand or direct action on the other.

De amor y de sombra (1984) and *Eva Luna* (1987) are both in the end about the evolution of a woman to greater self-awareness and to greater social and political awareness. In the former, the process is triggered by a

[23] Mario Rojas, '*La casa de los espíritus* de Isabel Allende, un caleidoscopio de espejos desordenados', *Revista Iberoamericana* 152/3 (1985), 917–25, p. 919.

[24] Philip Swanson, 'Tyrants and Trash: Sex, Class and Culture in *La casa de los espíritus*', *Bulletin of Hispanic Studies* 71 (1994), 217–37, p. 229.

crime, the murder of a young girl, Evangelina Ranquileo, by the villainous representative of the Pinochet regime, Lieutenant Ramírez. This shakes the heroine, Irene, out of the inauthentic, pampered existence she shares with her mother and eventually causes her to abandon her equally inauthentic love affair with another officer, Morante, and find true fulfilment with the strong but gentle and tender Francisco Leal. Their involvement with denouncing the crime leads to their exile, but love is their reward. Once more we are in the presence of a paradigmatic Post-Boom novel, plot-centred, reader-friendly with no fictional frills, optimistic, omnisciently written and fast moving, combining romance with politics, focusing on likeable young people and incorporating different social classes. It is melodramatic in the sense that it appeals to accepted values rather than challenging them, except in its presentation of more 'strong' women. To Moody, Allende affirmed that it offset the violence and horror of the regime with love and hope. The contrast is rather stark. One wishes that Morante had been more developed, so as to give Francisco a run for his money and present Irene with a real emotional test-situation. But that would have introduced ambiguities which Allende preferred to avoid. Love and hope are also the values of *Eva Luna* which chronicles the transformation of a young girl from the lowest social class into a popular writer of a television soap opera called *Bolero*. As with Puig's *Boquitas pintadas*, a kitschy 'pop' element becomes an integral part of the novel. But the originality in *Eva Luna* comes from the fact that, as we read on, we become less and less sure that Eva's autobiography has not been contaminated by the soap opera. This presents us with a problem. The novel is once more overtly feminist and in many respects social, concerned with Eva's upward mobility, while some episodes describe her temporary involvement with a revolutionary group. But the contamination by the fictional serial, which extends to the (sometimes parodic) use of clichés and stock situations as part of the narrative strategy, ultimately blurs the distinction between the 'reality' of Eva's life-story and the fantasy of the soap. The heritage of Borges and the Boom is not so easy to slough off.

Like Skármeta's *Match Ball*, Allende's *El plan infinito* (1991) is set outside Latin America and is a quest-novel in which the hero seeks escape from a sense of lack of fulfilment through love and sexuality. But whereas Papst reveals the failure of his quest with a certain amount of humour and irony, Allende shows Greg Reeves, whose story is partly inspired by experiences of her second husband, Willie Gordon, as achieving, through adversity and wrong choices, love and reconciliation with a world that finally makes some sort of sense. It is hard to think of a novel written after the end of the Boom which more explicitly replaces the Boom's disquieting metaphors of existence with a comforting one. But Allende cheats a little bit. In *De amor y de sombra* the main characters challenge an oppressive system. In *Eva Luna* and *El plan infinito*, they work successfully within the system but they enjoy special advantages. Eva is a talented writer, her friends Mimí and Rolf are respectively a brilliant actress and a successful photographer. In the same way Greg is a trained attorney working, at one point, for a prestigious firm. The dice are loaded in their favour. Greg is Allende's first male central character. Born of an American father and a Russian immigrant mother he is brought up in the latino barrio of Los Angeles. This is not casual: one of the main themes of the novel (which Allende came to understand more clearly after moving permanently to California) is the need for what she calls 'blending cultures'. The other two themes are Greg's quest for love and understanding and the pressures on him from the materialism and obsession with personal gratification typical of modern American society (in Allende's view). His redemption at the end of the novel is part of a wider pattern of achievement of harmony (spiritual, emotional, racial and social) towards which Allende's later work tends, and which the tragic death of her daughter Paula (commemorated in *Paula* 1994) has not compromised. *Hija de la fortuna* (1999) is another illustration of the theme. It is basically a female adventure story set in the nineteenth century in which the heroine, Eliza, follows the man she loves from Chile to California during the Gold Rush. There she breaks out of all contemporary social constraints, but in the end fails to track down her man, who may have become a famous bandit. None the less at the end she settles down comforted by the affection of a gentle and supportive Chinese doctor, much as Eva had found comfort and solace with Riad Halabí in *Eva Luna*. Carvalho has shown that, underlying the plot is the theme of Eliza's search for identity, in which 'the growth experiences generated by [Eliza's] journey result in a renewed vision of origin and self'. The journey is towards re-birth, self-discovery and self-empowerment.[25] In the foreword to the indispensible *Conversations with Isabel Allende*, which collects and translates major interviews,[26] Allende affirms that her aims in writing are to touch a few readers, to plant the seed of new ideas in them and make a difference to some people's lives. To do this she has not hesitated to borrow from popular forms of fiction to reach a wider audience. The success of her work and the interest taken in it by academic critics seem to justify her decisions.

The re-evaluation of love, significantly missing from Boom fiction, but so visible in the novels of Allende, is also prominent in those of Skármeta, as well as of Sainz and Bryce Echenique. It is perhaps most evident of all in the two novels of Laura Esquivel (Mexico, 1950–), *Como agua para chocolate* (1988) and *La ley del amor* (1995). Not by chance the former, which had a runaway success and sold tens of millions of copies in thirty or more languages, is set in a traditional family home in Northern Mexico in the early

[25] Susan Carvahlo, 'Transgressions of Space and Gender in Allende's *Hija de la fortuna*', forthcoming in *Letras Femeninas*.

[26] John Rodden, ed., *Conversations with Isabel Allende* (Austin, Texas U.P., 1999), pp. ix–x.

years of the twentieth century. As a young woman Esquivel accepted the youthful rebelliousness of the swinging sixties and later identified with Joan Baez, embraced Feminism and threw away her bra. But, as she explains in *Intimas suculencias* (1998), she came to believe in her thirties that something vital was being lost which had been present in traditional patterns of life. She began to feel a nostalgia for a more stable past in which certain behavioural rites and ceremonies connoted a more harmonious relationship between the individual and him/herself as well as with the collectivity. The incorporation of this nostalgia into *Como agua para chocolate*, which combines a cookery-book with fantasy characters and a soap-opera plot, proved to be a winner. The romantic formula of love, crossed by adversity, ending in death, exerted its age-old fascination. We read of Tita, the heroine, prevented from marrying by her selfish mother, resorting to a kind of magical cookery in which food can kill as well as nourish body and soul. After tribulations and madness, she is united with her lover, but when he dies after a night of love, she follows him to the grave. Some critics have hurried to hail the novel as 'transgressive' and 'subversive', as in some respects it certainly is, but García Serrano is right to draw attention to the darker side of the picture and to the ambiguities within Esquivel's outlook.[27] The important point is that cooking here is a symbol. It stands for the re-establishment of a more holistic, caring approach to living. But, like all ideals, this one runs into to the harsh reality of Tita's inner frustrations and the external pressures to which she is subjected.

La ley del amor is a pure fanstasy, set in the distant future. Its theme (like that of Valenzuela's *Hay que sonreír* and Allende's *El plan infinito)* is the human quest for love amid the forces of good and evil. In the end Azucena, the heroine, triumphs over all obstacles. Even her guardian angel and his devil-adversary settle down to matrimony. Without being a great novel it remains one of the high-water marks of Post-Boom neo-romanticism.

Arráncame la vida (1986) by Angeles Mastretta (Mexico, 1949–) belongs with Allende's *Eva Luna*, Esquivel's *Como agua para chocolate* and Ferré's *La casa de la laguna* in the sense that it deals with the obstacles to a woman's self-discovery and self-expression in a traditional society. In the case of *Arráncame la vida* the situation is pushed to an extreme because the heroine, Catalina, at a very early age, marries the Revolutionary general Andrés Ascencio and automatically becomes a public figure subjected to the social codes of Mexico in the 1930s and 1940s. The novel is thus closely connected on the one hand with the grand old theme in modern Mexican writing: the failure and corruption of the Mexican Revolution, and on the other with a prominent woman's desire for liberation from suffocating patriarchal

27 María Victoria García Serrano, '*Como agua para chocolate* de Laura Esquivel, apuntes para un debate', *Indiana Journal of Hispanic Literatures* 6/7 (1995), 185–205.

restraints. The myths, slogans and official discourses of the post-revolutionary period are remorselessly parodied and satirized from the inside by this deliciously forthright and humorous woman, who, nevertheless, is forced by her fear and economic vulnerability to stay with her cynical, self-serving and unscrupulous husband, even after he has her lover murdered. Catalina herself is not idealized. Initially complicitous and later passive in regard to her husband's political antics, she can also be cruel, vindictive and greedy. She rebels only by having adulterous relationships. What liberates her is her husband's death (though she may have poisoned him slowly). Inevitably, *Arráncame la vida* has been categorized superficially as Postmodernist, for example by Alicia Llerena, who uses criteria borrowed from Ruffinelli which cannot be taken seriously.[28] The obvious reader-friendliness and referentiality, the transgressive feminist agenda, the love plot, the use of 'pop' music as emotional commentary, and Mastretta's own rejection of 'obscurity' are all Post-Boom call-signs. When Mastretta said to de Beer, 'I want literature to seduce and move me before it appeals to my reason and my obligations' and 'I don't feel like writing obscure books',[29] she was speaking with much the same voice as Isabel Allende. *Mal de amores* (1996), Mastretta's second novel, won the prestigious Rómulo Gallegos Prize. Its protagonist, Emilia, belongs to an earlier generation than Catalina and is brought up in a freer atmosphere. She is another of the strong, liberated women, popularized by Allende, making her own way during the troubled times of the Mexican Revolution. In the process she turns herself into a doctor, caring for and healing people in the midst of blind, futile carnage. Once more this is in part a *Bildungsroman*, following Emilia's life and her love for two different men at the same time. As with Esquivel's *La ley del amor*, what is basic is the central role of love. No less typical of the Post-Boom is the warmth and affection with which Mastretta portrays all the characters. This is human nature as we should like it to be.

[28] Alicia Llerena, '*Arráncame la vida* de Angeles Mastretta: el universo desde la intimidad', *Revista Iberoamericana* 159 (1992), 465–75. Jorge Ruffinelli, 'Los 80 ¿ingreso a la posmodernidad?', *Nuevo Texto Crítico* 6 (1990), 31–42.

[29] Angeles Mastretta interviewed by Gabriella de Beer in the latter's *Contemporary Mexican Women Writers* (Austin, Texas U.P., 1996), pp. 228 and 231.

Further Reading

Shaw, Donald L., *The Post-Boom in Spanish American Fiction* (Albany, State University of New York Press, 1998).

Bacarisse, Pamela, *Impossible Choices: The Implications of the Cultural References in the Novels of Manuel Puig* (Calgary U.P. and Cardiff, University of Wales Press, 1993). Examines how references to culture underpin his themes.

Kerr, Lucille, *Suspended Fictions. Reading Novels by Manuel Puig* (Urbana, Illinois U.P., 1987).

Gelpí, Juan G., *Literatura y paternalismo en Puerto Rico* (San Juan, Puerto Rico U.P., 1993). One of the few useful books on modern Puerto Rican literature.

Lira, Constanza, *Skármeta: la inteligencia de los sentidos* (Santiago de Chile, Dante, 1985).

Brooksbank Jones, Anny ed., *Latin American Women's Writing* (New York, Oxford U.P., 1996). Good and up to date, though necessarily selective.

Davies, Lloyd, *Isabel Allende. La casa de los espíritus* (Grant & Cutler, 2000). In the excellent Critical Guides Series.

Hart, Patricia, *Narrative Magic in the Fiction of Isabel Allende* (London, Associated University Presses, 1989). The best monograph in English.

Riquelme Rojas, Sonia and Aguirre Rehbein, Edna, eds., *Critical Approaches to Isabel Allende's Novels* (New York, Lang, 1991). Some excellent essays.

Ibsen, Kristine, 'On Recipes, Reading and Revolution: Postboom Parody in *Como agua para chocolate*', *Hispanic Review* 63 (1995), 133–46.

Glen, Kathleen Mary, 'Postmodern Parody and Culinary Narrative in Laura Esquivel's *Como agua para chocolate*', *Chasqui* 23.2 (1994), 39–47.

Lawless, Cecilia, 'Experimental Cooking in *Como agua para chocolate*', *Monographic Review / Revista Monográfica* 8.26 (1992), 1–72.

These are all helpful in trying to categorize and interpret this hybrid text.

Gold, Janet, N., '*Arráncame la vida*: Textual Complicity and the Boundaries of Rebellion', *Chasqui* 17.2 (1988), 35–40.

Niebylski, Dianna, 'Transgressions in the Comic Mode: Angeles Mastretta and her Cast of Liberated Aunts', *The Other Mirror. Women's Narrative in Mexico 1980–1995*, ed. Kristine Ibsen (Westport, Greenwood Press, 1997), pp. 29–40.

Chapter 8

THE POST-BOOM CONTINUED

When the dust settles over the Post-Boom/Postmodernism question, it may be that we shall remember this period in Spanish American fiction chiefly for the triumphant emergence of a phalanx of major women writers, whereas the Boomers were all men. Allende (Chile, 1942–), Luisa Valenzuela (Argentina, 1938–), Rosario Ferré (Puerto Rico, 1942–), Cristina Peri Rossi (Uruguay, 1941–), Elena Poniatowska (Mexico, 1933–), Elena Garro (Mexico, 1920–), Diamela Eltit (Chile 1949–), Carmen Boullosa (Mexico, 1954–), Laura Esquivel (Mexico, 1950–), Angeles Mastretta (Mexico, 1949–), Claribel Alegría (El Salvador, 1924–) Gioconda Belli (Nicaragua, 1948–) and María Luisa Puga (Mexico, 1944–), amid a host of others, to say nothing of women writers of *testimonio* narratives, all testify to this remarkable change. It is impossible to deal with all of them, just as it is impossible to deal with all the men. One can only make a (more or less) informed choice and hope for the best. Having mentioned Allende, Esquivel and Mastretta, who form a sub-group, we may pass to Valenzuela and Ferré.

Valenzuela's fiction illustrates the difficulty of categorizing contemporary writers. *El gato eficaz* (1972), perhaps because it was written at the height of the Boom in the late sixties at Writing School in the University of Iowa (where Néstor Sánchez, Fernando del Paso and Gustavo Sainz also spent time) could easily be regarded as Postmodernist in the broad sense that it reflects a chaotic reality by means of a chaotic narrative technique. Sainz writes of it: 'Su protagonista piensa y sus pensamientos irrumpen en la narración sin aviso de ninguna clase. Los sueños son verdaderos. La realidad no es real. Lo absurdo irrumpe. Y nadie puede establecer qué es razonable y qué es locura, cuál es el orden del desorden.'[1] Critics remain baffled. Like Skármeta and Allende, Valenzuela has learned the lesson of Borges (a family friend) and the Boom: '*what we call* reality usually goes beyond tangible and explicable limitations' (emphasis added), she wrote in 1993.[2] *Como en la guerra* (1977) has already moved closer to the Post-Boom in that it begins in a torture-chamber and, although it is basically a quest-novel in which the pro-

[1] Gustavo Sainz, 'Prólogo: La narrativa de Luisa Valenzuela', in Valenzuela's *Cuentos completos y uno más* (Mexico, Alfaguara, 1998), pp. 20–21.

[2] Luisa Valenzuela, 'So-Called Latin American Writing', *Critical Theory, Cultural Politics and Latin American Narrative*, ed. Steven Bell (Notre Dame U.P., 1993), pp. 209–21, p. 214.

tagonist, AZ, seems to be seeking some form of life-enhancing absolute, it ends (very ambiguously) with what seems to be an act of political commitment. Nevertheless, both in content and technique, *Como en la guerra* seems to be dominated by a sense of 'la irracionalidad que implica la condición humana'.[3]

But meantime the collection of short stories *Aquí pasan cosas raras* (1975) had marked a shift in Valenzuela's outlook. Returning to Buenos Aires after working abroad as a journalist, she was appalled by the state terrorism and violence around her. To Gazarian Gautier she affirmed that 'the book became a metaphor for everything that was going on [in Argentina] at the time', and that thereafter she was 'trying to be very much in touch with what we call reality',[4] now, clearly, a terribly unambiguous reality. This is what makes her primarily a Post-Boom writer. The most important result was the collection of stories *Cambio de armas* (1982), probably her most memorable work. The title story, one of the finest modern Spanish American short stories, is an allegory of Argentina under military domination. The heroine, Laura, an ex-urban guerrilla has been captured and tortured by a military officer, Roque, who now keeps her as his mistress under the influence of drugs. As in Puig, sexual oppression is the paradigm of social oppression. With great narrative subtlety and the use of highly functional symbolism, Valenzuela follows Laura's gradual recovery of memory, until, as the military regime collapses, she takes the pistol he teasingly offers her and . . .? The open ending reminds us that Valenzuela's leading position in the Post-Boom is due to her avoidance of the simplified ideological positions we sometimes find in Allende and Skármeta. No one has expressed this better than Geisdorfer Feal.[5] From her earliest novel *Hay que sonreír* (1966), which is about male domination but also about female submission, Valenzuela has steadfastly refused to idealize the oppressed or to demonize the oppressors. Her aim is rather to show how very often the victim collaborates with the victimizer and how both, as individuals and symbols of the collectivity, have a 'dark side' to their personalities which has to be recognized before it can be exorcized. This is what gives her work depth.

A more careful reading of *Cola de lagartija* (1983) than that of Díaz[6] confirms such a view. Like Santiago Colás and Raymond Williams, to whose

3 Luisa Valenzuela, *Como en la guerra* (Buenos Aires, Sudamericana, 1977), p. 93.

4 Luisa Valenzuela in Marie-Lise Gazarian Gautier, *Interviews with Latin American Writers* (Elmwood Park [Illinois], Dalkey Archive Press, 1989), pp. 300 and 298.

5 Rosemary Geisdorfer Feal, 'The Politics of "Wargasm": Sexuality, Domination and Female Subversion in Luisa Valenzuela's *Cambio de Armas*', *Structures of Power*, eds. Terry Peavler and Peter Standish (Albany, State University of New York Press, 1996), pp. 159–88.

6 Gwendolyn Díaz, 'Postmodernismo y teoría del caos en *Cola de lagartija* de Luisa Valenzuela', *Letras Femeninas* (Número Extraordinario Conmemorativo 1974–1994), 97–105.

opinions we shall return in the next chapter, Díaz strives to accommodate Postmodernism to important aspects of contemporary Spanish American fiction, in this case to features of *Cola de lagartija*. But the task is difficult when we are dealing with what Fredric Jameson calls (Third World) 'national allegories'. Certainly Valenzuela here evokes, through aspects of fictional technique inherited from the Boom and sometimes regarded as Postmodernist – self-referentiality, fragmentation, shifting narrators and the use of a consciously nonrealistic approach – a chaotic reality. But she does so, not to comment on reality as such but to probe the mysterious irrationality of Argentine political life. In other words we must consciously separate the technique from the intentionality. The narrative strategies may approximate to those of First World Postmodernist writers. But the intention is concretely referential to the state of Argentina. The novel's main narrator/persona asserts: 'se trata de un perfecto juego especular con un superyó represor en la superficie (el gobierno) y su contracara represora bajo la tierra (el brujo).'[7] We notice the psychological terminology (with its implications of therapy). The object is to make the reader aware not just of the manifestations in the late Peronista regime of a negatively operating national superego but, much more importantly, of a terrible, irrational, national id. Together they explain both the brutal exercise of power and the admiration of, and submission to, the principle of authority. Like so many supposedly Postmodernist novels in Spanish America, beginning with García Márquez's *Cien años de soledad*, *Cola de lagartija* carries both the suggestion that all 'reality' is simply a mental construct and the urgent message that it is all-too-terribly real and that it demands a collective reaction.

In 1990 Valenzuela published both *Realidad nacional desde la cama* and the more important *Novela negra con argentinos*. The first is an absurdist allegory of the ongoing threat to Argentina (and, of course, other countries) of military dictatorship. It involves 'la señora', who is undergoing a rest-cure after returning from abroad, the military, under Major Vento (=blowhard), the Argentine middle-class, represented by la señora's doctor, and the masses. It is never clear whether the real danger comes from the comic-opera military or from the populace which is manipulated by media propaganda. What is fundamental is la señora's gradual *toma de conciencia* after chapter fifteen, during which she reproaches herself (and the reader) for unwillingness to think and remember the lessons of the past. *Novela negra con argentinos* has provoked an outpouring of critical reactions, both in the autumn 1995 issue of *World Literature Today* and in the special number of *Antípodas* (6/7, 1994–5) as well as elsewhere. In a cogent article,[8] Cook

[7] Luisa Valenzuela, *Cola de lagartija*, 2nd edn (Buenos Aires, Bruguera, 1983), p. 45.

[8] Alyce Cook, '*Novela negra con argentinos* and the Move towards Reconciliation', *La Chispa* (1997), 113–21.

points out that one of the keys to understanding the novel is the fact that it is symmetrical around a central episode in which the protagonists, Roberta and Agustín, who are exiles in New York, come out symbolically of the former's flat where they have been hiding after Agustín had committed a motiveless, irrational (and again surely symbolic) murder. The theme of the novel is the search for a motive for the crime. Once more the underlying metaphor is psychological analysis. The protagonists have to reach a greater understanding of themselves in order to be cured and to escape from the temptation to mindless violence or submission to violence. For that reason a sadomasochistic establishment figures prominently as another of the novel's basic symbols. Once again, Cook points out, characters vacillate between victim and oppressor roles. It is not clear, from these novels or from Valenzuela's recent short stories, whether Valenzuela in later life has moved closer to envisioning some sort of 'order' underlying the apparent chaos of experience which has always been an aspiration in her work, and indeed in that of other major contemporary writers. She tends to write as if she suspects that there is no such hidden order, no comprehensible explanations. But the fact that her work includes the notion that literature can be in some sense therapeutic shows that she has not lost hope.

If we accept that belonging to Postmodernism in fiction is not just a matter of using a certain repertoire of narrative techniques (self-reflexivity, fragmentation, parody, blending of 'high' and 'low' types of writing, double coding, predominance of sign over signified and so on); if we really think that it involves presenting a new vision of reality and the human condition (in which ideologies have crashed, there is a crisis of cultural authority, all knowledge is seen as a variable construct, and subversion of certainties tends to be prioritized), together with a new view of the writer's task, then strongly committed writing faces us with a difficulty. Rosario Ferré's work is a case in point. Her initially militant feminism and her assertive published criticism of Felisberto Hernández and Julio Cortázar from a 'committed' standpoint seem to conflict with current notions of Postmodernism as much as does the overt political commitment of Skármeta in *La insurrección*, Allende in *De amor y de sombra* or Valenzuela in 'Cambio de armas'. In *Sitio a Eros* (1986) she referred to 'la voluntad de hacerme útil, tanto en cuanto al dilema femenino, como en cuanto a los problemas políticos y sociales que también me atañen'.[9] The result is a strong endorsement of referentiality, linear narrative structure, unambiguous symbolism and emphasis on plot in her work, marking it unequivocally as Post-Boom writing. We see these characteristics very clearly in some of her best-known short stories, such as 'La muñeca menor', 'Mercedes-Benz 220 SL' and 'La bella durmiente', which have justifiedly attracted critical study. They deal with Puerto Rican society seen as patriar-

[9] Rosario Ferré, *Sitio a Eros*, 2nd edn (Mexico City, Mortiz, 1986), p. 22.

chal, racist and materialistic, that is, dominated by a false and oppressive value system. Her first novel, really a novella, *Maldito amor* (1988), uses, like her later *La casa de la laguna* (published in English, 1995, Spanish edition, 1996), the family-saga form to comment bitterly on socio-economic change in Puerto Rico in the twentieth century. In both novels, the central symbol is the family mansion, a symbol inherited from Poe's 'The Fall of the House of Usher' – perhaps via Cortázar's 'Casa tomada'. The destruction of the mansion symbolizes the family's collapse and the collapse of the social values and presumptions which the family had endorsed. In *Maldito amor* chapters 1, 2, 4 and 6 belong to a grotesquely overwritten romance written by the family lawyer, Hermenegildo, celebrating three generations of the de la Valles, representing the old, landowning, sugar-producing oligarchy and their (self-defeating) opposition to modernization of the industry with North American capital. The rest of the novel ironically deconstructs Hermenegildo's account, revealing the seamy side of the family's history, culminating with the burning down of the house by Gloria, the wife of one of the two third-generation sons. Thus female rebellion and social criticism are aptly combined.

La casa de la laguna seems at first sight to follow the same pattern. It deals autobiographically, from a woman's perspective, with two generations of the Mendizábal family in Puerto Rico. Their story is used to illustrate the rise of a new commercial oligarchy in the island, replacing that of the old sugar-planters with one that is just as feudal, exploitative and colonial. Human interest is added by centering the novel on the gradual failure of the marriage of the second-generation Quintín Mendizábal to the main narrator Isabel, whose feminism and support for Puerto Rican independence from the United States reflect Ferré's earlier radicalism. The time-span covered is from 1917, when the Puerto Ricans were granted United States citizenship, to the 1980s when Isabel leaves for North America disenchanted both with marriage and with her homeland. The chief technical feature, as in *Maldito amor*, is the use of a contrapuntal method of narration, with Quintín intervening to comment on and criticize his wife's account of the family, her experiences in it and recent Puerto Rican history. In this way the novel both foregrounds its own fictionality and discusses its own content. The result, despite the prominence of strongly surviving elements of social criticism and feminism, is now a growing impression of ambiguity. The reader is left to evaluate both the conflictive interpretations of events by Isabel and Quintín, and the subtle evolution which both undergo. The emancipation of Isabel from the bondage of marriage to an insensitive and unfaithful husband is intimately connected with the theme of Puerto Rican independence both from the United States and (more importantly) from a colonial, racist, patriarchal and materialistic mind-set. Irma López sees the novel primarily as an example of Hutcheon's category of 'historiographic metafiction', a revisionist reworking of recent Puerto Rican history by Isabel, in opposition to her husband's more traditional stance.[9a] But this is only one dimension of the novel. The other main dimension, associated with Isabel herself is much more ambiguous. We cannot interpret the burning down of the house on the lagoon as simplistically as the burning down of the mansion in *Maldito amor*. There it was an unequivocal act and symbol of protest. Here it is part of the anti-climactic ending in which in effect Isabel runs away from her problems and those of the island.

While *La casa de la laguna* marks a significant shift in Ferré's outlook, *Vecindarios excéntricos* (published first in English and then in Spanish in 1999) fails to develop it. Influenced perhaps by the approach to characterization initiated by García Márquez in *Cien años de soledad* and passed on to Allende in the first part of *La casa de los espíritus* and to Laura Esquivel in *Como agua para chocolate*, Ferré draws once more on her memories and creates a gallery of droll and eccentric figures, relatives of the female narrator, Elvira, whose life stories, stitched together episodically, create an entertaining family saga. Themes from her previous work (feminism, higher education for women, patriarchal oppression, social injustice, the industrialization of Puerto Rico, Puerto Rican politics, relations with the United States and so on) reappear sporadically, but are incidental to the portrayal of a family in which children can routinely be brought home from school in a fire-engine, the theft of a million dollars from the family coffers has no real importance, and people marry for insane reasons. This is humour, but not satire. It almost looks as though Ferré, writing now in English, is attempting to distance herself from some of her earlier stances.

To continue this rapid survey of some representative Post-Boom novelists, we may now glance briefly at Fernando del Paso and Gustavo Sainz. Del Paso (Mexico, 1935–), like Valenzuela, who published her first novel in the same year as his, 1966, has pursued a rather zig-zag course, but in many respects remains closer to the Boom and Modernism than to the Post-Boom or Postmodernism. There was no single novel in Mexico which marked a radical shift as early as Onetti's *La vida breve* did in Argentina. A pattern of narrative innovation can be traced through the work of José Revueltas (1914–76) and Agustín Yáñez (1904–80) with the former's *El luto humano* (1943) and the latter's *Al filo del agua* (1947) marking important stages in the renovatory process. But critics are agreed that the most important event in mid-century Mexican fiction was the publication in 1958 of Fuentes's *La región más transparente*. Like his compatriot, Sainz, and his fellow novelist in Chile, Donoso, del Paso was hugely impressed. Fiddian writes of 'decisive influence' and of Fuentes's novel as 'a template for *José Trigo*'.[10] This, del

[9a] Irma M. López, 'The House on the Lagoon: Tensiones de un Discurso de (re)composición de la identidad puertorriqueña a través de la historia y de la lengua', *Indiana Journal of Hispanic Literatures* 12 (1998), 135–44.

[10] Robin Fiddian, *The Novels of Fernando del Paso* (Gainesville, Florida U.P., 2000), p. 31.

Paso's first novel, which it took him seven years to write, breaks new ground by evoking urban working-class life (seldom present in Boom fiction), specifically a failed strike of railway workers, in a slum environment in Mexico City in 1960. But it is not primarily a novel of protest and del Paso played down its social content in a 1966 interview in favour of its linguistic and mythological aspects (Fiddian, p. 17). One of del Paso's obsessions is defeat: here the strike is defeated; the Cristero rebellion in the late twenties, in which members of the strike-leader (Luciano's) family took part, ended in defeat; the student rebellion in del Paso's next novel is crushed; the Emperor Maximilian goes down to defeat and death in *Noticias del imperio* and in a sense *Linda 67* illustrates the defeat of the American Dream. A second kind of defeat in *José Trigo* is that of the narrator who, like the narrator in Vargas Llosa's *Historia de Mayta*, seeks information about the title character, but similarly only finds contradictions which symbolize the impossibility of attaining insight into the lives and experience of others. Thus, like Asturias, Fuentes, Rulfo, García Márquez, Donoso and others, del Paso resorts to a typically Boom-type mythical vision of an otherwise inaccessible reality, expressing (and universalizing) themes of conflict and treachery, death and rebirth, by reference to Aztec and Christian mythology.

We have already alluded to what Carlos Fuentes in his influential *La nueva novela hispanoamericana* (1969) regarded as an essential feature of Boom fiction, the foregrounding of exuberant linguistic innovation and its prominence in the work of Cabrera Infante and Luis Rafael Sánchez, among others. It is a highly obtrusive feature of both *José Trigo* and *Palinuro de México* (1977) in which the influences of James Joyce and of Rabelais deliriously intertwine. Once more an affirmative vitality, manifested chiefly in terms of joyful sexuality and humour, is brought into contrast with the sense of anguish and existential solitude voiced by the doctor in chapter eighteen. This is an elephantine, rambling and episodic novel, dominated by the highly cultured, fun-loving medical student, Palinuro, and his many-faceted character, a much larger than life example of the carefree young protagonists we associate with Skármeta, Sainz, Bryce Echenique and other Post-Boomers. There is a certain totalizing tendency in *Palinuro de Mexico*, given that Palinuro himself expresses in his personality and experiences a kind of archetypal Mexicanness and even, like the protagonist of Carpentier's *Los pasos perdidos*, reflects Western man in general. This too links del Paso more with Modernism and the Boom than with Postmodernism. What, on the other hand, points directly towards the Post-Boom is what Fiddian calls del Paso's assertion of 'the marvelous beauty, the life-enhancing powers, and the liberating potential of erotic love' (p. 77), with which around a third of the novel is closely connected. The final crucial aspect of *Palinuro de México* from the point of view of the present chapter is the sudden emergence of the terrible here and now of Mexico at the end of the novel, when Palinuro is killed during the disturbances of 1968 in Mexico City. Precisely what the left-wing critics of the Boom considered to be its major failings: its turning away from external reality in Spanish America towards myth, 'inner journeys', the wider human condition, cosmopolitanism and linguistic play, are now brusquely shouldered aside by the massacre of Tlatelolco. In that sense the ending of *Palinuro de México* can be seen as another marker of the shift from Boom to Post-Boom.

Del Paso's best known work is his contribution to the New Historical Novel in Spanish America, *Noticias del imperio* (1987). As we already know, the New Historical Novel cuts clear across the main boundary concepts and cannot be seen as primarily associated with the Boom, the Post-Boom, Modernism or Postmodernism. The essential question is whether any given New Historical Novel offers a new (usually revisionist) vision of a set of historical events and their meaning, or whether it questions (through parody, incorporation of fantasy, or in some other way) the possibility of making sense of the past. In one sense, the fact that one of the principal narrative voices in *Noticias del imperio*, the Empress Carlota (wife of Maximilian, whose brief reign over Mexico (1864–67) is the subject of the novel), is insane, might be taken as symbolizing the impossibility of imposing an intelligible pattern on the events described. Again, she might be taken as a symbol of the irrationality both of the enterprise her husband undertook and of the assumptions by which that enterprise was justified at the time. On the other hand, the 'erudite' narrator, who offers a more objective version of events, and in addition openly discusses the difficulties involved in so doing, leaves us with the impression, as Elmore points out, that a consistent aim of the novel is not merely to elucidate a meaningful interpretation of what happened, but also to relate it to the situation of Mexico in the 1980s,[11] and in particular to 'the ethical issues left unresolved in the Mexican conscience' by the circumstances leading up to the execution of Maximilian (Fiddian, p. 108). Twelve of the novel's twenty-three chapters are monologues by Carlota, while the remaining eleven each contain three sections in which the 'erudite' narrator has his say and which contain more conventional fictional evocations of personages and events. There are other narrators, whose function is to vary the point of view, and a great deal of direct and indirect commentary having to do with the imperialistic ideology of the Western Powers at the time, the ambiguity of Maximilian's outlook and a variety of Mexican responses to his regime, especially that of Juárez, his main opponent. The question of whether *Noticias del imperio* is a Postmodernist novel depends ultimately on whether we regard del Paso as opting for a more radical denial of historical 'truth' than mere acceptance of relativism in historical judgement implies.

Del Paso's fourth novel *Linda 67* (1995) is chiefly important because it belongs to the growing number of Spanish American novels by major writers

[11] Peter Elmore, *La fábrica de la memoria* (Mexico City, Fondo de Cultura Económica, 1997), pp. 149–50.

which are set in the United States and sometimes contain an implicit or explicit critique of life there from a Spanish American viewpoint. Here the critique, as in parts of Donoso's *Donde van a morir los elefantes* or Allende's *El plan infinito*, is quite open (and in this case even surly).

Skármeta was not the first to explore the life-style of intelligent young people in Spanish America. The first really outstanding novel on this central Post-Boom theme was *Gazapo* (1965) by Gustavo Sainz (Mexico, 1940–) which caused great scandal to right-thinking Mexicans precisely because of its comic and irreverent exposure of certain aspects of the youth culture around them. A case could be made for seeing it as *the* inaugural novel of the Post-Boom (one only needs to contrast its presentation of young people with that of Vargas Llosa in *La ciudad y los perros*, or set Menelao, its central character, alongside Zavalita of *Conversación en la catedral*), but its date makes it more of a precursor. It already shows the same exuberance, erotic fixation, fusion of realism and fantasy and colloquiality of Skármeta's early short stories on the youth-theme. It is the story of two rites of passage to maturity: Menelao's unsuccessful attempt to break away from his family in order to live on his own and his equally unsuccessful attempt to seduce his girl-friend, Gisela. Underlying the episodes, as Brown lucidly explains,[12] is a crisis of late adolescence which Menelao is working through. As always in the Post-Boom, a key element is the treatment of reality. *Gazapo* should not be read as if it were a Boom novel. The erotic fantasies of the young men and other non-mimetic elements in the novel are not there to challenge or deconstruct our familiar sense of the real. Just as Skármeta accepted 'esta realidad que por comodidad llamamos realidad', so Sainz retains some confidence in 'the availability of reality'.[13] The novel deals sympathetically with a sometimes painful process of self-exploration, of coming to terms with a very real reality, which will lay the basis for Menelao's future development.

The pattern established in *Gazapo* is followed afresh in later novels, such as *Compadre Lobo* (1977) and *Muchacho en llamas* (1988) which again deal with growing up in Mexico City. But meantime Sainz had gone in other directions. *Obsesivos días circulares* (1969) is an enigmatic novel set in a Catholic Girls' School in Mexico City which is owned by a political Boss, Papa la Oca, who uses it for various illicit purposes. The central character is an unlikely janitor, Terencio, a published novelist. A parallel set of incidents to those which centre on the theme of abuse of power is concerned with Terencio's complex sexual and metaphysical problems. Somehow the novel does not quite jell. Sainz's next major contribution to the Post-boom is therefore his third novel, *La Princesa del Palacio de Hierro* (1974), without ques-

[12] James W. Brown, '*Gazapo*, modelo para armar', *Nueva Narrativa Hispanoamericana* 3.2 (1973), 237–44.

[13] Gustavo Sainz, 'Carlos Fuentes. A Permanent Bedazzlement', *World Literature Today* 57.4 (1983), 568–72, p. 569.

tion one of the most hilarious novels in all of modern Hispanic fiction. It is the Post-Boom's comic masterpiece. The heroine, a lively, deliciously funny, upper-class young woman looks back in a series of telephone monologues on her adolescence and early womanhood among the bright young things of upper-crust Mexico City. Drugs, sex, mindless violence, irresponsible devilment and criminal 'fun' dominate the narrative, but the criticism of the rich kids' life-style (and that of certain representative adults) is never explicit. The Princess views them merely as 'pequeños defectos nacionales' but her own innate decency and disgust with some of what goes on provides a form of moral commentary. Swanson and Jones[14] both focus attention on the Princess herself, her unhappiness, her lack of identity, her loss of innocence, her lack of parental love and support, in order to show convincingly that the novel is far from being an unproblematic entertainment, though Swanson's view that it might be all a compensatory fantasy seems rather extreme.

After this memorable novel, Sainz seems to have got into a blind alley. *Fantasmas aztecas* (1982), *Paseo en trapecio* (1985) and *Muchacho en llamas* (1988) have not received much critical attention. They appear to be in the nature of narrative experiments and contain a certain amount of self-referentiality. The last, like Sarduy's *Colibrí*, includes critical comments by the narrator's father as well as by Sainz's fellow-novelist Carlos Monsiváis which almost seem like warnings by the novelist to himself. In *A la salud de la serpiente* (1988), however, Sainz again found his true voice and produced a long, semi-autobiographical work looking backwards to when he was writing *Obsesivos días circulares* while he was in the Creative Writing Programme of the University of Iowa. The work is a gold-mine for critics as well as being another contribution to the interesting group of Spanish American novels set in the United States. Its great defect is its self-indulgence – Sainz has always loomed large in his own fiction. But it is required reading for the period. Taking himself as his theme, Sainz evokes himself as he remembers or imagines himself to have been in his late twenties, with his obsession with writing, his interest in other people's fiction, his admiration for the Boom writers, his different conception of the novel from theirs, his friendships, love affairs and interest in pop music and film, the scandal surrounding *Gazapo* and the impact on him of the Tlatelolco massacre. This is another of what Henry James called 'loose baggy monsters', like a Christmas pudding full of good and varied ingredients. In many ways it is a compendium of Post-Boom attitudes and themes.[15] Perhaps most importantly it echoes Allende's notion that fiction imposes an order on what 'los demás

14 Philip Swanson, 'Gustavo Sainz and *La princesa del Palacio de Hierro*: Funniness, Identity and the Post-Boom', chapter 7 (pp. 114–27) of his *The New Novel in Latin America* (Manchester U.P., 1995); Julie Jones, 'The Dynamics of the City: Gustavo Sainz's *La princesa del Palacio de Hierro*', *Chasqui* 12 (1982), 14–23.

15 See, *per contra*, Salvador Fernández, *Gustavo Sainz. Postmodernism in the Mexican Novel* (New York, Lang, 1999). Like Colás, Fernández accepts the idea of a social,

llamaban "realidad", "cronología", "tiempo", "verdad" '[16] which deludes us into thinking that we understand it. But in the end any doubts about our perception of the real or the ability of language to express it give way (in typical Post-Boom fashion) before indignation at the inescapable reality of Tlatelolco and, on the other hand, the equally inescapable reality of love which brings the narrator a sense of reconciliation with himself and with existence. Sadly, after making in the little novella *Retablo de inmoderaciones y heresiarcas* (1992) a contribution to the New Historical Novel dealing with the ideas (and tribulations) of the late colonial Mexican intelligentsia, Sainz tried to repeat *A la salud de la serpiente* in *La novela virtual* (1998). Once more heavily autobiographical and confessional, it deals often in sordid detail with the life and sexual frustrations of a fifty-nine-year-old professor of Spanish in a provincial North American university. Besotted with his nubile young women students, unable to get his life together after the death of his wife, in a love-hate relationship with his writing, carrying on a pathetic e-mail correspondence with a young, adoring, Mexican girl student in a distant university, the self-absorbed central character appears to be drifting intellectually, emotionally and sexually. While Skármeta's Papst in *Match Ball*, at fifty-two, risks all for love and sexual fulfilment with an outrageously younger partner, and is able to laugh at himself for doing so, the professor in *La novela virtual* struggles feebly and humourlessly against the banality of life in late middle age.

Three more novelists merit brief mention in this chapter. They are Reinaldo Arenas (Cuba, 1943–90), Alfredo Bryce Echenique (Peru, 1939–) and Mempo Giardinelli (Argentina, 1947–). That Arenas has a place in Spanish American Postmodernism has been postulated by Béjar,[17] who emphasizes uncertainty, decentralization and contradiction as underlying characteristics of his novels. Similarly Soto affirms that 'the concept of reality is fluid in Arenas's oeuvre', in the sense that 'so called real experience, as manifested in the way most people attempt to secure an unequivocal meaning of experience and of themselves, is never opposed to other forms of personal experiences, such as dreams, hallucinations and fantasy.'[18] But initially this was not much more than a blurring of the line between 'observed' and 'created' reality, such as we see in Arenas's first novel *Celestino antes del alba* (1967, reissued in 1982 as *Cantando en el pozo*). It is a long monologue by a perhaps slightly retarded child (one thinks of Rulfo's Macario and behind him Faulkner's Benjy) who finds relief from hunger, poverty and rejection by his family in fantasy and the poems Celestino carves on trees.

historical and political Postmodernism indistinguishable from earlier fiction except in terms of experimental technique.

[16] Gustavo Sainz, *A la salud de la serpiente* (Mexico City, Grijalbo, 1988), p. 87.

[17] Eduardo C. Béjar, *La textualidad de Reinaldo Arenas: juegos de la escritura posmoderna* (Madrid, Playor, 1987).

[18] Francisco Soto, *Reinaldo Arenas* (New York, Twayne, 1999), pp. 15 and 16.

We realize that Celestino is an imaginary creation of the narrator to help him overcome the hostility of his surroundings. The narrator's dreams and hallucinations do not in any sense deconstruct referential reality, except in so far as they challenge the idea of a fixed identity in the narrator himself. They are a refuge from the horror of the real. Like similar elements of fantasy to be found in Boom fiction, we cannot regard them as fully Postmodernist. Arenas, in the preliminary note to the 1982 edition, declared: 'la novela es una defensa de la libertad y de la imaginación en un mundo contaminado por la barbarie, la presunción y la ignorancia.' The sentence could stand as an introduction to all his work.

Celestino was the first of a set of five novels, which Arenas called a 'pentagony' and which he struggled to complete before his early death from Aids in the United States. The other four novels were *El palacio de las blanquísimas mofetas* (written between 1966 and 1969, but only published in 1980), *Otra vez el mar* (1982) which Arenas regarded as the 'obra central', *El color del verano* (1991) and *El asalto* (1991). In the preliminary note just mentioned, Arenas asserted that 'aunque el protagonista perece en cada obra, vuelve a renacer en la siguiente con distinto nombre pero con igual objetivo y rebeldía: cantar el horror y la vida de la gente'. The key word is horror: the horror of loneliness and alienation felt by the protagonists as they live among the other horrors: that of oppression, of being among people brutalized and desensitized by poverty, frustration and suffering, and that of being in a world without God and hence without any meaningful order. Soto identifies the themes of the pentagony as repression by abusive, authoritarian systems and discourses of power, and a troubled quest for sexual identity. The latter is both a reflection of Arenas's own appalling experiences of state homophobia in Cuba where he was both imprisoned and made homeless because of his homosexuality (shared, interestingly by Lezama Lima, Sarduy, Piñera and Senel Paz, all prominent twentieth-century Cuban writers).

Before proceeding with the pentagony, Arenas produced *El mundo alucinante* (1969). Based on the life and adventures in Mexico and Europe of fray Servando Teresa de Mier, a turbulent priest in constant trouble with the religious and secular authorities, it is an allegorical novel showing the influence of Quevedo, Rabelais, Gracián and perhaps Swift. Servando's life is a perpetual quest for liberty, justice and rationality which reaches a peak in chapter fourteen when he is brought up against the absurdity of his search. As in Voltaire's *Candide*, another obvious influence, his ingenuous optimism trips over reality. He has to recognize that his various escapes from prison are rendered pointless by the possibility that life itself may be a prison and that in any case we are trapped inside our own personalities. Moreover King Charles IV of Spain points out that what lies on the other side of liberation (in Arenas's case, the Castro regime) may be worse than what went before. The use of three simultaneous narrative viewpoints and the combination of fantastic episodes with 'real' events taken from Servando's memoires produces a novel and original effect. But it remains moot whether we are still in the realm of Magical Realism, or in that of incipient Postmodernism. Arenas insisted as late as 1980 that the real is not 'lo lineal ni lo evidente' and that 'el llamado realismo me parece que es precisamente lo contrario de la realidad'.[19] In this he is simply in agreement with Rulfo, for example, as well as with some other Boom writers. The idea of 'una realidad que puede ser múltiple'[20] hardly counts as a Postmodernist stance. It is really only with *El palacio de las blanquísimas mofetas* that Arenas approaches the line. Set in the small town of Holguín, it tells of Fortunato, a youth semi-employed in a dead-end job and his grotesquely dysfunctional family. To attempt to escape from his agonizing surroundings, Fortunato tries to join Castro's guerrillas, but he fails and is captured and tortured by the Batista forces. As in the rest of the pentagony, the historical situation of Cuba meshes with the frustration (social, physical and metaphysical) of Fortunato and the other characters. But now this is expressed via fragmentation and dislocation of chronological time such that, Olivares contends, 'Arenas's novel promotes a struggle between itself and the reader to make the text intelligible'.[21] The theme of sexual identity in relation to the wider issue of individual freedom surfaces again explicitly in *Otra vez el mar*. If the narrator in *Celestino* was a child and in *El palacio* an adolescent, here the central figure, Héctor, is a man, living under the all-pervading tyranny of the Castro regime. The novel is set in a small beach resort where Héctor has been allowed a short holiday. The text is made up of flash-backs, at first in prose, focalized on Héctor's wife. There are six parts, corresponding to the six days of the holiday (and of Creation). Later they become focalized on Héctor himself, a homosexual artist, this time in a mixture of prose and blank verse. Once we realize that the 'wife' in the first part is simply a fantasy of Héctor's, we are compelled to re-read the novel in order to reintegrate the two parts. The second part (as in many Borges short stories) comments ironically on the first, both in formal terms, since it is much less mimetic, and in terms of content, since Héctor's torturing homosexual desire (for a younger man who might just be a police informer) and frustration are more explicit. His repression of his true nature is an obvious symbol of socio-political repression under Castro and, indeed, is part of it. The sea (Arenas eventually escaped from Cuba by sea) stands for freedom. However, this is only an aspiration. The chief aim of the novel, explicitly stated, is that of communicating 'la verdad sobre la porción de horror que

[19] Reinaldo Arenas, 'Fray Servando, víctima infatigable', in *El mundo alucinante* (Barcelona, Tusquets, 1997), p. 20.

[20] Reinaldo Arenas, *La escritura de la memoria*, ed. Omar Ette (Frankfurt, Vervuert, 1992), p. 67.

[21] Jorge Olivares, 'Carnaval and the Novel: Reinaldo Arenas's *El palacio de las blanquísimas mofetas*', *Hispanic Review* 53 (1985), 467–76, p. 472.

hemos padecido y padecemos'[22] which ultimately drives Héctor to suicide. How much truth-telling in fiction can Postmodernism endorse?

The last two parts of the pentagony, written at speed as the author reached the end of his short life, show a decline in creativity. *El color del verano* is a fragmentary novel which partly satirizes Castro (as Fifo) and partly deals lightheartedly (but nevertheless tragically) with the bitter experiences of a young homosexual in the Havana of the 1980s. It grows by accretion of autobiographically inspired, satirical, erotic and often pathetic episodes in a process of carnivalization which the triple narrator, Reinaldo/Gabriel/La Tétrica Mofeta creates to hide his torturing sense of the uselessness and emptiness of his life. *El asalto* is a novel of dictatorship of the kind already seen in Asturias's *El Señor Presidente*, García Márquez's *El otoño del Patriarca* and Carpentier's *El recurso del método*. Inspired by futuristic fantasies like Huxley's *Brave New World* and Orwell's *1984*, it reveals the protagonist turning himself into the most sadistic police official of a cruelly authoritarian regime. A depressing aspect of Arenas's depiction of oppression is his recognition of the gullibility, slave mentality and degradation of the oppressed. The central character in this case understands this and despises the masses he victimizes. But at the same time he is full of self-hatred, since he perceives in himself the bestial instincts and the longing for certitude that he attributes to them. While in the end he destroys the 'Reprimerísimo' (associated with his witch-mother) we are not thereby entitled to jump to any hopeful conclusions.

Before the last two novels of the pentagony, Arenas published a separate one, *El portero* (1989), based on his experience of self-exile in Miami and New York. In the first part it joins those novels set in the United States by Spanish American writers (such as Del Paso's *Linda 67*) which satirize the North American life-style. Here Arenas uses the eccentricities of the tenants of a block of flats where Juan, the young Cuban exile, works. In the second, more fantastic, part he leads a string of their pets towards a new world of happiness, which he himself cannot enter. He is condemned to go on living in the real world (of horror). Arenas also wrote a handful of very fine short stories and novelettes, including *La vieja Rosa* (1972) and its sequel *Arturo, la estrella más brillante* (1971, published 1984), both on the theme of authoritarianism and persecution. The latter deals with the life of a sensitive, young homosexual condemned to a re-education camp. It is the nearest Arenas comes to documental writing, and reminds us afresh of how imprisonment and liberation (literal or figurative) constitute the deep theme of most of his fiction. That fiction, beginning with something very like Modernist fantasy, approaches Postmodernism in certain aspects of *Otra vez el mar*. Arenas never overcame the dichotomy in his work between the 'mimetic contract'

22 Reinaldo Arenas, *Otra vez el mar* (Barcelona, Argos Vergara, 1982), p. 387.

with the reader (used to express his passionate hostility to Castroism and homophobia) and the urge to explore narrative strategies which break that contract. Like other authors we have mentioned, he cannot be regarded as fully Postmodernist unless we are willing to accept that the term can cover an intense oppositional engagement with a national reality, which is regarded as all too real rather than merely as a mental construct.

From the beginning of his work, with *Un mundo para Julius* (1970) to *No me esperen en abril* (1995), one of the fundamental themes of the fiction of Bryce Echenique has been that of coming to terms unwillingly with reality. *Un mundo para Julius* is a story of loss of innocence. Julius, who is only eleven when the novel ends, belongs to the upper crust of Peruvian society, the oligarchy. The mansion he lives in is a microcosm of a Peru in process of change from a paternalistic feudalism to a more modern, more dehumanized relationship between the classes: the rich, represented by Julius's feather-brained mother and his stepfather, and the poor, represented by the (originally) six servants from different parts of Peru. As Julius grows, the old paternalistic pattern breaks down and, symbolically, his former nanny and substitute mother is forced into prostitution. Julius, deprived of parental affection, longs for love and security and finds it for a time with the servants and other workers, but he is always conscious of his class-difference, and is condemned to emotional and social marginalization. By the end of the novel he has been compelled to acknowledge defeat: 'Aceptó todos los diálogos que se había negado a sostener.'[23] With this awareness come the end of childhood, accompanied by a deep sense of emptiness and frustration, henceforth typical of Bryce's central characters. From the outset, the novel was recognized as a superb story, refreshingly reader-friendly, full of fun, of exuberant spontaneity and sentimentality, at the opposite extreme from the early work of Sarduy and Elizondo, for example. The narrator nudges the reader complicitously towards a reading of the text which caricatures the world of the rich and invites affection and understanding for Julius. Bryce invented a relaxed style based on free indirect speech, which enlivens the chronological string of often hilarious anecdotes that make up the story and foregrounds the role of language as the only major technical novelty in a work where, as Duncan correctly emphasizes, 'the traditional mimetic function of the novel is paramount'.[24]

Julius is too young to be an anti-hero, but we can already see that he is to some extent disarmed in the face of life and love. This vulnerability becomes the hallmark of Bryce's subsequent fictional heroes, beginning with the irre-

[23] Alfredo Bryce Echenique, *Un mundo para Julius* (Barcelona, Plaza y Janés, 1970), p. 426.

[24] J. Ann Duncan, 'Language as Protagonist. Tradition and Innovation in Bryce Echenique's *Un mundo para Julius*', *Forum for Modern Language Studies* 16 (1980), 120–35, p. 126.

pressibly romantic Pedro Balbuena of *Tantas veces Pedro* (1977). The 'tantas veces' are the many times he has fallen for young women behind whom he sees, like Borges's student pursuing Almotasim, the shadowy figure of his ideal beloved, Sophie. Like Julius, Pedro comes from a wealthy background, which he has abandoned to move to Europe in the hope of becoming a writer. Instead he adopts the life-style of a well-off hippy in rebellion against his background but with no ideological principles or direct engagement with the politico-social struggle. What governs his life is his obsession with love, which covers up the sense of emptiness he shares with Julius. The affectionate irony with which his obsession is treated makes the novel ultimately anti-romantic (in contrast to the neo-romanticism we find in Allende, Mastretta and Esquivel, for example). When Pedro finally discovers Sophie in Perugia, she kills him. But in a sense he dies of love. Bryce was as completely aware of the absence of the theme of love in the Boom as Allende. In 1977 he declared that *Tantas veces Pedro* 'Es una novela que tiene mucho de desafío. Creo que la novela latinoamericana de hoy, la que se escribe a partir de Asturias, Carpentier y los novelistas más jóvenes de hoy como Vargas Llosa y García Márquez, no han tratado el tema del amor, y a mí me interesa este tema. . . . Se trata de una novela de romanticismo nuevo.'[25] We have already alluded several times to this important shift.

Another Post-Boom characteristic of Bryce's fiction derives from his commitment to storytelling. In another interview he confessed to 'la emoción de contar, de narrar, de hacer que progrese la acción, no importa por qué camino'.[26] We recognize this priority afresh, along with humour and the now familiar oral style in *La vida exagerada de Martín Romaña* (1981) and its sequel *El hombre que hablaba con Octavia de Cádiz* (1985). As Sophie said of Pedro Balbuena, Martín is 'una máquina loca de recordar'. Another spoilt, upper-class Peruvian, vaguely bohemian, vaguely left-wing, he is in the Paris of the 1968 uprising, again with the intention of becoming a writer. Everything he touches goes humiliatingly wrong. Told nostalgically as a series of implicit dialogues, the two novels comment on themselves and make flexible use of the narratorial voice, but once more we are offered a proliferating series of (in this case, autobiographical) anecdotes in which Martín always comes off badly, never quite managing to belong to the left, never realizing his dream of writing, never finding the right partner. Now he looks back on his life reflectively, with sentimentality and humour. What the conventional reader misses is not so much a structured narrative – we enjoy the anecdotal approach and the slapstick – but we wait in vain for signs that his long

25 Alfredo Bryce Echenique, interview in *Cuadernos para el Diálogo* (30 April, 1977), cit. Jacques Soubeyroux in 'L'être et le désir', in *Co-Textes* [Montpellier], 9 (1985), 101–19, pp. 117–18.

26 Alfredo Bryce Echenique, in Leonardo Padura Fuentes, 'Retrato y voz de Alfredo Bryce Echenique', *Plural* [Mexico City], 224 (May 1990), 35–40, p. 37.

éducation sentimentale has made Martín, not just older and sadder, but also wiser. Unhappily, if he forgets nothing, he also seems to learn nothing. The ludic tone, the self-irony, the exuberance are not enough to conceal a certain gratuitousness underlying the episodes.

La última mudanza de Felipe Carrillo (1988) and *Reo de nocturnidad* (1997) continue the pattern of confessional novels on the theme of ill-assorted love. Carrillo and Max Gutiérrez, like Pedro and Martín, are stuck in a kind of prolonged adolescence, unable to take control of their emotional and sexual lives, which they see in terms of self-gratification. They can (and do) fall in love, but they are incapable of loving, of sustaining a mature relationship. The great defect of Bryce as a novelist is his inability to distance himself from his central characters, who are all cut from the same cloth. Of Carrillo, he said to Ferreira: 'Me inspiró cariño, ése es el problema de todos mis personajes.'[27] The same can be said of Manongo Sterne in *No me esperen en abril* (1995) in which Bryce returns successfully to the world of Julius. The novelty, both in *Un mundo para Julius* and here, is that the world of the rich is described, not bitterly from underneath, but humorously and satirically from inside. Manongo is a grown-up Julius, an outsider trapped inside his class, but different, refusing his class-mates macho outlook, serious and incurably romantic, seeing beyond gratification. We read *No me esperen en abril* with the same amusement as we read Sainz's *La Princesa del Palacio de Hierro*. The princess, too, is an in some ways slightly pathetic observer of the behaviour of the children of the top people. As he joins in the antics of his friends in a series of hilarious episodes which illustrate the life-style of the future ruling class, Manongo is always conscious of something rotten in the state of Peruvian high society, and, like Julius, feels a sense of emptiness and estrangement from his fellows. The two major symbols in the novel are the crazy, anglophile college Manongo attends, which assumes the function of the mansion Julius grew up in, and Manongo's eternal, unsuccessful love affair with Teri, his girl friend. In Bryce, star-crossed love, destined to failure, represents the difficulty of accepting life on its own (or on realistic) terms. Manongo is even less able to do so than Pablo or Martín or Max. In the end he kills himself. His suicide reminds us that, when Bryce regularly asserts in interviews that his humour is a way into reality, part of what he means is that his use of it leads us into areas of reality which produce the opposite effect from humour. His novels are not comedies; they are tragicomedies.

Like Giardinelli, in other words, Bryce has a soft spot for people who are not very good at getting their lives together. In that sense, *La amigdalitis de Tarzán* (1999) has something in common with *El cielo con las manos*. In

[27] Alfredo Bryce Echenique in César Ferreira, 'Entrevista con Alfredo Bryce Echenique', *Antípodas* 3 (1991), 41–7, p. 42.

both cases, the story combines exile with frustrated love, but in this case a real *amour-estime*. The narrator, Juan Manuel, is another re-make of the boy from Lima in Paris, slowly making it as a singer-songwriter. Separated from his wife, he is in love with a Salvadoran, Fernanda María, the Tarzan of the title, whose marriage to an itinerant, alcoholic photographer takes her from Chile to Paris, and thence to various parts of the Americas. In contrast to the soft-centred, sentimental, rather incompetent men of Bryce's novels, she is one of the strong women brought into prominence by Allende: Saint Tarzan to her children and 'la mujer más noble y limpia y buena del mundo'[28] to her sister. Unfortunately the failure of her marriage brings with it the recognition that even Tarzan can sometimes fail to measure up. The 'tonsilitis' stands for her brief interval of insecurity in the middle of the novel. But, caring for his two characters as much as ever, Bryce arranges a happy ending for her, if one that is not quite so happy for Juan Manuel. Unlike some of his earlier novels, this is an unalloyed example of Post-Boom neo-romanticism, perhaps now beginning to seem just a little over-ripe.

Mempo Giardinelli has never concealed his preference for plot-centred, reader-friendly novels. In 1986, he told Kohut: 'Yo me siento ante todo un narrador, en el sentido de que soy un contador de historias.' A long-time reader of detective stories, in which there is usually a carefully structured plot, he has suggested that what he learned from them was sequentiality: 'trato de presentar las situaciones en perfecta secuencia, con algunos recursos que indudablemente me vienen de la novela policial . . . porque este tipo de estructuras le da al lector la posibilidad de una lectura sencilla y accesible.'[29] Parts of this interview and other declarations by Giardinelli in Kohut's book and elsewhere (such as his 'Variaciones sobre la posmodernidad' in his magazine *Puro Cuento*[30]) deserve to be set alongside remarks by Skármeta and Allende which clarify rather well the relationship between their generation and that of the Boom.

Giardinelli's first novel, then called *Toño tuerto, rey de ciegos* (1976) had the honour of being suppressed by the censorship in Argentina as subversive. It was republished in 1983 as *¿Por qué prohibieron el circo*? and tells of a young intellectual who abandons the study of law (and his wife and child) to become a village schoolteacher in a tiny community on the far north of Argentina, dominated by its bullying Intendente and the local bosses. Toño leads an insurrection after a couple of failed strikes. We assume that it collapses and that he dies, but not before discovering his personal destiny in the

[28] Alfredo Bryce Echenique, *La amigdalitis de Tarzán* (Mexico, Alfaguara, 1999), p. 161.

[29] Mempo Giardinelli in Karl Kohut, 'La palabra, la imaginación, la vida', in the latter's *Un universo cargado de violencia. Presentación, aproximación y documentación de la obra de Mempo Giardinelli* (Frankfurt, Vervuert, 1990), pp. 51 and 48.

[30] 23 (1990), 30–32.

course of organizing the struggle. *La revolución en bicicleta* (1980) owed its considerable success to the figure of Bartolo, a Paraguayan army officer who in 1947 heads a failed coup against the then dictator of Paraguay. It collapses because of poor organization, inexperience and squabbling on the part of the leadership and lack of any clear ideology. Told from much later, when Bartolo is an old man, living in poverty in northern Argentina, after attempting other uprisings without success, it stands between Skármeta's *La insurrección*, glorifying revolution, and Vargas Llosa's *Historia de Mayta* which ridicules rebellion. Giardinelli conveys the drama and idealism of this *cuartelazo*, which grows into a popular movement, and the bitterness of failure. But Bartolo remains true to his ideals and thus undefeated, a symbol of courageous popular resistance to tyranny. Both this and its predecessor are very much early novels of the Post-Boom, plot-centred, engaged with the here and now of Spanish America, full of warmth, simple humanity and humour. Bartolo is as far from the intellectual hero of the Boom as Skármeta's postman, Mario, or Allende's Eva Luna. His bluff, oral style carries complete conviction. He withstands life's adversity without undue complaint. 'Es un derrotado', Gardinelli insisted, 'pero a la vez nunca lo vencen.'[31]

El cielo con las manos (1981) is Giardinelli's contribution to the novel of exile. It takes the form of a long nostalgic monologue by the narrator, in exile in Mexico, evoking his adolescence in northern Argentina and his calf-love for an older local beauty, Aurora. Once more it is a story of defeat, this time the defeat of an ideal of love. For, although the narrator finally runs into Aurora again in Mexico City and makes love to her, he discovers that only the past has any (bitter-sweet) value. Then comes the realization that there are only roads which lead nowhere and that the essence of the human condition lies in being able to face defeat with what dignity one can muster. *Luna caliente* (1983), which won the Mexican National Prize for Fiction, is strangely different from the rest of Giardinelli's work. In 1990, aligning himself with other Post-Boom writers, he asserted: 'Me nutrí y me nutro de los que se llama "realidad", y creo que mi deber de escritor es dar cuenta de ella.'[32] But in this case the reality is horrifying. The central character, Ramiro, practically rapes a thirteen-year-old girl, Araceli, and murders her father. Later, after avoiding arrest, he has a second torrid encounter with her and appears to kill her. But as he awaits arrest, she disconcertingly reappears (from the dead?), perhaps as an avenging fury. There is an overturning of values, underlined by the reactions of the local police chief, who seems willing to suspend prosecution if Ramiro collaborates actively with the mili-

[31] Mempo Giardinelli in Teresa Méndez-Faith, 'Entrevista con Mempo Giardinelli', *Discurso Literario* 5.2 (1988), 313–21, p. 318.

[32] Mempo Giardinelli, 'Fichero', *Nuevo Texto Crítico* 5 (1990), p. 187.

tary regime. But in the final pages we are given the eerie impression that he will suffer another kind of punishment.

The second of Giardinelli's novels to be set in Mexico is *Qué solos se quedan los muertos* (1985), which is not unrelated in some ways to Valenzuela's *Novela negra con argentinos*. In both cases a murder which occurs outside Argentina is indirectly related to events in the Dirty War there. Carmen, the mudered woman in Giardinelli's novel, is mixed up in the drug scene in Zacatecas. The narrator, her former lover, who tries to investigate her death, asks a key question: '¿de qué tuvo la culpa, si la hicieron vivir equivocada?'[33] and goes on to blame the violent events in Argentina which led to their joint exile, for pointing her in the direction which was to lead to her death. Even in Mexico, Carmen is a victim, less of some drug lord than of her background in the largely useless struggle against the authoritarian regime in her homeland. Thus, the plot remains largely separate from the commentary. The mysterious events in Zacatecas, which again illustrate Giardinelli's ability to put together a good story, are really a launch pad for a series of bitter reflections about the recent history of Argentina. In the above-mentioned interview with Méndez-Faith he insisted that this is how the novel must be read. Once more he concludes that 'quizá la única salvación para el hombre está en la dignidad con que recorre su propio camino' (p. 209). The narrator solves the mystery of the murder but, as the novel closes, seems likely to fall victim to the drug lord in his turn.

Santo oficio de la memoria (1991), which won the prestigious Gallegos Prize, illustrates the tendency of writers in Spanish America to appropriate Postmodernist fictional techniques and strategies and use them to create works (in this case another national allegory) which run against the grain of European and North American Postmodernism. Adapting the pattern of Faulkner's *As I Lay Dying*, *Santo oficio* is composed of one hundred and six sections, told by twenty-four narrators all of whom, however, turn out to be reported by El Tonto de la Buena Memoria, a mentally retarded member of the Domeniconelle family, whose story intertwines with and illustrates that of Argentina in the twentieth century. Pellón points out cogently that, however complex the presentation of reality is in Boom novels, there is always a key to the complexity, whereas (in the terms popularized by Hutcheon): 'True to its Postmodern moment, *Santo oficio* defies both closure and naturalization.'[34] Undeniably: but when Pellón goes on to point out that 'El Tonto de la Buena Memoria' functions in *Santo oficio* as an allegory of the national conscience, the national memory, the embodiment of all the *desaparecidos*, all exiles, and all internal exiles during the Dirty War, and

33 Mempo Giardinelli, *Qué solos se quedan los muertos* (Buenos Aires, Sudamericana, 1985), p. 178.

34 Gustavo Pellón, 'Ideology and Structure in Giardinelli's *Santo oficio de la memoria*', *Studies in Twentieth Century Literature* 19.1 (1995), 81–99, p. 91.

that 'El Tonto writes out of fury because he won't be silenced' (p. 92), we sense a discrepancy between the Postmodernity of certain aspects of the technique and the author's unabashed intentionality. As Pellón puts it, *Santo oficio* is 'the irregular sum of many subjectivities', but they combine to give 'an open ended and politically responsible account of Argentine history in this [i.e. the twentieth] century' (p. 92). Whether that can be a Postmodernist project is surely open to question.

The novel has two basic themes: that of the development of Argentina in the twentieth century, seen as producing '[un país] en el que la realidad se hace cada día más surrealista',[35] and that of the family spirit of the Domeniconelles: 'Libertario, indómito, rebelde' (p. 288), which includes the Feminism of Franca, shared by Pedro and passed on to his daughters, as well as Pedro's left-wing allegiances, rooted in the family's past, which force him into exile. This basic contrast is brought out through the interaction of the family members, their evocations of the family's past and their own life-stories. El Tonto explains the technique: 'las voces son muchas y todas disonantes . . . no hay voz omnisciente. . . . El único orden es que no todos hablan a la vez. Como los rayos de la rueda de una bicicleta . . . todo rayo confluye' (pp. 294–95). An important Post-Boom element is Giardinelli's evident confidence in the role of simple referential language: 'todo debe decirse . . . la palabra es noble, se adapta, crece con el bueno uso y alcanza la infinitud expresiva que necesitamos' (p. 289) and 'las mejores prosas siguen siendo las sencillas' (p. 300). Giardinelli's problem in *Santo oficio* is to render each of the narrators interesting and their self-reporting significant. This is difficult to sustain in more than a hundred sections. There is some dead ground. But taken as a whole *Santo oficio* seems likely to retain a place among the major works of its period.

One of the more charming (if old-fashioned) aspects of Giardinelli's fictional writing is his tendency to hold up the narrative for a while to give us, in one form or another, a piece of his mind. In *Imposible equilibrio* (1995) this takes the form of a dialogue between Cardozo, the principal narrator, and his friend Rafa. The latter, after calling attention to the corruption and immorality which have contaminated most aspects of life in the Chaco region of Argentina, asserts that man's basic characteristic is that he finds it impossible to strike a balance between reason and feeling. The context is the theft by a group of their cronies of a family of hippopotami which had been imported in the hope that they would clean up the local waterways by eating the vegetation. Reason suggests staying clear of the situation; Rafa's feelings require that he should help his friends to avoid the consequences of their crazy escapade. Once more the stress is on dignity and decency: 'tanto usted como yo

[35] Mempo Giardinelli, *Santo oficio de la memoria* (Bogotá, Norma, 1991), p. 372.

nos resistimos a que dé lo mismo ser derecho que traidor.'[36] The same applies to the cronies. They have released the hippos where they are likely to cause the most trouble to the authorities, whose aim had been to exploit their importation for political kudos. Victorio explains that behind the theft was a desire to rebel against an idiotic system, symbolized by the hysterical reaction of the authorities and the media to the loss of the animals: 'Nunca quise acomodarme a las miserias del sistema . . . No quiero vivir en equilibrio con esta sociedad de mierda' (pp. 200–01). The act of defiance succeeds, up to a point, though at the cost of the death of one of those involved. The others, assisted by Cardozo and Rafa, flee. But the ending, in which the survivors are shown to be what they are, characters in a novel, leaves the reader dissatisfied. As in other novels by Giardinelli, this is a study of how things go wrong. Like Toño, Bartolo and the unnamed narrator in *El cielo con las manos*, the hippo-snatchers are well-intentioned, even idealistic and self-sacrificing, but they come to grief partly through poor judgement, partly through lack of support from others and partly from their own personality defects. Giardinelli presents them non-judgementally, with a slightly ironic affectionateness and an inclination to share their tendency to blame life and/or society for what happens. An important theme in these novels is the way life humiliates us and frustrates our endeavours. Its hostility is seen with humour, but also with bitterness. Decency and dignity are not enough.

Further Reading

Díaz Gwendolyn and Lagos María Inés, eds., *La palabra en vilo: narrativa de Luisa Valenzuela* (Santiago de Chile, Cuarto Propio, 1996). Ten essays on different works or aspects of her writing.

Magnarelli, Sharon, *Reflections / Refractions: Reading Luisa Valenzuela* (New York, Lang, 1988). By Valenzuela's best critic.

World Literature Today 69.4 (1995). Valenzuela Number.

Hintz, Susanne S., *Rosario Ferré: A Search for Identity* (New York, Lang, 1995). The only general book in English.

Skinner, Lee, 'Pandora's Log: Charting the Evolving Literary Project of Rosario Ferré', *Revista de Estudios Hispánicos* 29 (1995), 461–76. An insightful overview.

Mansour, Mónica, *Los mundos de Palinuro* (Xalapa, Vera Cruz U.P., 1986).

Mata, Oscar, *Un océano de narraciones: Fernando del Paso* (Mexico, Universidad Autónoma de Tlaxcala-UAP, 1991).

36 Mempo Giardinelli, *Imposible equilibrio* (Buenos Aires, Planeta, 1995), p. 121.

Toledo, Alejandro, ed., *El imperio de las voces: Fernando del Paso ante la crítica* (Mexico City, Era, 1997). A very uneven anthology of critical essays.
All of these are less sophisticated approaches than Fiddian's.

Gunia, Inke, '*¿Cuál es la Onda?' La literatura de la contracultura juvenil en el México de los años sesenta y setenta* (Frankfurt, Vervuert, 1994). A helpful work for understanding the relation between La Onda and Post-Boom writing.

Cacheiro, Adolfo, *Reinaldo Arenas: una apreciación política* (Lanham, Maryland, International Scholars Publications, 2000).
Negrín, María Luisa, *El círculo del exilio y de la enajenación en la obra de Reinaldo Arenas* (Lewiston, Edwin Mellen Press, 2000).
Sánchez, Reinaldo, *Ideología y subversión: otra vez Arenas* (Salamanca, Centro de Estudios Ibéricos y Americanos, 1999).
All of the above are strong on ideas, less so on literary strategies and techniques.

Co-Textes, Montpellier, 34 (1997). Bryce Echenique Number.
Snauwaert, Erwin, *Crónica de una escritura inocente* (Louvain U.P., 1998).

Chapter 9

POSTMODERNISM

The lure of the term Postmodernism is irresistible; the difficulty of defining the term is inescapable. This is especially the case in regard to Third World literature where, in addition, it is apt to collide with the term Postcolonialism. Of the possible critical stances in the face of the problem one might mention four. The first and worst is the tendency to write about the topic making no reference to texts of any kind, but only to theory, as is the case, for example, with the articles of Nelly Richards and Ticio Escobar in the useful 1993 issue of the *South Alantic Quarterly* dedicated to Postmodernism. The second is that of Raymond Williams, especially in his *The Postmodern Novel in Latin America* (1995), the first chapter of which will remain required reading until much larger and more definitive treatments of the subject are published. The third is that of Santiago Colás in his *Postmodernity in Latin America. The Argentine Paradigm* (1994) which attempts to formulate a definition of Postmodernism which fits certain Argentine authors, or that of Salvador Fernández in *Gustavo Sainz. Postmodernism in the Mexican Novel*, which tries to do the same less successfully for Mexico. The fourth is my own in *The Post-Boom in Spanish American Fiction* (1998), where, influenced by the views of Ricardo Gutiérrez Mouat, Juan Armando Epple and Skármeta, I attempt (as here) to argue that we need to distinguish between writers whose work shows more possible conformity to canons of Postmodernism in Europe and North America, and writers like those discussed in the previous chapter, whose work tends to illustrate the notion of 'specificity' to Spanish America. The latter notion, as we have seen, tends to carry with it features like the survival of 'national allegories', politico-social commitment, ideology, and a reaction against narrative experimentation which make it hard to reconcile with some familiar conceptions of Postmodernism. The critical question is whether, as Williams, Colás and many other critics believe, we can stretch the definition of Postmodernism to include writers like Puig, Allende, Luis Rafael Sánchez, Sainz and del Paso, to say nothing of Boom writers like Cortázar, without risking a formulation which critics in the 'metropolitan' countries might hesitate to accept. A revisionist approach to Postmodernism, based on its alleged Spanish American form, that cannot be readily harmonized with conceptions of Postmodernism which are current elsewhere, is methodologically unsatisfactory. The litmus-test is referentiality. The more directly and unambiguously referential to the here and now of Spanish America (or in an increasing number of cases to North America), the less Postmodernist. The argument of both Williams and Colás that Spanish American Postmodernist narratives may express what the former calls 'the concrete, historical and political dimension of postmodern culture'[1] (which tends to imply an intelligible order detectable in reality) appears to conflict with Postmodernism's tendency to surrender to disorder, fragmentation and instability and, at times, to replace purposiveness and commitment with parody, pastiche and a ludic approach. There is also another issue. We know reasonably clearly when the Boom's creative cycle began and when it ended. Hence we can periodize the Post-Boom without undue difficulty. But in Latin American criticism the term Modernism, in the European and Anglo-Saxon sense, has hardly taken root as yet, so that we find ourselves discussing and attempting to periodize Postmodernism without any clear idea of when Spanish American Modernism was, or what it might mean. It is probably true, as Parkinson Zamora asserts,[2] that 'what has been called postmodern in New World writing represents neither a radical break with modernism nor a seamless continuity'. Williams (pp. 14–16) seems to agree, suggesting that the dividing line cuts across the Boom without necessarily compromising the unity of the movement, which he regards as predominantly Modernist. But until we have accepted definitions of both terms this is not very helpful.

Among the earliest Spanish American novelists to have been labelled Postmodern are Néstor Sánchez (Argentina, 1935–) and Salvador Elizondo (Mexico, 1932–). Both made their mark in the late 1960s, just as the Boom was at it height. Sánchez published four novels in rapid succession: *Nosotros dos* (1966), *Siberia Blues* (1967), *El amhor, los Orsinis y la muerte* (1969) and *Cómico de la lengua* (1973), before disappearing mysteriously from the literary scene. He began to be classed at once with Elizondo and Sarduy as representing a new stage in Spanish American fiction moving ahead from the Boom, though not in the same direction (as we can now see) as Puig, Skármeta, Allende or Sainz. Steven Bell[3] suggests that Sánchez and Elizondo carry to an extreme the questioning of our comfortable assumptions about reality which was already a major feature of Boom writing from Borges onward. For this process he uses Jean Ricardou's term 'anti-representational'. This emphasizes the crucial point; the non-referential use of narrative discourse. For that reason it is largely futile to attempt to convey the content of Sánchez's novels. Suffice it that the narrator in *Nosotros dos* reveals strong affinities with Onetti's Erdosaín and Larsen, as well as with Cortázar's

[1] Santiago Colás, *Potmodernity in Latin America. The Argentine Paradigm* (Durham and London, Duke U.P., 1994), p. 3.

[2] Lois Parkinson Zamora, *The Usable Past* (Cambridge U.P., 1997), p. 193.

[3] Steven Bell, 'Postmodern Fiction in Spanish America: the Example of Salvador Elizondo and Néstor Sánchez', *Arizona Quarterly* 42 (1986), 5–16.

Oliveira. Like them and like Valenzuela's AZ later in *Como en la guerra*, he is seeking an 'order', an intelligible pattern in things, which will allow him to make sense of life. He finds it briefly in marriage to Clara, but it slips through his fingers. A similar disquiet afflicts the narrator of *Siberia blues*, in which the outer slum suburbs of Buenos Aires seem to symbolize the kind of youthful vitality we find in the youngsters of Skármeta's early short stories and in Sainz's *Gazapo*. But here it has been lost and with it the narrator's life has lost direction. At the centre of *El amhor, los Orsinis y la muerte* is the distinction between 'lo orsínico' and 'lo felípico', as existential attitudes, in which the former represents a kind of ultimate stoicism in the face of the meaninglessness of life, the futility of suffering and the threat of death, while the latter is a mere escape mechanism. That Sánchez's novels are existential allegories is confirmed by *Cómico de la lengua*, whose theme is the struggle between 'lo leucémico', rejection of life, and what is called in capitals 'LA CONFIANZA EN LA VIDA', a Borgesian acceptance of its utter contingency.

Bell's article suggests that the incoherent fragmentation, the discontinuities, the suppression of normal chronology and spacial referentiality, the absence of plot and closure, the destruction of narratorial authority and the emphasis on 'the limitations of literature as a symbolic system' (p. 11) in Sánchez and Elizondo go beyond the usual practice of Boom writers and make these two novelists Postmodern in a sense that the latter are not. This seems debatable, when we think back to Donoso's *El obsceno pájaro de la noche* or to Cortázar's *62. Modelo para armar*, for example. In fact Cortázar is one of the main influences on Sánchez and thus emerges afresh as the main link between the Boom writers and their younger confrères. But this does not alter the critical questions: does there come a point when the intensification of certain characteristics of narrative discourse, already present in Boom fiction, amounts to a qualitative shift, and if so, how do we recognize it? Williams appears to argue that the shift occurs when writers finally renounce any 'truth-telling' function. If this is the case, it seems relevant to point out that Sánchez still believed in literature as 'un instrumento de conocimiento' and that his work contains a metaphysical quest like those in Arlt and Sábato. Such existential and epistemological searches seem a little too dated to be fully Postmodernist.

In 1968 Angela Dellepiane acutely postulated two divergent groups of novelists in Argentina. Of the one farthest away from old-style mimetic realism, Sánchez was clearly the extreme example. Similarly in Mexico in 1971 Margo Glantz discussed two divergent groups, 'Onda' and 'Escritura', the former with characteristics similar to those suggested by Skármeta in 'Al fin y al cabo . . .', the latter emphasizing linguistic and formal experimentation rather than referentiality and headed by Elizondo.[4] It is not hard to detect

4 See Angela Dellepiane, 'La novela argentina desde 1950 hasta 1965', *Revista*

in the existence of these pairs of groups the origins of the difference between the Post-Boom and Postmodernism. Elizondo became known in 1965 with *Farabeuf o la crónica de un instante*, which the author described as containing Farabeuf's 'mental drama' and, of course, that of his female partner. In his autobiography he described the novel as 'una historia turbiamente concebida sobre las relaciones amorosas de un hombre y una mujer'.[5] In one respect, it aspires, by dealing with taboo subjects (torture and sado-masochistic sexuality), to provoke and upset the reader and to question traditional moral assumptions. But Elizondo's other and more important objective is to try to overcome, by superimposed repetitions of the same three scenes, one of the problems enunciated by Borges: how can one 'fix' reality (like a photograph) in language, when reality is simultaneous and language, by its very nature, is successive and can only deal with one aspect at a time? In addition we have a further level of difficulty since, as Clark D'Lugo points out,[6] the text teasingly questions any referentiality it may appear to contain. Not only is it based on 'memories' of a non-event, but it regularly uses verb-tenses and other linguistic features to cast doubt on or question any affirmation. Hence we can talk again about 'subversion of certainty' and even 'ontological questioning', since the identity of the female character is undermined. There are hints that the text is a kind of extended riddle, but that the active reader (as in Cortázar's *Rayuela*, but with much more difficulty) can reassemble its elements so as to perceive a meaning. Unable to elucidate any such meaning, critics have tended to fall back on the notion that it must somehow have to do with the reader's perception of the novel's creative process. We are offered a mysterious visual equivalent in the mention of Titian's picture of 'Sacred and Profane Love', which Elizondo seems to regard as standing on the edge of the inexpressible in somewhat the same way as his novel does.

Elizondo's next novel, *El hipogeo secreto* (1968) attempts to carry the process of substituting the creative act for the created artefact a further stage. The author described it as 'un intento de salvar el abismo que media entre las concepciones de la mente y la posibilidad de ser concretadas real, visible y legiblemente mediante la escritura'.[7] That is, it is even more exclusively about the act of writing, the act of creating a mechanism for communicating without necessarily using it to communicate. But at the same time, in imagining a writer who in turn imagines a writer, Elizondo involves himself with the

Iberoameriana 160–61 (1968), 237–82, and Margo Glantz, 'Onda y Escritura en México: Jóvenes de 20 a 33', in her *Repeticiones* (Xalapa, Vera Cruz U.P., 1979).

5 Salvador Elizondo, *Salvador Elizondo* (Mexico City, Empresas Editoriales, 1966), p. 43.

6 Carol Clark D'Lugo, 'Elizondo's *Farabeuf*: A Consideration of the Text as Text', *Symposium* 39 (1985), 155–66.

7 Jorge Ruffinelli, 'Entrevista. Salvador Elizondo', *Hispamérica* 16 (1977), 33–47, p. 35.

Borgesian postulate that we ourselves may be fictitious. In fact, the novel alludes to that very possibility. Malva Filer has examined various ways in which this novel harks back to Borges,[8] especially in that it incorporates the same kind of search for an ultimate explanation that we find in the search for a catalogue of La Biblioteca de Babel, but she overlooks an important one which emerges when Elizondo suggests that imaginary descriptions of reality can proliferate endlessly, as Borges had postulated in 'Examen de la obra de Herbert Quain'. We are thus led to ask whether, for Elizondo, emphasis on the creative act is not a means of avoiding the contemplation of our possible unreality and of the meaningless chaos which any realistic account of reality would have to convey. It is possible that *El grafólogo* (1972) provides the answer. Once more a meditation on the act of writing leads to reflections about time and the enigma of the personality. These in turn produce the 'Tractatus rethorico-pictoricus' which contains the revealing statement: 'Todo tentativa de escritura de un tratado, aunque está condenado al fracaso – por el carácter imposible del lenguaje – es un intento de instaurar un orden.'[9] All writing is a search for, or an attempt to impose, a design on our experience. We have seen this notion already in Allende, Valenzuela and Sainz. In Elizondo it fails. In his interview with Ruffinelli he is already admitting that he has painted himself into a corner. The only escape is to write *as if* it could succeed. This is what eventually Elizondo does in *Elsinore* (1988). He returns to referentiality. But, just as Allende in *Eva Luna* presents the story as a soap-opera, partly in order to avoid the appearance of having gone back to straight mimesis, so Elizondo presents the story of a young cadet, with the same name as the author, in a military school in California, as a dream. It is not clear quite what difference this makes, apart from hinting to the reader that it is the mind which creates reality. What is crucial is the fact that Elizondo, like Sarduy, found it impossible to persevere in a radically anti-representational direction.

González Echevarría writes: 'The aesthetic of the Boom novel still contains fundamental elements of the traditional novel: characters that follow mimetic conceptions; time that is recoverable despite fragmentation; an implicit faith in the authenticity of local color as a source of truth about culture and the propriety of language.'[10] The writer who most clearly represents a break with this aesthetic is Severo Sarduy (Cuba, 1937–93). All his early fiction reveals a growing desire to thwart the traditional-minded reader who in *De donde son los cantantes* intervenes to expostulate: 'Lo que yo

[8] Malva Filer, 'Salvador Elizondo and Severo Sarduy. Two Borgesian Writers', *Borges and his Successors*, ed. Edna Aizenberg (Columbia and London, Missouri U.P., 1990), 214–26.

[9] Salvador Elizondo, *El grafólogo* (Mexico City, Mortiz, 1972), p. 57.

[10] Roberto González Echevarría, 'Plain Song: Sarduy's *Cobra*', *Contemporary Literature* 28 (1987), 437–59, p. 446.

quiero son hechos. Sí, hechos, acción, desarrollo, mensaje en suma.' Already the narratorial voice had retorted: 'Bueno, querido, no todo puede ser coherente en la vida. Un poco de desorden en el orden. ¿No?'[11] But it is not just a case of eluding the reader's desire for an orderly plot based on 'facts' which are related to one another by a process of cause and effect. This step had already been consciously taken by Borges and Cortázar. What Sarduy wants to do is to outrage and frustrate the conventional reader by using 'la idea de que el pensamiento pueda pensar sobre el pensamiento, de que el lenguaje pueda hablar del lenguaje, de que un escritor no escriba sobre algo sino escriba algo (como proponía Joyce)'.[12]

Gestos (1963), Sarduy's first novel, points in this direction by parodying the novels of the Cuban uprising against Batista by writers like Alejo Carpentier, Lisandro Otero, Edmundo Desnoes and others. There are residual references to an act of urban terrorism, which link the novel tenuously to the pre-history of the Castro revolution. But Sarduy's deliberate aim is already to convert a novel which is partly about revolutionary action into one which instead primarily presents itself to the reader as an 'actividad escritural'. Having by this time settled in Paris and come under the influence of the Tel Quel group, Sarduy, like Elizondo, had come to believe that writing was primarily concerned with consciousness of the act of writing rather than of what is being communicated. He was, of course, promptly excommunicated by the Castro critical establishment. *Gestos*, whose title suggests that meaningful revolutionary action is reduced simply to 'going through the motions', marks the first stage of Sarduy's evolution to the opposite extreme from that which is represented by a 'straight' Cuban revolutionary novelist like Manuel Cofiño.

A more radical stance is reached in *De donde son los cantantes* (1967). Here, as Méndez Rodanos emphasizes, 'no existe el plano histórico en una dimensión referencial'.[13] The spaces in which the episodes are set are obtrusively fictitious, though at one point the combination of modern urban architecture and a rubbish dump alludes to Havana, the characters are mere flat verbal entities without psychological depth, the authority of the narrator/author is regularly undermined and the reader has to figure out how to 'receive' the novel. It is made up of a trio of pastiches which relate to the three racial/cultural components of Cuban-ness: the Spanish, the African and the Chinese. The tone is predominantly ludic, though we notice in Part I that the two recurring characters Auxilio and Socorro are engaged in a hopeless search for a God who has taken flight. His absence symbolizes the absence of

[11] Severo Sarduy, *De donde son los cantantes* (Barcelona, Seix Barral, 1980), pp. 49 and 28.

[12] Cit. Emir Rodríguez Monegal, 'Las metamorphosis del texto', *Severo Sarduy*, ed. Julián Ríos (Madrid, Fundamentos, 1976), 36–61, p. 53.

[13] Adriana Méndez Rodanos, *Severo Sarduy* (Mexico City, UNAM, 1983), p. 35.

any meaningful 'order' for language to express. Similarly the search in the novel for an 'essential' Cuban-ness is doomed to failure. There are no essences. At the centre of *De donde son los cantantes* there is a nothingness, a *vacío*, for which the ludic tone and the cartoon-like episodes are merely a screen. Even the constant erotic quests which govern much of what 'happens' are futile, since the pseudo-characters possess no fixed gender and no predictable character traits.

Once more a residual element of parodic referentiality remains in the political satire of the third section 'Dolores Rendón'. We look in vain for an equivalent in *Cobra* (1972) which for that reason has been perceived as marking 'a turning point in the course of the novel form' in Spanish America.[14] The chains of grotesque and incoherent incidents in the novel represent a series of symbolic quests, which carry Cobra, an actress (i.e. one who keeps assuming new identities) to India, to Tangiers and ultimately towards Tibet. In each of these she undergoes a series of transformations before dying at the hands of a gang of drug-pushing motor-cycle toughs. It seems to be the case that the spiritual initiation rite carried out on her by the toughs corresponds on a different plane to the physical transformation which she undergoes in Tangiers. In the latter, she changes sex; in the initiation, she dies. Critics have struggled to relate the series of quests and transformations in *Cobra* to Sarduy's views on language and its relation to (any possible) reality, but without conspicuous success. What does not seem to have received enough notice is the fact that *De donde son los cantantes*, *Cobra* and *Maitreya* (1978) all contain parodies of spiritual quests. An absence of transcendence underlies Sarduy's humour, eroticism and emphasis on the process of literary creation, but hints remain of a nostalgia for lost meaning.

Colibrí (1984), *Cocuyo* (1989) and *Pájaros en la playa* (1993) are less ambitious than *Cobra* and reveal a gradual return to greater accessibility. *Colibrí*, set in a gay bar on the edge of a rain forest is told by a bi-sexual narrator and caricatures the values of heroism and endurance we find in Regionalist novels like Rivera's *La vorágine*. An interesting feature is the role of the narrator's father who intervenes to criticize what is recognizable as Sarduy's earlier work. *Cocuyo*, through an allegorization of a Cuban childhood, leads to a tragic *toma de conciencia* on the part of the central character, who comes to believe that life is no more than a peregrination through a disgusting labyrinth. The pessimism finds confirmation in Sarduy's last (posthumously published) novel, set in a nursing home for Aids victims. It is a bitter meditation in the course of which Sarduy's metaphysical malaise, which his concentration on writing had attempted to assuage, finally breaks surface.

Sarduy's early work contains 'writerly' elements of parody, pastiche, frag-

14 Suzanne Jill Levine, Preface to her translation of *Cobra* (New York, Dutton, 1975), p. vii.

mentation, non-referentiality, linguistic play, loss of authorial authority, discontinuity and reader-unfriendliness, combined with an awareness of the absence of any mentally or spiritually satisfying 'order' in things, which we recognize as Postmodernist. However, we cannot overlook the fact that Néstor Sánchez abruptly stopped publishing, while Elizondo and Sarduy both drew back from the radical break with mimesis which was made in their early work. Commenting on that early fiction in 1978, the Mexican novelist José Agustín who, it must be conceded, belonged like Sainz to 'La Onda' declared: 'I find only one serious flaw in Sarduy and Elizondo, both of whom have created a strong following in Latin America and also in Europe. They love their literary theories so much that they consider them the only valid ones, the ultimate truth of all artistic laws . . . But now . . . [fiction] needs to turn back to external reality.'[15] Similarly, the narrator in Sainz's in *A la salud de la serpiente*, after asking himself '¿no era un corsé espantoso el formato tradicional del libro?', decides that, while all kinds of extreme experimentalism in fiction are to be welcomed, unless there is a minimum of 'progresión' (i.e. linearity) and respect for 'nuestra concepción del espacio y el tiempo',[16] devotees of formal innovation are fooling themselves.

In *Cocuyo*, remnants of Sarduy's TelQuelism co-exist uneasily with a fierce criticism of Cuban life. By then, however, Diamela Eltit's *Lumpérica* (1983) seems to have taken over the imperative to try to harmonize a Postmodern narrative pattern with social protest. The novel was written when the Pinochet regime was at its height and power was often exercised less by direct violence than by channelling the Official Discourse through the media. We have already seen one form of protest against this in Valenzuela's allegorical *Realidad nacional desde la cama*. Eltit uses the figure of L. Iluminada, who functions in the novel like a screen super-star, to interact with a horde of homeless, pauperized people as if they were all initially involved in a film production, with a script and stage directions. That is, she uses allusions to the narcoticizing media both in order to find a new way of writing protest-fiction and to question the discourse of power which instrumentalizes the media. Kadir points out that the fact of Iluminada's being a woman is of central significance to the novel. There is 'a literal and metaphoric relationship between the fate of the disenfranchised and the condition of the woman protagonist'.[17] The novel is a confrontational and transgressive allegory, which functions at both the feminist and the political levels. So that Iluminada's self-wounding in the course of the novel and shaving of her head at the end symbolize frustration both with the feminine

[15] José Agustín, 'Contemporary Latin American Fiction', in his *Three Lectures. Literature and Censorship in Latin America Today: Dream within a Dream*, University of Denver Occasional Papers (1978), p. 9.

[16] Gustavo Sainz, *A la salud de la serpiente* (Mexico City, Grijalbo, 1988), p. 627.

[17] Djelal Kadir, *The Other Writing* (West Lafayette, Purdue U.P., 1993), p. 183.

condition under a regime which has reasserted traditional patriarchal values and solidarity with the suffering of the marginalized and dispossessed. The exercise of power and resistance to it are central concerns in Eltit's early work. Literary conventions are also a system of power to which authors submit. These too Eltit confronts and attempts to subvert. By placing her at the peak of a line of development beginning with Borges and developing through the Boom, Kadir is able to assert that her work is 'more radical and more radically revisonary' (p. 184) at the literary level than anything earlier, though he does not interpret this specifically as a crossing over into Postmodernism. That step is taken by Williams,[18] on the grounds that the main subject of the later chapters is language itself, that the setting in the city square is Baudrillardian, that the use of the different and the paradoxical corresponds to categories posited by Linda Hutcheon and that the novel deals in unstable, unsure, provisional truths. The critical questions are whether such extreme innovation, appealing as it must to a very small intellectual minority, can really be a suitable vehicle for social protest, and more specifically, how a novel which seems to question both mimetic reality and language as an instrument of communication can include protest at all.

Eltit complained that in her next novel, *Por la patria* (1986) she had merely used narratorial techniques 'que exploraron los del Boom',[19] an interesting comment which emphasizes that there is no clear dividing line between Boom and Postmodernism if we only look at experimentalism. The central character Coya-Coa lives with her all but destitute parents in a shanty town outside Santiago which in the course of the novel is raided by the army. She and three other women are arrested and taken to a prison where they are brutalized by Juan, who corresponds to the equally villainous Teniente Ramírez of Allende's *De amor y de sombra*. Speaking of *Por la patria*, Eltit made three points: 'Lo que más me importa es el asunto del poder y como se manifiesta en ciertos sectores oprimidos ya sea en forma de: la violencia, el desamparo, el desarraigo, la discriminación sexual, el silenciamiento.' Second, special emphasis on power and sexuality. Third, 'El significante es lo más relevante para mi trabajo narrativo'.[20] The first of these affirmations lists the themes of *Por la patria*.The second reminds us that they foreground the sexual taboo – incest (the Coya was an Inca princess destined to marry her brother). Kadir argues (p. 196) that Coya stands for 'imperial and cosmogonic orderliness', which is challenged and deconstructed by Coa and quotes:

18 See his *The Postmodern Novel in Latin America* (New York, St Martin's Press, 1995), pp. 73–75, and *The Modern Latin American Novel* (New York, Twayne, 1998), 134–36.

19 In Leonidas Morales, 'Narración y referentes en Diamela Eltit', *Revista Chilena de Literatura* 51 (1997), 121–59, p. 122.

20 In Sandra Garabano and Guillermo García-Corrales, 'Diamela Eltit' (an interview), *Hispamérica* 62 (1992), 65–75, pp. 68–69.

'Mi insurrección es total . . . Ya no Coya, incesto, hibridez. Renazco Coa.'[21] The strong undertones of imaginary incest with her father and lesbian relations with her mother at one level constitute a deliberately transgressive allegory of the yearning on the part of the marginalized for a return to the national family. However, after her experiences in prison, Coya/Coa achieves a *toma de conciencia* that allows her to confront sexual, social and patriarchal oppression. Even though she is in the same seedy bar as before, she has evolved.

The third affirmation links *Por la patria* with *El cuarto mundo* (1988) which has a double theme. Eltit explained to Garabano and García-Corrales that in one respect it figures forth an attempt to reveal the 'mecanisms' of its own writing-process. The first section, apparently told by a male twin, is more conventional and linear, that is, backwards-looking technically, while the second section, told by the female twin, 'representa la problemática de una novela que no se termina' (p. 69), deconstructing the metaphor of stability implied in the clear gender-roles of section one. The ambiguous sexual relationship of the twins, their implicit androgyny, manifest, like Coya/Coa's longing for a return to the family situation, a longing for unity, for overcoming rivalry, differentiation, male-only authority. At the same time, the incorporation into the twins' experience of the 'sudacas' (a contemptuous peninsular Spanish term for Latin Americans) reinforces this longing, extending it to the whole Latin American family of nations 'la fraternidad sudaca'. Eltit is a writer who is driven by a series of obsessions, 'sexuality and its deviations, unjust social inequality, the shame of convention and the arbitrary nature of a legality that is exclusionary',[22] and at the same time by a desire to write with risk, to explore new modes of narrative discourse. These come together in *El Padre mío* (1989) based on direct observation of street people. It consists of three monologues which Eltit had recorded. The speaker is a schizophrenic beggar whom she saw as representing 'el negativo de una sociedad, la otra cara del sujeto, la radical salida de un sistema productivo o laboral'.[23] *El Padre mío* carries testimonial literature to its farthest extreme while at the same time, since the Padre's incoherencies represent the final triumph of the signifier over the signified, it represents an extreme example of narrative discourse.

Although Eltit belonged originally to the bottom of the middle class she has always been interested in the lumpenproletariat, insisting to Piña (p. 242) that 'El lumpen de alguna manera es la metáfora mayor de todos nosotros'. In *Vaca sagrada* (1991) once more the female body represents marginality, pain, prohibitions and 'aquello minoritario postergado y oprimido por el poder central' (Piña, p. 244). Francisca is both lumpen and female. Her expe-

[21] Diamela Eltit, *Por la patria* (Santiago de Chile, Ornitorrinco, 1986), pp. 260–61.

[22] Diamela Eltit, 'Resisting', *Review* 49 (1994), 19.

[23] Diamela Eltit, 'Escritos sobre un cuerpo', in Juan Andrés Piña, *Conversaciones con la narrativa chilena* (Santiago de Chile, Los Andes, 1991), pp. 223–54, p. 238.

riences in the novel illustrate how oppression by a patriarchal, authoritarian state can operate both at the social level and at the level of personal relations. She is involved with Trade Union activities, but also with complex sexual partnerships. She loses out in both cases, achieving neither a steady job nor a satisfactory love-life. But Eltit avoids provoking pity for her. She takes drugs and abuses alcohol, she associates sex on occasion with masochism, and she has an abortion. Her life is anguishing and violent: she suffers political, economic and sexual oppression. Yet, despite elements of complicity with the system and with male machismo, her quest to construct a personality and life-style is, like Coya-Coa's, ultimately successful to the extent that she is able to 'invent' a meaningful narrative to interpret her experiences.

Los vigilantes (1994) is another national allegory. It takes the form of letters from a woman writer to her absent husband complaining of his censoriousness and that of his mother and the neighbours, who disapprove of her ideas, behaviour and life-style. The title refers to this hostile group. They represent the conformist middle class who felt supported by the Pinochet regime and who, after its fall, felt threatened by the proletariat. Anxious to hang on to middle-class hegemony, they scrutinize the new situation anxiously. The writer's crime is to have sympathized with the lumpen, so that she is regarded with anger and suspicion. Behind the 'vigilantes' stands the West, with its offer of economic well-being in return for neo-liberal social restraints. Eltit distrusts this new-style *gringuismo*. Her distant husband and father of her starving and freezing child is associated with the mentality of the fallen regime, now having retreated into the background, but still threatening. A key to the novel is the evolution of the son, whose two brief interventions frame the letters. Apparently feeble-minded to begin with, he is later able to take over the narrative so that the ending is not one of total defeat. The journey of mother and son towards the 'bonfires' which seem to symbolize warmth and human solidarity is not completed when the novel ends and may be a wild goose chase. But a residue of hope remains. *Los trabajadores de la muerte* (1998) returns to the family theme of *El cuarto mundo*, but in this case with the mother at the centre. The core episodes are framed by others at the beginning and the end which take place among beggars and street vendors in Santiago in an atmosphere of utter squalor with a curious admixture of dream-fantasy. The function of the frame seems to be to introduce the moral squalor of the family by means of references to its social/physical equivalent and to prefigure the theme of 'el poder que puede alcanzar el odio'.[24] In the central part of the novel we are given insight via the rancorous monologues of the wife into the frustrations and misery of her marriage to an insensitive, coarse-grained husband, who eventually leaves her with two sons to bring up, while he begins a new relationship in Concepción. A second set of chapters,

24 Diamela Eltit, *Los trabajadores de la muerte* (Santiago de Chile, Planeta, 1998), p. 31.

told partly in the second person and partly in the first, deal with the 'revenge' of the wife when one of her sons seduces and finally murders his half-sister, the child of the husband by his new partner in Concepción. The novel is divided into 'Acts' which suggest a tragedy on the Greek model, in which Destiny plays its implacable role. This is a new pattern of writing for Eltit and perhaps signifies a turning point in her work.

The fiction of Ricardo Piglia (Argentina, 1941–) illustrates afresh the difficulty of categorizing many Spanish American writers as Postmodernist. In 1991 he affirmed: 'Yo creo que toda buena novela es experimental',[25] and, in differentiating his generation from that of the Boom he foregrounded the relationship of writers after the Boom with mass-culture: 'cultura de masas y alta cultura, ese es el problema' (p. 133). Here are two recognizable Postmodernist features. Yet we notice that Piglia, whose allegiances are to the left, clings to the traditional idea of a causal relationship between social relationships and even the 'mecanismos' of fiction,[26] as well as arguing, like Allende and Boullosa, that it is writers who impose meaning on the raw data of experience to produce a form of 'truth', in his case making it possible to 'imaginar que uno puede vivir una vida que tiene sentido' (Viereck, p. 138). The notion of literature's 'making sense' of lived experience and being able to interpret our lives as social beings is not easily compatible with mainstream Postmodernism, which tends to problematize rather than interpret. We can see why Colás in his *Postmodernity in Latin America* has to stretch the definition of Postmodernism to include writers like Piglia and Tomás Eloy Martínez.

Piglia'a first two significant fictional works are literary 'investigations'. He implied to Viereck that he had learned from detective-story writers like Raymond Chandler the possibility of working with 'enigmas que no se resuelven, con esa manera particular de establecer una relación entre el que narra y el enigma' (p. 131). Having begun as a short story writer in *La invasión* (1967) which won the Casa de las Américas Prize, he included in a second collection, *Nombre falso* (1975) the story 'Homenaje a Roberto Arlt', described at the beginning, following Borges, as a report or an abstract (i.e. as non-fictional). It tells of the tracking down by the narrator of unpublished material by Arlt whom Piglia considered to be, along with Macedonio Fernández, the progenitors of modern Argentine fiction. The narrator writes: 'Un crítico literario es siempre, de algún modo, un detective.'[27] What we have, then, is a piece of literary research written up like a detective story. It leads the narrator to a short story, 'Luba', allegedly by Arlt but actually

[25] Ricardo Piglia in Roberto Viereck, 'De la tradición a las formas de la expresión. (Entrevista a Ricardo Piglia)', *Revista Chilena de Literatura* 40 (1992), 129–39, p. 137.

[26] Ricardo Piglia, *Crítica y ficción* (Universidad del Litoral, Cuadernos de Extensión Universitaria, 8, 1986), p. 45. This important series of interviews was later republished by Siglo Veinte (Buenos Aires) in 1990.

[27] Ricardo Piglia, *Nombre falso* (Buenos Aires, Siglo XXI, 1975), p. 136.

adapted by Piglia from one by the Russian writer Andreiev. It confronts a 'pure' political agitator who is on the run with a prostitute. In Piglia's version the girl embraces the agitator's ideals of revolution and redemption. The contrast between self-degradation and purity was highly relevant to the Argentina of the mid 1970s, but what mark the story as Postmodernist are its self-referentiality, its metafictionality and its element of literary parody.

Respiración artificial (1980) also contains an investigation, undertaken by Renzi (a recurring character in Piglia's fiction; Piglia's full name happens to be Ricardo Emilio Piglia Renzi) in conjunction with his uncle, Maggi, involving materials written by a distant relative, Senator Enrique Ossorio, who had been exiled by the nineteenth-century dictator Rosas. The novel has been seen as belonging to the branch of the New Historical Novel in Spanish America which utterly debunks the idea that we can ever possess real historical knowledge. De Grandis writes: 'El mundo narrado, lejos de establecer alguna relación con lo real, destruye la ilusión de la referencialidad. La autoreferencialidad es absoluta', and later: 'El sentido de los hechos históricos escapa a la interpretación.'[28] But this attempt to drag the novel into European and North American style Postmodernism overlooks both its context and Piglia's own remarks about it. Its context is the savagely repressive 'Proceso' in Argentina during and after 1976. Piglia has asserted that one of the novel's themes is Renzi's growing historical and political awareness which leads him to two conclusions. One is that the 'Proceso' is the modern equivalent of the Rosas dictatorship (1835–52) and will collapse in the same way. The other is that literary culture is inseparable from its politico-social background and interacts with it in a positive sense.[29] We can see why Colás asserts that this connection with developments in Argentina 'will recast all those devices and technical features that might make [*Respiración artificial*] a candidate for Euro-North American postmodernity in the light of a politically oppositional Argentine postmodernity' (p. 123). Can we really make such a distinction? The whole idea of relating Piglia's literary practice to the politico-social background and interpreting the fragmentary form of the novel in terms of subversion of the regime's official discourse is fraught with difficulty in this respect (just as it is in the case of Eltit's *Lumpérica*). In an important essay 'La poética de la novela. Polémica implícita de Macedonio con Manuel Gálvez', in *Prisión perpetua* (1998), Piglia makes it clear that he does not reject the social novel, but rather the old realist social novel as practiced by Manuel Gálvez (Argentina, 1882–1962). However, in the first part of *Prisión perpetua*, Piglia tells how he learned from a mentor, Steve Ratliff, a

[28] Rita de Grandis, 'La cita como estrategia narrativa en *Respiración artificial*', *Revista Canadiense de Estudios Hispánicos* 17 (1993), 259–69, pp. 264 and 265.

[29] Cf. Piglia's remarks about *Respiración artificial* in *Crítica y ficción*, esp. pp. 69–71. Maggi is described as rejecting the 'nihilismo deliberado que circula actualmente' (p. 69) which makes him hard to categorize as a Postmodernist character in such a context.

self-exiled North American writer, to 'negar la realidad'. In the second part, 'El fluir de la vida', the narrator tells how Lucía tells El Pájaro who tells Morán who tells the narrator a story which is partly Lucía's invention. As in Macedonio Fernández, we are compelled to address, not what is told, but the mode of telling, the procedures, the narrative strategy. The contrast with *Respiración artificial* shows Piglia zig-zagging, like Valenzuela, between two concepts of fiction, one of which contains a social metaphor and another which has an empty centre.

La ciudad ausente (1992) is set in 2004. At its centre is a talking machine invented by Macedonio Fernández to immortalize his dead wife, though its is not quite clear whether the talk is generated by the hallucinations of a psychotic woman. The machine, a metaphor for subversive writing, produces stories which the authoritarian regime wishes to silence. The stories and the attempt to deactivate their source are revealed to the reader in the course of an investigation by a journalist, Junior, whose efforts to discover what is going on constitute the main thread of the novel. Two symbolic spaces are dominant. One is the city of Buenos Aires fifteen years after the fall of the Berlin Wall, in which now only the machine represents the possibility of refusing to conform and accept the regime's official discourse. It is a city submissive to an authoritarian ideology which, as the police Chief tells Junior, creates 'reality' and the 'truth' which is imposed on the masses. The state systematically creates 'un mecanismo técnico destinado a alterar el criterio de la realidad',[30] whereas the machine keeps alive the collective memory of social conflict, plurality of belief systems and libertarian idealism. The other symbolic space is an imaginary island whose inhabitants are dominated by notions borrowed from James Joyce's *Finnegan's Wake* and from the Wittgensteinian idea of language as play. Language(s) create proliferating realities in playful contrast to the static reality of official discourse. The novel is at once a warning about the possibility of state-organized mind-control and an extended positive metaphor of the destabilizing and subversive power of fiction and language, both of which potentially can be used to safeguard freedom and the collective memories which preserve nationality.

In 1995 Carmen Boullosa took up some of the implications of *La ciudad ausente* in what almost amounts to a manifesto. Language, she asserted, is falsehood: the word 'fire' can never convey the reality of fire. Also, language belongs to the past, since the changing associations which words evoke are always associated with past experience. It is subject to time and change. But it is all the writer has to convert the 'miedo', the 'asombro', the 'pavor' and the 'sinrazón' which characterize our daily experience (experience of

[30] Ricardo Piglia, *La ciudad ausente*, 3rd edn (Buenos Aires, Sudamericana, 1992), p. 151.

destruction) into 'orden', 'coherencia' and even 'esperanza'. 'Los dioses que daban orden y sentido al mundo han muerto', she wrote, 'Nos espera un fin de siglo atroz, sin fe, sin utopías, sin convicciones.' Yet, 'el individuo reclama sentido' and only language can rescue (or create) 'unidad', 'armonía' and 'entendimiento' from the collapsing world around us.[31]

This sense of the horror of reality, combined with the assertion that writing can somehow salvage hope and values from the wreckage of our illusions, is an important key to understanding Boullosa's work, especially after her first two novels: *Mejor desaparece* (written in 1980, but not published until 1987) and *Antes* (1989). The first is a baffling novel composed of short pieces told by different narrators about a family which is disintegrating after the death of the mother. The incoherent and fragmented technique seems to be intended to figure forth the collapse of the family into solitude and lack of communication. There are two interconnected themes. One is the general nastiness of the father's response to his wife's death. He brings to the house, described as an 'estercolero', in which the children are confined, something disgusting (simply called 'eso'). It symbolizes the subtle cruelty and hypocrisy with which he will henceforth torment and humiliate the children. The other theme, identified by Clark D'Lugo,[32] is the subjection of women and the inauthenticity imposed on them by the men in the novel. It is seen in the fact that one daughter merely performs the music of others, another (an actress) merely mouths the words of others, while a third is converted into a waxwork. A fourth daughter has her face surgically removed. Boullosa sees life in terms of destruction. Here it is (as in Eltit's *El cuarto mundo*) the destruction of the nuclear family, traditionally the foundation of society, by patriarchal authority and mean-mindedness. At the end, however, the father's rejection of his children seems to rebound on him. He is unable to enter the house and is reduced to Lilliputian size.

Again like Eltit and Elizondo, Boullosa decided after writing this obscurely allegorical first novel that 'la literatura tiene que ser comprensible'.[33] *Antes* is slightly less elusive than *Mejor desaparece*. It evokes the childhood of the female narrator up to the age of eleven and the onset of puberty. To Hind, Boullosa said: 'la voz nunca pudo reponerse de la pérdida de la infancia', and that the novel represented a 'pesadilla'.[34] The child narrator suffers from an unspecified anguish, which Boullosa described

[31] Carmen Boullosa, 'El que gira la cabeza y el fuego: historia y novela', *Revista de Literatura Hispanoamericana* (Maracaibo, Universidad de Zulia), 30 (1995), 5–16.

[32] Carol Clark D'Lugo, *The Fragmented Novel in Mexico* (Austin, Texas U.P., 1997), pp. 210–15. She also has insightful comments on Elizondo and Sainz.

[33] Carmen Boullosa, in Ema Pfieffer, *Entrevistas. Diez escritoras mexicanas desde bastidores* (Frankfurt, Vervuert, 1992), p. 33.

[34] Emily Hind, 'Entrevista con Carmen Boullosa', *Hispamérica* (forthcoming in *Hispamérica*).

as 'un pánico de estar vivo' (Pfeiffer, p. 36) symbolized by the baby stuck all over with nails which the little girl draws for her dead mother. 'Clavitos' is the child herself, tormented by terrifying and inexplicable obsessions which she is trying to understand when she is dragged away into the world of adulthood into which she cannot fit so that all that remains is the memory of her difficult childhood. Ten years later, Boullosa returned to childhood memories from a totally new, comic, perspective. The first signs of a shift towards the views she expressed in 1995 become visible in *Son vacas, somos puercos* (1991) and its edition for younger readers *El médico de los piratas* (1992). A conventional autobiographical narrative based on a Dutch historical source, it tells of the adventures of a Dutch boy, Smeeks, in the Caribbean. He ultimately becomes a doctor, caring for pirates and participating in their expeditions. Unlike the earlier novels, this is exclusively a man's world. There is no fragmentation, no alteration of chronology, no questioning of authorial authority. But, crucially, Smeeks, discovers an 'order', the pirates' loyalty to 'La Ley de la Costa' which partly offsets the cruelty and destruction which he reports. In the light of Boullosa's 1995 statement we can see this novel and *Llanto* (1992) as allegories which in a way explain each other. *Llanto* deals with the reincarnation of the last Aztec Emperor, Moctezuma, in Mexico in 1989. He cannot conceive a world without a principle of order: 'se apegaba hasta la desesperación a las nociones de cómo debian ser las cosas.'[35] Boullosa deliberately compares the collapse of the Aztec Empire with the situation of late twentieth-century Mexico. The Gods have died; incertitude rules. Life 'deja de tener sentido y consigue un sinsentido helado y desolador' (p. 110). The encounter between Moctezuma and the three women who show him around modern Mexico City leads to a series of meditations in the text, on the incertitudes of the historical record of the fall of the Aztecs and the death of the Emperor, on writing in general and on the role of the writer in the Postmodern world. The fragmented technique, the different narrative voices and the complicated symbolism reflect that world. But Boullosa concludes that the best novels 'consuelan', breaking down otherness and solitude, and offering hope.

Boullosa's next three novels develop the allegorical mode. *La milagrosa* (1993) is a satire of Mexican political life, stressing the gullibility of the electorate and the cynical corruption of the politicos. Elena (La Milagrosa) can perform miracles on demand and does so at first with comic results. But when a drunken Private Eye is hired to check on her, he discovers that one of her clients has presidential aspirations, happily brought to nothing by his death. This leads into the novel's basic themes of the unwillingness of the Mexican electorate to envisage real democratic pluralism and its readiness to fall for the illusionism practised by the career politicians. There are interest-

[35] Carmen Boullosa, *Llanto* (Mexico City, Era, 1992), p. 97.

ing similarities with Valenzuela's *Realidad nacional desde la cama*. *Duerme* (1994) was dedicated, perhaps significantly, to the Mexican critic Margo Glantz and to Diamela Eltit. It is a curious mixture of the fantastic and the swashbuckling, set in sixteenth-century Mexico, with an adventurous heroine, Claire. She seems to represent both feminine emancipation and the mestizo population of Mexico who are destined to take over from the white descendents of the Spanish, but who (as *La Milagrosa* implied) will have no easy task in establishing a national identity or a workable politico-social system. *Cielos en la tierra* (1997) is set in the distant future after a nuclear holocaust. It deals with a community of survivors whose intolerance of the main, female, narrator, Lear, reflects the intolerance of minority opinion and racism which appear to have led to the catastrophe. Lear in the future, Estela in the present and father Hernández de Rivas in the past represent attempts to build a pluralistic culture linked to historical roots. But these are resisted by the majority. The future community even sets about giving up language itself. But Boullosa shows her three narrators as empowered to fight back by clinging to literary expression and a sense of history. Both in Piglia's *La ciudad ausente* and in *Cielos en la tierra* we perceive the common theme of connecting the present meaningfully with the past and the future so that history makes sense (so that an 'order' can be discerned). This is one of the basic aspirations of writers of fiction in Spanish America in the late twentieth century. In 1999, like Elizondo, Boullosa unexpectedly turned her back on those elements in her earlier work which might be regarded as Postmodernist and published *Treinta años*, in large measure a throwback to the type of fantastico-comic Magical Realism which we associate with García Márquez (whose *Cien años de soledad* is specifically mentioned). Boullosa has described it as 'prácticamente todo cuento de hadas al mismo tiempo que historia' (Hind). This first-person, delightfully reader-friendly narrative is the story of a young girl's childhood in an imaginary Tabasco where marvels occur on a daily basis, followed by her political awakening. Horses fly, there is an albino crocodile, old ladies levitate, rain can be bought for cash. This world of childhood imagination is abruptly destroyed by political conflict and repression and by the changes in the wake of oil prospecting. *Treinta años* represents a nostalgic parenthesis in Boullosa's work. The narrator, in fact, makes fun of herself (and indirectly of the younger Boullosa) for wanting to write a novel in which 'No había historia, no había anécdota, [los personajes] no interactuaban, no se gestaba algún nudo narrativo',[36] in other words, just like *Mejor desaparece*! No serious student of Postmodernism in Spanish American fiction can afford to overlook this self-satire.

36 Carmen Boullosa, *Treinta años* (Mexico City, Alfguara, 1999), p. 195.

Further Reading

Beverley, John, *et al.*, *The Postmodernism Debate in Latin America* (Durham, Duke U.P., 1995).

De Toro, Alfonso, *Postmodernidad y postcolonialidad: breves reflexiones sobre Latinoamérica* (Frankfurt, Vervuert / Madrid, Iberoamericana, 1997).

McGuirk, Bernard, *Latin American Literature: Symptoms, Risks and Strategies of Post-Structuralist Criticism* (London, Routledge, 1997).

Young, Richard A., *Latin American Postmodernisms* (Amsterdam, Rodopi, 1997).

Yúdice, George ed., *On Edge: The Crisis of Contemporary Latin American Culture* (Minneapolis, Minnesota U.P., 1992).

Viñas, David *et al.*, *Más allá del Boom* (Buenos Aires, Folios, 1984).

The above are some of the main books on the vexed question of how to label and approach Spanish American fiction after the Boom.

Rodríguez Padrón, Jorge, 'Néstor Sánchez: más allá de la novela', *Cuadernos Hispanoamericanos* 289 / 90 (1974), 457–64. Criticism of Sánchez is sparse and poor.

Bell, Steven M., 'Literatura crítica y crítica de la literatura: teoría y práctica en la obra de Salvador Elizondo', *Chasqui* 11.1 (1981), 41–52.

Graniela-Rodríguez, Magda, *El papel del lector en la novela mexicana contemporánea: José Emilio Pacheco y Salvador Elizondo* (Potomac [Maryland], Scripta Humanistica, 1991).

Incledon, John, 'Salvador Elizondo's *Farabeuf*: Remembering the Future', *Review* 29 (1981), 64–8.

The above may help in deciphering Elizondo's early work.

González Echevarría, Roberto, *La ruta de Severo Sarduy* (Hanover, New Hampshire, Ediciones del Norte, 1987). Not now up to date, but the best book so far.

Pellón, Gustavo, 'Severo Sarduy's Strategy of Irony: Paradigmatic Indecision in *Cobra and Maitreya*', *Latin American Literary Review* 11.23 (1983), 7–13.

Prieto, René, 'The Ambiviolent Fiction of Severo Sarduy', *Symposium* 39.1 (1985), 49–60.

Santí, Enrico Mario, 'Textual Politics: Severo Sarduy', *Latin American Literary Review* 8.16 (1980), 152–60.

Lértora, Juan Carlos, ed., *Una poética de literatura menor: la narrativa de Diamela Eltit* (Santiago de Chile, Cuatro Propio, 1993). Some help in understanding this very difficult writer.

Pratt, Marie Louise, 'Overwriting Pinochet: Undoing the Culture of Fear in Chile', *Modern Language Quarterly* 52.2 (1996), 151–63. A politically orientated approach.

Tierney-Tello, Mary Beth, 'Testimony, Ethics and the Aesthetic in Diamela Eltit', *Publications of the Modern Language Society of America* 141.1 (1999), 78–96.

Avelar, Idelber, *The Untimely Present. Postdictatorial Latin American Fiction and the Task of Mourning* (Durham, Duke U.P., 1999), Eltit, Piglia. Stresses the political background.

McCracken, Ellen, 'Metaplagiarism and the Critic's Role as Detective: Ricardo

Piglia's Reinvention of Roberto Arlt', *Publications of the Modern Language Society of America* 106.5 (1991), 1071–82.

Jagoe, Eva Lynn A., 'The Disembodied Machine: Matter, Femininity and Nation in Piglia's *La ciudad ausente*', *Latin American Literary Review* 23 (1995), 5–17.

Droscher, Barbara, ed., *Acercamientos a Carmen Boullosa* (Berlin, Frey, 1999). A symposium of generally useful essays. Good criticism of Boullosa is hard to come by.

Ortega, Julio, 'Carmen Boullosa: la textualidad de lo imaginario', *La Torre* [Puerto Rico], 10.38 (1996), 167–81.

CONCLUSION

In the foregoing we have seen that Spanish American fiction after the colonial period divides itself into four rather clearly defined periods:

1. From Fernández de Lizardi's *El periquillo sarniento* (1816) to Azuela's *Los de abajo* (1916)
2. From 1916 to Onetti's *La vida breve* (1950), that is, to the advent of the Boom.
3. From 1950 to about 1975, the main creative period of the Boom writers.
4. From around 1975 to the present, the period of the Post-Boom and of Postmodernism.

The first period, though containing interesting works, is still chiefly dominated by European models and movements. From a mid-Atlantic viewpoint, Spanish American fiction in this period remained outside the mainstream of Western fiction. There were novelists, now of interest chiefly to students and specialists, but no equivalent of Hawthorne, Melville or Henry James. We might draw a very rough analogy with fiction in the South of the United States before Faulkner. Only Sarmiento's *Facundo* (1845) stands like a solitary monument. It set the pattern of searching for a national or racial identity and of producing hybrid fictional works, as well as launching the long-lived theme of civilization versus barbarism.

The second period, dominated by Regionalism and Indigenism, shows Spanish American fiction writers coming to terms with the dual imperative to interpret their own Continent and at the same time to remain abreast of developments in fiction chiefly in Europe. It greatest success was in focusing attention on Spanish America itself, and especially its rural interior, its racial diversity, its struggle with the land itself and with a tradition of injustice and oppression. In the background, half-concealed, we perceive the beginnings of Modernism in the Anglo-Saxon sense of the word, which was to lead, via Borges, to the Boom. The rise of Modernism in Spanish American fiction still needs exploration.

The third period marks the coming of age of Spanish American fiction, its entry into the Western mainstream, the flowering of Modernism and the origins of Postmodernism. Both the vision of the human condition, of reality and of the writer's task evolve momentously at the hands of a galaxy of outstanding writers, some of whom are still producing at the end of the century. In the background, the older Realist tradition of fiction still has practitioners, who hand it on, in a form modified by the impact of the Boom, to the Post-Boomers.

In the fourth period a majority group, including for the first time a large number of women writers, initiates a reaction against the extremes of Boom-type cosmopolitanism, experimentalism and questioning of the referential function of language, with a return to greater reader-friendliness, plot and specificity to Spanish America. At the same time a minority group take up the heritage of the Boom's radical break with the Realist tradition and carry to a new level corresponding in some respects to what we think of as Postmodernism. But it remains unclear at the beginning of the twenty-first century whether critical attempts to stretch the definition of Postmodernism to include a wide selection of Spanish American writers after the Boom will meet with general agreement.

BIBLIOGRAPHY

Achugar, Hugo, *Ideología y estructuras narrativas en José Donoso*, Caracas, Centro de Estudios Rómulo Gallegos, 1979.

Adams, M. Ian, *Three Authors of Alienation*, Austin, Texas U.P., 1975.

Adelstein, Miriam, ed., *Studies on the Works of José Donoso*, Lampeter, Edwin Mellen Press, 1990.

Aizenberg, Edna, ed., *Borges and his Successors*, Columbia, Missouri U.P., 1990.

Agustín, José, 'Contemporary Latin American Fiction', in his *Three Lectures. Literature and Censorship in Latin America Today: Dream within a Dream*, ed. John Kirk and Don Schmidt, University of Denver Occasional Papers No. 1, 1978.

Alas, Montserrat, 'José Asunción Silva, *De sobremesa*. Etapas de una búsqueda simbólica', *RILCE* [Universidad de Navarra], 4.1, 1988, 9–15.

Alba-Koch, Beatriz de, *Ilustrando la Nueva España: texto e imagen en 'El Periquillo Sarniento' de Fernández de Lizardi*, Cáceres, Extremadura U.P., 1999.

Albónico, Aldo, 'Roa Bastos y el "Napoleón de la Plata" ', *Revista Iberoamericana*, 180, 1997, 467–84.

Alegría, Ciro, *Novelas completas*, Madrid, Aguilar, 1959.

Alegría, Fernando, *Nueva historia de la novela hispanoamericana*, Hanover [New Hampshire], Ediciones del Norte, 1986.

Alonso, Carlos J., *The Spanish American Regional Novel*, Cambridge U.P., 1990.

Altamirano, Ignacio M., *Clemencia*, Mexico City, Porrúa, 1944.

Anderson Imbert, Enrique, *El realismo mágico y otros ensayos*, Caracas, Monte Avila, 1976.

Arenas, Reinaldo, *Otra vez el mar*, Barcelona, Argos Vergara, 1982.

———, *El mundo alucinante*, Barcelona, Tusquets, 1997.

Arguedas, José María, *Yawar fiesta*, Santiago de Chile, Universitaria, 1968.

———, *Los ríos profundos*, Oxford, Pergamon, 1993.

Arlt, Roberto, *Obra completa*, Buenos Aires, Carlos Lohlé, 1981.

Asturias, Miguel Angel, *Hombres de maíz*, Paris, Klincksieck, 1981.

———, 'Paisaje y lengua en la novela hispanoamericana', *Rassegna Iberistica*, 54, 1995, 69–77.

Avelar, Idelber, *The Untimely Present. Postdictatorial Latin American Fiction and the Task of Mourning*, Durham, Duke U.P., 1999.

Ayora, Jorge, 'Psicología de lo grotesco en "El hombre que parecía un caballo" ', *Explicación de Textos Literarios*, 11.2, 1974, 117–22.

Azuela, Mario, *Obras completas*, Mexico City, Fondo de Cultura Económica, 1958–60.

Bacarisse, Pamela, 'Superior Men and Inferior Reality', *Bulletin of Hispanic Studies*, 66, 1989, 361–70.

———, *The Necessary Dream. A Study of the Novels of Manuel Puig*, Cardiff U.P., 1988.

———, *Impossible Choices. The Implications of the Cultural References in the Novels of Manuel Puig*, Calgary U.P. and Cardiff U.P., 1993.

———, ed., *Carnal Knowledge*, Pittsburgh, Tres Ríos, 1993.

Bacarisse, Salvador, *Contemporary Spanish American Fiction*, Edinburgh, Scottish Academic Press, 1980.

Balderston, Daniel, ed., *The Historical Novel in Latin America*, Gaithersburg, Hispamérica, 1986.

Barradas, Efraín, *Para leer en Puertorriqueño: acercamiento a la obra de Luis Rafael Sánchez*, Río Piedras, Cultural, 1981.

Barrenechea, Ana María, *Borges the Labyrinth Maker*, New York U.P., 1965.

———, 'Ex-centricidad, di-vergencias y con-vergencias en Felisberto Hernández', *Modern Language Notes*, 91, 1976, 311–36.

Barrios, Eduardo, *Obras completas*, Santiago de Chile, Zig-Zag, 1962.

Bazán-Figueras, Patricia, *Eugenio Cambaceres, precursor de la novela argentina contemporánea*, New York, Lang, 1994.

Beardsell, Peter, *Quiroga. Cuentos de amor, locura y muerte*, London, Grant & Cutler, 1986.

Béjar, Eduardo C., *La textualidad de Reinaldo Arenas: juegos de la escritura posmoderna*, Madrid, Playor, 1987.

Bell, Steven M., 'Literatura crítica y crítica de la literatura: teoría y práctica en la obra de Salvador Elizondo', *Chasqui*, 11.1, 1981, 41–52.

———, 'Postmodern Fiction in Spanish America: The Example of Salvador Elizondo and Néstor Sánchez', *Arizona Quarterly*, 42, 1986, 5–16.

———, *Critical Theory, Cultural Politics and Latin American Narrative*, Notre Dame U.P., 1993.

Bell-Villada, Gene H., *Gabriel García Márquez: The Man and his Work*, Chapel Hill, North Carolina U.P., 1990.

Benedetti, Mario, *El escritor latinoamericano y la revolución posible*, Buenos Aires, Alfa, 1974.

———, 'El escritor y la crítica en el contexto del desarrollo', *Casa de las Américas*, 107, 1978, 3–21.

Bensousson, Albert, 'Mario Vargas Llosa, le cannibale', *Magazine Littéraire*, 197, 1983, 76–81.

Beverley John *et al.*, *The Postmodernism Debate in Latin America*, Durham, Duke U.P., 1995.

Blest Gana, Alberto, *Martín Rivas*, Oxford U.P., 2000.

Bloom, Harold, ed., *Jorge Luis Borges*, New York/Philadelphia, Chelsea House, 1986.

———, *Modern Latin American Fiction*, New York/Philadelphia, Chelsea House, 1990.

Boldy, Steven, *The Novels of Julio Cortázar*, Cambridge U.P., 1980.

Bombal, María Luisa, *La última niebla*, Santiago de Chile, Nascimiento, 1962.

———, *La amortajada*, Santiago de Chile, Orbe, 1968.
Booker, M. Keith, *Vargas Llosa among the Postmodernists*, Gainesville, University Presses of Florida, 1994.
Borland, Roy, *Oedipus and the Papa State*, Madrid, Voz, 1988.
Boullosa, Carmen, *Llanto*, Mexico City, Era, 1992.
———, 'El que gira la cabeza y el fuego: historia y novela', *Universidad de Zulia* [Maracaibo], 30, 1995, 5–16.
———, *Treinta años*, Mexico City, Alfaguara, 1999.
Boyle, Catherine, ed., *Women Writers of Twentieth-Century Spain and Spanish America*, Lewiston, Edwin Mellen Press, 1993.
Brody, Robert and Grossman, Charles, eds., *Carlos Fuentes. A Critical View*, Austin, Texas U.P., 1982.
Brooksbank Jones, Amy, ed., *Latin American Women's Writing*, New York, Oxford U.P., 1996.
Brown, James W., '*Gazapo, modelo para armar*', *Nueva Narrativa Hispanoamericana*, 3.2, 1973, 237–44.
Brushwood, John S., *The Romantic Novel in Mexico*, Columbia, Missouri U.P., 1954.
———, *Mexico in its Novel. A Nation's Search for Identity*. Austin, Texas U.P., 1966.
———, *Genteel Barbarism. Experiments in the Analysis of Nineteenth-Century Spanish American Novels*, Lincoln, Nebraska U.P., 1981.
Bryce Echenique, Alfredo, *Un mundo para Julius*, Barcelona, Plaza y Janés, 1970.
———, *La amigdalitis de Tarzán*, Mexico City, Alfaguara, 1999.
Burgos, Fernando ed., *Las voces del kiraí; estudios sobre Augusto Roa Bastos*, Madrid, Edelsa, 1988.
Cabrera, Rosa M. and Zaldívar, Gladys B., eds., *Homenaje a Gertudis Gómez de Avellaneda*, Miami, Universal, 1981.
Cabrera Infante, Guillermo, 'Cain by Himself: Guillermo Cabrera Infante, Man of Three Islands', *Review*, 28, 1981, 8–11.
Cacheiro, Adolfo, *Reinaldo Arenas: una apreciación política*, Lanham [Maryland], International Scholars Publications, 2000.
Callan, Richard, *Miguel Angel Asturias*, New York, Twayne, 1970.
Calviño, Julio, *La novela del dictador en Hispanoamérica*, Madrid, Cultura Hispánica, 1985.
Camayd-Freixas, Erik, *Realismo mágico y primitivismo*, Lanham [Maryland], University Press of America, 1998.
Cambaceres, Eugenio, *Obras completas*, Santa Fe [Argentina], Castelvi, 1968.
Cardwell, Richard and McGuirk, Bernard, eds., *¿Qué es el modernismo?*, Boulder, Colorado, Society of Spanish and Spanish American Studies, 1993.
Carpentier, Alejo, *La novela latinoamericana en vísperas de un nuevo siglo y otros ensayos*, Mexico City, Siglo XXI, 1981.
Carvalho, Susan, 'Transgressions of Space and Gender in Allende's *La hija de la fortuna*', *Letras Femeninas* (forthcoming).
Castro Klarén, Sara, *El mundo mágico de José María Arguedas*, Lima, Instituto de Estudios Peruanos, 1973.

Castro Leal, Antonio, ed., *La novela de la revolución mexicana*, Madrid/Mexico City/ Buenos Aires, Aguilar, 1967.

Christ, Ronald, 'Interview with José Donoso', *Partisan Review*, 49, 1982, 23–44.

Coddou, Marcelo, 'Fundamentos para la valoración de la obra de Juan Rulfo', *Nueva Narrativa Hispanoamericana*, 1.2, 1971, 139–58.

Cohn, Deborah, 'A Wrinkle in Time: Time as Structure and Meaning in *Pedro Páramo*', *Revista Hispánica Moderna*, 48, 1996, 256–66.

Colás, Santiago, *Postmodernity in Latin America. The Argentine Paradigm*, Durham and London, Duke U.P., 1994.

Collazos, Oscar, *Literatura en la revolución y revolución en la literatura*, 2nd edn, Mexico City, Siglo XXI, 1971.

Compton, Merlin D., *Ricardo Palma*, Boston, Twayne, 1982.

Cook Alyce, '*Novela negra con argentinos* and the Move towards Reconciliation', *La Chispa*, 1997, 113–21.

Cordones-Cook, Juanamaría, *Poética de la transgresión en la novelística de Luisa Valenzuela*, New York, Lang, 1991.

Cornejo Polar, Antonio, ed., *José Donoso, la destrucción de un mundo*, Buenos Aires, García Cambeiro, 1975.

———, *La novela peruana*, Lima, Horizonte, 1989.

Cortázar, Julio, 'Algunos aspectos del cuento', *Casa de las Américas*, 15/16, 1962–3, 3–14.

Co-Textes [Montpellier], 34, 1977 (Bryce Echenique Number).

Craft, Linda J., *Novels of Testimony and Resistence from Central America*, Gainesville, Florida U.P., 1997.

Crystall, Elyse, Kuhnham, Jill and Layoun, Mary, 'An Interview with Isabel Allende', *Contemporary Literature*, 33.4, 1992, 585–600.

Cymerman, Claude, *Diez estudios cambacerianos*, Rouen, Rouen U.P., 1993.

Dauster, Frank, 'Notes on Borges's Labyrinths', *Hispanic Review*, 30, 1962, 142–48.

Davies, Lloyd, *Isabel Allende. La casa de los espíritus*, London, Grant & Cutler, 2000.

Davison, Ned J., *Eduardo Barrios*, New York, Twayne, 1970.

Daydí, Santiago, 'Drinking: A Narrative Structural Pattern in Mariano Azuela's *Los de abajo*', *Kentucky Romance Quarterly*, 27, 1980, 57–67.

De Beer, Gabriella, *Contemporary Mexican Women Writers*, Austin, Texas U.P., 1996.

De Grandis, Rita, 'La cita como estrategia narrativa en *Respiración artificial*', *Revista Canadiense de Estudios Hispánicos*, 17, 1993, 259–69.

De Toro, Alfonso, *Postmodernidad y Postcolonialidad: breves reflexiones sobre Latinoamérica*, Frankfurt, Vervuert/Madrid, Iberoamericana, 1997.

Dellepiane, Angela, 'La novela argentina desde 1950 hasta 1965', *Revista Iberoamericana*, 160/161, 1968, 237–82.

Díaz, Gwendolyn, 'Postmodernismo y teoría del caos en *Cola de lagartija* de Luisa Valenzuela', *Letras Femeninas*, Número Extraordinario Conmemorativo, 1974–1994, 97–105.

Díaz Rodríguez, Manuel, *Idolos rotos*, Paris, Garnier Hermanos, 1901.

———, *Sangre patricia*, Madrid, Sociedad Española de Librería, [no date].

Dictionary of Literary Biography, vols. 113 (1992) and 145 (1994), Detroit, Bruccoli, Clark Layman.

D'Lugo, Carol Clark, 'Elizondo's *Farabeuf*: A Consideration of the Text as Text', *Symposium*, 39, 1988, 155–66.

———, *The Fragmented Novel in Mexico*, Austin, Texas U.P., 1997.

Donoso, José, *The "Boom" in Spanish American Literature. A Personal History*, New York, Columbia U.P., 1977.

———, *El mocho*, Madrid, Alfaguara, 1997.

Droscher, Barbara, ed., *Acercamientos a Carmen Boullosa*, Berlin, Frey, 1999.

Duncan, J. Ann, 'Language as Protagonist. Tradition and Innovation in Bryce Echenique's *Un mundo para Julius*', *Forum for Modern Language Studies*, 16, 1980, 120–35.

———, *Voices, Visions and a New Reality. Mexican Fiction since 1970*, Pittsburgh U.P., 1986.

Durán, Gloria, *The Archetypes of Carlos Fuentes*, Hamden [Connecticut], Archon Books, 1980.

Early, Eileen, *Joy in Exile. Ciro Alegría's Narrative Art*, Washington, University Press of America, 1980.

Echevarren, Roberto, *El espacio de la verdad. Práctica del texto en Felisberto Hernández*, Buenos Aires, Sudamericana, 1981.

——— and Giordano, Enrique, *Manuel Puig, montaje y alteridad del sujeto*, Santiago de Chile, Monografías de Maitén, 1986.

Elizondo, Salvador, *Salvador Elizondo*, Mexico City, Empresas Editoriales, 1966.

———, *El grafólogo*, Mexico City, Mortiz, 1972.

Elmore, Peter, *La fábrica de la memoria. La crisis de la representación en la novela histórica latinoamericana*, Mexico City, Fondo de Cultura Económica, 1997.

Eltit, Diamela, *Por la patria*, Santiago de Chile, Ornitorrinco, 1986.

———, 'Resisting', *Review*, 49, 1994, 19.

———, *Los trabajadores de la muerte*, Santiago de Chile, Planeta, 1998.

Engelbert, Jo Anne, *Macedonio Fernández and the Spanish American New Novel*, New York U.P., 1978.

Enkvist, Inger, *La técnica narrativa de Vargas Llosa*, Gothenburg U.P., 1987.

Escajadillo, Tomás, *Alegría y 'El mundo es ancho y ajeno'*, Lima, San Marcos U.P., 1983.

Ette, Omar, *Reinaldo Arenas. La escritura de la memoria*, Frankfurt, Vervuert, 1992.

Faris, Wendy, *Carlos Fuentes*, New York, Ungar, 1983.

Feal, Rosemary Geisdorfer, *Novel Lives. The Fictional Autobiographies of Guillermo Cabrera Infante and Mario Vargas Llosa*, Chapel Hill, North Carolina U.P., 1986.

Fernández, Salvador, *Gustavo Sainz: Postmodernism in the Mexican Novel*, New York, Lang, 1999.

Fernández-Levin, Rosa, *El autor y el personaje femenino en dos novelas del siglo XIX*, Madrid, Pliegos, 1997.

Ferré, Rosario, *Sitio a Eros*, Mexico City, Mortiz, 1986.

Ferreira, César, 'Entrevista con Alfredo Bryce Echenique', *Antípodas*, 3, 1991, 41–47.
Fiddian, Robin, *Gabriel García Márquez*, London, Longman, 1995.
———, *The Novels of Fernando del Paso*, Gainesville, Florida U.P., 2000.
Fishburn, Evelyn, 'The Concept of "Civilization and Barbarism" in Sarmiento's *Facundo*. A Reappraisal', *Iberoamerikanisches Archiv*, 5 4, 1979, 301–8.
———, *The Portrayal of Immigration in Nineteenth Century Argentine Fiction (1845–1902)*, Berlin, Colloquium Verlag, 1981.
Flint, Jack, *The Prose Works of Roberto Arlt*, Durham U.P., 1985.
Flores, Angel, *Aproximaciones a Horacio Quiroga*, Caracas, Monte Avila, 1976.
Foster, David William, 'Pascal Symbology in Echevarría's "El matadero" ', *Studies in Short Fiction*, 7. 2, 1970, 257–63.
———, *Augusto Roa Bastos*, Boston, Twayne, 1978.
———, *The Argentine Generation of 1880. Ideology and Cultural Texts*, Columbia, Missouri U.P., 1990.
———, *Gay and Lesbian Themes in Latin American Writing*, Austin, Texas U.P., 1991.
——— and Altamiranda, Daniel, *Spanish American Literature. A Collection of Essays in English and Spanish*, Vols. III (from Romanticism to Modernism in Latin America; IV (Twentieth Century Spanish American Literature); V (Twentieth Century Spanish American Literature Since 1960), New York, Garland, 1998.
Franco, Jean, 'Image and Experience in *La vorágine*', *Bulletin of Hispanic Studies*, 41, 1964, 101–10.
———, *Society and the Artist. The Modern Culture of Latin America*, London, Pall Mall, 1967.
Fuentes, Carlos, *La nueva novela hispanoamericana*, Mexico City, Mortiz, 1969.
———, *La cabeza de la hidra*, Barcelona, Argos, 1978.
———, *Los años con Laura Díaz*, Mexico City, Alfaguara, 1999.
Gallegos, Rómulo, *Obras completas*, Madrid, Aguilar, 1959.
Gamboa, Federico, *Novelas*, Mexico City, Fondo de Cultura Económica, 1965.
———, *La novela mexicana*, Colima U.P. [Mexico], 1988.
Garabano, Sandra and García-Corrales, Guillermo, 'Diamela Eltit', *Hispamérica*, 62, 1992, 65–75.
García Barrragán, María G., *El naturalismo literario en México*, 2nd edn, Mexico City, UNAM, 1993.
García Serrano, María Victoria, '*Como agua para chocolate* de Laura Esquivel, apuntes para un debate', *Indiana Journal of Hispanic Literatures*, 6/7, 1995, 185–205.
Gazarian-Gautier, Marie-Lise, *Interviews with Latin American Writers*, Elmwood Park [Illinois], Dalkey Archive Press, 1989.
Geddes, Jennifer L., 'A Fascination for Stories, the Call to Community and Conversion in Mario Vargas Llosa's *The Storyteller*', *Literature and Theology*, 10, 1996, 370–77.
Gelpí, Juan G., *Literatura y paternalismo en Puerto Rico*, San Juan, Puerto Rico U.P., 1993.
Gerdes Dick, *Mario Vargas Llosa*, Boston, Twayne, 1985.

Ghiano, Juan Carlos, *Análisis de 'La guerra gaucha'*, Buenos Aires, Centro Editor de América Latina, 1967.
Giacoman, Helmy F., *Homenaje a Carlos Fuentes*, New York, Anaya/Las Américas, 1971.
———, *Homenaje a Ernesto Sábato*, New York, Anaya/Las Américas, 1973.
———, *Homenaje a Juan Rulfo*, New York, Anaya/Las Américas, 1974.
Giardinelli, Mempo, *Qué solos se quedan los muertos*, Buenos Aires, Sudamericana, 1985.
———, 'Fichero', *Nuevo Texto Crítico*, 5, 1990, 185–88.
———, *Santo oficio de la memoria*, Bogotá, Norma, 1991.
———, *Imposible equilibrio*, Buenos Aires, Planeta, 1995.
Glantz, Margo, *Repeticiones*, Xalapa, Vera Cruz U.P., 1979.
Glen, Kathleen Mary, 'Postmodern Parody and Culinary Narrative in Laura Esquivel's *Como agua para chocolate*', *Chasqui*, 23.2, 1994, 39–47.
Gligo, Agata, *María Luisa (Sobre la vida de María Luisa Bombal)*, Santiago de Chile, Andrés Bello, 1985.
Gold, Janet N., '*Arráncame la vida*: Textual Complicity and the Boundaries of Rebellion', *Chasqui*, 17.2, 1988, 35–40.
Gómez de Avellaneda, Gertrudis, *Sab*, Madrid, Cátedra, 1997.
González, Aníbal, *La novela modernista hispanoamericana*, Madrid, Gredos, 1987.
González, Manuel Pedro, *Antología crítica de José Martí*, Mexico City, Cultura, 1960.
González Echeverría, Roberto, *The Voice of the Masters*, Austin, Texas U.P., 1985.
———, 'Plainsong: Sarduy's *Cobra*', *Contemporary Literature*, 28, 1987, 437–59.
———, *La ruta de Severo Sarduy*, Hanover [New Hampshire], Ediciones del Norte, 1987.
———, *Alejo Carpentier. The Pilgrim at Home*, Austin, Texas U.P., 1990.
Graniela-Rodríguez, Magda, *El papel del lector en la novela mexicana contemporánea: José Emilio Pacheco y Salvador Elizondo*, Potomac [Maryland], Scripta Humanistica, 1991.
Gras Balaguer, Menene, 'Entrevista con Antonio Skármeta', *Insula*, 478, 1986, 1 & 14.
Graziano, Frank, *The Lust of Seeing. Themes of the Gaze and Sexual Rituals in the Fiction of Felisberto Hernández*, Lewisburg, Bucknell U.P., 1997.
Guerra-Cunningham, Lucía, *La narrativa de María Luisa Bombal: una visión de la existencia femenina*, Madrid, Playor, 1980.
Guibert, Rita, 'Entrevista con Guillermo Cabrera Infante', *Revista Iberoamericana*, 76/77, 1971, 537–54.
———, *Seven Voices*, New York, Knopf, 1973.
Güiraldes, Ricardo, *Obras completas*, Buenos Aires, Emecé, 1962.
Gullón, Germán, 'Técnicas narrativas en la novela realista y en la modernista', *Cuadernos Hispanoamericanos*, 286, 1974, 173–87.
Gunia, Inke, *¿Cuál es la Onda? La literatura de la contracultura juvenil en el México de los años sesenta y setenta*, Frankfurt, Vervuert, 1994.

Harss, Luis, *Los nuestros*, Buenos Aires, Sudamericana, 1966. (English translation: *Into the Mainstream*, London, Harper and Row, 1967).

Hart, Patricia, *Narrative Magic in the Fiction of Isabel Allende*, London, Associated University Presses, 1989.

Hart, Stephen, 'Current Trends in Scholarship on *Modernismo*', *Neophilologus*, 71, 1987, 227–34.

———, *A Companion to Spanish American Literature*, London, Tamesis, 1999.

Harter, Hugh A., *Gertrudis Gómez de Avellaneda*, Boston, Twayne, 1981.

Hayes, Aden, W., *Roberto Arlt, la estrategia de su ficción*, London, Tamesis, 1981.

Henríquez Ureña, Max, *Breve historia del modernismo*, 2nd edn, Mexico City, Fondo de Cultura Económica, 1962.

Hernández Felisberto, *Diario de un sinvergüenza y últimas invenciones*, Montevideo, Arca, 1974.

———, *Piano Stories*, New York, Marsilio Publishers, 1993.

Higgins, James, *A History of Peruvian Literature*, Liverpool, Cairns, 1987.

Hind, Emily, 'Entrevista con Carmen Boullosa', *Hispamérica* (forthcoming).

Hintz, Susanne S., *Rosario Ferré. A Search for Identity*, New York, Lang, 1995.

Hirsch, Marianne, *Beyond the Single Vision*, York [South Carolina], French Literature Publications, 1981.

Ibieta, Gabriela, *Tradition and Renewal in 'La gloria de Don Ramiro'*, Potomac [Maryland], Scripta Humanistica, 1986.

Ibsen, Kristen, *Author, Text and Reader in the Novels of Carlos Fuentes*, New York, Lang, 1993.

———, 'On Recipes, Reading and Revolution: Postboom Parody in *Como agua para chocolate*', *Hispanic Review*, 63, 1995, 133–46.

———, *The Other Mirror. Women's Narrative in Mexico 1980–95*, Westport, Greenwood Press, 1997.

Icaza, Jorge, *Obras escogidas*, Mexico City, Aguilar, 1961.

Incledon, John, 'Salvador Elizondo's *Farabeuf*: Remembering the Future', *Review*, 29, 1981, 64–8.

Ivask, Ivan and Alazraki, Jaime, eds., *The Final Island. The Fiction of Cortázar*, Norman, Oklahoma U.P., 1978.

Jackson, Richard L., 'Black Phobia and White Aesthetic in Spanish American Literature', *Hispania*, 58, 1975, 467–80.

Jagoe, Eva, 'The Disembodied Machine: Matter, Femininity and Nation in Piglia's *La ciudad ausente*', *Latin American Literary Review*, 23, 1995, 5–17.

Jansen, André, *Enrique Larreta*, Madrid, Cultura Hispánica, 1967.

Jiménez, José Olivio, *Estudios críticos sobre prosa modernista hispanoamericana*, New York, Eliseo Torres, 1975.

Jiménez, Yvette, '*El llano en llamas*', *La Torre*, 2.5, 1988, 139–59.

Jitrik, Noé, '*Paradiso* entre desborde y ruptura', *Texto Crítico*, 13, 1979, 71–89.

Jones, Julie, 'The Dynamics of the City: Gustavo Sainz's *La Princesa del Palacio de Hierro*', *Chasqui*, 12, 1982, 14–23.

Kadir, Djelal, *The Other Writing*, West Lafayette, Purdue U.P., 1993.

Katra, William H., *Domingo F. Sarmiento: Public Writer (Between 1839 and 1852)*, Tempe, Arizona State U.P., 1985.

Kerr, Lucille, *Suspended Fictions. Reading Novels by Manuel Puig*, Urbana, Illinois U.P., 1987.
———, 'Conventions of Authorial Design: José Donoso's *Casa de Campo*', *Symposium*, 42, 1988, 133–52.
King, John, *Modern Latin American Fiction*, London, Faber and Faber, 1987.
Kirkpatrick, Susan, *Las Románticas. Women Writers and Subjectivity in Spain, 1835–1850*, Berkeley, California U.P., 1989.
Kostopoulos-Cooperman, Celeste, *The Hybrid Vision of María Luisa Bombal*, London, Tamesis, 1988.
Kristal, Efraín, *The Andes Viewed from the City*, New York, Lang, 1987.
Langford, Walter, *The Mexican Novel Comes of Age*, Notre Dame U.P., 1971.
Larco, Juan ed., *Recopilación de textos sobre José María Arguedas*, Havana, Casa de las Américas, 1976.
Lasarte, Francisco, *Felisberto Hernández y la escritura de "lo otro"*, Madrid, Insula, 1981.
Lastra, Pedro, *Relecturas hispanoamericana*, Santiago de Chile, Universitaria, 1987.
Latin American Literary Review, 15.29, 1987.
Latorre, Mariano, *Autobiografía de una vocación. Algunas preguntas que no me han hecho sobre el criollismo*, Ediciones de los Anales de la Universidad de Chile, 1955.
Lawless, Cecilia, 'Experimental Cooking in *Como agua para chocolate*', *Monographic Review/Revista Monográfica*, 8.26, 1992, 1–72.
Leal, Luis, *Mariano Azuela*, New York, Twayne, 1971.
———, *Juan Rulfo*, Boston, Twayne, 1983.
Leland, Christopher T., *The Last Happy Men: The Generation of 1922. Fiction and Argentine Reality*, Syracuse U.P., 1986.
Lértora, Juan Carlos, ed., *Una poética de literatura menor: la narrativa de Diamela Eltit*, Santiago de Chile, Cuarto Propio, 1993.
Lewald, H. Ernest, *Eduardo Mallea*, Boston, Twayne, 1977.
Lichtblau, Myron I., *The Argentine Novel in the Nineteenth Century*, New York, Hispanic Institute, 1959.
———, *Mallea ante la crítica*, Miami, Universal, 1985.
Lindstrom, Naomi, *Macedonio Fernández*, Lincoln [Nebraska], Society for Spanish and Spanish American Studies, 1981.
———, *Twentieth Century Spanish American Fiction*, Austin, Texas U.P., 1994.
Lira, Constanza, *Skármeta: la inteligencia de los sentidos*, Santiago de Chile, Dante, 1985.
Llerena, Alicia, '*Arráncame la vida* de Angeles Mastretta: el universo desde la intimidad', *Revista Iberoamericana*, 159, 1992, 465–75.
López, Lucio V., *La gran aldea*, Buenos Aires, Plus Ultra, 1965.
López de Martínez, Adelaida, 'Dynamic of Change in Latin American Literature: Contemporary Women Writers', *Studies in Twentieth Century Literature*, 20.1, 1996, 13–40.
Lorenz, Guther W., 'Diálogo con Miguel Angel Asturias', *Mundo Nuevo*, 43, 1970, 35–51.
Loveluck, Juan, '*De sobremesa*, novela desconocida del modernismo', *Revista Iberoamericana*, 31, 1965, 17–32.

———, *La novela hispanoamericana*, 3rd edn, Santiago de Chile, Universitaria, 1969.
Lyon, Thomas E., 'Motivos ontológicos en los cuentos de Juan Rulfo', *Anales de la Literatura Hispanoamericana*, 4, 1975, 305–12.
MacAdam, Alfred, 'The Art of Fiction LXXV. Guillermo Cabrera Infante', *Paris Review*, 25, 1983, 156–95.
McCracken, Ellen, 'Metaplagiarism and the Critic's Role as Detective: Ricardo Piglia's Reinvention of Roberto Arlt', *Publications of the Modern Language Association of America*, 106.5, 1991, 1071–82.
McGrady, Donald, *Jorge Isaacs*, New York, Twayne, 1972.
McGuirk, Bernard and Cardwell, Richard, eds., *Gabriel García Márquez. New Readings*, Cambridge U.P., 1987.
McGuirk, Bernard, *Latin American Literature: Symptoms, Risks and Strategies of Post-Structuralist Criticism*, London, Routledge, 1997.
McMurray, George, 'The Absurd, Irony and the Grotesque in *Pantaleón y las visitadoras*', *World Literature Today*, 52.1, 1978, 44–53.
———, *José Donoso*, New York, Twayne, 1979.
———, *Jorge Luis Borges*, New York, Ungar, 1980.
———, ed., *Critical Essays on Gabriel García Márquez*, Boston, G. K. Hall, 1987.
Madrigal, Luis Iñigo, ed., *Historia de la literatura hispanoamericana II. Del neoclasicismo al modernismo*, Madrid, Cátedra, 1987.
Magnarelli, Sharon, *The Lost Rib. Female Characters in the Spanish American Novel*, London, Associated University Presses, 1985.
———, *Reflections/Refractions. Reading Luisa Valenzuela*, New York, Lang, 1988.
———, *Understanding José Donoso*, Columbia, South Carolina U.P., 1993.
Mansour, Mónica, *Los mundos de Palinuro*, Xalapa, Vera Cruz U.P., 1986.
Martin, Gerald, *Journeys Through the Labyrinth*, London, Verso, 1989.
Martín, José Luis, *La narrativa de Vargas Llosa*, Madrid, Gredos, 1974.
Martínez, Z. Nelly, 'Entrevista: José Donoso', *Hispamérica*, 21, 1978, 53–74.
Martínez Morales, José L., *Horacio Quiroga: teoría y práctica del cuento*, Xalapa, Vera Cruz U.P., 1982.
Masiello, Francine, *Between Civilization and Barbarism*, Lincoln and London, Nebraska U.P., 1992.
Mata, Oscar, *Un océano de narraciones: Fernando del Paso*, Mexico City, Universidad Autónoma de Tlaxcala-UAP, 1991.
Mattalia, Sonia, *La figura en el tapiz*, London, Tamesis, 1991.
Matto de Turner, Clorinda, *Aves sin nido*, Buenos Aires, Solar/Hachette, 1968.
Martel, Julio, *La Bolsa*, Buenos Aires, Emecé, 1942.
Martí, José, *Lucía Jerez*, Madrid, Gredos, 1969.
Méndez-Faith, Teresa, 'Entrevista con Mempo Giardinelli', *Discurso Literario*, 5.2, 1988, 313–21.
Méndez-Ramírez, Hugo, 'El narrador alienado en dos obras clave de la narrativa latinoamericana moderna', *Hispanic Journal*, 16, 1995, 83–93.
Méndez Rodanos, Adriana, *Severo Sarduy*, Mexico City, UNAM, 1983.
Mendoza, Plinio A., *El olor de la guayaba. Conversaciones con Gabriel García Márquez*, 2nd edn, Barcelona, Bruguera, 1983.

Menton, Seymour, *Latin America's New Historical Novel*, Austin, Texas U.P., 1993.
———, *Historia verdadera del realismo mágico*, Mexico City, Fondo de Cultura Económica, 1998.
Mercado, Juan C., *Building a Nation. The Case of Esteban Echevarría*, Lanham, University Press of America, 1995.
Merrim, Stephanie, 'Felisberto Hernández's Aesthetic of "lo otro": the Writing of Indeterminacy', *Revista Canadiense de Estudios Hispánicos*, 11, 1987, 521–40.
Michalski, Andre S., '*Doña Bárbara*: un cuento de hadas', *Publications of the Modern Language Society of America*, 85, 1970, 1115–22.
Miller, Yvette E. and Tatum, Charles M., eds., *Latin American Women Writers. Today and Yesterday*, Pittsburgh, The Review Press, 1977.
Millington, Mark, *Reading Onetti: Language, Narrative and the Subject*, Liverpool, Cairns, 1985.
——— and Smith, Paul Julian, eds., *New Hispanisms*, Ottowa, Dovehouse, 1994.
Moody, Michael, 'Interview with Isabel Allende', *Discurso Literario*, 4.1, 1986, 41–53.
Morales, Carlos Javier, *Julián Martel y la novela naturalista argentina*, Logroño, La Rioja U.P., 1997.
Morales, Leonidas, 'Narración y referentes en Diamela Eltit', *Revista Chilena de Literatura*, 51, 1977, 121–59.
Moran, Dominic, *Questions of the Liminal in the Fiction of Julio Cortázar*, Oxford, Legenda, 2000.
Morello-Frosch, Marta, 'La sexualidad opresiva en las obras de Manuel Puig', *Nueva Narrativa Hispanoamericana*, 5.1/2, 1975, 151–7.
Moreno Turner, Fernando, 'Un lugar sin límites, la inversión como forma', *Cuadernos Hispanoamericanos*, 295, 1975, 19–42.
Negrín, María Luisa, *El círculo del exilio y de la enajenación en la obra de Reinaldo Arenas*, Lewiston, Edwin Mellon Press, 2000.
Nelson, Ardis L., *Cabrera Infante in the Menippean Tradition*, Newark, Juan de la Cueva, 1983.
Oberhelman, Harley D., *Ernesto Sábato*, Boston, Twayne, 1970.
Ojeda, Enrique, *Ensayos sobre la obra de Jorge Icaza*, Quito, Casa de la Cultura Ecuatoriana, 1991.
Olivares, Jorge, *La novela decadente en Venezuela*, Caracas, Armitano, 1984.
———, 'Carnaval and the Novel: Reinaldo Arenas's *El palacio de las blanquísimas mofetas*', *Hispanic Review*, 53, 1985, 467–76.
Onetti, Juan Carlos, *El pozo. Para una tumba sin nombre*, Barcelona, Seix Barral, 1979.
———, *La vida breve*, Madrid, Anaya y Mario Muchnick, 1994.
Orjuela, Héctor, *De sobremesa y otros estudios sobre José Asunción Silva*, Bogotá, Instituto Caro y Cuervo, 1976.
Ortega, Julio, 'Carmen Boullosa: la textualidad de lo imaginario', *La Torre*, 10.38, 1996, 167–81.
———, *Reapropriaciones*, Río Piedras, Puerto Rico U.P., 1991.

Oviedo, José Miguel, *Mario Vargas Llosa, la invención de una realidad*, 3rd edn, Barcelona, Seix Barral, 1982.
Padura Fuentes, Leonardo, 'Retrato y voz de Alfredo Bryce Echenique', *Plural*, 224, 1990, 35–40.
Palmer, Julia, 'Some Aspects of Narrative Structure in José Asunción Silva's *De sobremesa*', *Revista Interamericana de Bibliografía*, 41, 1991, 470–77.
Parkinson Zamora, Lois, *The Usable Past*, Cambridge U.P., 1997.
Peavler, Terry J. and Standish, Peter, eds., *Structures of Power. Essays on Twentieth Century Spanish American Fiction*, Albany, State University of New York Press, 1996.
Pellón, Gustavo, 'Severo Sarduy's Strategy of Irony: Paradigmatic Indecision in *Cobra* and *Maitreya*', *Latin American Literary Review*, 11.23, 1983, 7–13.
———, *José Lezama Lima's Joyful Vision. A Study of 'Paradiso' and Other Prose*, Austin, Texas U.P., 1989.
———, 'Ideology and Structure in Giardinelli's *Santo oficio de la memoria*', *Studies in Twentieth Century Literature*, 19.1, 1995, 81–95.
Pérez, Trinidad, *Recopilación de textos sobre tres novelas ejemplares [La vorágine, Don Segundo Sombra* and *Doña Bárbara]*, Havana, Casa de las Américas, 1971.
Pfeiffer, Ema, *Entrevistas. Diez escritoras mexicanas desde bastidores*, Frankfurt, Vervuert, 1992.
Phillips, Allen W., *Estudios y notas sobre literatura hispanoamericana*, Mexico City, Cultura, 1965.
———, 'El arte y el artista en algunas novelas modernistas', *Revista Hispánica Moderna*, 34, 1968, 757–75.
Picón Garfield, Evelyn, *Cortázar por Cortázar*, Xalapa, Vera Cruz U.P., 1978.
Piglia, Ricardo, *Crítica y ficción*, Universidad del Litoral [Argentina]. Cuadernos de Extensión Universitaria, 8, 1986.
———, *La ciudad ausente*, 3rd edn, Buenos Aires Sudamericana, 1992.
Piña, Juan Andrés, *Conversaciones con la narrativa chilena*, Santiago de Chile, Los Andes, 1991.
Polo García, Victorino, ed., *Conversación de otoño, homenaje a Mario Vargas Llosa*, Murcia, CAM, 1997.
Portal, Marta, *Proceso narrativo de la revolución mexicana*, Madrid, Cultura Hispánica, 1977.
Pratt, Marie Louise, 'Overwriting Pinochet: Undoing the Culture of Fear in Chile', *Modern Language Quarterly*, 52.2, 1996, 151–63.
Prieto, René, 'The Ambivalent Fiction of Severo Sarduy', *Symposium*, 34.1, 1985, 49–60.
———, *Miguel Angel Asturias's Archeology of Return*, Cambridge U.P., 1993.
Pupo-Walker, Enrique, *El cuento hispanoamericano ante la crítica*, Madrid, Castalia, 1973.
Quintero, Isis, *José Donoso: una insurrección contra la realidad*, Madrid, Hispanova, 1978.
Rama, Angel, *La novela hispanoamericana, panoramas 1920–1980*, Bogotá, Instituto Colombiano de Cultura, 1982.
———, '*La guerra del fin del mundo*: Vargas Llosa y el fanatismo por la literatura', *Antípodas*, 1, 1988, 88–104.

Recopilación de textos sobre Juan Rulfo, Havana, Casa de las Américas, 1969.
Reedy, Daniel, R., *El ensayo y la crítica literaria en Iberoamérica*, Toronto U.P., 1970.
Rincón, Carlos, 'Entrevista con Antonio Skármeta', *Caribe* [Caracas], 4 January 1976, pages unnumbered.
Ríos, Julián, *Guillermo Cabrera Infante*, Madrid, Fundamentos, 1974.
———, *Severo Sarduy*, Madrid, Fundamentos, 1976.
Riquelme Rojas, Sonia and Aguirre Rehbein, Edna eds., *Critical Approaches to Isabel Allende's Novels*, New York, Lang, 1991.
Rivera, Eustasio, *La vorágine*, Santiago de Chile, Zig-Zag, 1965.
Roa Bastos, Augusto, *Hijo de hombre*, Buenos Aires, Losada, 1976.
Rodden, John, ed., *Conversations with Isabel Allende*, Austin, Texas U.P., 1999.
Rodríguez Alcalá, Hugo, ed., *Nine Essays on Rómulo Gallegos*, Riverside, California U.P., 1979.
Rodríguez Luis, Julio, *Hermeneutica y praxis del indigenismo*, Mexico City, Fondo de Cultura Económica, 1980.
Rodríguez Monegal, Emir, 'Las fuentes de la narración', *Mundo Nuevo*, 25, 1968, 41–58.
———, *El arte de narrar*, Caracas, Monte Avila, 1968.
———, 'The New Latin American Novel', *Books Abroad*, 44, 1970, 45–50.
———, *El Boom de la novela latinoamericana*, Caracas, Tiempo Nuevo, 1972.
Rodríguez Padrón, Jorge, 'Néstor Sánchez, más allá de la novela', *Cuadernos Hispanoamericanos*, 289/90, 1974, 457–64.
Roffé, Reina, *Espejo de escritores*, Hanover [New Hampshire], Ediciones del Norte, 1985.
Rojas, Mario, '*La casa de los espíritus* de Isabel Allende, un caleidoscopio de espejos desordenados', *Revista Iberoamericana*, 152/3, 1985, 917–25.
Rossman, Charles and Friedman, Allen W., eds., *Mario Vargas Llosa. A Collection of Critical Essays*, Austin, Texas U.P., 1978.
Ruffinelli, Jorge, *Juan Carlos Onetti*, Montevideo, Marcha, 1973.
———, 'Entrevista. Salvador Elizondo', *Hispamérica*, 16, 1977, 33–47.
———, *Crítica en Marcha*, Montevideo, Premia, 1979.
———, 'Los 80, ¿ingreso en la posmodernidad?', *Nuevo Texto Crítico*, 6, 1990, 31–42.
Rutherford, John D., *Mexican Society during the Revolution. A Literary Approach*, Oxford U.P., 1971.
Sábato, Ernesto, *El escritor y sus fantasmas*, Buenos Aires, Aguilar, 3rd edn, 1967.
———, 'Entrevista', *Cuadernos para el Diálogo*, 195, 22–28 Juanuary, 1977, 53.
Sackett, Theodore A., *El arte en la novelística de Jorge Icaza*, Quito, Casa de la Cultura, 1974.
Sainz, Gustavo, 'Carlos Fuentes. A Permanent Bedazzlement', *World Literature Today*, 57.4, 1983, 568–72.
———, *A la salud de la serpiente*, Mexico City, Grijalbo, 1988.
Salomon, Noël, 'La crítica del sistema colonial de la Nueva España en *El Periquillo Sarniento*', *Cuadernos Americanos*, 138, 1965, 166–79.

Sánchez, Luis Rafael, *La guaracha del Macho Camacho*, Buenos Aires, De la Flor, 16th edn, 1994.
Sánchez, Reinaldo, *Ideología y subversión: otra vez Arenas*, Salamanca, Centro de Estudios Ibéricos y Americanos, 1999.
Sandoval, Alejandro, ed., *Los murmullos: antología periodística en torno a la muerte de Juan Rulfo*, Mexico City, Katún, 1986.
San Román, Gustavo, *Onetti and Others*, Albany, State University of New York Press, 1999.
Santí, Enrico Mario, 'Textual Politics: Severo Sarduy', *Latin American Literary Review*, 8.16, 1980, 152–60.
Sarduy, Severo, *Cobra*, [trans. Suzanne Jill Levine], New York, Dutton, 1975.
———, *De donde son los cantantes*, Barcelona, Seix Barral, 1980.
Schulman, Ivan, *Símbolo y color en las obras de José Martí*, Madrid, Gredos, 1960.
Shaw, Bradley and Vera-Godwin, Nora, eds., *Critical Persectives on Gabriel García Márquez*, Lincoln [Nebraska], Society for Spanish and Spanish American Studies, 1986.
Shaw, Donald L., *Gallegos. Doña Bárbara*, London, Grant & Cutler, 1972.
———, 'Gallegos's Revision of *Doña Bárbara* 1928–29', *Hispanic Review*, 42, 1974, 265–78.
———, 'Narrative Arrangement in *La muerte de Artemio Cruz*', *Forum for Modern Language Studies*, 15, 1979, 130–43.
———, 'Concerning the Structure of *Facundo*', *Iberoamerikanisches Archiv*, 6.3, 1980, 239–50.
———, 'Notes on the Presentation of Sexuality in the Modern Spanish American Novel', *Bulletin of Hispanic Studies*, 59, 1982, 275–82.
———, 'Concerning the Interpretation of *Cien años de soledad*', *Antípodas*, 4, 1992, 121–38.
———, *Alejo Carpentier*, Boston, Twayne, 1985.
———, 'Inverted Christian Imagery and Symbolism in Modern Spanish American Fiction', *Romance Studies*, 10, 1987, 71–82.
———, *Borges's Narrative Strategy*, Liverpool, Cairns, 1992.
———, 'More Notes on the Presentation of Sexuality in the Modern Spanish American Novel', in Pamela Baccarisse, ed., *Carnal Knowledge. Essays on the Flesh, Sex and Sexuality in Hispanic Letters and Film*, Pittsburgh, Tres Ríos, 1993, 113–27.
———, *Antonio Skármeta and the Post-Boom*, Hanover [New Hampshire], Ediciones del Norte, 1994.
———, *The Post-Boom in Spanish American Fiction*, Albany, State University of New York Press, 1998.
———, *Nueva narrativa hispanoamericana*, 6ta ed. ampliada, Madrid, Cátedra, 1999.
———, '*La boda del poeta*: Skármeta's Parody of Post-Boom Themes', *Language Quarterly* 49.1, 2001, 1–10.
Silva, José Asunción, *Obra completa*, 2nd edn, Barcelona, Biblioteca Ayacucho, 1985.
Silva Cáceres, Raúl, *Del cuerpo a las palabras: la narrativa de Antonio Skármeta*, Madrid, LAR, 1983.

Skármeta, Antonio, 'Tendencias en la más nueva narrativa hispanoamericana', *Avances de Saber, Enciclopedia Labor*, 11, 1975, 751–71.
Skinner, Lee, 'Pandora's Log: Charting the Evolving Literary Project of Rosario Ferré', *Revista de Estudios Hispánicos*, 29, 1995, 461–76.
Sklodowska, Elzbieta, *La parodia en la nueva novela hispanoamericana*, Amsterdam, Benjamins, 1991.
Smith, Verity, *Carpentier, Los pasos perdidos*, London, Grant & Cutler, 1983.
———, ed., *Encyclopedia of Latin American Literature*, London, Fitzroy Dearborn, 1997.
Snauwuert, Erwin, *Crónica de una escritura inocente*, Louvain U.P., 1998.
Solotorevsky, Myrna, 'El cliché en *Pubis angelical* y *Boquitas pintadas*, desgaste y creatividad', *Hispamérica*, 38, 1984, 3–18.
Doris Sommer, *Foundational Fictions. The National Romances of Latin America*, Berkeley, California U.P., 1991.
Sommers, Joseph, ed., *La narrativa de Juan Rulfo*, Mexico City, Sepsetentas, 1994, 174–7.
Sosnowski, Saúl, *Augusto Roa Bastos y la producción cultural americana*, Buenos Aires, Ediciones de la Flor, 1986.
Soto, Francisco, *Reinaldo Arenas*, New York, Twayne, 1999.
Soubeyroux, Jacques, 'L'être et le désir', *Co-Textes* [Montpellier], 9, 1985, 101–19.
Souza, Raymond D., *The Poetic Fiction of José Lezama Lima*, Columbia, Missouri U.P., 1983.
Spell, Jefferson Rea, *The Life and Works of José Joaquín de Lizardi*, Philadelphia, Pennsylvania U.P., 1931.
Suárez-Marías, Marguerite C., *La novela romántica en Hispanoamérica*, New York, Hispanic Institute, 1963.
Swanson, Philip, *José Donoso. The "Boom" and Beyond*, Liverpool, Cairns, 1988.
———, *Landmarks in Latin American Fiction*, London and New York, Routledge, 1990.
———, *Cómo leer a Gabriel García Márquez*, Madrid, Júcar, 1991.
———, 'Tyrants and Trash: Sex, Class and Culture in *La casa de los espíritus*', *Bulletin of Hispanic Studies*, 71, 1994, 217–37.
———, *The New Novel in Latin America*, Manchester U.P., 1995.
Tauzín Castellanos, Isabelle, *Las tradiciones peruanas de Ricardo Palma. Claves de una coherencia*, Lima, Universidad Ricardo Palma, 1999.
Taylor, Lewis, 'Literature as History: Ciro Alegría's View of Rural Society in the Northern Peruvian Andes', *Iberoamerikanisches Archiv*, 10, 1984, 349–58.
Tierney-Tello, Mary Beth, 'Testimony, Ethics and the Aesthetic in Diamela Eltit', *Publications of the Modern Language Society of America*, 141.1, 1999, 78–96.
Toledo, Alejandro, ed., *El imperio de las voces: Fernando del Paso ante la crítica*, Mexico City, Era, 1997.
Tittler, Johnathan, *Manuel Puig*, New York, Twayne, 1993.
Toledo, Alejandro and González Dueñas, Daniel, 'Entrevista', *Universidad de México*, 484, 1991, 37–41.
Valenzuela, Luisa, *Como en la guerra*, Buenos Aires, Sudamericana, 1977.

———, *Cola de lagartija*, 2nd edn, Buenos Aires, Bruguera, 1983.
———, *Cuentos completos y uno más*, Mexico City, Alfaguara, 1998.
Valera, Juan, *Obras de Don Juan Valera*, Madrid, Aguilar, 1949.
Vargas Llosa, Mario, 'The Latin American Novel Today', *Books Abroad*, 44, 1970, 7–16.
———, *Historia de un deicidio*, Barcelona, Barral, 1971.
———, *Historia secreta de una novela*, Barcelona, Tusquets, 1971.
———, *Pantaleón y las visitadoras*, Barcelona, Seix Barral, 1978.
———, *La utopía arcaica: José María Arguedas y las ficciones del indigenismo*, Mexico City, Fondo de Cultura Económica, 1996.
———, *La fiesta del chivo*, Madrid, Alfaguara, 2000.
Various Authors, *Primer encuentro de escritores peruanos*, Lima, Casa de la Cultura del Perú, 1969.
Various Authors, *Historia de la literatura argentina*, Buenos Aires, Centro Editor de América Latina, 1980.
Vidal Hernán, *José Donoso, surrealismo y rebelión de los instintos*, San Antonio de Calonge, Aubí, 1972.
Viereck, Roberto, 'De la tradición a las formas (Entrevista con Ricardo Piglia)', *Revista Chilena de Literatura*, 40, 1992, 129–39.
Villa, Alvaro de and Sánchez Boudy, José, *José Lezama Lima: peregrino inmóvil*, Miami, Universal, 1974.
Viñas, David, *et al.*, *Más allá del Boom*, Buenos Aires, Folios, 1984.
Walker, John, *Metaphysics and Aesthetics in the Works of Eduardo Barrios*, London, Tamesis, 1983.
———, *Rivera, La vorágine*, London, Grant & Cutler, 1988.
Warner, Ralph E., *Historia de la novela mexicana en el siglo XIX*, Mexico City, Robredo, 1953.
Williams, Raymond L., 'The Boom Twenty Years Later: An Interview with Mario Vargas Llosa', *Latin American Literary Review*, 15.29, 1987, 201–6.
———, *The Postmodern Novel In Latin America*, New York, St Martin's Press, 1995.
———, *The Modern Latin American Novel*, New York, Twayne, 1998.
World Literature Today, 69.4, 1995.
Young, Richard A., *Carpentier. El reino de este mundo*, London, Grant & Cutler, 1983.
———, *Latin American Postmodernisms*, Amsterdam, Rodopi, 1997.
Yovanovich, Gordana, *Julio Cortázar's Character Mosaic. Reading the Longer Fiction*, Toronto U.P., 1991.
Yúdice, George, ed., *On Edge. The Crisis of Contemporary Latin American Culture*, Minneapolis, Minnesota U.P., 1992.
Zubieta, Ana M., *El discurso narrativo arltiano, intertextualidad, grotesco y utopía*, Buenos Aires, Hachette, 1987.

INDEX